WALTZING
AUSTRALIA

And he sang as he looked at his old billy boiling,
"Who'll come a-waltzing Matilda with me?"

-from "Waltzing Matilda" by A.B.Paterson

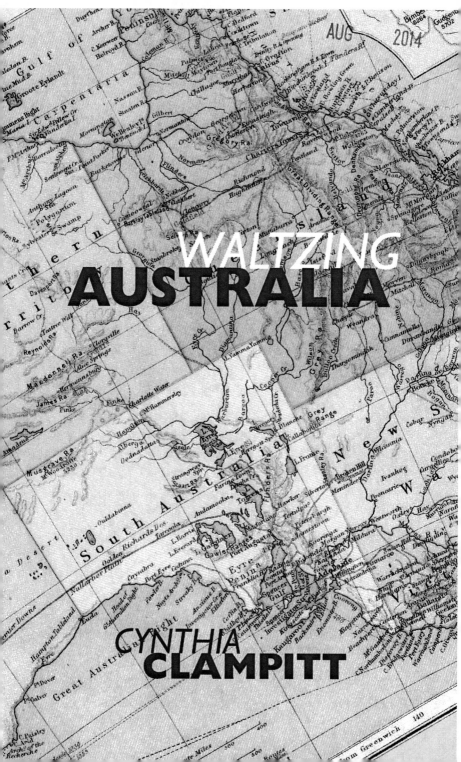

WALTZING
AUSTRALIA

CYNTHIA
CLAMPITT

[eucalyptus-leaf art] The eucalypt, or gum tree, is the "signature" tree of the Australian landscape. In its myriad variations, it accompanied me throughout the country. Hence, it seemed fitting to picture a gum leaf throughout the book.

Excerpt from the poem "In the Droving Days" by A. B. "Banjo" Paterson is from *The Collected Verse of A. B. Paterson*, forty-seventh printing, 1983, from the Australian Literary Heritage Series, published by Angus & Roberson, a division of HarperCollins Australia.

Excerpts from poems by Adam Lindsay Gordon from *Bush Ballads and Galloping Rhymes: The Poetical Works of Adam Lindsay Gordon*, published by Currey O'Neil in the Australian Classics series, 1980.

Dedication

To mom and dad—for believing in me, even when my dream seemed crazy, and for raising me to be the kind of person who would even consider doing some of this stuff.

Acknowledgements

Thanks to my parents for encouraging me to dream.

Thanks to my very talented brother, Darch Clampitt,
for the artwork and the design and layout of the book,
and to his wife Margaret, for technical advice
and general hand-holding.

Thanks to Ro Sila and Jeannette (Jay) Allen for
proofreading the manuscript, and special thanks to Ro
for her unflagging enthusiasm and
continued efforts to promote my work.

And thanks to everyone at BookSurge, but particularly
Maureen Cody and Bethany Snow, for making the
publication of this book such a painless process.

Cynthia Clampitt is a freelance writer specializing in food, travel, and history. The life she leads today began with a dream, a dream that seduced her away from her corporate career and led her to the Australian outback—and beyond.

Since the dream took hold, Cynthia has been a-waltzing in China, Cambodia, Morocco, Ecuador, Mongolia, Turkey, Iceland, Vietnam, India, Thailand, Mexico, and many other countries—and she has returned to Australia, as well.

At Cynthia's blog, you can find photographs from the trip described in *Waltzing Australia,* learn about other destinations and adventures, and get updates on writing projects.

http://waltzingaustralia.wordpress.com

Table of CONTENTS

WALTZING AUSTRALIA

Looking Back —————————————— **p. 1**

August 17–September 6: *Queensland* ———— **p. 2**

September 7–27: *Northern Territory* ———— **p. 56**

September 28–October 19: *Western Australia* —— **p. 124**

October 20–30: *South Australia* ———— **p. 177**

October 31–November 25: *Victoria* ———— **p. 205**

November 26–December 4: *Tasmania* ———— **p. 274**

December 5–8: *Canberra & Environs* ———— **p. 312**

December 9–January 6: *New South Wales* ——— **p. 325**

January 7–24: *Back to the bush and flash flood* —— **p. 382**

January 25–February 2: *Sydney and environs* —— **p. 452**

Epilogue: *The Next Step* ———————— **p. 463**

Glossary: Aussie slang and terms used in book. —— **p. 467**

Appendix ————————————————— **p. 477**

"G'day, Mate"

WALTZING QUEENSLAND

Sometimes things work out.

Dreams come true, though usually not as quickly as one hopes. In fact, my dreams have taken a lot of time—and a lot of work. However, once the dream took on the solidity of real life, the risk, the worry, and the hardship began to fade, leaving me with what I had accomplished—and the memory of the dream.

My dream still whispers to me sometimes, speaks to me not as the present reality but as the dream that once was. Even now it makes my heart beat faster, as I remember the beginning of the dream, the hope and eagerness with which I set off on the path down which it sent me.

I pull a battered loose-leaf binder off the shelf. It bulges with lined notebook paper—hundreds of pages, some dirty or torn, all hand written with an exhilaration that I can still feel when I think back to the early days of the dream. It is the record of the first step. I had known that it would take a drastic step to get me headed in the right direction, to cut me free from what I had always done. But I had underestimated how much it would change me. It seems long ago—and yesterday. The road that has led me to where I am today has been long, but I know that it is the right road—and for me, Australia was the beginning of that road. Settling down to read and remember, I turn to the first page. . .

Wednesday, August 17

Sitting at a small desk in a small hotel room, I gaze at my surroundings and wonder out loud what I've gotten myself into. I think of all the studying and work that went into getting me here and try to imagine where it will lead. As I organize pens, writing paper, and the few books I thought worth bringing, I think of all the work that will be needed to justify having come. Starting from scratch is not easy—but then, nothing important is.

There are so many dreams tied up in this: starting over; writing; Australia; finding out what I can do, what I need, and maybe who I am. The prospects are both wonderful and frightening.

Starting over is a relatively recent dream, not more than six years old. I have for too long been a prisoner of expectations and what I thought was my career. I worked hard, then harder, till there was nothing except work, and it was not enough. I continued to work and started graduate school part time. Still, it was not enough. I spent ten years working my way up the corporate ladder, trying not to notice the persistent dream that kept whispering, "Jump."

Writing is an enduring friend and my oldest dream. I have always loved it, and have spent free moments since childhood jotting down thoughts, stories, poems. Even as my corporate career eclipsed everything else, I still wrote. In hotel rooms on business trips, during pauses between meetings, I would dash off poems filled with bits of dreams and memories and burdened with longing for beauty and a different life. But my writing became as tied to the corporate world as I was, and soon I produced little besides business documents, marketing plans, and press releases. I wanted to write something else, but I didn't do anything else.

Australia is the love affair that tipped the scales toward leaving. For as long as I can remember, Australia was there, waiting for me, though it is only in the last three years that she has become an obsession. Photographs and stories through the years built my fascination, but then something clicked, and Australia became my focus, the one thing I had to discover. Expectations, security, and fear outweighed my dreams of writing and of starting over, but as this new obsession grew, the balance changed. Australia beckoned, and I had to go.

The dreams are different, yet all are tied together, each affecting the others. My desire to write helps me justify coming, but I would have come anyway, I think—unless, of course, it is because I am a writer that I have such dreams. Who knows for sure? What I do know is that if I'd stayed at home, in the corporate world, the dream would have died.

So I studied and planned, went to Australian movies and read Australian books. I sold my wine collection, books, music, clothes, and, finally, my car. I bought a plane ticket, quit my job, and came. The dream is coming true.

This morning, after eternity in flight, Sydney slid beneath my wings, the harbor, the Opera House, all startlingly familiar. I just touched down before turning north, but I shall return. I traveled on to Brisbane, to— what? The beginning of a new life? A will-o'-the-wisp? I guess time will tell.

At this point, all I have—besides my dreams—is this hotel room, two pieces of over-stuffed luggage, several broken ribs (I thought horseback riding lessons would help prepare me for the trip), and a rough idea what I want to see over here: Everything. But I am in Australia, and right now, that is all I need.

So here I sit, cup of tea nearby, pen in hand, and try to do one of those things for which I came—write: write about Australia, about change and learning, about dreams coming true. I don't know what will happen, but dreams evolve in unexpected ways, so I shall just let this unfold, day by day.

Thursday, August 18

Just after dawn, a gentle, perfumed breeze slid past the curtains and touched my hair, and I awoke as if it had been lightning. I'm really here. Whatever doubts or fears I had dissolved in Brisbane's clear, innocent, morning light. I arose and strolled out into my new life.

I am not the first to start a new life in Brisbane. Australia's history is largely a history of new starts: convicts, explorers, soldiers, refugees of war or poverty, scholars, fortune-hunters, and dreamers have, for 200 years, come here and begun again.

Like much of Australia, Brisbane has a history that begins with convicts. In 1823, explorer John Oxley headed north from Sydney to find a site for a new convict settlement. Entering Moreton Bay, which was mapped by Captain Cook in 1770, Oxley discovered a large river, which he named for Thomas Brisbane, Governor of New South Wales. The soon-to-be-notorious Moreton Bay penal settlement was established 12 miles above the river's mouth. The first convict "settlers" and their guards began to build (some of their work still stands) and farm. The area developed, though slowly and often painfully.

In time, and in defiance of a government ban on free settlement, free men came—explorers, land-seekers, cattle and sheep ranchers—and pushed back the boundaries, opened new land, developed the port, domesticated the settlement. Brisbane, named for the river it straddles, was declared a town in 1834, and in 1859, became the capital of the newly independent state of Queensland.

I started off early to explore this lovely town so inauspiciously begun. Brisbane spread voluptuously before me, a sea of red tile roofs and green trees washing over low, rolling hills. I breathed deeply the tropical air and stopped to examine every tree, flower, building, and sign as I walked along Albert Street, past Wickham Park and the Roma Street Gardens, down the hill to City Hall, with

its soaring clock tower, and across King George Square.
The sunny, open square, with its crowds, fountain, and
highly polished, dark-wood benches, is like a broad foyer
for the city's heart.

The central downtown area nestles in a bend of the
broad, meandering Brisbane River. Bright towers of glass
and steel stand behind historic churches or spring up at the
ends of blocks of stately, old buildings with elaborate
façades of carved wood or iron lace. Shops have awnings
or overhangs that extend to the curb, so the sidewalk seems
like a broad veranda around the whole of each city block.

Through the shaded streets I wandered, arriving before
long at the Queensland Government Tourist Bureau. I have
been a tourist before, but not an "adventurer." I started in a
city because I know cities. When I was very young—
before I loved theatre, cinema, ballet, and before I wore
make-up, or worried about my hair, or took on any of the
other baggage that makes the wilderness seem over-
whelmingly inconvenient—I loved the out-of-doors. I
have always remembered that love, have written love
poems to that memory, but I no longer know the wild
places and do not know how I shall react to them now,
after so many years. Slowly, I'll edge away from
civilization—day runs into the mountains, trips to animal
reserves—and ease myself into a lifestyle where blue
suits and high heels have no part.

I made plans for seeing sights around Brisbane and
made hotel reservations for other destinations in
Queensland. Despite all the maps I've seen, it is only now,
as I plan to cross her, that Australia's vastness is really
registering. There's so much I want to see and do, and I
can't fit it all in. *I've been here one day, and I already
feel like I'm running out of time!*

I strolled on through Brisbane, past many of the city's
beautiful, 19th-century buildings: Parliament House,
designed along French Renaissance lines; the profusely

detailed, Italian Renaissance-style Old Treasury Building;
the General Post Office, adorned with colonnaded balcony
and arched entry-ways. This Second Empire opulence
nestled amid palm trees, hibiscus, and bougainvillea
appears odd but charming. Combined with the surrounding
red tile roofs and Victorian gingerbread, it seems more
eclectic than incongruous: a delicious mélange of London,
New Orleans, and Santa Barbara.

Crossing through the city, I headed toward the Botanic
Gardens. Sunlight danced in the swaying palms and sparkled
on the nearby water. Surrounded by strange trees and
brilliant flowers, I became giddy with delight. I raised my
face to the sun and laughed out loud. The joy and beauty of
the day reconfirmed for me that coming to Australia was
the right thing to do, and this was the right place to start.
This fragrant, sun-washed city soothes my soul, and my
tightly wound, rat-racing soul needs to be soothed.

Jet lag, compounded by exposure to unaccustomed
amounts of fresh air, caught up with me after sundown.
So, with the flickering on of the streetlights, I wended my
way wearily, happily, back to the hotel.

Friday, August 19

One week ago, I still had a job. I had given notice, but I
was still at work. I'm not certain how much it has sunk in
that I'm not going back, that I'm unemployed and without
prospects. I've managed to snatch a few one-week vacations
over the years, so I haven't actually been gone long
enough to truly believe that I won't have to go to the
office on Monday. I wonder how long it will take my head
to catch up with my actions. However, it's another glorious day—dazzling, clear, warm—and I find it impossible
to really worry about it.

The warmth here in Brisbane seems to come from more

than just the sun. There is a warmth of spirit that flows from the country itself and is reflected in its people. A joyous energy pervades the air, like the first spring day after a hard winter. The warmth and energy have wrapped around me, filled me, augmenting my excitement, and at the same time making me feel at home.

I spent the early morning wandering, photographing old houses and strange trees. Most of the older houses are built up on "stumps," wood or concrete stilts that permit breezes to pass beneath houses to cool them. Newer homes have air conditioners, which are probably more effective, but are not nearly as picturesque. As for trees, I loved the African tulip trees, with their circles of bright, orange, cup-shaped flowers, and the dramatic, leafless coral trees, with their clusters of hard, spiky, curving, scarlet blooms. Odder still were the sausage trees, which bear long, sausage-shaped fruit that hang down on cord-like stalks.

Around 9:30, I headed up past the Grecian-columned Anzac Memorial and over to the Central Railway Station for a short ride to the fairgrounds. From the train, I could see the tall, glittering rides of the fairway, the sea of metal-roofed exhibition halls, and the milling crowds of people and animals as we approached. This is the last day of the Royal Brisbane Show.

The show is a celebration of Queensland, of the land— farming, ranching, mining, nature—and of the people. Here, I found myself immersed in the vigorous, healthy exuberance of an Australia that seemed even more enthusiastic, friendly, and sporting than I had imagined.

The miles of exhibits delighted me. Here was a concentrated dose, a rich cross-section of everything I've read, everything I associate with vast, sprawling Queensland: sugar refining and bauxite mining; forestry and wildlife; exotic fruit and brilliant flowers; horses, dogs, sheep; and people— lots of wonderful, outgoing people. Food vendors, ranchers, guides, exhibitors, other visitors, all would stop whatever they were doing to have a chat with (apparently) the only American at the show. They were cheerful and charming, proud of Australia, Queensland, their hometowns, or their prize bulls, and glad to have someone to share it with.

At home, I am accustomed to "Hanging in there" or "Not too bad" (even from my own lips) as the response to "How are you today?" Here, everyone is "Fantastic," "Terrific," "Any better and I'd be dangerous." The difference is startling, refreshing, and encouraging. The easy, natural joy seems to be contagious.

I wandered for hours among elaborate arrangements of vegetables and fruit, pens of newborn lambs and calves, resource conservation displays, rows of bright tractors, contests for every skill and/or animal imaginable, and demonstrations of everything from weaving to mining. Everything was raised to the level of high entertainment by the unrelenting, wry wit of the Aussies.

Australian humor is sort of a cross between the dry understatement of England and the wild hyperbole of the American West, but tempered and augmented (and a little twisted) by the hardships and peculiarities of Australia. Everyone today had a joke or a witty rejoinder (for example, when asked if he'd lived here his whole life, one farmer responded, "Not yet.").

At the exciting finals of the state wood-chopping competition, I met Harold, a station owner from north of Brisbane. (A station is what we Yanks refer to as a ranch.) White-haired and broadly smiling, with his bushman's hat pushed back from a deeply tanned, well-creased face, he appeared the quintessential rural Aussie.

Harold flooded me with information about the area, the show, and raising cattle. He explained the classes of wood-chopping events, and told me about the competitors in the contest (many of whom are policemen—no wonder the crime rate's so low). Time is used for handicapping, with the top choppers starting later than their challengers. And, boy, could the champs make the chips fly.

His grandfather, Harold told me, was among the earliest settlers in the area near Conandale where his family now lives. He described a place near his home named Maleny. "It's so beautiful," he said, "they had to shoot someone to start the cemetery—no one wanted to leave."

Harold talked of his station, of the horses needed to run it, and of the skillful riders he employs. He created for me visions of hearty stockmen riding flat out through the scrub, ringing the mob (rounding up the herd) and driving it across wide, golden plains. I was truly sorry to have to tell Harold that I've planned too much and couldn't accept his invitation to come out and ride the range for a few days. It's only been a week since the last horse I rode pitched me into a wall, breaking my ribs—but that probably wouldn't keep me from trying if I had the time. It is a part of the Australia I want to know. Perhaps someday I shall have another chance.

Parting company with Harold, I wandered off to enjoy an evening filled with horses. Australians have always been a people who love horses and admire skilled horsemen, so neither the quality of the equestrian events nor the crowds in attendance came as a surprise. From the formal elegance of dressage to the excitement of Roman chariot races, the skill of the riders, and the beauty and power of those glorious animals delighted everyone.

Totally new to me was tent-pegging, a sport of skill and daring, in which mounted lancers try to spear wooden pegs (originally the tent pegs in an enemy camp) while riding at a full gallop. I was enthralled.

Finally, near midnight, a huge fireworks display brought my bright day to a dazzling close. Time to find the train station and head "home."

Saturday, August 20

It was a brilliant day, and the sunlight sparkled on the dancing, silver-edged surf. My southbound bus stopped frequently to drop off swimmers and sunners. After little more than an hour, I disembarked near the lush, wooded Currumbin Wildlife Sanctuary.

I walked through the entryway, past the visitors' center, and out into the sanctuary, the wonderful sanctuary. Something snapped, like an over-wound spring, and I felt the reserve and the years fall away, and I was a kid in a candy store, capable of few comments more sophisticated than "Wow."

Among the tall gum trees, dozens of koalas nibbled leaves or slept, curled into tight balls, wedged in the forks of higher branches. A mother koala ambled from limb to limb, her baby clinging to the fur on her back.

Winding paths led me between shade trees and across grassy clearings, where kangaroos and wallabies wandered, grazed, relaxed, played, and watched their visitors. As I walked along, kangaroo after kangaroo bounded past me or crossed my path. Grazing or resting they look something like over-sized rabbits, but in "flight" they are a delightfully strange sight, with their powerful legs and big feet bouncing them along, and their great tails balancing them. I thought of Rudyard Kipling's "Sing-Song of Old Man Kangaroo," where the kangaroo asks of the Big God Nqong, "Make me different from all other animals." Nqong was very successful.

More than anything else, at Currumbin I saw birds, and Australia has some wonderful ones. Emus, five feet tall, stalked between paperbarks and grass trees. Sulphur-crested cockatoos searched for gum nuts, or greeted visitors with a tilted head and a rasping "hraw." Parrots competed in brilliance with flowering hibiscus and other exotic blooms. Mud hens, black with red faces, dashed through the papyrus, and pale gray Cape Barren geese snorted through the shrubs. Egrets waded and pelicans glided across the lake. The rarest birds were in cages, but everything else flew, fluttered or strolled around the grounds. Particularly abundant were the rainbow lorikeets—dazzling, multi-colored little parrots—which come by the thousands to feed at the sanctuary each day.

I even saw a kookaburra (as in the song "Kookaburra sits in the old gum tree"—which, when I learned it as a child, I thought was about a make-believe creature). The kookaburra is the largest member of the kingfisher family and is best known for its rollicking "laughter" (". . .merry, merry king of the bush is he"). However, this stocky, brown-and-white bird with the light blue-spattered wings sat in absolute silence, just staring back at onlookers. But its over-sized beak did seem ever-so-slightly curved up at the edges into a little smile.

Dinner at the hotel brought me into contact with another of Australia's delights—the hospitable Australian. At the little restaurant at the hotel, Margot is hostess, waitress, and cashier, and her husband Carl is the cook. After relaying my order to Carl, Margot pulled up a chair and sat with me until my food arrived, asking what I've been doing and what my plans are.

After dinner, Margot returned, this time with a steaming kettle. She poured two cups of tea, and we chatted until Carl was through in the kitchen and could join us. Statistics indicate that Australians are generally well read (in fact, they're among the biggest book buyers per capita in the world), and Margot and Carl certainly seemed to bear this out, so we had no problem finding topics of conversation. Talking until after 10:30, we covered topics ranging from history to current politics, and pumpkin scones to wheat prices. Of course, they also wanted to know if I like Australia. Absolutely!

Sunday, August 21

Passing the Old Mill, a convict-built relic of Brisbane's early history, I headed into town to catch a tour to a different part of the area's history. I was soon speeding southward, toward Beenleigh and Australia's oldest rum distillery.

The Beenleigh Rum Distillery has a museum filled with artifacts and displays detailing the part rum played in the early days of colonial Australia. It was a more significant part than might be imagined. Always a valued commodity in a harsh, thirsty land, rum, with the help of the New South Wales Corps,* became the colony's primary currency. Wages were paid and purchases made with rum. Through import monopolies, the Corps maintained control of the trade, and therefore of the colony, for nearly 20 years.

Such liquid assets were easily forged, and illegal stills abounded. Of course, the problems involved in an economy built almost entirely on an illicit liquor trade are legion, and England eventually sent a stern disciplinarian out to solve the problems. Captain William Bligh (of *Bounty* fame) was installed as Australia's fourth governor.

The scope of the problem had been underestimated, as almost all military officers and free settlers were involved in the rum trade at some level, and Bligh's interference and accusations merely served to precipitate the Rum Rebellion. Bligh was arrested by Major Johnston, Commander of the New South Wales Corps, in January 1808, and spent more than a year in confinement. When news finally reached London, a new governor, Lachlan Macquarie,* was sent out, this time accompanied by a full regiment to back up any orders he might wish to make. Macquarie was a bit more judicious than Bligh, and, rather than directly attacking the rum trade, he simply worked on expanding and developing the colony until land became more profitable than rum.

Interestingly, the current legal distillery was founded in

*See appendix

1884 from an earlier, illegal distillery that was housed offshore on a ship. Moored not far from the entrance of the distillery's amiably sprawling wooden buildings and walkways is a 3/4-size replica of that ship, the *Walrus*. I guess it shouldn't be surprising that a land that cherishes its convict past would fondly remember past bootlegging.

Aside from the history lesson, I also learned about rum making. It is distilled from molasses, which arrives in great carriers from the sugar refineries up north. The smell of the rum aging in oak casks was delicious and heady— but the fumes are highly flammable, and signs abound warning visitors not to light anything.

On the bus again, we were off for what proved to be the highlight of my day—Mt. Tamborine and the rainforest. As we ascended Mt. Tamborine, our guide stopped to point out the ancient and primitive macrozamia palms. These stunted, shaggy, rather fern-like palms, also known as cycads, are living relics of prehistoric times. Many of the slow-growing little palms are hundreds—some even estimate a thousand or more—years old. A spectacular view of plains stretching toward the ocean greeted us as we crested the mountain. Then we were dropped off at the beginning of a narrow, rough path, and on foot, we descended into the rainforest.

It is almost beyond words to describe the beauty of the rainforest. It is harder still to express how that beauty affected me. My reaction was almost physical—an intense serenity, an elated peacefulness poured through me, like cool water in a dry land.

The forest is rejoicingly beautiful and incredibly green. As one descends, the trees close overhead, so even the sunlight filtering in seems green. Water trickles over moss-covered rocks, joins with other trickles, forms streams that end in waterfalls and great, deep pools that spill endlessly down the mountainside, disappearing and reemerging from the fabulous tangle of undergrowth. Fig trees with fantastic aerial root systems twist into weird, intricate shapes. Palms, mahogany trees, figs, and gum trees stretch high overhead. Ferns attain amazing sizes. Trees drip with vines. We could hear the calls of wild birds and see an occasional flash of vivid color, but the only creature we saw clearly was a brush turkey building its nest.

Most of the trees grow straight and tall, trying to reach above the green canopy and into the sunshine. Some grow at precarious angles, wedged into gaps in the mountain's side, clinging to boulders for support. Fallen trees have become gardens of moss, ferns, and shelf-like, orange fungus, but even the living trees support mosses and ferns. Creeping vines carpet the forest floor in green. Climbing vines, some with thorns, twist up, over and around, hanging in festoons from tree to tree. Small, subtly colored flowers peek through the leaves of many bushes. The rich beauty of the place is almost overwhelming.

By the time we had descended to Cedar Creek Falls, we were breaking out of the rainforest and getting back into eucalypt forest. There, a great slash of bare, gray rock cuts through the trees, where Cedar Creek bursts through a broad cleft and falls to a series of deep pools connected by cascades and rapids.

Stained, stone walls rose up on the far side of the pools, but the slope on the side where we stood was like giant, uneven steps, broken and worn. We climbed down through the rocks for a better view, balancing along stone ledges paralleling the rushing water, hopping across boulders. There were people swimming in one of the lower pools, and boys diving from the cliffs into the deep water below.

"Idyllic" was the first word that came to mind, but it is not strong enough. This, to me, this whole day was far more wonderful than "rustic contentment." It was a revelation. I wanted to stay, and my gaze clung to everything around me, trying to hold me there.

I am beginning to understand that nice landscaping

around the office and the occasional sunset during the drive home are not enough, at least for me. This beauty, this wildness, this everything real and alive is something I must have as part of my life. My mind may be well served indoors, but what my starving spirit craves can only be found outside. I need culture, but I need nature, too—and maybe more.

Monday, August 22

The first order of business this morning was getting to the Northern Territory and Western Australia Government Tourist Centres, to book rooms for Alice Springs and Darwin, and to collect information on how to access some of the less accessible areas in which I'm interested. Brochures full of alien words such as "hike," "climb" and "camp" were spread before me. My excitement mounted, however, as I looked at pictures of glorious wilderness, of remote gorges and forests and deserts, of the kind of natural beauty with which I hope to saturate myself.

The ambitiousness of my plans might be daunting, if I thought of them practically. One day in the rainforest, and I suddenly seem completely unable to keep my inexperience and possible limitations (can I really do this?) in mind. I said "yes" to everything.

After lunch, I headed down to Hayles Wharf to catch a boat to Lone Pine Koala Sanctuary. Lone Pine is a non-profit organization operated for the benefit of the animals, not for the tourists. They just let us visit, both to raise support for their efforts and to educate the public about Australia's native fauna. The sanctuary normally has around a hundred koalas, one of the largest colonies in Australia. Lone Pine has been so successful at breeding the animals that they have been able to return large numbers of them to the wild.

"Koala" is an Aboriginal word for "never drink" or "no

water." Koalas get almost all the moisture they need from the eucalypt leaves they eat. However, they do occasionally drink, but only small amounts, and only in the summer, when the leaves dry out. Adult koalas come in a surprising range of sizes: from 10 to 30 pounds, and two to three feet in length. They have remarkably soft fur, but their long, sharp claws make them less than ideal as cuddly toys. Due to the heavy eucalyptus consumption, they smell a lot like cough drops. A few of the colony's koalas were feeling romantically inclined, and we could hear their startling mating calls. It's sort of a snore/snort for the males and like loud hiccups for the females.

Lone Pine also has a selection of other Aussie fauna: kangaroos, wallabies, dingoes, wombats, emus, pythons, cockatoos, and a duck-billed platypus (which in real life doesn't look any more probable than it does in pictures). As I strolled around the park-like sanctuary, 'roos, wallabies, and emus kept coming up to me for hand-outs (animal treats were available at the entrance, and I'd filled all my pockets). It was wonderful. I loved watching small children react to the animals. (Just as in the U.S., the wild creatures of field and forest do not normally show up in urban backyards, so even for many Australian children this is a first-time encounter.)

Dingoes are confined to large, fenced-in runs. These wild dogs, apparently introduced from Asia by sea travelers about 4,000 years ago, are similar to domestic dogs in structure and habits. They stand about two feet tall at the shoulder. Dingoes are generally loners, and they don't bark, just yelp or howl. Seeing them here, it is hard to imagine these rather handsome, sad-eyed, yellow dogs as big problems. I've read, however, that in many areas they are a real nuisance, as poultry and sheep are easier prey than the kangaroos and rabbits they normally hunt.

Too soon, it was time to catch the boat back to town. During the return trip, the boat captain pointed out the mangrove trees studding a large, low swamp island cradled in a broad meander of the river. Hanging from the trees were thousands of fruit bats, or flying foxes. Fruit bats are the largest bats in the world, with body lengths of around 16 inches and wingspans of five feet. Their furry, fox-like faces and large, dark eyes make them more attractive than other bats. "Unknown to most people," we were told, "the bat is a very affectionate animal and makes an ideal pet." Sure.

The sun was slipping toward the horizon, and the city was outlined against the frail pink of the twilight sky as the boat pulled in once more to Hayles Wharf.

--- *Miscellany* ---

I have said nothing thus far of the foods I've enjoyed here in Queensland, and that's not like me. Of course, the biggest news is seafood when staying in a seaport. The indigenous delights I have sampled thus far have included mud crabs, sand crabs, king prawns, tiger prawns (really huge), Moreton Bay "bugs," and barramundi.

"Bugs" are sweet, flavorful crustaceans that look something like small, flattened lobsters. Barramundi is a massive saltwater fish that is also called giant perch. Not only is it indigenous to Australia, its range is limited even here, being found from Queensland to the Kimberleys (northern Western Australia). The name is Aboriginal and means "big fish." The flesh is dense, white, and delicately flavored—definitely something to add to the "favorites" list.

Fruit is also abundant and often exotic (had my first passion fruit here).

I've always considered discovering new foods to be one of the joys of travel. I didn't come to Australia looking for exceptional new foods, but I'm happy to be finding them.

Tuesday, August 23

Once again I was on a bus heading south. We drove almost to the New South Wales border before turning inland. Mountains rose up as we wound through a green valley of farms and villages.

In a tiny town called Canungra, the bus driver suggested we stop for morning tea. (Tea breaks are almost as deeply rooted in Australian life as in British.) Lush, tropical plants framed clean, white cottages that were, like the older houses in Brisbane, perched on stumps. I sat in the shady garden of a small, charming, dark-wood hotel, surrounded by flowers and immense staghorn ferns, enjoying tea, clear air, and chatting with people from the bus.

While in Canungra, the bus driver walked over to the post office and picked up the local mail. As we continued up into the mountains, the driver would honk the horn and, as we rounded a corner, we'd see someone emerging from a house or the forest to come down to the road to get their mail. They'd talk with the driver and wave to friends on the bus. Then we'd drive on.

I am delighted by this interdependency, this drawing together bred of isolation. Without realizing it, I think that this sense of community (so intrinsic a part of this isolated land as to border on the legendary, woven unconsciously through nearly all of Australian literature) is one of the things I came looking for.

The winding, unpaved roads carried us upward. We ascended more than 2,000 feet into the McPherson Ranges, which are actually the eroded remnant of a massive caldera from long-vanished volcanoes. I watched pastureland give way to eucalypt forest, which changed and intensified as we approached the range's rich, wet, green crown. An hour and a half after leaving Canungra, we reached O'Reilly's Guesthouse, one of only two entryways into Lamington National Park.

This spot was settled by the O'Reilly family in the early

1900s. When the area was designated a national park in 1915, the O'Reillys realized that they, who knew the area so well, were in the perfect position to introduce others to the wonders of this region. They opened their guesthouse in 1926. The rambling, wooden buildings of the rustic mountain lodge are set in a broad, grassy clearing near the edge of a cliff. Below and beyond lie the Canungra Valley, rolling green foothills, and the misty blue of other mountains. And surrounding O'Reilly's is the glorious rainforest. Lamington National Park encompasses the largest preserved stand of sub-tropical rainforest in Australia—and I was ready for more rainforest.

I entered the rainforest, alone, eagerly descending into its green heart. Huge ferns and palms towered overhead. Fantastic trees spread immense wings and buttresses to support themselves in the soft, cushiony forest floor. Hugely tangled root systems wrapped around rocks and snaked across the footpath. The dense vegetation shut out all outside noises. I could hear only the sounds of the forest: bird calls, dripping water, rustling leaves, scurrying feet, and beating wings.

As I wound down the path, I occasionally startled pademelons—tiny, bush-dwelling wallabies. Each one would look at me for a moment, then dart off through the undergrowth. I frequently saw brush turkeys trotting along, enjoying the comparative ease of the footpath. The sight of a beautiful gold and black Regent bowerbird stopped me in my tracks, and I stood, watching, as long as it was near.

It began to rain, but the trees overhead were so dense that, though I could hear the rain, it never reached me. The path was only visible for a few feet before and behind me, with the forest closing in around it. It was so peaceful, and so intensely green, and so beautiful and wild that it left me helplessly and deliciously captivated.

After descending for nearly an hour, I turned around and

headed back up the mountainside. Everything looked so different from the other side, it was hard to believe I was covering the same ground.

As I neared the lodge, I took a side path up the hill to the Botanical Garden and Orchid Sanctuary. Left as close as possible to its natural state, the garden was lush and chaotic, and so vast and dense that one might easily become lost. Transplanted samples of the local flora grew in dazzling profusion. There were cascades of orchids: pale yellow and deep red, speckled pink, dark gold, rust and white. Swarms of small, fragrant jasmine flowers covered tall bushes. Grass trees, lilies, fuchsia, cyclamen, grape hyacinth, bright yellow acacia, pink gardenias, and orange hibiscus abounded. Some of the bromeliads had flowers that looked like cascades of bright-pink, purple-tipped wax matches. There were low clusters of pale lavender flowers, plants that looked like ice and smoke, brilliant red daisy-like blooms, and great bushes of deep purple or delicate pink blossoms. The rainforest wrapped snugly, possessively around the garden, overlapped the boundaries, and the garden flowed out into the forest.

When at last I walked back to the lodge, I was given a grand tour. The lovely mountain resort is still run by the O'Reillys. The walls of the music room are lined with family photographs of the earliest arrivals on the scene, with the teams of horses (massive, Australian-bred draft horses called Walers, after New South Wales) they used to haul equipment up the mountain.

After the tour I bought some birdseed, because (I had been told) if you feed them, the parrots will come right out of the rainforest. Within seconds I was besieged by the most astonishingly beautiful birds I've ever seen. Brilliant red and royal blue, they're called crimson rosellas. As greedy as they were, they got tired of waiting for the seeds to hit the ground and started perching on my hands, arms, shoulders, head. As D.H. Lawrence noted, "That is another

of the charms of Australia: the birds are not really afraid."
I was delighted. I sat on the ground and poured the rest of
the seeds into my skirt, then photographed the birds as
they perched on my knees, munching, and snapping and
flapping their wings at newcomers. They were so beautiful,
I could hardly believe it.

It was desperately hard to leave. I feel like all I'm doing
here is finding out what plans I should have made; I should
have stayed longer at O'Reilly's, spent more time in the
rainforest. Instead, I was booked on the late afternoon bus
heading back to the city. It didn't help that the woman
seated next to me had just spent three days at O'Reilly's
and was fairly bursting with stories. She told me about
waterfalls, nighttime rainforest tours, creeks illuminated
by thousands of glowworms, and waking to mountain-
fresh air and the sounds of myriad birds.

I guess there was no way to foresee what all this would
mean to me. Some hidden part of my being must have had
a hint, seen some glimmer of it, or I wouldn't have come.
But I didn't really know it would touch me so profoundly.

I'll just have to come back.

Wednesday, August 24

Morning found me headed east, along the Warrego
Highway, out through Ipswich and the broad, verdant
Lockyer Valley. On the far side of the valley, the Great
Dividing Range rose, its slopes splashed yellow, pink,
orange, and white by an unrestrained riot of lantana. We
ascended 2,000 feet, topped the rim, and rolled onto the
wide plains of the Darling Downs.

We passed through Toowoomba, the "Garden City" of
Queensland, then swung slightly north. We were nearly
100 miles from Brisbane, in the small rural town of
Oakey, when we stopped for lunch. An English girl on the

tour joined me, and we bought sandwiches and ate outside, strolling up the parkway of Oakey's wide main street.

At the edge of town, we saw a sign that directed us to a museum situated behind a small tea room. At the back of a building that must once have been a warehouse was the Darling Downs Aviation Museum. The room was filled with propellers, engines, instrument panels, and navigational equipment. Placards gave detailed explanations of the bits of equipment and the area's aviation history.

During World War II, there was a large military airfield nearby. Most of the planes were destroyed at war's end, but locals, veterans, and military history buffs are working to collect anything that escaped destruction.

We hurried back to the bus after enjoying our little discovery and were on our way to Jondaryan. Jondaryan Woolshed was the first sheep station in this area, dating back to 1859. It's a wonderful-looking place. The work buildings are of weathered wood with corrugated iron roofs. The houses are classic colonial Australian, with wide verandas and steep roofs. Nearby, old windmills pumped water from deep wells. Great draft horses hauled heavy loads across the yard, past the many sheds, work buildings and animal enclosures.

We crossed the wide, dusty yard and entered the large, low shearing shed. In the shed's interior, the wood is dark, but light seeps in through cracks and openings everywhere, making a wonderful play of shadows in the spacious main room. The floor slats are laid in geometric patterns, and the many sheep pens further enhance the design. Small, low doors, through which the sheep are released once shorn, let in patches of light and glimpses of the greenery growing thickly at the building's edge.

Jondaryan used to handle 200,000 sheep each season. It is quieter now, but is still used for shearing. Rough-coated Border Leicesters and Suffolks were on hand, but the sheep we saw shorn were the great, cloud-like Merinos, which are possessed of the finest wool in the world. The belly wool is removed first and kept separate. Then the rest of the wool is taken off in one piece. It's amazing to watch them spread out the huge blanket of wool that comes off one sheep. The wool is folded, shoulder wool outermost, as this is the best wool. A greasy fringe is removed and saved—it is the source of lanolin—then the wool is baled, ready for market.

Leaving the shearing shed, we wandered back across the compound. At the forge, the blacksmith made a horseshoe, then admitted that they now usually buy ready-mades. A stockman drove bullocks into the yard. At the cooking shed, damper and billy tea were being removed from the fire.

Damper and billy tea are staples of bush cooking, referred to frequently in literature and legend and still commonly consumed around campfires. Damper is a very basic bread made of flour, water, and baking powder and baked in a cast-iron camp oven buried in the coals. Sitting near it on the fire would be the billy, a blackened bucket, in which water for tea was boiled. (If a boiling billy doesn't ring a bell, it's been too long since you last heard "Waltzing Matilda.")

While I enjoyed my first damper and a mug of tea, I talked with an Aussie who'd appeared from behind one of the work buildings and strolled over in search of refreshment. He told me tales of his youth, growing up in the Outback. He was rugged and not past being handsome—and he looked entirely capable of the things he described: cattle drives and sheep shearing; tea and damper around real campfires; education in a one-room school house, where you stayed until you were 14, then went to work full-time on the station. He said he was back in this area looking for a property of his own. He'd worked for 20 years in the city, saving his money, and now he was ready to make his move back to the land.

I looked around me, at the broad fields, the buildings, the gum trees standing tall and gaunt against the pale sky, and thought,

"Yes, this is good land to move back to."

Thursday, August 25

Today was a day for farewells, as I explored Brisbane for the last time. I revisited many of the city's grand buildings and window-shopped the length of Queen's Mall. I wandered through town and along the river, pausing to watch the ferries and sailboats glide across the water.

Several hours were spent in exploration of the Botanic Gardens. High hedges of poinsettias bordered the walkways. Aloes and yuccas crowded the sunniest corners. Outlining the gardens, shading the river bank, and dotting the lawns and flower beds everywhere were exotic trees: tall, slender palms; massive, spreading figs; heavily laden sausage trees; coral trees, with their brilliant, flame-colored, spiky crowns of flowers; monkey puzzle trees, with great, swooping branches of thick, rigid leaves. I stopped for a while to watch an impromptu soccer game on one of the broad lawns. The sun was bright and warm, and the whole world seemed to sparkle.

The bell in the clock tower at Town Hall was tolling as, at long last, I crossed King George Square. The setting sun gilded the trees of Wickham Park and set the horizon ablaze. Finally, I arrived back at the hotel for an evening of organizing and packing.

Tomorrow I leave Brisbane. I'm excited about the rest of my trip, but I'm still sorry to leave. I have truly enjoyed my stay here. But I didn't come this far to settle in—so onward, and maybe upward.

Friday, August 26

A bus ride is still an intrinsically romantic experience: gliding down a ribbon that's tied to the horizon. It was raining, which seemed appropriate for departing. As we rolled northward, I leaned back and became absorbed by the journey, listening to the singing of the tires, looking out the window at the rain, the city, suburbs, wilderness— always changing, with the radio playing, and I can hear the movie cameras rolling in my mind.

Driving city to city in Australia, there's a lot more in-between than city, and not all the roads are paved (or sealed, as they say here). Some of the unsealed roads became a bit tricky in the rain, and our driver stopped a couple of cars coming from the opposite direction to make certain the roads were still open. The streams running across our path only slowed us slightly, however.

Saturday, August 27

I awoke (if I ever actually slept) to a glorious dawn, sun rising over fields of sugar cane, sky streaked pink and mauve. We rolled into Airlie Beach at 8 a.m., 18-1/2 hours after leaving Brisbane, and I disembarked.

I never thought I'd make it the five blocks to my hotel. Not knowing what to bring, I brought everything. With riding boots, hiking boots, running shoes, tennis shoes, flats, pumps, and three pairs of sandals, my footgear alone could sink me. Aside from a huge suitcase, I have an amoeba-like, green, nylon duffel bag that keeps slithering off my little, wheeled luggage cart, and my camera equipment (my trusty Nikon, lenses, tripod, and 120 rolls of film). My ribs, having already been rebroken once during the trip over, are far from being sufficiently healed for me to be toting all this, and even pulling the cart is far from painless. I struggled along, but hadn't gone more than a few yards before a strapping Aussie shopkeeper saw me and came zipping out of his store. With a grin and a "Where you headed, luv?" he grabbed my luggage and set off down the street. He dropped my gear at the front desk of the Airlie Beach Hotel/Motel, said "Have a nye stye," (have a nice day? a nice stay?—I love the accent, but I'm still not completely adjusted to it), and ambled back to his shop.

I slept for a few hours, making up for last night on the bus, then spent the balance of the day hiking around the area, climbing hills and strolling along beaches. I am now well above the Tropic of Capricorn, so the weather is hot, even though it is still winter. The attitude here is tropical, too—laid-back, easy-going, and friendly.

Airlie Beach is a delight. It is one of those lovely, small places you hope not too many people hear of—although too many have probably heard already. She sits snugly, amiably, nestled at the base of lushly forested hills, with the unbelievably clear, turquoise ocean at her feet. The Whitsunday Islands float on the horizon, easily visible from town.

There are flowers everywhere, perfuming the clean sea air, dazzling the eyes. Palm trees sway along the shore. The streets are lined and gardens filled with frangipani trees, mango trees, African tulips, flame trees, and innumerable others. It is intoxicatingly exotic.

Dark green mangrove trees, with searching, arching, stilt roots, grasp at the sand, gathering silt where a stream empties into the ocean. The ancient, sun-bleached remains of a boat wrecked along the shore, among the mangroves, was half buried by the collecting silt. The pale, curving, wood ribs sticking out of the mud in this dazzling location looked like a story waiting to be told. Of course, I imagine there are many stories here.

Sunday, August 28

I caught an early bus to Shute Harbour, for a cruise of the Whitsunday Islands (so called because Captain Cook discovered this area on Whitsunday in 1770). It could not possibly have been a more beautiful day—sunny, with a light, fresh breeze. From Shute Harbour we cruised north. The islands around us were hilly and green and lush. Some met the water with gentle beaches, others, with rugged cliffs. We passed South Molle and Mid Molle Islands and stopped at Daydream Island. We took on more passengers, then headed for Hayman Island, across the Whitsunday Passage.

The thing I could not, and still cannot, get over is the water. It is as clear and brilliant as a flawless aquamarine, varying in hue from dark turquoise to rich peacock blue to delicate crystal green nearer the islands. I could see through the waves; I could see the keels of boats at anchor. It was incredible.

After 1-1/2 hours we pulled into the dock at Hayman Island, a verdant, steep-sided, submerged mountain surrounded by broad, white beaches. Bougainvillea grew in bright pink and fuchsia cascades the size of houses. African tulips, with their brilliant orange flowers, blazed in the sunlight. Frangipani scented the air. Cockatoos screeched from palm trees and peacocks wandered about looking for handouts.

The only habitation on the island is an attractive resort village. Almost all the islands are part of the National Parks system, which protects them and prevents exploitation. Resorts lease their land from the Department of Parks and Wildlife.

The morning passed quickly in these lovely surroundings. Then, after lunch, those of us who wished to visit the underwater observatory at Hook Island reboarded the boat. We crossed miles of bright water, circling Hook Island to the side opposite Hayman. A hundred yards offshore, we were met by glass-bottom boats, which ferried us out over the reef.

The Great Barrier Reef is 1,250 miles long and supports more animal life per square mile than any other region on earth. It is the largest structure ever built by living creatures, constructed over thousands of years by tiny coral polyps. But even more impressive than its size is its beauty. Nowhere else in the world is the marine life so varied and colorful. Nearly 400 species of coral provide an opulent backdrop for the sparkling dance and drama of reef life.

The coral was 20 to 30 feet below us, but looked close enough to touch, the water was so clear. As the boat edged away from the island, we peered intently through the glass and were entranced by the changing panorama. We saw fan coral and mushroom coral, fire coral and leathery coral, blue coral and red organ pipe coral. Schools of vividly colored fish darted through the almost luminous seascape, among starfish, sea anemones, and giant clams.

After about 20 minutes, we putt-putted toward the island. A long, narrow pier led us out to the observatory. I descended the steep, winding staircase through an immense steel tube and emerged in the observation room 30 feet below the water's surface, right in the heart of the reef. There were small, heavy windows all around me, and I was surrounded by coral and fish.

The colors that seemed pretty from the glass-bottom boats became breathtaking at close quarters. Tiny, brilliant yellow fish darted among the channels of enormous, green brain corals. Giant clams, some four feet across, turned out their mauve, purple, and green mantles to collect food. Red and yellow fans, and delicate, silver fire coral (named for its sting, not its color) waved in the crystalline water.

Bright orange and white clownfish nestled among the gracefully undulating tentacles of great, flower-like sea anemones. Green and peacock-blue parrotfish glided under extended shelves of plate coral. Pink and purple staghorn corals stretched long fingers toward the surface. Enormous blue sea cod and tiny butterflyfish, shimmering damselfish and ponderous batfish, royal blue surgeonfish and glittering jewelfish, angelfish and harlequinfish, and too many others to name, even if I could, wove around and through the maze of coral, sea urchins, seashells, and anemones.

A group of tuna came and hovered outside one of the windows for a while, no doubt trying to identify the strange creatures captured inside. I went slowly from window to window, taking more than an hour to make my way around the small room.

Long ago, I planned to become a marine biologist, but I got sidetracked. Now, my love for the wonder and complexity of the sea came back in a rush. I don't know if it was the memory of this old love, or my newly awakened passion for nature's beauty that made leaving so hard, but I found it difficult to tear myself away from this living fantasy of color, form, and movement.

When I did reemerge from the observatory, I headed inland, to explore the island. The steep, circuitous route I chose cut through the foliage then climbed to a cliff-side path that rewarded me with breathtaking vistas of sea and island. The greenery around me was lush and fragrant, and the air on the island was full of butterflies—tiny white and yellow ones and large purple and black ones.

Finally returning to the beach, I walked along the sand, collecting small, sun-bleached bits of coral that had washed ashore. Too soon, it was time to reboard the glass-bottom boats for the ride back to our ship. During the return trip to Shute Harbour, still awed by the beauty and clarity of the water, I hung over the ship's railing, gazing through the waves created by our bow.

At Shute Harbour, I purchased a Map Cowrie to add to my shell collection, then caught the bus back to Airlie Beach. I wandered along the shore until the lavenders and golds of sunset faded, and the outlines of the waving palms were only dimly visible against the star-reflecting sea. Then I headed back to the hotel to prepare for tomorrow's onward journey.

Miscellany

I have been delighted to hear in common usage expressions which until now I have encountered only in stories set in Australia. "Too right" and "my word" no longer belong only to characters in Nevil Shute's novels. "You beaut" is not now cried in an Arthur Upfield tale, but by real people, and I even saw a sign advertising "Beaut Pools." The relentlessly optimistic "She'll be right" is felt as much as heard. And, as literature indicated, so life bears out, everything is "she"—Australia, towns, cars, the weather, even life.

Monday, August 29

A true daughter of the big-city suburb, I'd grown up with the strongly held belief that taxis abounded throughout the civilized world. This is not true. I'm not sure, but I think Airlie Beach has only one.

When the taxi called by the hotel receptionist failed to materialize, I began to panic; only one bus goes through Airlie Beach each day, and I wanted to catch it. (It takes more than a few days in paradise to alter a hair-triggered, schedule-dominated, rush-hour mindset.)

The receptionist called a store across the street from the bus stop and asked them to make sure the bus waited for me. Then I headed back outside and started dragging my belongings across the unpaved yard, in the direction of the bus stop. The wheels on my cart wouldn't turn on the rocky ground, so I tried to carry everything. An awful, grinding feeling—something like the way fingernails down a blackboard sound—let me know that I'd pulled my ribs apart again, so I had to stop.

As if on cue, the second my ribs gave out, the taxi pulled up. The girl behind the wheel (who I think just woke up) failed to understand my anxiety. "Don't worry," she said with drowsy calm, "we'll make it." Through clenched teeth I said, "wonderful," as I wrestled my bags into the cab.

The shopkeeper had flagged down the bus, and he was standing at the curb, chatting with the bus driver. But as soon as I arrived, my luggage was loaded, and we were off. (The Australian bus services are, I was told, justly proud of their on-time records.)

The weather was, again, beautiful. The road north wound through miles of cane fields, which spread in all directions, framed by green mountains and blue sky. The sugar cane was seven feet tall and impossibly lush. At intervals, wonderful Victorian Queensland Plantation-style homes, all sloping roofs, verandas, and white woodwork, interrupted the undulating sea of green.

Just past noon, we rolled into Townsville, Queensland's second-largest city. Townsville sits astride Ross Creek on Cleveland Bay, which was discovered (what wasn't on this coast?) by Captain James Cook in 1770. In 1864, sea captain Robert Towns recognized the need for a port to serve the expanding inland cattle stations and founded the town that bears his name.

I checked into the large, modest Peoples Palace, which I'd chosen for its location and its low rates (being unemployed and uncertain about my future, luxury is not a consideration). Then I walked the two blocks to Flinders Street Mall, where I wandered among the ivory, white, and pastel, 19th-century buildings and abundant palm trees and flowers of the city's bright, lively heart.

After getting my bearings, I searched out the local Queensland Tourist Centre, where I booked an afternoon tour of the city and a tour for tomorrow to Charters

Towers, site of one of the state's great gold rushes.

The city tour gave me a wonderful overview of the town and the history of this region. From the Strand, a garden-lined beachfront boulevard that is home to parks and old Victorian buildings, I could see Magnetic Island. Captain Cook, who named it, thought the island affected his compass, but it isn't really magnetic—apparently, all it attracts is tourists.

At the Jezzine Barracks Military Museum, I learned of Townsville's surprisingly impressive military history. The tale begins in 1877, when this area was the location of Australia's main defenses against Russian and Chinese pirates, and continues through to World War II, when, after the fall of Guam, Pacific Operations relocated to Australia. During the war, there were upwards of 50,000 troops stationed in this area.

The Australian Army Captain who showed us through the museum overflowed with stories, many amusing— such as the tale of the bombing of Townsville. It was bombed three times during WWII. The first time, the only casualties were four chickens and a palm tree. There was also a very big hole in the ground, which, our Captain averred, was immediately claimed by the Department of Highways as a future source for potholes.

We spent more than an hour perusing photographs, maps, and souvenirs, listening to our host describe the pain, the difficulties, and the camaraderie of the many Pacific campaigns. Pictures of Borneo, New Guinea, Truk Island, Guadalcanal, Java, Guam, the Philippines, and Indonesia were testaments of the steaming, slogging horror of tropical jungle warfare, while medals, mementos, and stories bore witness to the strength, humor and heroism that arose from the hardship. As an American, I tend to think of World War II in terms of the United States and Britain, but Australia had a huge part in the war.

Castle Hill offered an excellent view of the town, valley,

and nearby islands. The hill is 997 feet high. In Australia, to be considered a mountain, the elevation must be 1,000 feet or more. So last year, local school children took buckets of dirt up the hill, three feet worth, to see if they could get it reclassified. Unfortunately, when the rains came, they lost their three feet, so it's still a hill.

At a nearby flora and fauna sanctuary, misleadingly named "Town Common," the Kangaroo Crossing road signs hinted at the possibility of wildlife lurking in the sea of tall grasses around us, but the only fauna we saw was a large number of kites, impressive members of the hawk family, soaring overhead.

Back at the People's Palace, I headed to the coffee shop for dinner. A young man at another table grinned when he saw me and asked, "You were just in Airlie Beach, weren't you?" When I responded in the affirmative, he grabbed his coffee, came and sat with me, and said, "I thought I recognized you. You were there yesterday." (It really is a small town.) He chatted while I ate, telling me with considerable excitement about his current plans. He is heading inland to Julia Creek to work as a "jackeroo," or ranch hand. By the time my meal was through, he was done with his tale, and was obviously pleased to have had someone with whom to share his great good fortune. I smiled as he headed off to find a pub to celebrate his last night in the big city.

One of the things that I had wondered about was how I would handle the solitude of a six-month solo tour. At home, I live alone, but work, church, family, and friends provide me with lots of human interaction. I like having time alone, but I also like people. I like talking and sharing. So I had thought that perhaps being on my own for so long a period might be a problem. However, I am beginning to think that Australia is not really going to give me much opportunity to feel lonely.

Tuesday, August 30

Charters Towers is 84 miles and a hundred years from Townsville. So well preserved is the town's antiquity that, when they made the period film *The Irishman* here, all they had to do was take down a few signs and cover the now-paved streets with dirt. Ornate buildings and impressive homes interspersed between simpler, more rustic shops, testify to the wealth of the gold rush days in this charming, turn-of-the-century country town.

The discovery of gold, which is where the town's history began, came in December 1871. A group of prospectors located the site, then traveled to Ravenswood to apply for a claim. The claim was awarded, in January 1872, by Mr. W.S.E.M. Charters, the mining warden at Ravenswood, and the prospectors named the spot Charters Tors, in his honor. Before long, common usage had changed the name to Charters Towers.

Charters Towers exploded into a bustling boomtown of 30,000 people. From 1872 to 1911, 6,800,000 ounces of gold were produced. Then, around 1916, gold production began to decline, so other industries were developed in the already dwindling town. There is still some mining going on around a greatly reduced Charters Towers, but the area's wealth now lies mainly in cattle raising and fruit growing.

For hours, I walked through Charters Towers' streets and shops, admiring the iron lace, curved awnings, pillared verandas, and interesting façades. I strolled by wonderful old homes, most on stilts, most richly burdened with Victorian "gingerbread" and surrounded by wildly luxuriant gardens. I passed the tall, stately City Hall and turned into the main street. In the wood-interiored saddlery shop and general store, even the air seemed old, and I could almost feel time slow down.

Most of the buildings in the town's center were built in the late 1800s. The 1887 Stock Exchange, where the price of gold was announced daily during the rush, now houses the mining museum. The old Imperial Hotel is run by the daughters of the man who built it. Both in their 80s, the two women are still waiting for the next big gold strike, which they are certain is imminent.

I rejoined my seven-member tour group at the Excelsior Hotel. The owner treated us to a tour of the large, lovely, old building, which dates to the 1880s. Velvet drapes frame tall windows. Original furnishings fill high-ceilinged, wood-floored rooms and halls of the well-maintained hotel. But beyond the lush, Victorian decor there was, in the air or the light, a sense of remoteness, an edge of rustic wildness that made me feel like ghosts of exuberance and golden possibilities still lurked just around the corner.

Just outside Charters Towers, we stopped at the home of Henry Weare. Henry is a prospector and a poet—the kind of character you hear about in tales of bygone days but never actually expect to meet. Snowy-haired, tan and broadly smiling, he greeted us at the entrance to the tangled, over-grown garden that surrounds his less than tidy house.

We wound through a yard littered with various tools for mining and refining precious metals, following the barefoot poet/prospector to the clearing where he works. Henry smelts gold in his bare feet, because "the hot coals would ruin the leather if they fell on your shoes."

A fire was burning when we arrived, and Henry stoked it till it was almost white hot. He removed a crucible from the inferno. Flames danced over the clay surface, and container and contents glowed fiercely. Henry tipped the crucible and poured molten gold into an ingot mold. During the entire operation, he recited his poetry for us.

Henry told us about prospecting in this area, where he thought reefs of gold might be found (usually under some new highway), how to mine and refine gold and silver, and about his life and travels. When the ingot was cool enough, he passed it around, along with some silver he'd smelted previously. Then, reciting a poem that began "Leave a footprint on my garden path," he requested that we sign his guest book, so he'd have a memento of our visit.

We drove on, back across the wide, open plains beneath the wide, empty sky. The remoteness, the sense of isolation attracted me strongly, and I gazed intently at the subtle, seemingly empty grasslands.

Around us, hundreds of rough, gray "anthills," three to five feet high, pointed—like gnarled, old fingers—out of the golden grass. They are actually the mounds of some of Australia's many varieties of termite, which are also called "white ants." Our driver told us that, in the old days, the hard, clay-like mounds were ground up, mixed with water, and used for making footpaths and tennis courts.

We crossed bridges over broad beds of sand that become powerful rivers during "the Wet," the summer rainy season. In clumps of brush, we saw jabirus: Australian storks, black and white, with long, red legs.

Too soon, civilization began to creep back into the picture. I was dropped off once more in the center of Townsville.

Wednesday, August 31

Today is the last day of winter—tomorrow spring begins. It was another gloriously sunny, warm day.

I walked into town for a bit of shopping and soon found a delightful, little country and ranching clothing store. The shopkeeper was great—not a hint of condescension in his manner when the crazy American woman tugged at an invisible hat brim and asked if he'd seen the movie version of "The Man From Snowy River." He smiled and politely said, "Of course," glanced at my head, and brought me the right size of the right hat. It's a gray, fur felt, Akubra

"Snowy River" stockman's hat with a tan, braided leather hatband. I've wanted this for a long time. My delight at finally having it was nearly unbounded. I love the look of it, the feel of it.

I spent some time window shopping—well, actually, admiring the reflection of my new hat in store windows. Then it was time to pick up my gear at the hotel and taxi over to Greyhound, to continue my journey north.

Views of the jeweled ocean, with its long, pale beaches, alternated with handsome sugar plantations, where the tall, supple cane rippled in the wind like another sea. Low mountains, their eroded ridges and cliffs softened by a thick blanket of greenery, rose before and around the road, approaching and retreating as we rolled on. We passed over bright rivers, through small towns, and along broad stretches of lush, tropical rainforest.

At 6 p.m., the bus pulled into Cairns. I disembarked and headed toward the sea and my hotel—the Silver Palm.

The Silver Palm is a "private hotel," i.e., a converted house. Although modest in itself, it has a fabulous setting, crowded on all sides by palms and flowers and facing the tree-lined Esplanade and beautiful Trinity Bay.

The whole outside wall of my room is louvered and can be opened to take full advantage of the fragrant tropical breezes and wonderful view. I watched the sun disappear, in a colorful blaze, behind the mountains that surround the town.

I'm sitting now, enjoying the evening breeze, listening to the sound of lapping waves and chirping crickets, watching the big ceiling fan turning lazily overhead. This is wonderful. I think I'm going to like it here.

Thursday, September 1

Up early, I had the Esplanade almost to myself as I strolled toward the harbor. The light was brilliant and the

day was already becoming warm. I turned up Shields
Street and stopped at the Queensland Government Tourist
Centre, to make arrangements for coming days and to pick
up a local bus schedule. Then I struck off through town,
along the wide, veranda-lined streets of very tropical, very
laid-back Cairns.

Down a side street, I came across the Aboriginal Craft
Centre. Spears, woomeras, boomerangs, churingas,
bullroarers, and didgeridoos lined the walls. A woman
there explained to me that they are trying to interest young
Aborigines in making traditional items in traditional ways,
both to keep the crafts alive and to keep the teens
employed. She also told me much about how the objects
on display were made.

She explained that the making of didgeridoos is something
of a joint effort. "White ants" eat only the heart of a tree,
leaving the trunk and branches hollow, so Aborigines look
for termite mounds near trees, then tap on branches until
they find a hollow branch the right size and shape. They cut
it, smooth the outside, and paint it—*et voilà,* a didgeridoo.

I made my way across town to the Royal Flying Doctor
Base and School of the Air. There are 14 Royal Flying
Doctor bases serving two-thirds of Australia. Each base is
connected by two-way radio to outlying stations in an
approximately 450-mile radius. All service is free of
charge; the entire operation is financed by donations. I
contributed a few dollars and was thrilled to get a "Keep
the Doctor Flying" bumper sticker as thanks.

Employing the same facility, and the same radios, as the
Flying Doctor is the School of the Air. In Queensland, 750
children, on distant, scattered stations and outposts,
"attend" school by shortwave. I watched a teacher conducting a class and listened as the young voices of her
widely dispersed pupils crackled back over the radio.
Though they talk daily during the school term, teachers
generally see their pupils only once each year.

I was delighted beyond words with the Royal Flying Doctor and School of the Air. They seem so much a part of a distant, romantic time, part of stories I read while I was growing up, and here they were before me, an ongoing reality. I wanted to be part of it, wanted to be at the other end of the radio signal, listening, depending on providence and the airwaves.

A short bus ride took me to the Botanical Gardens. Planted in 1886, the sumptuous, densely planted gardens feature more than 10,000 trees, shrubs, and flowers. I stopped to splash on a little bug repellent, as I noticed a humming shimmer rise from a shaded pool. Then, otherwise undaunted, I plunged into the crowd of greenery.

Brilliant cascades of red-flowered Flame of the Jungle spilled through the lush foliage. Cannonball trees appeared to be growing rows of rusting cannonballs. Large purple and small yellow water lilies thronged glassy ponds. Delicate, lavender Australian wisteria hung in festoons and curtains above masses of ferns, and fragrant clusters of ginger lilies crowded between royal palms and travelers palms.

After a few hours in the gardens, I was off again. I crammed the day with sights and sounds (add to the above a tour of Cairns Brewery and a visit to a marine research facility that specializes in coral and the Great Barrier Reef), tackling Cairns with the same kind of thoroughness and zeal I bring to business projects. But I guess this really is sort of a business project, this starting life over—happy but serious business. Besides, I hate wasting opportunities, and worry that, if I slow down, I'll miss something important.

As evening approached, I headed back toward my hotel. Instead of going inside, I crossed the Esplanade, sat down beneath the tamarind trees along the shore, and watched the sunset over the bay. The water was mauve and lavender, the surrounding mountains, dark purple, and the sky, pink and gold with lilac clouds. The many graceful, white seabirds gathered near the shore stood out in strong relief against the background of pastel sky and sea.

I felt absorbed by the beauty. I sat, listening to the waves, and permitted myself, for the first time in years, to do nothing. I looked at the stars, breathed the fragrance of the sea, felt the breeze teasing the hair on my neck and around my face, and I had nothing to do but enjoy it.

Sometimes stillness accomplishes as much as industry. Sitting there, unmoving, surrounded by the tranquility and warmth of the night, I felt like a patient who realizes for the first time that there really is a chance of getting well.

Friday, September 2

This morning, I was down at the boat docks on Trinity Bay bright and early for a cruise to Green Island. Green Island is part of the 80,000 square miles of reefs, islands, and protected waterways that make up the Great Barrier Reef. It is one of many islands along this coast that are true coral cays—that is, Green Island is not surrounded by reef, like the Whitsundays, it is reef. The highest point on the island is only about two meters above sea level at high tide.

As soon as I arrived on the island, I headed for the underwater observatory, which was a joy. Once again, the myriad forms and colors of reef life danced before my eyes, even more resplendent in their beauty and variety than I had remembered.

After an hour of rapturous observation of fish, coral, clams, rays, and sea anemones, I explored the beautiful, little island. The center of the island is lush and green, with palms and stilt-rooted pandanus, cascades of golden orchids, and magnificent deep pink and red hibiscus. From this bright cluster of tropical vegetation, glistening white beaches run down to the sparkling water. The mountains of the mainland rise, blue, rugged, and misty in the distance.

I left the shore, wading out a short distance onto the sharp, uneven coral. I was wearing tennis shoes—considered *de rigueur* for reef walking—but I still picked my way carefully. The tide was out, so the bright water was shallow, and I could see the coral sloping away from the island toward the brilliant blue of deeper water. I must come back someday without broken ribs, and try snorkeling in these waters.

Along the shore, there was much worn, twisted driftwood, and hundreds of small, white, spiraling seashells. I wandered about, photographing trees and beaches, egrets and hibiscus. At the island's outdoor cafe, tiny, exquisite, green and yellow birds perched on the rims of plates at abandoned tables, searching for crumbs. I explored until it was time for the last boat returning to the mainland.

Back in Cairns, I strolled under the tamarind trees along the Esplanade, trying to identify the many birds there. Most abundant were Australian pelicans, plumed egrets, honeyeaters, and silver sea gulls.

Finally, about 6 o'clock, I came back to the hotel to pack and get ready for tomorrow's trip to Cooktown.

Saturday, September 3

Tropic Wings Tours collected me at 8 a.m., then zipped over to the airport, where a small, twin-prop, bush-hopping plane and six other passengers awaited me.

After take-off, I got some nice aerial shots of Cairns, cane fields, mountains, sea, and islands. But then the "trouble" began. In order to show us something directly below, the pilot banked sharply, so we were perpendicular to the ground. "And now, so the passengers on the left side can see..." he announced, and he rolled the plane to its other side. He did this several times, even though we encountered turbulence over the mountains. Fortunately, even very small planes have airsick bags. I occasionally stole a sidelong glance out the window, to see whatever was being described, but mostly I kept my eyes closed, resting my reeling head against the cool glass. Thankfully, it was only a forty-minute flight.

On the ground, walking down the runway in the sunshine, I quickly recovered my equilibrium. By the opening in the fence that surrounds the grassy landing field, a bus awaited us. I boarded it and was ferried to the James Cook Historical Museum.

The museum is a gracious, two-story, Victorian composition of brick, white wood lace, and pillared verandas. Inside are exhibits covering the area's natural history (animals, plants, minerals, and a dazzling array of seashells), displays detailing the history and development of the town (including a restored Chinese shrine from the gold rush days), and an extensive collection of Captain Cook memorabilia. An avid little cluster of "Cook groupies" were in this last section—and, after a little study, I understood (and came to share) their enthusiasm.

James Cook was the son of a migrant Scottish farmhand who had married and settled in Yorkshire, England. The little boy's exceptional intelligence caught the attention of a farmer for whom his father worked, and this led to an opportunity for an education—though learning was a lifelong passion, and Cook never stopped studying. While working near the port of Whitby, the teenaged Cook fell in love with the sea and ships. He was skilled at business, but eventually turned to sailing the wild and dangerous North Seas. Hoping to see more of the world, he joined the British Navy when he was 27. Within two years, he became master of a ship and saw action in the Seven Years War.

Cook excelled as a mathematician and surveyor, and his surveys of the New World and his data on the solar eclipse of 1766 brought him to the attention of the scientific community. He was commissioned to observe the transit of Venus from the South Pacific, and in August 1768, he sailed from England in the *Endeavour*, a ship measuring less than 98 feet in length.

After accomplishing his primary mission in June 1769, Cook made his first reconnaissance of southern waters, to determine the location of the Antarctic Continent. During the course of this voyage, he found and charted all of New Zealand and discovered and surveyed the east coast of Australia (which he called New South Wales).

Captain Cook traveled north along the coast of Australia, naming bays, islands, and landmarks as he went, picking his way carefully as he sailed around and over the jagged coral of the Great Barrier Reef. On the night of June 10, 1770, his ship struck the reef. With two pumps going full tilt, and all hands working to lighten the load (they even jettisoned the cannons, one of which, recently recovered, now resides in the Cooktown museum), it was still a couple of days before they floated free of the coral, and another three days before the weather permitted them to limp into the narrow channel of a bay on the coast. The bay turned out to be the mouth of a river, which Cook named the Endeavour, after his ship. Years later, the town that grew up on the site, Cooktown, was named for the intrepid navigator who had been forced to beach there.

After Captain Cook's return to England in 1771, he was immediately commissioned to lead another expedition into Antarctic waters. The voyage lasted from 1772 to 1775 and covered 70,000 miles. During this time, Cook discovered New Caledonia, precisely located many little-known South Sea islands, and, crossing the Antarctic Circle, penetrated farther south than anyone had previously dared.

Upon his return to England, Cook was awarded the Copley Medal by the Royal Society of London for his work against scurvy, the most common cause of death at sea in those days. Then he was commissioned to lead another expedition in 1776, to approach the quest for a sea route north of the

American Continent from the Pacific side.

En route, Cook rediscovered Hawaii, previously known only to the Spanish, who discovered it in the 16th century. He then surveyed the coast of North America from Oregon northward through the Bering Strait to the Arctic Ocean. But when a sudden storm demasted one of the ships, Cook was forced to return to the Hawaiian Islands.

Cook did not want to return to Hawaii, as cultural conflicts and misunderstandings had led to growing tensions between crew and natives. However, the crippled ship left him no choice. When the natives' continual thieving culminated in the disappearance of one of the ship's boats, Cook, wanting to peacefully put an end to the harassment, confronted the Hawaiian king. He was assured that the boat would be returned, and the king accompanied Cook to the beach, where they were greeted by a crowd of young warriors carrying stones, knives, and spears.

Not wanting any bloodshed, Cook had his men fire a warning shot into the air. When the natives saw the muskets go off but no one falling, they assumed the guns were harmless. Too much in awe of Cook to attack while he faced them, the Hawaiians waited till he turned his back and was walking toward the shore before they pounced on him, stabbing him repeatedly. They soon learned that the muskets were far from harmless, as the frantic sailors tried to reach their Captain. Firing volley after volley, they finally cleared the beach. But Cook was gone.

Captain Cook would never have condoned retaliation, so there was none. The natives kept his body for a few days, then returned what was left—only bones—to the shocked and saddened sailors. His remains were buried at sea on February 21, 1779.

At news of Cook's death, the King of England wept. David Samwell, surgeon's mate on this final voyage, wrote of Cook, "The trust we placed in him was untiring. Our admiration of his great abilities unlimited. Our esteem for his good qualities affectionate and sincere. He was our leading star, which at its setting left us involved in darkness and despair."

Cook established new standards of thoroughness in discovery, navigation, seamanship, map-making, and shipboard health (in 10 years at sea, he never lost a man to scurvy—virtually a miracle for his time), and he was the first person to combine science with exploration. As it states on his coat of arms, awarded posthumously by King George III, "He left nothing unattempted." Captain James Cook peacefully changed the map of the world more than any other single man in history.

Quite a life. Quite a man. Certainly worthy of the admiration of the small gathering of devotees studying the displays in "his" museum.

Cooktown was founded in 1873, during the Palmer River gold rush. By 1874, the population exceeded 30,000, and the town boasted 94 hotels. But after only 10 years (and $10 million in gold), the rush was over. Today, Cooktown is a small, quiet, rugged country town. There is a vibrancy and adventurousness behind that quiet, however, no doubt born of remoteness and a colorful past.

Here, prefab butts ghost town, elegantly columned arcade overlooks corrugated roof, gold rush excess stands beside rustic practicality, all softened by palm trees and cascades of bougainvillea. There are three hotels, a few stores, some offices, and clusters of tidy homes. Everything has a veranda. The grocery store was a bank during the gold rush days and, with its high, arched entryways, is one of the town's more impressive buildings. The office of a public accountant is an iron-roofed, eucalyptus-wood shanty the size of a tool shed on an otherwise deserted dirt track. Rutted, red roads disappear into the green of the surrounding bush. Barefoot Aborigines wander the dusty streets or sit in the shade talking and watching their children play.

Nearby, the sky-blue, mangrove-bordered river sparkles in the bright light. Low, green hills rise at the town's edge and roll, unevenly, into the distance. The town's odd, seemingly contradictory combination of rustic and exotic appeals to me immensely. The warmth of the equatorial sun seems to permeate everything, including the friendly people I met as I strolled around town.

In the afternoon, I joined a small group for a tour of the area. We divided our time between past and present, with the past mostly represented by graves and memorials. The town's old cemetery was populated with explorers, folk heroes and heroines, prospectors, early settlers, and infants. Low, iron fences enclosed small, dry plots, where weathered gravestones, some grander than I would have expected in this remote place, rose out of the golden grass. One stone heralded accomplishments, another told of a 3-year-old "accidentally drowned." Though ancient, the stones bore familiar sentiments: "beloved wife," "he died too young," and sad poems by parents and friends.

At the river's edge, we viewed the grand, column-crowned Captain Cook monument. Farther out, in a small forest clearing, we came to a tall monolith decorated with red and black Chinese characters. This isolated shrine was erected by the Chinese community in memory of those who never returned from the gold rush.

We were dropped off near a billabong covered with water lilies and circled by paperbark trees. We walked along the water's edge, in the warm, sun-dappled shade. A small snake raced away as we approached, disappearing in the fallen leaves. Here were subtle colors and soft edges, like a Monet, but with bold strokes and a sort of primitive vibrancy, like a Gauguin. It was beautiful and strange, and I wanted to stay.

When we stopped again, we were near the coast. A hike through the trees and up a sand dune brought us to a wide beach near the mouth of the Endeavour River, near the

place where Captain Cook beached his ship for repairs.
We walked across the wet, rippled sand, down to the
water's edge, where we had a glorious view of the ocean
and coastal mountains. Off to our right, a dense fringe of
mangrove trees outlined the river's tidal inlet. I broke
away from the group and headed towards it.

"You might not want to get too close to the mangroves,"
our guide called after me.

I glanced back at him. "Snakes?"

"No—crocs. Big ones."

I turned back and scanned the line of mangroves.
Playing across my mind was the thought, "This is it. This
is the edge, where civilization runs out and wild is simply
status quo." My spirit seemed to vibrate in sympathetic
response to something in that wildness. I felt drawn to the
innocence, the fierceness, the solitude. My gaze trailed
again across the rippling sand, with its hundreds of sand
crab burrows, out toward the bright, blue sea, up to a
small, pale explosion of birds lifting into the air, then back
to the mangroves. I studied them a while longer, smiled,
then turned and walked back across the sand.

Back at Cooktown's bay, we watched the crews of the
prawn trawlers prepare their picturesque, net-festooned
vessels for the next day's work. Then, lastly, we drove to
the top of a high hill for an unobstructed view of our surroundings, to imagine ourselves as Captain Cook surveying the new land.

I dined this evening with the delightful people from the
tour. Sheila and Leontyne, sisters, are students from
Sydney. Joyce is a surgeon from Melbourne and is especially knowledgeable about Australian history and lore.
Traveling with her is Gwinny, who is a nurse. John and
Pauline are a charming couple from Adelaide. We had a
jolly time at dinner, swapping jokes and stories, recounting
our travels inside and outside Australia.

Sunday, September 4

Yesterday, in Cooktown, I saw a T-shirt printed with "I made the drive from Cairns to Cooktown" accompanied by a picture of a shattered-looking individual holding a detached steering wheel and a fender, with a tire on the ground nearby. Today I found out why that is, and is not, funny. You can't do it. Not in a regular car, anyway. Many wrecked and abandoned autos along the route testify to that. Up on the Cape York Peninsula (where Cooktown is located), everyone drives a pickup truck (called a "ute" here—short for utility), a dirt bike, or some form of 4WD vehicle. Even with 4WD, the rutted, red dirt road was a challenge, and we actually had to get out and push once.

For 240 kilometers, we bounced, bumped, and thumped along, stopping frequently to explore. Early on, a long hike took us deep into the woods, where wild kapok bushes, with bunches of yellow flowers, and pale paperbark trees, with tattered, soft, many-layered bark, surrounded us. Nearby grew the awesomely fragrant blooms of the frangipani tree. John picked some for me, and I stuck the blossoms in my hatband. We saw (and I collected) "matchbox beans," large, dark, smooth, squarish, hard-shelled seeds that used to be hollowed out and used as watertight matchboxes by early bushmen.

Driving farther on, we came to the mysterious Black Mountain—an enormous pile (more than 1,000 feet high and two miles long) of huge, black boulders. Almost nothing grows on this mountain. The Aborigines call it Kalcajagga—Mountain of Death. Aboriginal legend says that during "Dreamtime" (Aboriginal pre-history), two brothers fell in love with the same girl. Because they were brothers, they could not use spears to fight each other, so they decided to amass a great number of rocks, which each could shower down on his rival. They collected this immense pile of stones, but before they could duel to the death, a terrible storm came. In it, the brothers died on the

mountain, and the girl died at its feet. Cheerful tale.
However, the story sounds as reasonable as any other
explanation when you're standing beside that ominous,
jumbled, barren mountain.

Before long, we reached the Lions Den Hotel, a historic
old Outback pub that figures in many stories of this area.
It is of dark, weathered wood and corrugated iron construction, with trees crowding around and bright, flower-
covered vines clinging to the walls. The yard is "decorated" with old mining equipment. The rustic interior of
unadorned wood planks and beams, rough tables, and gas
lamps conjures up visions of rugged bushmen and miners
gathering, before the turn of the century, to tell tales and
drink their earnings.

The landscape's muted greens gave way to muted reds
and golds, as we rolled into a great emptiness that was
dwarfed by the immensity of the clear blue sky. Overhead,
fork-tail kites soared. We passed occasional clumps of
tamarind and royal poinciana trees, some filled with beautiful pink and gray galahs. (A galah, accent on the second
syllable, is an Australian parrot related to the cockatoo.)

A great swath of black rock interrupted the rippling, red-
gold countryside at Annan River Gorge. Steep, ragged,
water-sculpted walls rose on either side of the narrow
gorge. The bright stream that had shaped the gorge rushed
and sparkled, then cascaded down the sharp drops it had
created for itself. We spent an hour clambering around the
worn, layered rock, enjoying the beauty of the spot and its
openness to the wide, bright sky.

The place where we stopped for lunch at first appeared
unpromising: a modest-sized, aging building in the middle
of a barren nowhere, with rusting cars and old mining
equipment cluttering the yard. But, as with so many
things, outward appearances can be deceiving; the interior
was delightful. The owner, an energetic man in his early
50s, had paneled the inside walls with black slate that he

quarried and polished himself. It looked fabulous and made the restaurant surprisingly cool.

A room at the front offered a small, carefully laid out museum. Here, shelves were lined with the owner's carefully labeled collection of minerals found in the area, as well as seashells, crocodile skins and jaw bones, old mining equipment, and preserving jars filled with local crawlies: snakes, spiders, scorpions. It was a marvelous one-man effort.

On the road again, we crossed the Palmer River, once called the "River of Gold," and drove through the old mining towns of Mt. Carbine and Mt. Molloy. We climbed onto the Great Dividing Range, stopping occasionally at high, forested lookouts, then descended through the rainforest on the other side.

The last hundred kilometers of our 380-kilometer drive were paved, for which we were all grateful. Finally, I was dropped back at my hotel in Cairns. I was sorry to say good-bye to my new friends, but perhaps we shall meet again.

Monday, September 5

With only two more days in Queensland, I wanted to cram in a bit more greenery before heading for the desert. I caught a bus up to a place called Mountain Groves, where "ducks"—W.W. II army amphibious vehicles—are used for tours of the rainforest.

As the old "ducks" lumbered through the forest and across rivers, our bright, funny guide pointed out the delights surrounding us. Growing in chaotic profusion were orchids, coffee plants, cork and sarsaparilla trees, stinging trees, and "wait awhile" vines (if you get tangled in the barbed vines, you have to wait because it will be a while before you free yourself). Fluttering and flying about us were iridescent-blue Ulysses butterflies, four inches across; electric-green and yellow Cairns Birdwing butterflies; kookaburras and parrots. In and around the streams we saw water dragons and other lizards, as well as a variety of turtles.

Next, I bussed over to Kuranda, to see the famous train station and ride the scenic railway back to Cairns. The station is renowned because, decades ago, a stationmaster who was an avid horticulturist got a little carried away with his hobby. In his spare time, he planted gardens around the station, put flower boxes in the station, hung baskets of ferns and vines from the station's eaves. Soon the place became something of a tropical paradise in its own right. It has been maintained in this condition ever since.

The delightful, little, narrow-gauge railroad that runs from Kuranda to Cairns was completed in 1888. The 21-mile line has 15 tunnels and 37 bridges. It passes through some glorious scenery as it descends 2,000 feet from the edge of the Atherton Tableland, past steep, stone walls and lush rainforest. Waterfalls descended in shimmering curtains beside the tracks. Deep, rugged, rock-lined Barron Gorge, far below the train's narrow trestle, was filled with the sound and spray of Barron Falls. Closer to Cairns, rolling hills were dotted with yellow wildflowers and looked positively Alpine.

Sharing the wooden bench with me on the train was a young couple from Sydney. They have traveled all over Australia and were eager to share with me all the places they thought I should go. The list continues to grow.

When I got back to Cairns, I stopped to buy some of the lovely fruit so abundant here in the tropics, including some three-inch-long "sugar bananas," which I have been told are a specialty of the area. I also got some macadamia nuts, which are indigenous to this part of Australia and are often called Queensland nuts here. Then I headed to the hotel for a short siesta. My ribs are pretty sore after the jarring drive from Cooktown, so I'm fairly tired just from hurting.

At 7 p.m., a tour bus picked me up, and I was off to the Hambledon Sugar Mill. The sun had set, but the sky was alight with the glow from the fires burning off the cane. Great pillars of white smoke billowed into the night sky. Heavy stands of sugar cane, seven feet tall, were silhouetted black against the leaping orange and yellow flames. The burning gets rid of leaves and weeds, and drives away pests, leaving behind nothing but the bamboo-like cane stalks, ready for cutting.

Cutting machines come through during the day, harvesting the cane, chopping it into 8- to 10-inch lengths, and loading it into tram "cars," steel baskets about six feet cube. The trams are operated by the mill, and tracks run out to all the plantations that supply the mill with cane. The baskets, which hold more than a ton of cane each, are numbered to identify suppliers. Once loaded, the trams head for the mill, which is where we joined them.

The mill at night is one of the most visually exciting places I've ever seen—all fire and steam and motion, giant machines and endless conveyors and bins. There is a roof, but no walls, so everything plays against a backdrop of dark, starry sky or flaming fields. The lighting is fantastic—flood lights in strategic places, immense boiler fires, dramatic shadows, dancing bright and dark. And everything is moving: spinning, churning, crushing, turning.

When the tram cars enter the mill, they are weighed, then put on the cane tippler, which turns the bins upside-down and empties them onto the carrier, a conveyor belt that moves the cane into the shredder then on to the crushers. The cane is crushed in four separate crushers, to make certain all the juice is extracted. The cane fiber, called bagasse, is used as fuel in the mill boiler, providing nearly all the power and heat required by the factory.

Next, the juice from the cane is clarified: cleaned of dirt and impurities. The dirt removed at this step is mixed with a small amount of bagasse, producing an excellent fertilizer. Talk about an operation that wastes nothing!

After the juice has been clarified, it is concentrated. At this point, the product is raw molasses. Our guide drew off a cup of it for us to sample—delicious. Next, crystals begin to form. Through microscopes, we could see the tiny crystals take shape. Then the crystals are separated from the syrup. We were treated to this warm, rich, moist, raw sugar—mmm!

The molasses separated out during this last step is mostly sent to distilleries for rum. Now I feel like I have that whole process tucked away, having seen the vats of molasses being turned into rum at the Beenleigh Rum Distillery.

Before we left, we were given stalks of sugar cane. Childhood ambition realized! I have always remembered the longing I felt as a child when I read about children in far-off places chewing on sweet sections of sugar cane. At last, I could do it, too. It was heaven.

Tuesday, September 6

The morning sunlight glittered on the water of Trinity Bay, and in the freshness of the early hours, my eyes consumed the beauty of Cairns, as I stood on the Esplanade waiting for one last Queensland tour bus.

We headed southwest, up the Gillies Highway, to Lake Barrine, for a cruise on the deep, clear, glassy-calm crater lake. Below us we could see perch, turtles, and freshwater eels. On the water's surface, pelicans and black ducks swam and dove. Overhead, kites wheeled in the air, swooping down to catch their prey, or occasionally catching in mid-air a treat tossed to them by our guide. Along the shore, there were mud hens, amethyst pythons, and water dragons. Butterflies flitted and fluttered everywhere—in fact, the entire day was filled with butterflies.

Our guide pointed out plants and trees lining the shore: giant kauri pines, purple water lilies, golden orchids, "umbrella trees" (schefflera) two stories high, with stalks of red flowers spreading out from their tops, black bean trees, strangler figs, immense king ferns, and great stands of elegant bamboo.

We had some time to explore on our own, and I disappeared down a cool, green tunnel that paralleled the shore, stopping often to photograph plants. But soon we continued on, to Lake Eacham, another ancient, steep-sided crater lake. The high ridge surrounding the deep, blue lake is blanketed by rainforest, the rich greenery cascading down the crater walls to the water's edge.

We hiked to nearby Yungaburra, which is famous for its Curtain Fig. (*Yungaburra* is Aborigine for "fig tree.") The Curtain Fig is a strangler fig. Stranglers begin their lives in crevices of other trees, then drop down aerial roots to the ground, becoming steadily stronger. The roots begin to wrap around the host tree, constricting, strangling, and eventually killing it, leaving the strangler fig standing alone. At Yungaburra, before the fig was strong enough to stand on its own, the host tree fell, its fall stopped short by another tree, so it rested at an angle. The strangler continued dropping aerial roots from along the entire length of the original host tree, forming a huge, plaited wall of roots. Both the original host and the second tree died and rotted away years ago; now all that remains is that vast curtain.

Driving across the Atherton Tableland, we saw beautiful dairy farms and fields of maize and tobacco settled in between tiny towns and dense stands of rainforest. The brolgas (Australian cranes) have arrived early this year. We saw them wading in rice paddies and streams and flying in great flocks overhead. During one of our stops, by the side of a lake, I got to hear the wild, giddy laughter of the laughing kookaburras—at last.

We headed off through the rainforest again, to visit some of the area's many waterfalls. My favorite was Millaa Millaa Falls. Moss and ferns hang from the underside of a high, ragged, jutting cliff, over which the water flows in a long, silvery cascade. The surrounding tropical greenery is so dense that it also appears to be flowing over the cliff. The waterfall is reflected in the pool at its base, which gives the impression of two falls rushing toward each other and meeting at the water's surface. As always, I would have liked to have stayed for days.

Continuing down the Palmerston Highway, we traveled through a green tunnel of lush rainforest. Around us, amid the surrounding trees and vines, were basket ferns and staghorn ferns; the red, heart-shaped leaves of the bleeding heart bush; gympi gympi, or nettle trees; giant philodendrons; and wild orchids.

Rainforest alternated with lush plantations. Emerald green fields of tea bushes stretched to the feet of the green, forest-clad mountains, then blurred into more rainforest. Finally, miles of sugar cane led us back into Cairns.

I had to pack, but I prepared for my departure with mixed emotions. It has been a glorious three weeks. All that I have seen in Queensland I have loved, and I must return someday. But I must also move on.

Wednesday, September 7

Miles of rugged, nearly uninhabited red terrain spread below me as I winged toward the center of the continent. I feel that, somehow, the real adventure is now beginning, as I leave the somewhat familiar behind and head for the Outback—and for camping out. But this is the only way to see all that I want to see, the only way to become intimate with Australia. I think back to a passage that I underlined in *Voss,* a novel by Australian and Nobel laureate Patrick White, words that resonated for me then—and still do.

> *"Can you tell me," LeMesurier had asked, "if you are coming to [Australia] for any particular purpose?"*
> *"Yes," answered Voss without hesitation. "I will cross the continent from one end to the other. I have every intention to know it with my heart."*

We touched down in the mining town of Mt. Isa, then continued on to Alice Springs. At the bright, airy, little Alice Springs airport, I collected my bags from the luggage truck, which pulled up near the front door. I set my watch back the half-hour time difference between here and the East Coast, then caught the bus into town.

"The Alice" is as strange and beautiful as you could possibly imagine. I might have fallen completely in love at the instant, if it weren't for the flies, which are a bit annoying.

The town is set on the banks of the Todd River, a broad swath of deep, soft, red sand that is visited by water only on rare occasions. In fact, the famous Henley-on-Todd Regatta, which is run each year, is done in boats without bottoms. Teams stand inside the boats, carrying them, and run the course along the dry riverbed. Only once in the race's history have they had to cancel due to water.

Alice keeps a low profile. Tidy, one-story cottages surround a downtown area of one-story shops, with only a few hotels aspiring to second or third stories. It is the country, not the town, that dominates the scene. One cannot escape the red land, or the immensity of the sky that embraces the town, as it does the desert at the town's edge. Alice Springs feels open and honest to me, without the edge, the electricity of a big city, but also without the chilly shadows and flickering anxieties.

Alice Springs is quite unlike anywhere I've been before, but is exactly what I had hoped it would be. It is strange, but with a tantalizing strangeness. As Patrick White wrote, *"In this disturbing country . . .it is possible more easily to discard the inessential and to attempt the infinite."*

And that's just what I want.

Thursday, September 8

It has not taken me long to develop an "Alice twitch," a sudden twist of the head followed by the flick of a hand before your face which keeps the flies away, if just for a moment. But, in spite of the flies, this charming, semi-rugged, little town has won me over. The streets are clean, the houses tidy, the denizens casual, friendly, and easy going. The air is redolent with the scent of orange blossoms, as well as the fragrance of blooms I do not know, and is so clear, it is as if the world were created yesterday. The light is incredible, bright and silvery, with the sky rising like a sheet of burnished metal from the red earth. The plants are entirely different from those on the coast—smaller blooms, a few with heady fragrances, some strange, all fascinating.

When I stopped to photograph some beautiful pink flowers, a white-haired Aborigine passing by stopped and told me that they were oleanders and picked a branch for me. His English was limited, but we still managed to talk for a while, and he pointed out several other plants he thought I might find interesting. Then he continued on his way.

A construction worker, seeing my camera, stopped to tell me some good places to photograph. He also recommended "Panorama Guth," a gallery with a cyclorama-style painting by Dutch artist Henk Guth of the Centre's natural wonders (Ayers Rock, the Olgas, etc.). "It's wonderful. It's all around you, just like it's real," he explained enthusiastically, "with the sunlight coming in from above, and you can see everything in all directions. It's the best dollar I ever spent." How could I resist?

The panorama, which is 20 feet high and 200 feet in circumference, was worth seeing. However, the part of Panorama Guth that interested me even more was the large collection of Aboriginal artifacts housed there. Glass cases were filled with spears, woomeras (spear throwers), and boomerangs. There were human-hair belts and armbands, tjeringas (or churingas—sacred stones that embody mythical spirits), and bullroarers (wooden objects which, when whirled at the end of a string, produce a deep "roar," to call spirits or the tribe together). A ngangkari's (medicine man's) implements, mostly sticks and bones, assist in the casting and breaking of spells, which are sung into the implements. (If someone is said to have been sung, or had the bone pointed at them, they are under a death curse, which can only be broken by a more skillful ngangkari.) Rain stones are rubbed to make clouds appear. And feather shoes are used by kaditja men, tribal executioners, who wear the oval, feathered footwear to obscure their footprints while tracking their victims.

Leaving Panorama Guth, I continued my exploration of Alice Springs. Nothing was crowded, but all was busy— until the shops and businesses closed, and then I might have been in a ghost town. It was a bit eerie, strolling along the completely deserted streets. But things began to pick up again around 7 p.m., when the restaurants started opening.

After dinner, I walked back to my hotel, stopping at every darkened corner to gaze up at the millions of unfamiliar stars. Australia faces toward the center of the Galaxy, instead of outward, like the Northern Hemisphere, and the nighttime sky is dazzling.

Miscellany

There are a lot more Aborigines here than I have seen up till now. They are, as the name implies, an ancient people— *ab origine* (Latin), "from the beginning." Australia's Aborigines are Australoids—dark-skinned, but descended from an early Caucasoid race (probably the same as, or similar to, the race that gave rise to the Ainu, Japan's aboriginal people). They have silky, dark brown, curly to wavy hair, which is sometimes tipped in blond or red. It is believed they came from Asia, thousands of years ago, in boats or across an ancient land bridge. I hope that Panorama Guth is just the beginning of expanding my knowledge of this ancient people and their culture, which I have up until now only been able to gain from books.

Friday, September 9

"What does the country look like?" she enquired.
"It's red," he said. "Red around Alice and where I come from, red earth and then, the mountains are all red... great red ranges of bare hills against the blue sky."

- from *A Town Like Alice* by Nevil Shute

And it is red. And fascinating. I spent the morning walking all over Alice Springs. I strolled down to Leichhardt Terrace and waded out into the deep sand of the Todd River. Then I headed across town to where rocky, red, scrub-covered Anzac Hill rises near the intersection of Wills and Railway Terraces. I climbed to the top, to see the white obelisk that stands as a memorial to Alice's war dead and to get a good look at the Alice, a patchwork of green and white in the midst of the red land. The wilderness closes in around the town, laps at its edges, and spills in through Heavitree Gap, the break in the rugged, red MacDonnell Ranges that permits the passage of the Todd River and the road from the south. It's not a very large town, which adds to the feeling that it could easily just melt back into its surroundings.

The afternoon held much buying of necessities for "going bush." It's amazing to me that I could bring so much and still have so little I need. A sleeping bag, canteen, and flashlight ("torch" here) topped my shopping list. I probably ought to get some shorts, too, but I'm so accustomed to skirts, I'm not sure I'd find shorts all that comfortable.

I returned at last to the hotel to begin packing for tomorrow's safari. At the back of my mind was the thought: What if I've overestimated my ability to tolerate all of this? It's been a long time since the summer camps of my childhood. For the last ten years, the great outdoors was the garden room at the Ritz-Carlton, and physical exercise was a heavy day of shopping downtown.

But this is what I came for—stretching myself, reaching that new level—to boldly go where no high-heeled, over-urbanized, corporation refugee has gone before. And, in a way, to never come back. This should be interesting.

Saturday, September 10

On Saturdays, Adelaide House is open to the public as the John Flynn Museum, and seeing it proved to be an excellent way to spend the morning. John Flynn was the Presbyterian clergyman who founded the Australian Inland Mission and developed the concept of a flying doctor service. He also designed and built Adelaide House, the Alice's first hospital. He was aided in his effort to spread "the mantle of safety over inland Australia" by Alfred Traeger, who established the first radio base in Alice Springs in 1926. Traeger perfected a pedal-operated, two-way radio for use by isolated settlers, which made Flynn's flying doctor service viable.

The museum is filled with maps, books, old medical equipment, and the first radios used by doctors and stations to communicate. Photographs detail the difficulties Flynn faced as he built, staffed, and equipped the hospital. The only way to bring in medical equipment, building supplies, nurses, doctors, and anything else they needed, was across the desert on camels. The hardships were exceeded only by the dedication of those involved.

At 1:15, I rolled into the Bill King office for the beginning of my "Nine-Day Red Centre Four-Wheel-Drive Camping Safari." Not all the members of our group had arrived, but those of us who were there were carted over to a campground on the far side of the Todd River, where we got a quick lesson in putting up tents. Then we piled back into the desert cruiser for a tour of the area.

We drove out to the old Telegraph Station, which is where Alice Springs began. Charles Heavitree Todd (for whom the Todd River and Heavitree Gap were named), Superintendent of Telegraphs and Postmaster General of South Australia, sent telegraph surveyor William Whitfield Mills into the Northern Territory to survey a route for a telegraph line that would link Adelaide with Darwin, and Australia with the world. Mills was also instructed to find suitable sites for telegraph repeater stations.

Following the route of explorer John McDouall Stuart, Mills came, in March 1871, to a permanent waterhole, which he named for Todd's wife, Alice. The central telegraph station was built adjacent to "Alice Springs." This would be the midway point of the 2,230-mile Overland Telegraph Line, which was built in record time and opened in 1872.

By 1900 the isolated telegraph station was home to a cook, a blacksmith-stockman, a governess, four linesmen-telegraph operators, and the Station Master and his family. The town that grew up nearby was originally named Stuart, after the intrepid Scotsman who, in 1862, made the first successful south to north crossing of the continent. But because the area was so widely known for the water-hole and its attendant telegraph, the town was renamed.

The handsome buildings of the telegraph station, all solidly constructed of locally quarried stone, with white roofs and broad verandas, are still standing. The Station Master, head of the largest station on the telegraph line and the only magistrate in Central Australia, was an important man, and his residence, though modest in size, occupies a suitably preeminent spot in the station com-pound. Behind it is the kitchen, separated from the main house, as dictated by the heat. Nearby is the Post and Telegraph Office, the heart of the station, with wires radi-ating out toward Adelaide and Darwin, as well as to the power house. Messages telegraphed along the line had to be electrically boosted, the power being supplied by huge wet-cell batteries stored in this building. Rounding out the compound are a buggy shed, forge, storage area, and large barracks that combined sleeping quarters, schoolroom, and dining facilities.

Massive, old gum trees shade the wide, dusty, red yards, where ancient, wooden wagons stand in brittle retirement. The spring called Alice is nearby, at the base of a rugged, boulder-strewn hummock, encompassed with grass and trees and full, at least when we were there, of delighted children, both Aborigine and white, playing and splashing in the water.

Leaving the station, we drove across town to the MacDonnell Ranges and out through Heavitree Gap. The ragged, red MacDonnells, which stretch east and west of Alice Springs, once stood 9,000-13,500 feet high. Today, the highest peaks of the ancient, eroded ranges reach only to about 4,500 feet. But in the gap, the bare, sharply angled rock ribs do not seem so old. The towering, striated stone slabs look as though they have just been forced through the earth's crust, shooting skyward, crashing into each other, splitting, shattering. It is gorgeous.

On the other side of the gap, we visited a camel farm. There were no roads or rails coming inland for much of the Centre's history, and horses were not really suited to desert travel, so camels—one-humped dromedaries from India—were imported during the 1800s to help conquer the sand and dryness of this part of Australia. They were perfect for the job. Aside from their ability to get by without drinking for many days, camels could thrive on desert vegetation that would not support other mammals.

After the camels had served their purpose, many of them were released into the desert, where their numbers quickly multiplied. Today, there are an estimated 15 to 20 thousand wild camels in Australia. The only country in the world with disease-free camels, Australia now exports healthy, domesticated thoroughbreds to the Middle East.

Following camel-riding lessons, we headed for the camel museum. The museum has photos, camel saddles, mementos from the days of the early desert explorers, and a taped talk on camels. Camels can carry loads of 600 pounds and more. The males can be dangerous during the mating season; they become agressive, and they are capable of tearing a man's arm off. The rest of the time, they are quite manageable. Camels cannot be bridled with a bit because they are cud-chewing animals and would choke to death, so they are controlled by reins attached to a peg through one nostril.

Then it was time to head out to the airport, to pick up the late arrivals, and we were a "family" at last.

The Cast

Hugh – our "coach captain" (a near-legendary title for the driver-guides of the Outback that has even been immortalized in song)—in his 30s, bearded, tan, smart, funny, resourceful—able to rebuild a 4WD, find water, climb mountains, and put up with a new group of campers every week.

Carrie – our cook—young, giddy, vivacious, dark-haired, cute, and capable.

Marge – my tent mate—successful, well-educated woman, charming, attractive, and lots of fun.

Judy – English girl transplanted to Australia—dark-haired, sparkling, energetic, positive—radiologist in Melbourne (she visited Australia several years ago, loved it, found out what job skills were needed at the time, then went back to England and retrained in radiology).

Sue – Australian—red-headed, energetic, tomboyish, fun—a pharmacist, she works at the same hospital (Royal Melbourne) as Judy, but never met her before this trip.

Barbara – delightful, enthusiastic German woman—loves collecting Aussie colloquialisms—Ph.D.—works in the German State Library, where she is responsible for all English translations of works in the library—her first trip to Australia, two years ago, was as a lecturer in this field.

Bärbel – another German woman, a friend of Barbara's (they belong to the same hiking club)—quiet and serious, but friendly and always showing concern for others.

Willy and Anna – German couple—both charming and adorable—he's especially lovable, and very funny, but a little self-conscious about his limited English—she's dear, but quieter than he is.

Denny – retired from the Australian Air Force, now works in the Federal Patent Dept. in Canberra—his father was a British Army officer stationed in India, which is where Denny was born—moved to Australia when India gained independence.

Jeff and Robyn – delightful couple from Melbourne—both are sharp professionals; intelligent and fun.

Stephen – serious and relatively quiet, but clever—works for the government in Sydney.

John – another Melbournian—tall, athletic, sports enthusiast—outgoing, always offering whatever he has to those nearby.

Ray and Auriel – lovely, older couple from Toowoomba—they're both full of marvelous stories, many of them hilarious—he used to be a cattle drover, she was raised on a sugar plantation, cooking on a wood-burning stove and enjoying all those other "amenities" of the good old days—warm and thoughtful people. (It was Auriel who told me, as I waved the flies from my face, that what I had dubbed the Alice Twitch is actually known almost universally as the Great Australian Salute.)

Gerhard and I Ching - he's German—works in the Immigration Office in Hamburg; she's Chinese, from Taiwan— teaches Mandarin Chinese at the University of Hamburg.

We sat around the campfire, enjoying wine and cheese and conversation. Carrie crouched near the blaze, cooking steaks for our first meal together. The evening got cooler as the sun went down, so we pulled closer to the fire as we talked after dinner. Then, before it got too late, we headed for our tents, so we can get an early start tomorrow.

Sunday, September 11

We rolled out of our sleeping bags at 5:30 and started to pack up camp and load our gear into the four-wheel-drive Bedford desert cruiser. After breakfast, we doused our fire, then climbed on board. Before taking off, Hugh announced the demonstration of our "individually controlled air-conditioning units," then leaned forward and slid his window open.

We headed south, through Heavitree Gap and out into the rolling, red land of Australia's heart. After eighty miles of easy driving, just past Henbury Homestead, we swung west, off the Stuart Highway and onto a dirt road. Not far from this turn-off, we stopped to see where a shower of meteorites crashed to earth 2–3,000 years ago. The cluster of craters produced by the shower covers an area of 49 acres. The craters vary in size from 40 feet deep and twice the length of a football field, to a mere 20 feet across.

Fascinated by the great, overlapping craters, I was equally delighted with the area itself. Acacias with masses of yellow flowers, silvery-green saltbush, bunches of wildflowers, and bright green shrubs filled the hollows and dotted the walls of the craters. Overhead, a couple of wedge-tailed eagles—magnificent birds with six-foot wingspans— circled slowly in the bright sky.

We continued along the dirt road, stopping at Wallara, a station (ranch) that is so accustomed to visitors that the owners stock soft drinks, beer, and batteries for travelers heading through this region.

We had lunch at a beautiful spot in the middle of a red, rolling nowhere. The hills around us were veiled with muted greens and gold. During the break, we collected firewood for our next two nights, because we are camping at Uluru National Park, and you can't collect wood on park property. Brittle branches and great, dead limbs were handed up to Hugh, who strapped them to the roof of the cruiser.

The only other stops we made were on those occasions

when Hugh spotted things he thought would interest us:
trees (graceful desert oaks, with their slender, needle-like
leaves; light green poplars; and yellow-flowered mulgas,
members of the acacia family), plants (red-beige-flowered
wild hops; spidery, golden honey grevillea; soft, fuzzy,
purple-blossomed mulla mulla; and witchety bushes, in the
roots of which can be found the Aboriginal delicacy,
witchety grubs), and birds (mostly galahs and blue and
green budgerigars).

At one point, Hugh scooped up a thorny devil he'd seen
sleeping on the red dirt road. The ferocious-looking but
harmless horned lizard blinked sleepily as we examined it.
The spiny, four-inch-long *Moloch horridus* was patterned
in a dozen shades of brown and, despite the thorns covering its entire body, was quite handsome. Hugh then
released the drowsy little creature well off the track.

We pressed on, because Hugh wanted to make certain
we arrived at Ayers Rock in time for the sunset. "Sunset
Strip," the most popular spot from which to view the Rock
at this hour, was already well populated when we arrived,
ten minutes before sundown. We proceeded on foot, winding between beautiful green and silver bushes and purple,
white, and yellow wildflowers, plodding through the dark,
red sand, to a good position on the crest of a dune.
Cameras snapped away until the light was gone.

We pitched our tents at Yulara, the campsite nearest
Ayers Rock. Our cooking fire became the center of a tight
circle, as we ate dinner, then sat talking, drinking tea, and
enjoying the silence and clarity of the desert night.

Sue pointed out the Southern Cross to me. I was delighted
to see the cruciform constellation at last. This time of year,
it is relatively low on the horizon, so up until now it has
been obscured by buildings or mountains. Tonight, I could
see more stars than I would ever have thought possible.

Monday, September 12

Ayers Rock, called Uluru—sacred and permanent—by the Aborigines, is an important feature of Dreamtime legend. Dreamtime is the time of the giants, when the earth was formed, and every feature of Uluru bears the mark of some event from this period. It is where the Rainbow Serpent dwells when he is not arched across the sky. Many of the sacred caves around the Rock's base are fenced off. Still used in rituals by local tribes, these areas are off limits to outsiders. However, though these are the most sacred sites, the entire Rock is holy to the Aborigines.

Ayers Rock is immense, imposing, beautiful. It is the biggest monolith in the world—a giant stone in the middle of a long-extinct river, exposed and shaped by millions of years of erosion—rising 1,143 feet above the surrounding desert. And what you can see is only the tip of the proverbial iceberg. The Rock ripples and undulates, soars and breaks, has caves and formations of great size and curious shape. The base of the Rock is six miles in circumference. The walls are sheer, the top is a maze of ridges and gorges. Its "skin" is a weird flaky-smooth, like a cross between stone and rusting metal. And it is the color of rust, due to the oxidation of iron contained in the sandstone of which the great monolith is composed.

Many of those who visit Uluru come for the purpose of climbing it. The distance to the top is just over a mile. At the highest point in the Rock's rumpled back is a cairn, where a steel box holds a book with the signatures of all those who have succeeded.

The first hurdle to get past is Chicken Rock, so called because this is where most people realize how tough the climb is and chicken out. (Tough for a non-climber, that is. If you've done Everest, this is a piece of cake.) After that, you face the first ascent, at a point known to the Aborigines as Webo, where, in Dreamtime, the rat-kangaroo men crouched, their tails falling to the ground, form-

ing the slope. On most maps it is simply called The Climb.
It is steep and smooth, and is the most difficult part of the
endeavor. In 1963, the elders of the Yankuntjatjara and
Pitjantjatjara tribes—the tribes traditionally responsible for
"tending" the ceremonial and spiritual sites in this region
—permitted the installation of a chain to aid climbers
along part of Webo, for Webo, though a site of significance, is not a major Dreaming site.

The rest of the climb consists mainly of scrambling up
and down ridges, balancing along stone rims, and climbing
in and out of small gorges. A faint, white, dotted line runs
across the back of the Rock, marking the safest path to the
top, and climbers are instructed to follow it. Uluru is not
treacherous, but neither is it totally harmless—there have
been a fair number of deaths (though more heart attacks
than falls) and many injuries.

As we climbed the long, narrow fold in the Rock's flank
that carried us skyward, we stopped often to enjoy the
view. Around us there was only sandstone and space, with
the desert retreating to our rear. Then, with one last, short,
almost perpendicular scramble, we were on top.

The wind whipped around us as we clambered over the
rippling back of the monolith. It snatched Gerhard's sunglasses, which disappeared into space. It whistled in our
ears and sang among the stones. We braced ourselves
against it and plodded on.

The summit can only be seen when you are within a
hundred yards of it. Often we thought our destination was
at hand, only to find, on topping a ridge, that another
stretch of undulating red rock awaited us. But at last, the
cairn came into view. Denny took our photographs by the
cairn as we signed the climbers' book. We rested and
stretched, and then it was time for the descent.

As we crested a ridge, the Rock's broad back stretched
before us, with the white line running, curving, disappearing, and reappearing among its myriad folds. The tiny

forms of distant climbers made Uluru's great size even more apparent. Before descending The Climb, we stopped to admire the seemingly endless quilt of red and gold desert below us. The narrow, winding ribbon of road was a deeper red, with a pale, geometric fringe of buses and cars clustered at the bottom of the rock wall.

As we arrived at the base, we were greeted by Willy, smiling broadly, congratulating us heartily, and bringing us glasses of cold orange cordial. "You have made it! Wonderful!" he announced. And it was wonderful.

We headed off to explore those of Uluru's strange formations, caves, and sites not forbidden to us. Maggie Springs, a permanent water hole at the Rock's base, is known as Mutitjula (or Mutitjilda) among Aborigines. It was important to local tribes both for water and for the wildlife attracted to it. Leading down to the water hole is a chain of depressions in the stone, looking like the backs of hands with fingers tightly interlaced, which becomes a series of pools and waterfalls when it rains.

Following the path away from Maggie Springs, along the smooth, red wall and among the tumbled rocks, we came to a low-ceilinged cave. Hugh urged the women in the group to rub a large, round stone in the cave, but, on a hunch, I refrained. My guess was right—this was the fertility cave. Aboriginal women believed that rubbing the stone would make them pregnant. Bularri, after whom the cave is named, was a Dreamtime heroine who gave birth at Uluru, and the cave is said to be her womb. In addition to conception, the cave is traditionally a site for birthing, and some Aboriginal women still return to Bularri to have their children.

Outside the cave, I recognized from my reading features of a great Dreamtime battle: an enormous, smooth slab of stone with a small round hole in it—the shield of one titan pierced through by another's spear; a great, cleanly sheared-off rock that was Kulikudjeri's severed nose; the

stains on the wall from the ochre with which Ingridi decorated her body when mourning the death of her son; the
bodies that became boulders at the Rock's base, and the
spears that became trees.

A little farther along we entered a small cave created by
an overhang of rock. Aboriginal paintings decorated the
walls and ceiling. Hugh pointed out the numerous concen-
tric-circle drawings depicting water holes—the primary
concern of natives in this arid part of the country. There
were handprints and images of animals and plants, as well.

We headed around the end of Uluru, passing the boulder
called Tuppudji, or Little Ayers Rock. Above us, on
Uluru's northern face, was The Brain, an immense, fretted,
skull-shaped formation almost in the center of the stone
wall. It really does look like a brain—to us. To the
Aborigines, who call it Ngoru, it looks like rows of ceremonial scars on a young man's chest. We stopped next to
view the Kangaroo Tail, a 300 foot-long stone shaft that is
attached at its top and base to the Rock, but is otherwise
separate from the main body of the Rock along its entire
length. To the Aborigines, it is Ngaltawaddi (or
Ngaldawata), the sacred digging stick. Completing the circuit, we once more passed The Climb, which was completely deserted. This was a bit eerie, but understandable,
because climbing is possible only in the early morning,
before the heat and wind get bad.

A dust storm was blowing up, and we drove on through
great clouds of red sand. When we got to camp, we found
most of the tents down, and the ones that were still up had
accumulated drifts inside. We secured everything, then
huddled around the cruiser for lunch. Fortunately, red sand
is tasteless and is not gritty like regular sand. And the
wind does keep the flies away.

Back in the 4WD, we turned toward the Olgas, a cluster
of more than 30 bizarrely shaped monoliths. The Olgas are
similar in origin to Ayers Rock, except this giant stone

shattered, and millions of years of wind, sand and water have turned the pieces into "truly wonderful....rounded minarets, giant cupolas, and monstrous domes," as Ernest Giles (the explorer who, in 1872, discovered and named the formation) described them. The Aborigines call them Katajuta, which means "many heads."

The distant domes of the Olgas rose blue and purple at the end of the long, red dirt road. Then, as we got closer, they changed to the region's familiar rust color. We drove around the strange, impressive formation, stopping finally at Mt. Olga, which is about 600 feet higher than Ayers Rock.

We hiked into Olga Gorge. Gum trees, gray-green bushes, and tall, golden grasses lined the red-floored passage. The rough, scarred, red walls drew together as they rose higher against the blue sky. As we wandered through the steep-sided ravine, we could hear the wind moan and sigh as it rushed through the Valley of the Winds on the far side of the towering domes.

Eventually, we returned to our vehicle. We drove the rest of the way around Katajuta before turning once more toward Uluru and Sunset Strip. Again, I stood on a soft, dark-red dune, surrounded by wildflowers and silvery scrub, watching Ayers Rock blaze red in the late afternoon light, shadows moving across its face, color deepening as the sun rode down the sky. Behind me, the Olgas stood out darkly against the lowering, golden sun. The light played across the rolling desert, faded, then disappeared, leaving only warm shadows and bright stars.

I am in love with this place.

Tuesday, September 13

We made an early stop at Curtin Springs, where postcards were dropped off, to be entrusted to the next travelers headed for the Alice. Then we were on the road again.

Ahead of us, and to our right, a great, sheer-sided, flat-topped mountain rose above the rolling dunes. Mt. Conner, one of this region's three lonely titans (along with Ayers Rock and the Olgas), is called Artila by the Aborigines, who believe it is home to the spirits responsible for cold weather. We stopped to admire the strange, impressive island-mountain. A high, red sand dune dotted with yellow and white wildflowers stood behind us, and we scrambled up its soft side. Before us lay one of the area's many salt lakes—lakes that rarely have water in them, just salt, which stretched away in a great, unbroken sheet, blazing white in the sunshine.

Flocks of budgerigars rose in clouds beside us as we drove, flashing green and blue in the sunlight. Yellow honey-eaters and pied butcher birds flitted through the brush.

We had lunch by a small, weathered corral, an outpost of the old Angus Downs station. A windmill pumped water into an aluminum reservoir, which fed a low, wooden trough. The spot, visited by free-roaming cattle throughout the year, is heavily employed at roundup time (called "muster" here). No cows were in sight, but dozens of galahs and a few magnificent kites found the water attractive.

We stopped for firewood, which was again secured by Hugh to the roof of our vehicle. After that, our only stop was when we got bogged in bull dust and had to switch to four-wheel drive.

By late afternoon, we reached a remote wilderness site near Reedy Rock Hole, where we set up bush camp. Bordering red cliffs and tall trees offered shade, while throngs of yellow-flowered acacia bushes perfumed the spot. When the tents were up, we hiked the short distance to the rock hole. A high, sheer, stone wall rose straight up from the back of the pool, and enormous, smooth boulders hedged in and protruded from the clear, cold water.

Back in camp, I grabbed a stool and settled down in

front of my tent to write. While I was so occupied, Willy came over, smiling and laughing as always, bearing cheese and crackers. My *danke schön* elicited such joy and approval that I could only regret that I do not know more German. A little later, Bärbel came over with a mug of wine for me, and others stopped by to see how I was doing.

When the light finally failed, I joined our merry band around the campfire for another pleasant evening in excellent company. After dinner, a sing-along seemed like a natural, and we launched into a few Aussie standards—"Pub With No Beer," "The Road to Gundagai," "Waltzing Matilda," "Click Go The Shears." Denny sang a moving ballad about a stockman whose life was saved by the Flying Doctor. Then our German contingent presented several rousing folk songs.

For a late night snack, Auriel made a "bushman's plumcake," which is damper with a little sugar and some dried fruit added. For me, the pleasure of eating it extended far beyond its taste. Sitting around the fire at night, in the middle of the Australian bush, having billy tea and damper really made me feel like part of the Outback, part of the continuity that runs from past to present, that connects legend with everyday life.

Wednesday, September 14

It was another spectacularly crystalline day. Again, as we do each day, we scanned the sky, the immutable sky, in silent amazement. Never a change. Never a hint of cloud to interrupt the bright, shimmering expanse. No haze. Nothing. Just radiant, metallic blue from one infinite horizon to the other. I would not have imagined that this inevitable clarity could seem so strange. But we all feel it, and look at each other to confirm our common awe.

We drove to a spot about two miles from the head of

Kings Canyon. Undulating, scalloped stone walls fell from the plateau above like a great, ragged, red furbelow. Hugh led us up one of the steep, broken stone pleats. A 700-foot climb brought us to the top of the canyon wall, where the scene before us was wonderful, but almost too strange to describe. Surrounding us were bizarre domes, shelves, steps, and sculptures of layered, fractured, red rock. A sea of what looked like giant, worn, red beehives, four feet to 20 feet tall, stretched into the distance.

Crossing this remarkable terrain, we wound between humps and mounds, clambered up and down broken stone slabs, and crawled through a long, low cave. We explored the area known as the Lost City, which, with its domes, spires, and terraces of red rock, does look like the half-buried ruins of some Eastern citadel.

On cliffs and in crevices grew lone ghost gums—graceful trees with chalk-white trunks and slender, pale, olive leaves. Twisted, weather-blasted cypress trees clung with gnarled roots to splintered shelves and inclines of rock, and ancient, feathery cycads grew lushly in the shadows and valleys. The cycads here are the rare *Macrozamia macdonnellii,* which may have grown in this area for as long as 200 million years. In places where the terrain was flat, the ground was dotted with the wonderful, round, golden "pillows" of spinifex grass. The leaves of spinifex are tender and green when young, but as they mature they roll up into pale "needles," which one quickly learns to avoid. But I love the look of them—like herds of huge, gold and green hedgehogs.

We hiked on through the weird, inspiring, rust-colored landscape. Near Aladdin's Lamp, a four-foot-long rock sculpture balancing a few feet above our heads, we came to a rather scary but safe (we were assured), narrow bridge of flat sandstone slabs wired to tree branches, which had been dropped across a 90-foot-deep crevice. Only a few people were so daring as to stop in the middle of the bridge to pose for photographs.

On the other side of the crevice, we continued on till we reached the impressive, precipitous North Wall of Kings Canyon. At the canyon's edge, Hugh climbed a rise, then strode out onto a sturdy rock shelf projecting into space. Quickly, others followed, to enjoy the unexcelled view of the canyon below and the land we had just traversed.

We skirted the North Wall, then turned and followed another of the many deep crevices that wind through the rock. At the bottom of the crevices, crowds of trees and acacia bushes grew among tumbles of boulders in the narrow strips of cool, damp, shaded ground. In the rocks around us, we were occasionally surprised by sprays of wildflowers, all the more beautiful for their isolation. Tiny lizards dashed for cover on our approach.

After two hot hours of scrambling around on top of the canyon, we descended 100 feet into the sheer-sided, hidden valley named the Garden of Eden. Lush vegetation—palms, reeds, cycads, vines, and flowering bushes—crowded around a narrow stream running the length of the valley. Pushing our way through the tangle of plants, we followed the stream to where the valley suddenly widens, and the clear stream becomes a large pool. Here, we stopped. Hugh's backpack yielded up a treasure of oranges, and we sat in the sun enjoying the much-needed refreshment. Then, a few people went swimming, while the rest of us explored paradise further.

Not far beyond the pool we found that the valley ends at a narrow gap. There was a trickle of water escaping through the opening—a trickle which, when the rains come, becomes a waterfall cascading into Kings Creek 500 feet below. Bracing ourselves against the stone, we edged out through the fissure until we had a glorious view of the perpendicular rock faces of North Wall and South Wall, stretching away from us on either side, and the tree-lined floor of the canyon far below. The South Wall is so sheer, it looks as though it has been sliced by a giant knife, while the smooth, curving, pale North Wall, with its strange, dark brown stains, looks very much like burnt wood.

Eventually, we departed the lovely Garden of Eden. A few more hours of climbing and hiking, and we were out of the canyon and on our way back to camp. Parrots quarreled in the trees overhead as we hiked to Reedy Rock Hole to wade and splash a bit, and rinse off some of the day's heat and dust. Then we headed back to camp to help Carrie with the evening meal.

Dinner, garlicky roast lamb with pumpkin, was cooked in the traditional bush style, in a cast-iron camp oven buried beneath the coals. Preparing the food in this manner was almost as much fun as eating it—though not quite.

Thursday, September 15

This morning we arose at 6:30, packed camp, and hit the road, headed for Palm Valley. It was a long day of driving through beautiful, rugged terrain that really tested the capabilities of the cruiser and its driver. We drove through the George Gill Ranges to Carmichael Crag, then across rocky, broken red ground, hills and desert, and onto Aboriginal Reserve property. On all sides were vistas of jagged red rock and strange, beautiful plants—mulla mulla, acacia, saltbush, spinifex, and scattered clusters of small, yellow and white wildflowers.

Crossing the Palmer River we headed for the Areyonga Native Settlement. Hugh pointed out the burned vehicle of "bootleggers" who had tried to bring liquor onto Aboriginal land. By tribal law, no liquor is permitted on the reserves. Hugh told us that they take these laws very seriously, and once you're on their property, you're governed by their laws—it is wise to obey them. Hugh also explained that, should we ever consider coming this way ourselves, we should know that permission is required for driving onto Aboriginal property.

Areyonga was very quiet. Barefoot women wandered down the street with babes in arms and toddlers at their heels. Behind the houses, naked children played in the dust. The men sat in small circles, talking amongst themselves. The only person who spoke to us was an earnest, young government worker, there to encourage children to pursue education and to aid any natives who wish to pursue more traditional Aboriginal lifestyles.

There is a shop at Areyonga where Aboriginal arts and crafts are available for purchase. The things sold there are made at the settlement, in an effort to preserve some of the old skills. Some of the work was particularly nice, especially some of the bark paintings and coolamons (carved, wooden bowls).

We visited the settlement store, because it's the only place in this area where we can replenish our supplies. In addition to necessities, the store offers comic books, music cassettes, ice cream, soda pop, canned spaghetti, and a PacMan machine. It makes you wonder what happens psychologically to those who are growing up under the mixed influences—how close do they feel to which culture? But then, I guess the history of world cultures is largely a history of people adopting what they like and leaving behind that which is not useful to them.

Leaving the James Range, we continued on through the Krichauff Range, in the direction of Palm Valley. To get into Palm Valley, which is not always accessible, you must drive down the bed of the Finke River—a really rough ride. When we weren't bumping over rocks or fording streams, we were slogging through deep sand. We got bogged several times, even with 4WD, and everyone had to get out and push.

We stopped at a huge, rock "bowl" called the Amphitheatre. Climbing to the top of Initiation Rock, we could see, across a broad stretch of scrub, Cathedral Rock, the Battleship, and other aptly named, red rock formations on the far side of the bowl.

Hugh took off in the cruiser, after pointing the way for us, and we walked the two kilometers to the campground, arriving just before dark. The first thing we did was head for the showers, having been without this luxury since Ayers Rock. Water was limited, so we had to be quick, but nothing ever felt better. After all the climbing and hiking and firewood gathering, we were pretty grubby. One thing that made showering a bit tricky was the fact that the facilities here have no lights (the hot water is the top handle, and watch the step down).

Friday, September 16

I was awakened by the singing of butcher birds, which sound like someone whistling the opening strains of Beethoven's Fifth Symphony—da, da, da, dum. They would repeat this several times, then go off on some other little melody, always returning eventually to the Beethoven. I listened, amused and delighted, until it was time to rise. Then we were off to see the valley.

Palm Valley is most notable as the only place you can find the *Livistona mariae,* the Palm Valley palm, one of the rarest trees in the world.

We hiked into the valley. Climbing a narrow, steep shelf in one of the rough, stone walls, we gained a glorious view of the place. The valley is not particularly wide, but it is so open to the sky that there is a tremendous feeling of light and spaciousness.

The valley floor is water-smoothed stone. Large boulders are scattered everywhere. The tall, slender-trunked palms cluster around the many permanent pools, in company with ferns and moss. Ghost gums cling to the cliffs and crevices in the rock walls. Ancient cycads abound.

There is a profusion of wildflowers, including the lovely mauve-pink Sturt desert rose, floral emblem of the Northern Territory.

Hugh played shepherd as far as Cycad Gorge, then pointed the direction back to camp and left us to our own devices, instructing us only to be back by noon. We wandered; photographed trees, flowers, rocks, and each other; and enjoyed the beauty of the spot and the (as always) dazzling, warm, blue-skied day.

After lunch, we packed up camp and headed back up the bed of the Finke River. We then turned down the rugged, rocky, pitted, hilly, almost indiscernible Mereenie Track.

Our first stop was at Hermannsburg Mission, the oldest Aboriginal mission station in the Northern Territory. It is not a mission anymore, however, but an Aboriginal settlement. The government provides meals and medical care, as well as primary education for the children and technical training for the young adults, but otherwise, the Aborigines run the settlement themselves. There is a large cattle station (1,500 square miles) at Hermannsburg, where many of the men work as stockmen, and it is the site of the annual all-Aborigine rodeo.

Thanks to the missionaries who founded Hermannsburg, the local tribe, Western Aranda (or Arunta), was protected, kept together, and so retained its tribal identity. The Aranda (which means the "Wrathful") is one of the few tribes whose cultures received detailed, early study, again thanks to Hermannsburg.

The son of one of those early missionaries, Theodore Strehlow, shared his father's interest in the Aranda people, with whom he grew up. Strehlow became an eminent anthropologist and spokesman for the Aborigine. Though he struggled to rescue Aranda heritage, he realized that it was impossible to turn back the clock. As he pointed out, much of the drift from the tribal areas was not due to violence on anyone's part, but to the attractions of a stronger culture. Those who remained faithful to the old ways soon found that they had become forsaken relics. Before his death in 1978, Strehlow, along with the older, more traditional Aborigines with whom he'd grown up, watched with alarm the growing dissatisfaction and anger among the younger natives.

We were warned not to take photographs—don't even let the cameras be seen. The children were cheerful, laughing and waving as we drove in, but the adults glowered or turned away. We are not welcome here (or, as one guidebook stated it, "Visitors are not encouraged").

Hermannsburg has a long-standing reputation as a training ground for Aboriginal artists and craftsmen. The most renowned of all native artists, the gifted Aranda watercolorist Albert Namatjira, was born here. He was the first in a long line of painters that became known as the "Aranda school."

Unfortunately, the strain of straddling two dramatically different cultures—as a famous artist treated with distinction in the white man's world (Namatjira was even presented to Queen Elizabeth) and, among his own people, as just another member of the tribe, expected to share everything he earned—drove him to drink, which eventually killed him. Other factors may have been involved, but this tension is generally acknowledged as the root cause of the talented painter's sad demise. Today, Namatijira's sons, Ewald, Oscar, and Keith, and grandson Gabriel, carry on the painting tradition—and still deal with the difficult dichotomy of operating in two worlds.

The only evidence we saw of the settlement's artistic tradition was a large, vividly colored mural painted relatively recently by two local artists. It is on the wall of the general store, which is where we stopped. We were there to buy supplies. We also picked up some goodies for a farewell party this evening.

Continuing along the Mereenie Track, it was quite a

while before we stopped again, this time at Gosse's Bluff. Not really a bluff, this formation is the remains of a massive crater. Though greatly diminished from its original size, it is still impressive—nearly four miles in diameter, with walls more than 600 feet high. This is just the central uplift of the impact structure. It is estimated that the crater was originally 15 or more miles in diameter.

No trace of the bolide (fireball or exploded meteorite) remains, so it is believed that the comet or meteorite that struck this spot created an explosion sufficiently great to vaporize itself. It is estimated that the energy expended in such an explosion would be something in the neighborhood of 200,000 times greater than the bomb dropped on Hiroshima. The convulsion from such an event would have been felt over the entire planet.

The shock wave of the impact caused phenomenal compression of the rocks, followed immediately by a tremendous rebound, which created the enormous crater and brought to the surface a central core of very resistant rock layers (the present-day Gosse's Bluff) which formerly lay approximately 9,000 feet under ground. The outer rim of the giant crater is now gone, eroded away by millions of years of wind and rain. Gosse's Bluff now stands alone, a huge ring of shattered-rock hills rising abruptly out of the broad expanse of Missionary Plain.

We drove on, crossing the MacDonnell Ranges at Tyler Pass, skirting the mountains, and arriving finally at Glen Helen Gorge, a great slash in the range cut by the Finke River. White sand covers the floor of the gorge, and dramatically striated red walls rise up on either side, looking something like the pipes of a giant, stone pipe organ. The broad waterhole that completely blocks the gap at this end is known to the Aranda as Japala and is, according to Aranda myth, the place where the first formless humans emerged.

The gorge explored, we moved on to this evening's bush camp. We set up near a crystal-clear stream that reflected the graceful gum trees growing beside it. Reeds and water lilies lined the stream's banks, and numerous herons and cormorants fluttered and waded at its edge. The rolling terrain surrounding us was dotted with spinifex. To the northwest, Mt. Sonder, one of the Centre's higher peaks, rose impressively, blue and purple in the late afternoon light.

Dinner was a fairly festive occasion, as this was our last night all together. Happy hour lasted longer than usual and included much exchanging of addresses. When Carrie started dinner, I Ching pitched in, preparing an Asian-style vegetable dish. After dinner, we presented Hugh and Carrie with cards we had all signed, as well as an "honorarium" we had collected. None of us could believe the time was so nearly over.

Before the evening ended I saw a shooting star—the second I've seen this week. I'm told they occur frequently in this hemisphere. Beautiful!

Saturday, September 17

We got off to a very early start for our last day of hardcore sightseeing. Our first stop was Ormiston Gorge, a large and breathtakingly spectacular canyon where Ormiston Creek cuts through the MacDonnells. With all that we have seen this last week, we were still astonished by the beauty of this spot.

The complexity of Ormiston Gorge's geological structure is evident in the folding and layering of the rocks, the overlapping of colors, the variety of forms and shapes. The towering orange and red quartzite walls have been wildly fractured. The floor of the gorge is strewn with fallen boulders and rocks of every hue: pink, brown, cream, red, orange, black, purple, yellow, gray. The patterns are as diverse as the colors; rocks have been shattered into squares and slabs and steps, or have been worn into

smooth, strange, gracefully curving designs. The walls are
ragged and scarred in some places, in others, they look
sculpted or quarried. Slender ghost gums cling to the cliffs
and ledges of the splendid, rust-colored mountain walls.

All this magnificence is mirrored in wide, serene pools
of clear, cool water. Just above these pools, the iron oxide
that stains the walls higher up has been washed away,
revealing white bands of quartzite. We hiked and climbed
in this glorious place for more than an hour. Some of us
went wading (the water spirits here are said to be friendly), then sat on the white sand in the shade of the massive,
smooth-barked river red gums that line the watercourse.
Nearby, crested spinifex pigeons—adorable, tuft-headed
birds that live in the prickly spinifex—dashed between pillows of the golden grass.

We headed next for Serpentine Gorge, which is smaller
than Ormiston, but nearly as lovely. Here, we wandered
amid more trees and worn rocks before continuing on to
Ellery Gorge, a permanent water hole protected from the
sun by close, high cliffs.

We reached Standley Chasm before noon. The chasm is
named for Mrs. Ida Standley, the first school teacher in
Alice Springs, who was noted for her work with
Aboriginal children. A group of Mrs. Standley's students
discovered the spot in 1929. Standley Chasm is now
owned and administered by the Jay Creek Aboriginal
Settlement.

It is a half-hour hike to the chasm, through a gorge filled
with ghost gums, cycads, spinifex, and flowering bushes.
Running down the center of this shaded valley is Jay
Creek, a clear stream that winds among boulders and
plants, gurgling merrily as it tumbles down short falls and
over rocks. The sunlight sparkled on the orange quartzite
of the chasm's sheer, 250-foot walls. The floor of the 15-
foot-wide fracture in the range was bare, rocky, and partially in shade. The sun only reaches into this narrow fis-

sure for a few hours around midday, so the rock was cool, as were the pools of water that stood near the tumbled boulders at the far end of the chasm.

After a few hours of wandering, we returned to the entrance of the gorge that leads to Standley Chasm. Carrie had lunch waiting for us. As we ate, we noticed something skulking in the shadows nearby. Hugh tossed some food into the clearing, and out dashed a yellow dingo to snatch it up. "Mulga," as the wild dog has been nicknamed, is far from tame, but tolerates the proximity of humans because of the possibility of leftovers.

We drove to the site of the twin ghost gums made famous by the great Aboriginal painter, Albert Namatjira. The two, tall, white trees, outlined against a red mesa and blue sky, have been much photographed since Namatjira originally set them down on canvas.

Then it was on to Simpson's Gap, a high-walled break in the MacDonnell Ranges notable for its large colony of rock wallabies. In the middle of the gap, there is a steep tumble of boulders where an entire canyon wall collapsed. This is home to nearly 50 of the diminutive, doe-faced marsupials. The adorable, two-foot-tall creatures hopped among the rocks, then stopped to watch us watching them. They are almost exactly the same reddish-brown color as the rocks, so when they stop moving, they practically disappear, which is, of course, their greatest defense.

Beyond this chaos of fallen rock, there is a large water hole. Huge, spreading river red gums, pale and twisted, stand in the entrance of the gap. The trees were filled with pink and gray galahs when we were there.

Our last stop was at John Flynn's grave. A bronze plaque informs readers that "Beneath this stone rest the ashes of 'Flynn of the Inland'—1880-1951." The block to which the plaque is affixed is surmounted by one of the Devil's Marbles. The Marbles, another of the Territory's many unusual rock formations, stand in the desert about 300 miles north of Alice Springs. These massive, round, granite balls, often balanced on one another, offer the only shade available to travelers in that area. One traveler who often rested by these strange stones was the Reverend John Flynn, so an eight-ton Devil's Marble was brought down to shade his final resting place.

The entire drive along the MacDonnells today was delightful. The mountains are wonderful, of course, but the whole area is fascinating. I feel strongly drawn to the strange beauty of the place. I love the golden clumps of spinifex; the shimmering white ghost gums; the dark green, narrow-leafed desert oaks; the twisted corkbark trees; the mulgas; and the small clusters of wildflowers. After just a couple of weeks, the red earth is no longer peculiar, merely beautiful, and the only thing that seems strange is that the soil elsewhere should be any other color.

We arrived back in Alice Springs at about 4:30. First to leave the "nest" were Gerhard and I Ching, who had an evening flight to Brisbane. Gerhard in particular had enjoyed our group, and he didn't want to say good-bye. We were all having a tough time making the break. There was much hugging and kissing and well wishing; then they were off.

The rest of us put up our tents for the evening, then scurried for showers and washing machines. Stephen and I took turns watching each other's laundry as we dashed back and forth trying to get organized. I headed for the campground office to reclaim my luggage, having taken only my green duffel on this trip. Marge, my tent mate, retrieved her bags, too. We sat on the grass in front of the tent, repacking, then left everything outside, because there was no room inside the tent for all our gear.

After dinner we sat around the campfire together, enjoying billy tea and conversation until 8:30. Then Denny, Marge, John, Stephen, Judy, Sue, and I called taxis and went over to the Casino. We all had wine and wandered around the gaming room, watching people lose money.

Our group played a few games of Keno, which only costs $1. Marge was our big winner of the night, netting $4 on her second game. I just picked "lucky" numbers for Denny, losing him $2. Then, at 11 o'clock, we cabbed it back to the campground. Robyn, Jeff, Ray and Auriel, who had remained behind, had the fire blazing and a billy boiling when we returned, so we joined them for a last cup of tea before crawling off to our waiting sleeping bags.

Sunday, September 18

This morning, we said good-bye to Hugh and Carrie; they're heading out on another tour. Then we all went off in different directions. I went for a long hike along the river and through the town, but eventually turned my steps back toward the campsite. I am now sitting in the sun, beneath a tree full of sweetly scented, purple flowers and squawking galahs, thinking and writing.

Much has happened in the last nine days—internally as well was externally. It seems not to have been so much a matter of change as it has been a discovery of what I really am. I have taken to this life with my whole heart, and almost find it difficult to remember why I worried about how I would react to the wilderness, to camping. Sleeping outside, on the ground, has seemed, not a challenge, but a natural progression, a way to more nearly embrace the compelling beauty of this land. That peace has settled over me that one associates with coming home. Sleeping bags and billy cans, starry nights and whispering trees—these are the things I have always needed, and I didn't realize it till now.

As I finished writing, the rest of our intrepid band returned to camp, gathering around a liter of wine. I joined them, and we sat in the shade, toasting each other's health, happiness, and safe journey. Ray and Auriel left after we'd finished the wine, amidst a hail of affection and good wishes. Then the rest of us had lunch together, during which we began planning our reunion. Because I'll be in Melbourne in early November, and because most of the Australians in our group are Melbournians, the time and place seemed obvious. Denny and Stephen were even talking about flying in from Canberra and Sydney.

Soon it was time for Denny, Marge, Sue, Jeff, and Robyn to catch their plane. The rest of us decided to ride out to the airport on the bus with our dear departing, so we could see them off properly. We talked until our friends had to board their flight. We waved, and they were off.

Stephen, John, Judy, Barbara, Bärbel, and I bussed back to town. We'd heard that this was the last day of the Central Australian Football League season, so we headed for the game.

Four different types of football are played in Australia: Soccer, Rugby League, Rugby Union, and Australian Rules Football. No one is entirely like the others, and none bears any resemblance to the game we call football in the U.S. I've been a huge fan of soccer since college, but came to Australian Rules Football more recently, via cable TV—and I find the relentless excitement of Aussie Rules quite intoxicating.

In Australian Rules Football, there are 18 players on a side. The oval field is roughly 180 yards long by 150 yards wide. Quarters last 25 minutes, with no time-outs, and every player plays the whole game. Only two substitutes are allowed; if more than two players are injured, the team plays short-handed. But no player leaves the field if he can still stand.

The ball is moved by hand-passing (similar to a volleyball serve) or awesomely accurate kicking. To score, the ball must be kicked through the goal posts without being touched by another player. Going between the tall inner pair of uprights nets six points, while a ball through the short outer, or "behind," posts scores one point.

Action is fast-paced and continuous. The size of the field and the speed of play push players to the limits of endurance. Though it is a game of constant physical impact, no protective gear is worn. Players are attired only in shorts, knee socks, and jerseys, usually sleeveless. It's a wild game.

In Alice Springs, the football is Aussie Rules. The Rovers, in blue, faced the green and gold Pioneers, an almost all Aboriginal team that was favored to win. It was a close game until the fourth quarter, when the Pioneers ran over the Rovers for a 107 to 63 victory.

After the game, the six of us stopped for dinner— Australian pizza, which offers such unusual toppings as shrimp, eggs, or ham and pineapple. We lingered over our cappuccino; then John, Stephen, Barbara, and Bärbel walked Judy and me to the Greyhound station. Judy is booked on the same wildlife tour out of Darwin as I am, so we'll be traveling together for a while longer. Everyone waited with us until our bus came at 7:45, then stood outside waving good-bye until we disappeared from sight.

It was nice having Judy along on the bus—made the previous farewells less of a wrench than if I'd been alone. We chatted, about life and travel, for most of the 200 kilometers between Alice Springs and Ti Tree Well.

It was after 11 p.m. when we reboarded the bus and roared off into the night. The lights were turned off inside the bus, and the headlights—the only lights for hundreds of miles—seemed to accentuate the profound darkness of our surroundings. With the stars appearing to be so close at hand, and nothing else visible anywhere, it almost seemed as if we were traveling in space.

Monday, September 19

Is it really Monday? After spending 21 hours on the bus, I feel a little disoriented. I guess it must be Monday, though—that's when the schedule says the bus arrives in Darwin.

We slept fitfully during the night, waking for a refreshment stop at 2:45 a.m. Once daylight returned, we were too interested in viewing our changing surroundings to sleep more. As we journeyed up the Stuart Highway, we watched the scenery change from the rocky, red beauty of the Centre to the starkness of the desert to the green and gold savannah of the Top End. We lost the spinifex and mulga and desert oaks. For a while, the area through which we passed was fairly desolate, then gum trees and sand palms began to appear. The temperature rose steadily as we got farther north, approaching 100 degrees as we approached Darwin.

The termite mounds, which were always with us, got steadily larger—we saw some near Darwin that were seven or eight feet tall. Most of the termites eat grass, but a few species prefer trees, and we saw collapsing, hollowed-out trunks from time to time.

Parrots and bougainvillea are more plentiful in the tropic North. So are flies (364 species up here). However, here as elsewhere, complaints about the flies bring the inevitable response, "What flies?" (A wonderfully quirky aspect of Australian personality is the ability to ignore—and sometimes actually revel in—things that might be considered hardships, while still genuinely delighting in the things that are good and pleasant.)

About eight hours outside Darwin, one of the passengers asked our driver if we could take a short detour and drive past the almost legendary Daly Waters Pub, which she'd always wanted to see. It wasn't far off the track, so no one objected. Daly Waters is much like other Territory towns—small, clean, nicely kept up, but with a certain ruggedness. We drove past the renowned pub, a low, charmingly rustic, stone building whose hard-working, sunburnt patrons you could imagine without even venturing inside. This is the oldest pub in the Territory. It was licensed in 1893 and was once a stop for drovers on the great overland cattle drives.

Our bus stopped at the Daly Waters police station, where our driver got out for a brief chat with one of the local Territory police. A third man joined the group, an Aborigine, also in uniform, with a stripe of office on his sleeve embroidered with the word "Tracker." Talk about legendary. It is said that these native trackers can follow a man through rivers and across stone. Their familiarity with the land gives them an uncanny ability to pick up a trail. Almost any decent manhunt story in Australia, fact or fiction, past or present, involves one of these remarkable men.

We continued north, through Katherine and Adelaide River, past the Northern Territory prison, into Darwin's tacky periphery of industrial developments, half-finished railroad, and abandoned W.W. II airstrips, and finally into the city's attractive, tropical center. The bus dropped us in front of the Lameroo Lodge at 4:30 p.m.

The great, sprawling Lodge sits, pale, plain, and boxy, surrounded by flame trees, on the beautiful, beachfront Esplanade, a half block from city center. There are no attached baths, and only the registration office is air-conditioned, but it's cheap, there is a swimming pool, and dinner is included in the single room rate. After we'd settled in, Judy and I crossed the courtyard to the Lodge's huge cafeteria. The first and most obvious thing we noticed about the place was that, at the time, we were the only women in it. But the price was right, so we got in line behind the miners, truck drivers, and dock workers awaiting dinner.

The simple but generous roast chicken dinners were dispensed with military chow-line precision by a couple of gruff, muscular men in white T-shirts. When Judy and I reached the first gent, he stopped dead, spluttered a bit, then brightened and asked if we wanted "upper portions or lower portions." His sidekick turned and stared at him. "What're you talkin' about—upper portions or lower portions?" In a loud, rough whisper, the first cook snapped back, "These are ladies, mate. I can't ask 'em if they want breasts or thighs!" Judy and I share the belief that chivalry must never be discouraged, so we bit our lips, demurely requested "upper portions," and waited till we got to our table before collapsing with delighted laughter.

I have encountered as much bias in the business world (and elsewhere) as any woman my age, and more than some, and I have worked hard, proven myself, and succeeded, but I have been saddened by the general perception that equality negates chivalry, and even civility. I have been reminded in Australia of how pleasant it can be to be "treated like a lady." Here, men rise when I enter, offer seats, do not swear in my presence, and help me with my luggage. For years, I have been told that I should resent courtesies such as these, but I have never been so insecure that I felt threatened by good manners. There is, after all, a great deal of difference between being called "honey" in the boardroom and having a door cheerfully and politely opened for you. I've worked for and deserve equality, but I'm still a lady, and I enjoy being treated as one. Some tell me you can't have it both ways, but it sure doesn't seem like a problem here.

Tuesday, September 20

Darwin is hot. Too hot to be comfortable for sleeping, at least until you get used to it (if you can get used to it). And it's humid. The ceiling fan in my room kept the air moving, which helped some. But even with the fan, I awoke at 5:30 with perspiration pouring off of me. I had thought that I had already shed as much of my civilized veneer as was possible for me, having jettisoned complex hair care and most of my make-up, but here, even a bit of blusher seems unimaginable, so with wet hair and no more than a splash of sun-block on my face, I headed out into the day.

Judy and I checked out of our rooms, stowed our excess baggage in the Lodge's storage room, then waited in front of the motel for our tour to begin. We struck up a conversation with Susan, who, we found out, was also going on the tour. Susan is an attractive, funny, strapping blond English woman who has lived in New Zealand for three years. She's a nurse/midwife, has a fabulous sense of humor, and has traveled all over the world.

By 8 o'clock, we were bouncing along in the back of a khaki-colored Toyota land cruiser, with our sleeping bags and duffels strapped to the roof rack. Henk, our lanky, tanned bush guide, launched immediately into introductions. Clary and Fay, a couple from Sydney, are avid scuba divers, and this is their first non-underwater holiday together. Kim and Marilyn are from England, but have been in Australia for four years, traveling on work/holiday visas. Outgoing, athletic, fair-haired Helen is a postal worker from Alice Springs. And Judy, Susan, and I are the remainder of the group.

We headed out of Darwin on the Stuart Highway, turning off on the Arnhem Highway for the 200-kilometer trip into the heart of Kakadu National Park on the edge of Arnhem Land. Arnhem Land is a 96,000-square-kilometer Aboriginal reserve. Kakadu is actually part of the reserve, but the local tribes lease the 6,000-square-kilometer property to the National Parks and Wildlife Services, so that the beauties of this tropical wilderness can be shared with others. It is still, however, under Aboriginal management, with Aboriginal rangers. The park derives its name from the people who traditionally lived in part of this area, the Kakadu, or Gagadju, tribe.

We crossed the broad, flat Marrakai Plains, which stretched away toward a distant shimmer of heat. Mangrove forests interrupted tidal flats, where brolgas searched for food. Just beyond the Mary River, we stopped at The Bark Hut. We bought fruit juice and sat outside in the shade, breathing the heady fragrance of frangipani and watching huge, black cockatoos soar from tree to tree.

Soon we left the highway, turning onto the dirt road that leads into Kakadu. By the side of a lovely billabong, we stopped for lunch. I volunteered to build the fire to boil our billy and quickly discovered that shreds of paperbark are just as effective for starting a fire as the birch bark I once relied on as a young camper in the North Woods. But here we did not huddle around the fire. I made it just big enough for the billy can, then backed off quickly and watched it, reveling in the realization that I was sitting by a billabong waiting for my billy to boil (though not, alas, under the shade of a coolibah tree). Within minutes, several magnificent kites appeared on the scene, figuring, where there's smoke, there are leftovers. No problem with garbage disposal out here.

We didn't stop again until we were within hiking distance of Nourlangie Rock, a great, craggy, red outcrop of sandstone, a massive outlier of the Arnhem Land Plateau. At Nourlangie there is an important "gallery" of Aboriginal artwork in caves and along the undersides of overhangs. This region is filled with such sites, offering the most extensive examples of ancient art in the world. Some of the work is relatively recent, but much of it dates back an estimated 20,000 years or so.

The earliest paintings are the *Mimi,* or dynamic spirit figures, produced in fine, fluid lines of red ochre. They mostly depict scenes of movement, such as running, dancing, hunting, and fighting. It is possible that these paintings were created by a people that preceded the current race of Aborigines, for local legend says that these paintings were here when the first Aboriginal ancestors arrived, and attributes them to the *Mimi,* a spirit people that live inside the rocks.

The X-ray paintings, which are also very old, show the internal parts of human and animal bodies. These are done in a variety of colors, consisting of pigments from ochre, clays, and charcoal. Another common style is stencil painting, where the artist chews the pigment, then spits it over the stencil, usually a hand or foot, leaving the outline on the rock. In light of the Aborigines' uncanny ability to identify each member of their tribe by their tracks, one can appreciate the significance of these hand and foot "prints." They were a means by which the artist could be identified with the paintings and the sacred sites in which they were produced.

We saw the different styles of art and their various themes: humans and spirits, hunters and prey, legendary creatures that eat natives and everyday creatures the natives eat —fish, turtles, kangaroos. There are crocodiles and barramundi. A red man spears a white kangaroo. There are strange things, too: antennae spring from the head of a bizarre, skeletal figure; an animal-headed monster prepares to pounce on a victim; X-ray spirit figures wear elaborate headdresses. Many of the paintings overlap one another. This is because the satisfaction sought in such endeavors was found in the ritual act of painting, rather than in the completed picture. Nearby, bowl-shaped indentations have been worn into the rocks by centuries of artists grinding their pigments, and overhead, the stone ceilings are blackened from the artists' fires.

After about two hours at Nourlangie Rock, we started the long walk back to the 4WD. The senses are almost overwhelmed by the intensity of everything here—vivid colors, heady perfumes, lush beauty, heat, strangeness. It is so awesomely untouched and wild.

Henk pointed out many of the fascinating plants of the area. We saw paperbark trees (Melaleuka), with their wonderful, pale, papery, many-layered bark; bloodwoods, with their thick, dark-red sap; the wild kapok bush, with its yellow flowers and green seed pods; the red-flowered kapok tree; acacia bushes, laden with sweet-smelling yellow blooms; hibiscus in many colors; bright, spidery grevillea; fragrant gardenias; and the wonderful *Pandanus spiralus*, or screw palm, with its long, green fronds spiraling up the trunk, like a tall, shaggy corkscrew.

We saw a feral pig rooting around under a clump of mangroves nearby. As we walked, we startled mobs of red-winged parrots, rainbow bee-eaters, and red-collared lorikeets. Henk caught a tiny, slender, pale rock dragon, which strolled up his arm as we examined it.

Many of the gums had dark, rough bark half way up their trunks. Henk explained that this protects the trees from the fires that flash through this area at the end of the dry season. Spear grass, which is six feet tall when green and new, becomes a thick, flammable, tangled mat in the dry season. Even when it isn't set off by lightning, fire is certain, as the Aborigines regularly "clean the country," burning off the undergrowth, as they have done for countless centuries, to make hunting and traveling easier.

Back at the jeep, we eagerly gulped the contents of our canteens before continuing on to another billabong, to look for more birds and plants. Henk identified the water pandanus and saltwater mangrove, both of which have elaborate systems of arching stilt roots to support themselves in the soft, wet soil. We saw raintrees and got our first whiff of Melaleuka in bloom—a heavy, sweet scent like honey.

Then we drove to Cooinda, a tiny settlement consisting of one small pub and a few trailers. In a clearing less than a mile away, we set up camp (no tents, though—too hot). Amazing numbers of frangipani trees—many with the familiar white flowers with yellow centers, and others with bright pink blossoms, which I've never seen before—clustered around the site, flooding it with their gorgeous fragrance. Wallabies dashed through the trees and peeked through the bushes around us. The species common to this area is the Agile wallaby. They watched most of what we were doing with great interest.

When camp was up, we hiked back to the Cooinda pub, behind which there is a small, inviting swimming pool. We splashed and swam until dinnertime. Swimming made my side ache, but it was the kind of good ache that feels beneficial, like I was strengthening the long-inactive muscles around my nearly healed ribs.

By the time dinner was ready, I was too tired to eat, as all the camping, overnight bussing, hiking, and heat suddenly caught up with me. And I certainly didn't feel like trekking back to the pub with the others after dinner. When everyone had gone, I rolled my swag out on the warm ground, beneath the stars and swaying gum trees. Alone in the little clearing, I could feel the peace of the bush close in around me. Except for waking a few times because of the dingoes howling, the wallabies searching for leftovers, or the full moon directly overhead, I slept heavily, blissfully through the night.

Wednesday, September 21

Yellow Water Lagoon, with its many branches and inlets, was as still as glass when we arrived just after dawn. Reflected in the smooth, silver-blue water were the willowy paperbarks, dark-leaved mangroves, and densely clustered groves of pandanus that grow along much of the shoreline. A small, flat-bottomed, aluminum boat was tethered to a tree at the lagoon's edge, and in this we launched out onto the bright water.

Like most of the estuaries and lagoons of Australia's north, Yellow Water is home to the enormous (adults 15-25 feet in length) and dangerous saltwater, or estuarine, crocodile—"salty" for short. You stay out of the water. Not only can salties make an easy meal out of any human foolish enough to go for a swim, these monsters think nothing of tackling water buffalo, grabbing them by their faces when they come down to wallow and pulling them under water. Though massive, salties can move with incredible speed, even on land. They have reactions fast enough to catch a diving bird in flight, lurking below the water's surface, then exploding into action.

Most of the salties we saw were lazing in the sun or cruising through the water lilies. We did see one, though, who'd just caught dinner—a 20-pound ox-eyed herring—and we watched as he calmly crushed his struggling prey, the sound of crunching bones echoing across the still lagoon. Then he deftly tossed the fish into the air, catching it so it would go down head first, and with one gulp it was gone.

A large goanna moved cautiously into a clearing at the water's edge. Goannas are monitor lizards, of which there are about 19 species in Australia. The largest is the giant perentie, which can grow to more than eight feet long. The goanna before us was no giant, but was at least four feet long. We went ashore to get a closer look, approaching slowly and quietly. The lizard's forked tongue flicked in and out as it "tasted" the air, and it could tell something was going on. I was closest to it, and I could hear it hissing. Then it reared up, and I froze. Eventually, the goanna moved off into the brush, and we returned to our boat.

Yellow Water is so called because after the rainy season the water's surface is entirely covered with yellow water lilies. The lilies we saw were either purple or white, and clung mostly along the shore. But it is feathers, not flowers, that draw visitors to Yellow Water, for here one of the largest selections of Northern Territory birds congregates.

More than 270 species of birds can be found in the Kakadu region. Though not all of them gather at Yellow Water, those that do reside at the lagoon are astonishing in variety and in sheer numbers. In the trees and among the flowers on shore there were parrots, cockatoos, kingfishers, warblers, lorikeets, rainbow bee-eaters, honeyeaters, finches, and martins.

Clouds of black-and-white, hump-headed magpie geese passed overhead (an estimated 100 thousand reside in this area). Blizzards of white egrets swirled in the air and descended, blanketing nearby fields. Jacanas, which are also called lotus birds, waded among the lilies, their tremendously long toes permitting them to walk on top of the floating vegetation. Tiny green-winged pygmy geese swam by, always in pairs. Darters, also known as snake-birds, submerged themselves until only their heads and long, slender necks showed above the water, darting snake-like from side to side as they searched for fish. Pied cormorants dove into the lagoon, swimming underwater to catch dinner, then reemerged, heading for shore to eat their meals and fan their wings to dry the feathers.

Stalking along the shore were tall, graceful brolgas (Australian cranes), soft gray, with reddish-orange heads; and red-legged, black-and-white jabirus (Australian storks). White-breasted sea eagles perched on treetops or soared high in the blue sky. Called *Marawuti* by the area's Aborigines, this magnificent bird is said to rule the flood plains and carry off dead-men's souls. Clustered along the shore or in shallow water were Nankeen night herons, masked plovers, grebes, black ducks, Australian pelicans, sacred and white ibises, and Burdekin ducks, which are said to signal the presence of a saltwater crocodile

After three hours of rapturous bird watching, we headed back to the landing and then to camp for lunch. With lunch, as with breakfast, the kites began to gather shortly after we began preparations for the meal. Black, or fork-tail, kites and whistling kites circled, perched and waited. When we finished eating, we threw our scraps around camp and watched as the magnificent birds swooped and dove with unerring accuracy, picking up every morsel of bread and meat. What a show.

We packed our gear and turned our wheels down the rough but negotiable dirt road. The only thing we could see that marred the purity of the primeval landscape flanking the road was the occasional survey marker or splash of paint on a tree trunk: signals that this region is scheduled to be "improved." I'm glad to be here now, before they bring any more "progress" to the area.

Before long, we reached an almost over-grown turn off to a rough bush track. A sign warned that only 4WD vehicles were allowed along this stretch and stated that no guarantee was made that it was actually passable. We turned onto this track, with only inches of clearance between our vehicle and the trees on either side.

The land became more rugged, the forest denser, and we climbed higher as we approached the escarpment of the Arnhem Land Plateau. The sandstone escarpment rises suddenly out of the forest, 500-600 feet of sheer rock, topped with a riot of lush vegetation that spills over the edges in great, green cascades. Tales of lost worlds whirled through my delighted mind as I focused on the escarpment, and I could almost imagine that a dinosaur might appear at any moment over the edge of one of the forest-crowned cliffs.

Driving farther into this wilderness, we finally came to Jim Jim Creek, which is the site of our bush camp for the next two nights. Four hours in the confines of a slowly moving metal box, combined with the dirt we accumulated on the occasions when our vehicle got bogged in the deep, soft soil of the forest floor and we had to get out and push, made the creek a particularly welcome sight. We were in the water within moments of stopping at the stream's edge.

We swam for a while, then just sat near shore with the water chest deep. Henk decided this was the right time for happy hour. He carried a small folding table, cheese, sausage, and flagon of wine out to where we were and set it up, with the tabletop just clearing the water. We soon found that the snack-filled plastic bowls would float, so rather than passing things, we could just let them drift. It was one of the most unusual and pleasant happy hours I've ever enjoyed.

Eventually we set up camp. Clary and Fay put up a tent, because the mozzies are bad, but the rest of us just threw our lilos (a "lilo," pronounced lie-low, is an air mattress) on the beach, preferring the bugs to the heat.

While it was light, we frequently saw brilliant flashes of color as parrots flew through camp. After dark, different things on wings appeared. Insects were attracted to our camp, and bats were attracted to the insects, so we saw a veritable aerial ballet of swooping, squeaking creatures having a field day thanks to our gas lamps.

After dinner, as we sat around talking, Henk pulled out his didgeridoo and taught us how to play. I love the sound of this instrument. I quickly got the hang of making the right noise come out of it, but it takes a lot of time and practice to master the breathing techniques that permit the uninterrupted flow of sound produced by a skilled musician. Henk demonstrated his proficiency at this, and we were all duly impressed.

The didgeridoo actually originated and was traditionally only played in this part of Australia. The Arnhem Land Aborigines have the most complex traditional culture of all the Aboriginal groups in Australia. It has been enriched by centuries of contact with outsiders. The Chinese, probably sandalwood cutters from Timor, only 310 miles away, were here as early as the 13–1400s. Malay, Indonesian, and Macassan traders and fishermen frequented these shores. Also, it is likely that Arab sailors, who reached Indonesia by the 13th century, touched here, too. Intermarrying occurred, and customs, tools, and weapons were selectively absorbed. Asian influence was most likely responsible for development of the didgeridoo.

As the evening wore on, Henk unfolded to us tales of his experiences with the Aborigines here in the Top End. The natives in this area have managed, to some extent, to preserve their culture. Corroborees, magic, rock painting, and hunting still fill lives lived as nearly as possible to the ways of their ancestors. Henk said the elders have great dignity and power within the tribe. The people are friendly, though still frequently cryptic. Once, when he was hunting with several young Aboriginal men, Henk asked them what significance the name Jim Jim had, what it meant. They were evasive, but finally said they would tell him in the morning. When Henk awoke, he was alone. Their secrets are still very much their own.

Before going to bed, we piled the leftovers we had saved from dinner at the edge of camp—this time for the dingoes. The food was only a few yards away from us, so we could hear the dingoes crunching the bones and see shadowy forms moving in the bright, moon-lit clearing.

We went to bed wearing little more than insect repellent, not even bothering to climb into our sleeping bags. We just lay on top of them with a sheet or sarong tossed over us and stared at the stars until oblivion swept over us.

Thursday, September 22

Up bright and early, we headed off to the bush loo ("loo" is slang for restroom or toilet, the "bush" preceding the term signifies that there isn't actually any loo, just bush). Henk warned us to look out for Joe Blake. They occasionally use Cockney rhyming slang in this part of the country, and Joe Blake means snake. Other phrases I've encountered up here are jog a mile (crocodile), dead horse (tomato sauce—sauce being pronounced more like "sorse" by those with extremely broad accents) and titfa (short for tit for tat, hat). Happily, we did not run into Joe Blake. About all we saw were frogs, lizards, and more insects—especially green ants, which Henk, cheerfully downing a handful, tells us are high in Vitamin C (I'll stick to my tablets, thanks). But we were still careful.

After we were attired in our hiking gear, we left for Jim Jim Gorge. The drive was short, but filled with wonderful sights—cockatoos, parrots, and rainbow bee-eaters; flowers and trees of awesome variety; water buffalo peering at us through the foliage.

The gorge is a spectacular "fold" in the formidable plateau, craggy, chaotic, sheltering a dense pocket of rainforest. A broad, incredibly clear stream runs down the center of the gorge, its still, unbroken surface reflecting the trees and rocks surrounding it. We stopped and filled our canteens with the bright, cool water before beginning our trek.

The hike/climb/scramble up the gorge was rough, over house-sized boulders and down steep tumbles of rock. Susan twisted her ankle, and all of us came away with some bruises and scratches, but the place was well worth the difficulty of traversing it.

The sandstone walls of Jim Jim Gorge provided a dramatic backdrop for the rugged, tropical beauty of the location. Palms, pandanus, and strangler figs grew among the rocks, at the base of the escarpment, and up fissures and breaks in the stone walls. Moss, ferns, vines, and flowers ran riot along the length of the gorge. Parrots flitted through the trees.

Awaiting us at the head of the gorge was an enormous rock pool, 500 feet across and 250 feet deep, with the rock escarpment rising straight up on three sides to a height of more than 600 feet. During the wet season, Jim Jim Falls, the largest waterfall in Arnhem Land, thunders into this huge pool. Even now, at the end of the dry season, with the spectacular falls reduced to a broad trickle easing down the sandstone face, the spot is breathtaking.

We had swimsuits on under our hiking clothes, and in minutes we had removed the outer layer and were diving into the crystal-clear water. We swam for about 45 minutes, then Henk herded us out of the water, and we clambered back down the gorge.

We arrived back in camp a little more than five hours after we left it. We ate a quick lunch, then loaded the lilos on the Toyota's roof rack, and we were off again. We parked our vehicle about 15 minutes later, unloaded the lilos, and headed into Twin Falls Gorge the only way you can—by water.

Henk told us that the crocodiles in this gorge are all the harmless, freshwater Johnston crocodiles. You wouldn't want to corner a freshie, but given a choice, this fish-eating variety of croc would rather slip away. The freshies are smaller, too, averaging five to nine feet when mature. Henk said that if we were very quiet, we would probably see several of the crocodiles as we swam up the gorge. We made as much noise as possible.

All this "freshie," "saltie" business brings up another point—Australians love to shorten things. The abridged words are affectionate diminutives, which sound perky and positive, and are even capable of making the ferocious saltwater crocodile seem somehow less intimidating by reducing it to a saltie. Mosquito becomes mozzie, barbecue becomes barbie, football is footy, a Salvation Army worker is a Salvo, compensation is compo, breakfast is brekkie, surfing enthusiasts are surfies, and so on.

We hiked a short way to a good launch site, then threw our lilos into the water, jumped on, and started the one-kilometer paddle to the falls. As we wound between high, wildly fractured, green-clad, sandstone walls, our lilos slid over great, submerged boulders in the cool, glassy water. About half way up the gorge, we had to get out of the water and portage across a stretch of shattered rock, where one of the walls had collapsed. Then it was back in the water for the rest of the distance into paradise.

The Twin Falls were falling, two shimmering, cold sprays spilling over the edge of the escarpment into the pool below. The wide, green pool was warmed by the sun and was absolutely clear. Sand spits along two sides were crowded with palms, pandanus, and other tropical plants. Henk climbed a fissure in one of the ragged stone cliffs that towered above us. We explored the lush vegetation on the strips of white sand, floated on our lilos, swam, or stood under the waterfalls, drinking our fill of the wonderful, bright, fresh water.

We stayed for more than two hours, which means most of us got a bit too much sun, but we wouldn't have wanted to leave a minute sooner. The gorge was mostly in shadow as we paddled back out, which took us a lot longer than our trip in, as we were feeling rather playful, and none of us was really eager to leave such an idyllic spot.

But camp wasn't too bad, either. Again, we had happy hour in the river. Everyone told stories of their travels, and we traded jokes. We had a fairly late dinner, because no one wanted to break up happy hour. When we did get around to eating, Henk grilled lamb chops, which pleased us and delighted the dingoes, as they got the bones.

Friday, September 23

It was still dark when we arose at 5:30. As dawn broke, the parrots set up their usual racket, to which we had risen each morning. By 6:45 we'd eaten breakfast, broken camp, and loaded the 4WD—we're getting good at this!

As we drove back down from the edge of the escarpment, we saw black cockatoos, wallabies, wallaroos, and water buffalo. Wallaroos, or euros, are heavy-built kangaroos with shaggier fur than the more familiar gray or red kangaroos. Water buffalo, which can weigh up to 3/4 of a ton, with horns that measure ten feet from tip to tip, watched us with looks of bewildered innocence, as they tried to decide whether they should stay, run, or attack.

One of the most amazing things we saw were the giant termite mounds—much larger than any we had seen previously. The giant mounds stand up to 20 feet tall. They are slightly rough, like coarse, unglazed pottery, in shapes like huge, melting sand castles. Henk knocked off a bit of the hard, gray shell to show us the honey-combed interior. The mounds are not the actual nests of the grass-eating termites, but are food storage facilities and air-conditioners. They expand and contract as the sun hits different parts, causing air to circulate in the deep, extensive complex of tunnels and chambers of the nests below.

At lunchtime we stopped by a large water hole surrounded by hundreds of paperbark trees. Stretches of dried mud showed that the water hole was greatly diminished, but the spot was still lovely, and the surface of the water was covered with thousands of water lilies.

As we ate, Henk suddenly appeared in our midst holding a very unhappy, three-foot-long goanna. We grabbed our cameras and gathered around Henk and the big lizard, photographing the two of them as Henk described the goanna's habits. Then Henk dropped the lizard in the middle of our little circle, noting cheerfully, "Well, he'll either run or attack." (Some people have strange senses of humor.) We scattered. The goanna stood in the center of the clearing, hissing and roaring and flickering its long, forked tongue. Goannas are not poisonous, but they do have powerful jaws that can inflict unpleasant wounds. Besides, who wants to be attacked by a mad lizard? We watched from a safe distance, as the angry creature began to slowly stroll around camp, trying to determine where its enemy had gone. Eventually, the goanna gave up on the vendetta and walked back into the brush.

After lunch we did a bit of "bush bashing"—traveling,

without benefit of roads, across open bushland. It was a very rough ride. Henk wanted to find us more wildlife to photograph, so we bashed about till we all felt as though our teeth and brains were loose. Then we headed back to the road, for the long drive to Darwin. We crossed the South Alligator River and passed Black Jungle Spring. The dirt road rejoined the Arnhem Highway near Wildman River. We passed the settlements of Annaburoo and Humpty Doo, the Marrakai Reserve, Buffalo Plain and Leaning Tree Billabong. Finally, we turned once more onto the Stuart Highway, driving past lagoons, reserves, and Yarrawonga Park Zoo, and finally rolling into the city's center.

The sun was setting as Judy, Susan, and I were delivered back to the Lameroo Lodge. First thing we did was head for the showers, then we met at 7 p.m. at the Lodge's cafeteria for dinner. When we'd finished, Judy and I went for a long walk. We stopped at the Moka Bar for gelato (the chocolate-hazelnut is sublime), before heading back to the lodge. Susan had stayed behind to do laundry, but was nearly finished when Judy and I returned. The three of us bought fruit juice and sat outside, in front of the hotel, chatting—mostly about Kakadu—late into the steamy night.

We talked about the impending "improvement" of the region, and sadly realized that Kakadu will never again be as we have seen it. I don't want to sound greedy—I want to share much of what I've seen, but there should be some special places reserved for those who are willing to work a little harder for it, "pay the price." Not everything should be easy. Here, the challenge is part of the place; reducing the challenge reduces the magic, the meaning of this glorious, remote wilderness.

Saturday, September 24
This morning I headed into town to do a little shop-

ping. I bought a lot of postcards and a beautiful, hand-printed, blue sarong. Sarongs are popular up here. They're cool and, for travelers especially, very practical, since they work as sheets, skirts, sundresses, whatever.

After stopping again at the Moka Bar for another gelato, I headed back to the lodge. I found Susan sitting outside in the shade, and I joined her. We talked until it was time for her next tour to start, then I went inside to tackle my laundry. Everything I wore on this last little jaunt was basically the same shade of dark gray. But then, even before we left town, Henk had promised that we would all soon be indistinguishable from the earth around us. After a bit of effort, however, my clothes were free of the sweet, hard-earned earth and smelled once more of detergent and civilization.

At four o'clock, I was picked up at the lodge and was off on a sunset tour of town. Darwin, the capital of the Northern Territory, is 954 miles northwest of Alice Springs. The location for Darwin was selected in 1869, after several disastrous attempts to found settlements at other sites across the Top End. The city is situated on a deep harbor called Port Darwin, named for naturalist Charles Darwin, who visited Australia in 1836. Originally called Palmerston, the town was renamed after its harbor in 1911.

Our driver kept us entertained with a constant stream of information about the area. We learned that Darwin is so close to the equator that almost every day has 12 hours of daylight, with the length of day varying by only about half an hour throughout the year. Darwin also has tremendous tides, with the water rising as much as 27 feet during high tide.

As we toured bright, modern Darwin we saw remains of the old Darwin, and reminders of the cyclone that cleared old Darwin away. Cyclone Tracy, which struck Darwin on Christmas Day 1974, was a ferocious storm. The anemometer at the airport registered a wind speed of 170 mph, then broke. In less than seven hours, the cyclone leveled the city. It damaged 90 percent of Darwin's buildings, destroying 97 percent of those, and devastated 25 out of 30 ships in the harbor. Sixty-five people died, 150 were injured. All that was left of many houses were the stumps that supported them and, usually, the floor. Because of this, our driver told us, Darwin was jokingly referred to at the time as a "city of raised dance floors." I've read stories of how people all over Australia came to the assistance of Tracy's victims. The one benefit of the cyclone, most people say, is that a prettier, cleaner city was rebuilt after the storm.

We drove down the Esplanade toward Government House, a beautiful, seven-gabled mansion that has been built (and rebuilt) in stages since 1870. You can hardly see the house for the luxuriant gardens surrounding it. We then swung past the old Police Station and Court House, which were built in 1872. Actually, this is the second pair of buildings on the site. The original ones were constructed of wood by builders unacquainted with Australia's voracious "white ant" (termite). By the time the roofs went on, the wooden structures were already coming down. Their second attempt was in stone, and the buildings survived.

We turned down Smith Street, passing Christchurch Cathedral. The bright, new cathedral incorporates an old, stone porch—all that Tracy left of the original church. Despite its solid Victorian construction, the Old Town Hall (1883) was virtually destroyed by Tracy, and only the walls remain. Across the street, Brown's Mart (1885) was damaged, but salvageable. The stone Commercial Bank (1883) at the corner of Smith and Bennett Streets, still stands, but the Chinese temple a few blocks up Bennett had to be completely replaced.

Driving along Fannie Bay, we stopped to walk along the beautiful, pale cliffs that rise precipitously out of the water. We passed Fannie Bay Gaol, which was built in 1883 and used until 1979, and headed to East Point, where Darwin's defenses against invasion were built during

World War II. Because it had the airstrips and harbor nearest to Indonesia of any spot in Allied territory, Darwin was bombed heavily by the Japanese. The first bombing raid, on February 19, 1942, killed nearly 300 people, wounded or maimed 400 more, and destroyed planes, ships, harbor facilities, and the hospital. A few of the lonely, concrete bunkers and gun turrets built to defend this shore still stand at East Point, not far from the War Museum.

The tour ended with a view of the sunset from the beach. The thing that is amazing about Darwin's sunsets, aside from the fact that you have a totally unobstructed view of the sun dropping into the equatorial sea, is the afterglow. About half an hour to 45 minutes after the flaming red and orange sun disappears beyond the horizon, the sky begins to turn pink, then deepens into red, then purple—all without clouds. The sky from horizon to horizon (which at the equator seems to involve the whole of the universe) goes through this incredible color change.

By 7 p.m. I was back at the hotel, where I bought a half liter of chocolate milk for dinner (you don't eat much in this heat, you just drink all the time), then headed up to my room. Judy, who'd been visiting her roommate's sister all afternoon, dropped by at around 7:30, and the two of us went for a long walk in the warm, frangipani-scented evening air.

We'd been walking for about an hour, when a 4WD Toyota pulled up next to us and Henk popped his head out the window and asked where we were going. Then he asked if we'd like to join him for coffee and cake at this great little place he knew—his shout. (When you "shout," that means you're buying, it's your treat.) Judy and I laughed when he pulled up in front of the Moka Bar, as we've both been haunting the place since our arrival in Darwin. To get out of Henk's Toyota, we had to roll down the window and use the outside handle. We thought it suited Henk, though—he's a bit quirky, too.

We ordered cappuccino and cannoli, and chatted. Henk had just come from the hospital, where he'd been visiting a fellow bush guide. It seems Henk's friend got a little careless, lulled into a false sense of security by the infrequency of mishaps in the area. He was at Cooinda just two days after we were. He'd gone bush loo at night, without a flashlight and in his bare feet. Strolling through the dead leaves, he felt the needle-like burning pain of a snake bite—death adder. (Most Australian snakes will get out of your way if they can tell you're coming, but the nocturnal adder, though it doesn't go after you, will hold its ground.) Fortunately, he was with someone who knew how to drive the 4WD, and they got him out of Kakadu and to medical attention. He had gone into a coma, and had just regained consciousness a short time before Henk arrived.

Henk's warnings about Joe Blake came back to us, and we wondered if we ever came close. But even Eden had its serpent. The story wouldn't keep us from going back—it would just keep us from getting careless.

After we finished our treat, Judy suggested that we go over to the Hotel Darwin's Green Room for a drink. The Hotel Darwin is one of those airy, elegant, white hotels that the British build in tropical climates. Judy says it reminds her of Raffles in Singapore. The Green Room is all green and wicker and ceiling fans, the kind of place where even the heat seems intrinsically romantic, a necessary part of the ambiance.

Judy shouted the first round, and the three of us talked, about travel, about adventure, about Australia and the Northern Territory. After a while, Henk started to get restless, almost vibrating in place. Suddenly, he stood up, mumbled something about this being "too civilized," apologized, and disappeared.

Judy and I stayed. I shouted the next round of drinks. A band played soft music out on the veranda. The old, dark, hardwood fans turned lazily overhead. We watched the condensation drip down the sides of our cold glasses, enjoyed lounging in the big wicker chairs and wearing clean cotton dresses, and agreed that, as much as we loved Kakadu, as much as we wanted to go back, we wouldn't want to be forever without pleasures like the ones we were experiencing at the moment.

We left the Green Room before midnight and walked back to the Lameroo Lodge along the beautiful, frangipani-lined Esplanade.

Sunday, September 25

This morning I rose at 7 o'clock—reluctantly, since I had to pack last night and didn't get to bed until 1:30. I met Judy for breakfast at 7:30, then the two of us strolled down to Doctor's Gully.

Doctor's Gully is the location of a thing called Aquascene, which we had been told is one of the "must sees" in Darwin. Many years ago, someone living in a house on this spot began throwing bread and scraps to the fish near shore at high tide. Over the ensuing years, more and more fish started showing up for the free food. Now, at high tide, thousands of fish swarm to shore for the handouts. You can stand in the water and feed them by hand, or toss bread farther out for the larger fish. The water boils with bodies as the fish try to get as much as possible before the tide begins to turn. Near the feeding ramp were diamond-scaled mullet, blue catfish, and bream (it's interesting to note that, despite the large numbers and heated competition, the fish stay almost entirely together by species). A little farther out were the milkfish or giant herring. Occasionally, an enormous, strange-looking creature emerged from the depths to grab a slice of bread—it was a hump-headed batfish, and we read on the way out that they are rarely seen, and only at the highest tides.

It was particularly fun watching the delighted, giggling children wade among the churning fish, some of the youngsters so excited that they almost forgot to feed the fish the slices of bread they had clenched in their little fists. The fish swirled around Judy's and my legs as well, as we stood knee-deep in the bright water. It was all pretty astonishing, and just a little weird.

After Aquascene, Judy and I headed back to the hotel, as check-out time is 10:00. We left our luggage in the storage room, then took off for a last wander around Darwin. I saw a few things during last night's tour that I wanted to photograph, and, as Judy hadn't seen them yet, I acted as tour guide. We passed a park hedged with the marvelously spiraling screw palms, then headed on up to the end of Mitchell Street to Government House, the Old Police Station, and Court House. Then we turned down Smith Street and wandered back toward Darwin's lovely, palm- and bougainvillea-adorned pedestrian mall. We stopped at the Northern Territory Tourist Bureau, so Judy could sign up for the same Katherine Gorge tour I'm going on. Then we went back to the hotel, had orange and mango mineral water (they put some terrific stuff in cans over here) for lunch, and got ready to catch the 1:30 bus to Katherine.

We arrived in Katherine at 5:30, at which time I threw away my poor, battered luggage cart. It has gone through a lot of loading and unloading in a short period of time, and the strain of this last bus trip was more than its little frame could bear. At least it waited till my ribs were healed.

The next local bus out to Springvale Homestead was scheduled for 6:15, so we didn't have long to wait. The drive out to Springvale took us through an alternating land-scape of eucalypt forests and undulating pastoral properties.

Springvale Homestead is a delight. This was one of the first homesteads in this area. The original, salmon-colored brick buildings are still in use as the main offices for the compound. The extensive, wooded property is bordered by a wide, shaded stream. A clear, natural spring, surrounded by large old trees and other greenery, bubbles up near the main house. A little wooden bridge crosses the spring, and several varieties of ducks waddle up and down the spring's banks.

A tall, bulging boab tree squats near the homestead buildings. Related to the African baobab, this peculiar-looking tree is most plentiful a few hundred miles west of here, though it obviously strays a bit. Its bulbous trunk and usually bare limbs give it a bizarre appearance. Aboriginal legend tells that the boab tree was once tall, proud, and beautiful. However, the tree's conceit and air of superiority when comparing itself to other trees angered the spirits, and they bewitched the tree so that from that time forward it would grow upside-down. When you hear the legend, then look at the boab, you can't help being amused at how utterly the tale suits the tree—it really does look like it has been uprooted and stuffed head first into the ground.

The budget room I had requested was in a cabin-like building at the far end of the compound. The tiny room, with its bare wood walls, had just enough space for the two low beds and little nightstand that furnished it. Through the screen door, I looked out at the eucalypt forest that came almost to the edge of the veranda.

I started to do some writing, but Kim, Marilyn (from the Kakadu trip—they're down here, too) and Judy showed up at my door within an hour of my arrival, and we talked until well after 10 o'clock.

Monday, September 26

All tours around Katherine originate at Springvale Homestead, which is wonderfully convenient. This morning, I wandered around the homestead, taking photographs, while I waited for the bus that would carry me to Cutta Cutta Cave.

The explored section of Cutta Cutta Cave extends for about half a mile and lies approximately 45 feet below the surface. The cave, a series of limestone caverns connected by narrow passages, is unusual in that it is tropical, whereas most caves occur in temperate areas. During the rainy season, the cave fills with water, which washes away whatever is on the ground. This explains the almost total absence of stalagmites. The cave, though dark and damp, is not cool. In fact, it will be closed after October 1, because it becomes stifling during the summer. Today, the temperature was about 98 degrees, with an effective humidity of 100 percent.

A park ranger accompanied us, to identify the various formations and explain how they came about. An inverted forest of stalactites clung to the cave roof, with the long, thin, hollow, calcite "straws" from which they form crowding between them. There is an abundance of flowstone. Flowstone is formed from films of calcite left by flowing water. It takes the shape of ribbons, undulating shawls, and frozen waterfalls. Helictites, also called mysteries, form tangled clusters of knotted, stone "twigs" growing in all directions, with no consideration for the laws of gravity (hence the mystery).

The cave was called Cutta Cutta by the Jawoyn (or Djauan) tribe. The name means devil devil. The belief that evil spirits did, indeed, inhabit the site kept natives from using it as a shelter, though nearby caves have had considerable use. The reason the word is repeated in this and so many other Aboriginal names is that in Aboriginal languages there is no way to make a word plural, so words are repeated to denote quantities greater than one.

After a very hot hour in the cave, we reemerged into the dazzling morning sun and hiked the mile back to our bus. A container of cold water awaited us, and was both necessary and welcome. Then we started off for Mataranka.

Mataranka was dry and dismal, surrounded by dusty

fields dotted with anthills. In all fairness, I was not seeing the spot at its peak. It is the end of the dry season, so everything is pretty crisp. Plus, the forests around Mataranka have just been burned off, so there is no under-growth—just a lot of charred stubble and blackened tree trunks. It looked unpromising, though it was still fascinat-ing, in its weird desolation, with the smoldering termite mounds standing like eerie, twisted gravestones in the denuded fields and forests. On faith, I changed into my swimsuit and hiked across the hot, barren clearing around the homestead. I came over a little hill, through a gate, and suddenly I was in paradise.

At Mataranka there is a thermal spring, and the spring feeds a stream that flows into a large, unbelievably clear pool. The water coming out of the spring is hot, but it cools quickly as it travels downstream through the shade of the myriad palms and general tropical lushness growing in such profusion around it. By the time it reaches the pool, the crystal blue water is quite refreshing, though still warm.

In this astonishing place, I whiled away a couple of hours. I swam in the glorious water, reveling in the beauty of the pool, of the lush, overhanging greenery, and of the short, exuberant waterfall where the stream continues on. I wandered through the dense foliage of the oasis and stopped to admire the apparently bottomless, turquoise spring from which the water issues.

Mid-afternoon, we drove to the Elsey Cemetery. Here are buried many of the people who populate Jeannie Gunn's classic tale *We of the Never-Never,* including her husband, Aeneas Gunn. Mrs. Gunn was one of the first white women in the Territory. Her books are fascinating accounts of station life at the end of the 1800s, and also give interesting insights into the lives and traditions of the Aborigines who inhabit this area.

Then it was time to head back to Springvale. I dropped by to see Judy, Kim, and Marilyn, and I was introduced to

Sheena, Ann, and Mary, who are from Scotland. The seven of us chatted for a while, then I dashed off for a shower prior to the start of the evening's festivities.

A corroboree was to be held this evening, and at 8 o'clock, we gathered in the clearing near the homestead for its beginning. A corroboree is an Aboriginal get-together that can either be a time of instruction in rituals and sacred rites or, as was the case tonight, just a festive occasion with music, singing, and story telling.

Participants were members of the Jawoyn tribe. Before things could really get under way, a fire had to be started, and two natives appeared and tackled this task in traditional fashion. The two took turns rubbing a stick between their palms, rotating it rapidly in an indentation in a woomera. (A woomera is a spear thrower, but most utensils have multiple uses, to cut down on the number that have to be carried when the tribe goes "walkabout.") Soon, enough heat was generated to kindle the dry grass around it.

A good fire was built up, and the rest of the group entered. The men and boys who made up the ensemble were all dressed in red loin-cloths. Some had red arm bands, and a few had clusters of feathers in their red headbands. (In *The Little Black Princess,* Jeannie Gunn explains that red is a significant color, for if, during the rainy season, the powerful thunder spirit is "roaring dreadfully, and happens to catch sight of an old man with plenty of red handkerchiefs, and scarves of red feathers tied around him, it puts him into such a good temper that . . .nobody gets hurt.") The natives all bore extensive body decorations, elaborate designs in white paint. They looked very impressive.

The musicians came in, one with a didgeridoo, another with clap sticks. The didgeridoo does not supply a changing melody, but rather a deep, undulating tone which, with the clap sticks, is intended to keep time, establishing rhythm for dances and songs.

The dances all tell stories, and a narrator explained to us

before each began what story we would see. There were hero/ancestor stories, a kangaroo hunt, and a tale of a man getting bitten by a snake then being cured by the medicine man. As each story unfolded, at intervals there would be a shout, and each dancer would stamp his foot. When the story was finished, the entire ensemble stamped feet and clapped hands in rapid rhythm. We were expected to clap along and call out the names of the dancers, which we did enthusiastically. Each dance was repeated on the side of the fire opposite its first run-through, to make certain details and nuances were not missed by anyone present.

Following the dancing, there was a demonstration of spear throwing using the woomera. Several of the natives demonstrated their skill with these, then asked if any of those watching would like to try. Of course, the volunteers were all moved closer to the target than the Aborigines had stood, but still no one could even get near to hitting the mark. One guy even got the woomera to go farther than the spear—and you're not supposed to let go of the woomera.

I made the mistake of mumbling, "I bet I could do that," and suddenly six pairs of hands were propelling me forward. "Go on," the girls urged, "give it a go." I was the only American there, and the only woman to volunteer. Dressed in my sarong, with a hibiscus behind my ear, I probably didn't look too threatening. I listened carefully to the native's instructions—depend on the woomera rather than on your own strength. (It may be primitive, but it's a brilliantly effective piece of equipment.) My first shot was clean and straight, but fell a bit short. I retrieved my spear from where it lay in the dust and fitted its end back into the woomera. I nailed my second shot right into the center of the bale of hay we were using as a target. What amazed me was the amount of congratulation I received—everyone was quite excited about my success (especially the women) and very flattering.

Finally, we were all invited to join in the dance, which we did. It was great fun, clapping hands and stamping in the dust around the fire, and it continued until the fire had died out.

Tuesday, September 27

I was up early, getting myself and my luggage ready to face a day of adventure and travel. Today I was heading for Katherine Gorge, and I had Judy, Kim, and Marilyn, as well as Sheena, Ann, and Mary, along with me. The bus picked us up at 7:15, and we were off. We stopped to drop my luggage at the Ampol Roadhouse in Katherine, where it would await my return this evening.

Before long, we were standing on the banks of the Katherine River, waiting for our guide. The seven of us were among the few who had booked the full day tour. Only six other people were going with us, as not many people want such a strenuous trip—there's a lot of climbing between gorges, and the temperature on the rocks can be 110 degrees by late afternoon. It was a brilliant day, with not a cloud in the sky, and it was already getting hot.

I recognized our guide, Peter, from the corroboree last night. He was the "emcee" and narrator for the story dances. Aside from us seven girls and the guide, there were two bronzed, male surfers from Queensland's Goldcoast, a man from Perth, another from Sydney, and a young couple from Melbourne.

We started our jaunt at the end of the gorge, where the sheer stone walls give way to gently inclined beaches. Our flat-bottomed boat moved up the first gorge, passing the crowded boats for the two shorter tours.

When we got to the top of the first gorge, Peter secured the boat, and we scrambled over the rocks to the next section. This particular barrier in the gorge is not very difficult to negotiate, and handrails and steps have been installed in strategic locations, so nearly everyone can make it through the first two gorges. (Actually, technically speaking, there is only one gorge, with several sections, but everyone here refers to the different sections as gorges.) A second boat was tethered on the other side of the barrier, and we launched out onto the next stretch of water.

The second gorge is spectacular. The tan- and black-streaked, reddish-brown cliffs rise 200-300 feet straight up on both sides, and the water stretches from wall to wall. Fissures in the rock walls overflow with tropical greenery. The clear, perfectly serene water reflects the towering cliffs and blue sky.

Katherine Gorge bends frequently, as the river follows fault lines in the stone. As we turned one sharp corner in the river's course, we gained an excellent view of imposing Jedda Rock. It is a sheer, 200-foot precipice that figured in Aboriginal legend, as well as in the 1950s movie *Jedda*.

The climb to the third gorge was more difficult than the previous passage had been, but we were rewarded with increasingly beautiful scenery. Another boat awaited us, and we cruised up this stretch of water to the top of the section. The climb to the fourth gorge was lovely. The surrounding cliffs, ledges, and boulders were enriched by ferns, figs, orchids, silver-leafed paperbark trees, fan palms, eucalypts, lilies, and pandanus.

The fourth gorge is one of the longest, so it took us a while to reach the top. By the time we arrived at the barrier separating the fourth and fifth gorges, the day was warming up, so it was time for a swim while the billy boiled for tea. The water here is clean and pure, as it has been everywhere I've ventured in the Top End, so Peter filled our billy right from the river.

After tea, we headed for the fifth gorge. It was a spectacular climb, taking us high up one of the gorge walls for more breathtaking views than we had previously experienced. As we scrambled among outcrops of stone and along narrow ledges, we came to a spot where wild passion fruit was growing in abundance. As I clambered up and down that magnificent, shattered, chaotic landscape—towering, water-sculpted rock walls, fascinating plants, the sparkling river, dazzling scenery on all sides—munching on warm, tangy-sweet wild passion fruit, soaking up the gloriously brilliant sunlight, I could not help but think to myself, "I don't know what the rest of the world is doing right now, but it couldn't be this good."

About half way up the fifth gorge, Peter slowed the engine and pointed out a huge cave in the rock wall beside us. The ceiling of the cave was covered with the wonderful, bottle-shaped mud nests of the fairy martin, just one of the many birds I've seen in my wanderings.

The climb to the sixth gorge was the most difficult, over an absolute chaos of tumbled boulders. The rocks were worn smooth and into fantastic, weird shapes by the action of the water. We swam for about half an hour in this gorge, some people even heading to the top of the section to see if they could make it to the seventh gorge. I swam along the cliff walls, examining some of the caves, trying to spot some of the area's wildlife. Then it was time to head back.

By the time we had swum, climbed, boated, and climbed again back to the top of the fourth gorge, we were ready for lunch. We had another long swim while Peter got the food ready. (Jumping into the water every few minutes definitely makes the hot rocks and blazing sun seem more amiable.)

After a leisurely meal, we hopped back on the boat and set off down the fourth gorge. About 20 yards from shore, Peter cut the motor and asked who'd like to go overboard, to hold onto the ropes along the side and be dragged through the water to the end of the gorge. Almost everyone jumped in. One of the non-participants steered the boat while Peter ran up and down taking our pictures with each of our cameras. It was great. Then, at the beginning of the gorge, Peter joined us in the water for a while before we had to climb back to the third gorge. We then boated downstream to the climb into the second gorge.

Half way down the second gorge, we stopped again to swim, and Peter climbed one of the stone walls to demonstrate cliff diving. He was soon joined by the two guys from the Goldcoast, though Peter continued to dive from a far higher perch than they would dare.

After another half hour of playing in the water, it was time to continue on. We got back into the boat and puttered to the beginning of the second gorge, then climbed back to the first section. The cruise back to the dock seemed far longer than the trip out had been, but eventually we arrived—nine hours after our departure.

The bus dropped me off at the Ampol Roadhouse in Katherine, where I bid a fond farewell to my new friends before they headed back to Springvale Homestead. At least I will be seeing Judy again, when I get to Melbourne in November.

After everyone left, I headed for the shower in the ladies' room. It's funny how things change your perspective. When I was in the bus depot in Brisbane a month ago, I saw the shower stalls in the restroom and thought it must be pretty strange to bathe in such a public place. Now it seems perfectly natural to shower anywhere there's running water.

I bought fruit juice and went outside to one of the tables in front of the roadhouse. I settled down with paper and pen to fill the pages and the hours till the arrival of the 12:45 a.m. bus that will carry me away from the Northern Territory. How I have loved this place. My time here was wonderful and exciting, but it was more—it has given me myself. As the dream unfolds, I'm finding that it is better than I ever imagined.

Now, if all goes as planned, tomorrow night at 10:40, I'll pull into Broome, Western Australia, where I'll join up with my next tour—another camping safari. Till then, I have a long bus ride ahead of me. It should be an interesting drive, during daylight hours—but now it is 1 a.m., the bus is about to leave, and I'm going to try to sleep. It's been a long day.

Wednesday, September 28

One of the things that delight me about Australia is the speed and ease with which one can make new friends. In the front of the bus were the driver (of course), the back-up driver (out here, the towns are so few and far-between that there's nowhere to pick up a new driver, so the relief driver travels with you), Ron from Sydney, Jenny from Darwin, with her 17-year-old daughter, Joanne, and me. Within an hour of leaving Katherine, we were chatting as though we had been acquainted for years. Jenny told me about life in Darwin, Joanne talked of school, Ron described what he hoped to see in Perth, and the two drivers recounted tales of life on the road.

After a while, we decided to try and get some sleep before the night was completely gone. Fortunately, the bus was half empty, so we could all stretch out over two seats. Susan (from the Kakadu trip) had told me that I should take my sleeping bag on the bus with me next time I was making a long haul like this, and I had taken her advice. It really went a long way toward smoothing out the bumps and softening the seats.

I managed to get a couple of hours of sound sleep before our first refreshment stop. Around 5 a.m. we rolled into Kununurra, just over the W.A./N.T. border. I stumbled sleepily off the bus and, over tea and toast, renewed my acquaintance with my traveling companions.

WALTZING
WESTERN AUSTRALIA

It was still dark when we reboarded the bus, but it was not too long before the sky began to lighten and we could see the countryside through which we were passing. The northern part of Western Australia is beautiful, a seemingly endless, red terrain dotted with buttes, plateaus, mountains, spinifex, and ghost gums. I loved the scenery, but the people on board were the highlight of the drive. The joyous group surrounding me made the whole day a party on wheels.

In the early afternoon, several miles outside Fitzroy Crossing, we saw some poor guy peeling himself away from the motorcycle he had just totaled. Our driver stopped the bus and offered the biker a ride, which he cheerfully accepted. He was in frightful condition, with his clothes in tatters and blood on most visible parts of his body. But he was charming and happy, and shrugged off his extensive lacerations with the greatest of nonchalance. The incident—both the driver's stopping and the wounded man's cheerfulness—brought to mind the very familiar (to Australians, anyway, almost proverbial) lines from Adam Lindsay Gordon's* poem "Ye Wearie Wayfarer":

> *Life is mostly froth and bubble,*
> *Two things stand like stone,*
> *Kindness in another's trouble,*
> *Courage in your own.*

We dropped our unlucky motorcyclist off in town, and he

*See appendix

trudged merrily up the street—I hope to the doctor's office. Actually, he really did have something to be cheerful about—the bus only comes through twice a week, and in this heat, he never would have made it walking.

As we neared Derby in the late afternoon, we began to see increasing numbers of the astonishing boab trees. Some of them are so bulbous, squat, and peculiarly formed that they look like something out of a weird dream. It was dark by the time we rolled into Derby, but you could still discern the unmistakable outlines of the boabs lining the street.

In another three hours, we pulled into Broome, almost exactly on time. I was met at the bus stop by Stuart and Jeanette, the coach captain and cook for my latest tour. Stuart is a dashing Scot, in his late 40s, with thick, wavy, graying hair and a marvelous Scottish burr. He is powerfully built and reminds me a little of James Mason. Jeanette is 22, cute, pert, and very friendly. She is slender, tallish, and has long, straight, light-brown hair. The two of them whisked me off to a nearby campground, where Stuart had already thoughtfully set up my tent.

This tour has been in progress for a while. They left Darwin while I was still in the wilds of Kakadu and arrived in Broome yesterday. The group was gathered in a circle, listening to Jimmy Howard, an itinerant, Aboriginal country /western musician. Stuart told me that this is Jimmy's last night in Broome; he'll be hitting the road tomorrow, wandering who knows where. The sounds of the singer and his guitar rose into the immense, crystalline silence of the night, as rough, warm, and inviting as a campfire. I listened as I settled in, but was too tired to face meeting new people tonight.

Thursday, September 29

A fresh breeze and the cries of birds awoke me, and I lay in my sleeping bag, watching the long, narrow wedge of sky framed by my open tent flap brighten, turning from silver to blue. The camp was still silent as I crawled out of my tent and into the morning. But before long, others stirred, and soon everyone was up and about, preparing for the day and introducing themselves to the newcomer.

After breakfast, we boarded the coach, some for a ride to town, some to the beach, and some of us to a mother-of-pearl "factory," where we saw a slide presentation on the history of pearling in Broome.

Broome was once known as the pearling capital of the world. Large, beautiful, exceptionally white natural pearls were found in the waters off this coast. However, there was even greater profit in collecting pearl shells. Broome supplied more than three-quarters of the world's requirements for mother-of-pearl. A decline began in the 1930s, with the appearance of the first synthetic buttons. As plastics improved, the mother-of-pearl industry disintegrated. The luggers (pearling boats) were requisitioned by the armed forces during W.W.I, and in W.W.II, Broome was heavily bombed. It seemed unlikely that the town would survive. Fortunately, the demand for cultured pearls kept Broome from becoming a ghost town. In 1956, a pearl farm was established at Kuri Bay, and luggers from Broome began fishing for live shells to be seeded for producing cultured pearls.

One thing I found amusing was how they used to clear the old luggers of cockroaches. At high tide, the crew would pull the plugs out of a boat and let it sink. The cockroaches, to avoid drowning, would run up the masts. When all but the tops of the masts were submerged, someone would row out and scrape the bugs off the masts. When the tide went out, the vessel was left high and dry and pest-free. Then it was replugged. (This worked because the tides here are enormous—more than 30 feet in the spring.)

Following the slide show, we picked our way between huge piles of turban and oyster shells to an area where artisans were cutting, carving, and polishing mother-of-pearl. A slender, bearded young man, wearing only white pants and a deep tan, showed us how shells are selected and prepared. Then we watched as gleaming white bracelets and baubles took shape at a dozen rough tables in the large, light, open room.

It was a free afternoon, so everyone headed off to swim, sunbathe, or go fishing. Stuart said he would drive me to a couple of the more remote spots (places the others saw yesterday), then drop me in town, so I could explore on my own.

Stuart took me first to the Japanese Cemetery at the edge of town. Pearl divers once came by the hundreds from Japan to work in the waters off Broome's coast. In the early days, when the wildly unpredictable weather changed for the worse, divers were quickly hauled up, regardless of the depths at which they were working, as the concept of decompression was unknown. Hence, most of the 919 individuals buried here died of the "bends," or divers' paralysis. The cemetery, with its simple headstones and carefully raked, bare ground, looks much like one of those austere, elegant "gardens" of rock that one associates with Japanese temples.

We drove next to Gantheaume Point, where I got my first view of the dazzling, inviting, bright clear turquoise of the Indian Ocean. This stretch of waterfront was bounded by a high, rugged, broken wall of oddly worn, tan, red, and orange rock. The contrast with the vivid blue water and pure white sand of the nearby beaches was startling and beautiful. Stuart and I climbed among the strangely shaped, eroded rocks. At the top of the cliffs, Stuart pointed out large, cement casts of dinosaur footprints. The actual 130-million-year-old, fossilized footprints lie about 25 yards off shore at this point, but can only be seen at extremely low tide.

Soon, I was back in town, on foot and on my own, with a few hours to discover Broome. The site on which Broome eventually grew was discovered in 1699 by buccaneer/explorer William Dampier. Broome's primary waterway, Roebuck Bay, derives its name from Dampier's ship, the *Roebuck,* and Dampier Creek flows nearby. The town was not officially established, however, until 1883, when pearls were discovered.

Broome doesn't really look much like the center of a still-thriving pearl industry. With its broad, dusty streets, wide verandas, and modest, iron-roofed buildings, it looks more like a sleepy little outback settlement that time forgot, in its beautiful setting by the Indian Ocean.

Broome's citizens are of Japanese, Chinese, Sinhalese, Malay, Koepanger, European, and Aboriginal origin. All of these cultures contributed heavily to Broome's history and development. I strolled down Napier Terrace, toward Chinatown, and turned into Carnarvon Street, where the small shops, restaurants, and multi-lingual street signs reflect this multi-racial heritage.

I stopped at the memorial to Mr. Kuribayashi, who founded the cultured-pearl industry in this region. Nearby stood a fully rigged pearling lugger, which commemorates the deaths caused by the pearling industry. The twin-masted, wood-hulled lugger was handsome, but small enough to make it easy to see why crews would panic when the weather turned mean. (The fear was not unfounded, either. I've read that, among the many disasters, 150 members of lugger crews were killed in 1908 when a cyclone struck, and even as recently as 1935, 141 drowned when they got caught at sea by a storm.) I browsed through the surprisingly exotic shops, then headed down Short Street, to Streeter's Jetty, which, nestled amid the mangroves that throng the shore, is only accessible to luggers at high tide.

Back in camp for the evening, I worked on getting to know my new "team mates." It's a larger group than I've been with before, diverse of age, largely Australian, but with a good number of visitors. It's an interesting mix, and nearly everyone is enthusiastic and friendly.

Friday, September 30

This morning, we were up before 5 a.m. It's odd—back in the "real world," it would take an event of astonishing magnitude to get me up before 6:30 (and I'd rather sleep till 8), but out here, waking when the earth does seems right and good—and possible.

Soon we had camp broken and were on the road. It was basically a driving day, because many of the sights to be seen out here are hundreds of miles apart. We had our first break at Sandfire Flat Roadhouse, which stands in the approximate middle of nowhere, on the edge of the blindingly hot and monotonous Great Sandy Desert. It consists only of a couple of gas pumps, a garage, restrooms, and a little necessities shop—but it's the only spot out here for hundreds of miles on an otherwise empty road, so it's on the map.

Lunch was 100 miles later, at Goldsworthy, an iron-ore mining town that made its final shipment about six weeks ago. We saw a few people moving around the depressing rows of single-men's quarters, and saw clothes drying on lines behind a few of the houses, but the town is already showing signs of impending desertion. Most of the buildings are empty, and the mines and trains are silent. Grass is growing around the benches in the open-air cinema. Doors stand ajar. Goldsworthy will probably be a ghost town soon.

In another hundred miles, we reached Port Hedland, from which port much of the iron ore mined in northern W.A. is shipped. Port Hedland is also a major center for the production of sea salt, and we passed immense salt-pans and glistening, white mountains of sun-dried salt. We drove along the waterfront, where we saw the massive machinery used for moving and loading iron ore and salt, and caught sight of the huge freighters floating offshore. Piers, tugboats, and thousands of sea gulls were silhouetted against the brilliant sea, which glittered like crumpled silver foil in the late afternoon sun.

We had an hour free to explore the town. After buying

half a dozen handsome seashells at the local shell shop, I wandered back down to the waterfront, to get a closer look at the mountains of salt and ore.

It's funny, but as small as this town is, it seems too populated for my current wilderness, camping-out mindset. I am interested to see the ships and salt pans, but I am not interested in staying here.

After dinner, five of the women from the tour invited me to join them for a little "nightlife." At the pub adjoining our camp ground, we bought soft drinks and took the opportunity to get better acquainted. Jill and Jo are policewomen from London, England. Nikki is a veterinarian from Manchester, England. Gay is a nurse from South Australia. Angela is a nurse from Arizona, USA. All were friendly, but I could tell early on that Nikki and Jo would be the ones who were most likely to become friends.

We stayed up too late for our incredibly early start tomorrow, but that was okay. We finally headed back to our tents feeling more connected. In a few hours, we'll be on the road again. I'll be glad to get back to the wilderness.

Saturday, October 1

We spent the day in transit—very rough transit, so sleeping on the bus was out of the question. Just as well, though, as there were wonderful things to see: the burnt, red plains of the North, dotted with spinifex; great, shimmering ghost gums; and emus dashing for cover. Then there was desolation—long stretches of bare sand and burned-out trees.

As we drove farther, there were signs of renewal: huge, strange, twisted limbs which might have appeared dead except for a flourish of green at the base; the reappearance of spinifex, but greener than before; then wildflowers in widely separated bunches, like small bouquets left on lonely, deserted graves. Before much longer, the Hamersley Range began to rise in the distance, wonderful and weathered, striated in reds, blues, greens, and blacks.

The Hamersley Range is a 200-mile-long rock mass believed to have been one of the first sections of the earth's crust to cool. The range is renowned for the many deep, spectacular, water-worn gorges that crisscross its high, ancient tableland, and we soon encountered our first, Yampire Gorge.

Yampire is one of the broader gorges, and one of the few that can be entered by road. The dark red walls rise in tiers, with pale golden grass topping each layer. White-trunked ghost gums, with their slender, olive green leaves, contrasted dramatically with the rust colored cliffs around them. Lovely mauve-pink blossoms of the Sturt desert rose decked twisted, brown branches growing amid the sea of shattered rock that covers the gorge floor.

We stopped for lunch in Yampire Gorge, near the site of an abandoned blue asbestos mine. The mine is no longer operating, because blue asbestos has been found to be dangerous to those who come in frequent contact with it. After eating, Jo, Nikki, Jill, and I wandered off to photograph trees and rocks and to admire the many finches flitting from perch to perch. We could see seams of blue asbestos running across some of the rock walls. There was also a lot of blue asbestos lying around—dark blue with silvery fibers, it is an amazing stone, the way it breaks into shimmering, supple threads. Had Stuart not forbidden the bringing of asbestos on the bus, I would probably have collected several pieces.

Not far from the gorge, Stuart stopped by one of the local giant termite mounds (the mounds here are rougher, redder, and more slap-dash looking than those in Kakadu), allowing a few minutes for all to stand in awe then photograph the prodigious construction. Then we were off to Dales Gorge and Fortescue Falls.

With Dales Gorge, as with most gorges in the Hamersley Range, you start at the top and climb down. About halfway down the tiered, red wall we got our first glimpse of Fortescue Falls below us. The falls cascade down slopes that are worn in layers like a series of terraces. The pale green water separates and reunites, like fluid lace, as it splashes over the rocks, descending from one pool to another. On one side, the rock wall rises straight out of the water, but on the other, the pools are fringed with reeds and bordered by trees and shrubs.

But as beautiful as the falls are, what fascinated me most were the rocks. As we descended farther into the gorge, we saw more formations, layering, diversity. The red walls are splashed with black and tan and touched with white and blue and purple. Quartzite, shale, iron ore, and other minerals run in slabs and ribbons and stripes. In many spots, the sharp, clean angles make the rock look as if it has been quarried, rather than worn by wind and water.

We continued our drive along the rim of the 25-mile-long gorge, stopping again near the site of the Circular Pool. The walls here were steeper than at the first place we descended, so I did not climb the entire distance to the bottom, just far enough down to view the great, round Circular Pool at the base of a perpendicular rock wall. I spent my time instead exploring the gorge's perimeter. The ground is red, pebbly, and metallic looking. It is almost pure iron ore. Spinifex and ghost gums, a few acacia bushes, and widely scattered wildflowers dot the strange, austere, beautiful, red landscape.

By late afternoon, we reached Wittenoom, the small town at the mouth of Wittenoom Gorge. Actually, it almost isn't a town anymore. Since the nearby blue asbestos mines were closed, Wittenoom has been creeping towards ghost town status. There are still people living here, still a police station and a pub, still a service station and a few shops. But many of the streets are deserted. Spinifex has started to reclaim the unsealed and unused side streets. Walls of empty houses are vanishing, leaving only geometric skeletons in the middle of weed-covered yards. It is a sad sight, especially when you see the tidy homes of those who are still trying to hold on, to not let the town die.

After pitching camp at the edge of town, we took a ride through Wittenoom Gorge. This gorge is wider than Yampire or Dales Gorges, with higher walls. The sun, which was low in the west, set the rock faces ablaze with color. Wallabies darted through the undergrowth. Giant termite mounds perched on precipitous slopes. Trees and bushes clustered thickly at the base of the red walls.

Before dinner, Melva and Roberta, two delightful, soft-spoken Aussies, asked if I'd like to join them for a wander around Wittenoom. We strolled down the main street, with its one pub and tiny hospital, past rows of deserted houses, to one inhabited street on the far side of town, where we browsed through a small art gallery/souvenir shop.

Across the street from these homes, the wilderness stretched toward the horizon, bordered on one side by the colorfully striated Hamersley Range. The blood-red earth was dark between the widely spaced clumps of spinifex, the tops of which shimmered with the last rays of the setting sun. The sky was paling to a soft mauve. A few, lonely ghost gums stood like eerie sentinels on the twilight desert, their white trunks turned pink by the pastel sky. We stood and watched the desert and the mountains till there was no sunlight left. Then, by the light of the stars, we made our way back to camp.

Sunday, October 2

This morning, we rose at our usual early hour. (I've never before seen so many sunrises.) A windstorm last night kept most of us from sleeping, so everyone was tired, but those of us who stayed up late Friday were dying. Even with the bumpy roads we dropped off to sleep minutes after boarding the coach—but not for long.

We were soon at Hamersley Gorge, renowned for its folded rocks. The remarkable, layered walls of this gorge wave, bend and bow as if they had once been fluid. It's hard to imagine the kind of pressure necessary to do this to solid rock.

The immense, striated ripples rise out of the bright green water at the bottom of the gorge and run along the faces of the cliffs on both sides. We climbed down into the gorge, where we spent a good deal of time scrambling up and down paths and over boulders, admiring the great, buckling ribbons of red rock around us.

Leaving Hamersley Gorge, we continued to drive through a dramatic landscape of red, gold, and green. Our next stop was at Oxer's Lookout, which overlooks a great, deep, sheer-sided hole where Weano, Hancock, Joffre, and Red Gorges come together like a titan pinwheel.

We stood for a while on the brink of the cluster of gorges, then skirted the rim of Weano Gorge until we came to the steep, narrow path that leads to the bottom. Only a few members of the group tackled the 300-foot descent, but those of us who ventured down into the gorge were abundantly repaid for our efforts. We descended into the widest part of the gorge, where the walls are rough and offer good handholds and relatively easy climbing.

The vegetation in Weano Gorge was sparse, with a few flowering bushes standing amid shaggy tufts and straggles of golden grass. The dry grass often rustled as we approached, and we would see little lizards that had been sunning on the rocks disappear into the safety of the brush.

As we continued along the floor of the gorge, the ragged, red walls began to close in on both sides. Soon we were winding through a narrow, undulating passage where there was only a thin strip of light far overhead. The walls of the crevice now rose cool and purple, in smooth, water-sculpted ripples. We climbed over slabs and plates of shattered rock, as we followed the twisting path, trying to avoid the spots where trickles of water made the well-worn stone slippery.

We emerged from the long, dark channel into a bright opening. A clear, jade-green pool filled the space where the chasm suddenly widened and dropped dramatically. Here the walls were again red and rugged, rising straight up out of the water on all sides. The narrow passage continued on the far side of the pool, but was submerged.

After a few hours of delighted exploration, we resurfaced from the depths of the gorge. Jeanette had a late lunch waiting for us. As we ate, several crested spinifex pigeons came bobbing over searching for handouts. These adorable little birds are predominantly pale brown, with black and white markings on their heads, red "masks" around their eyes, and brown crest feathers that stick straight up from their little heads like a severe cowlick.

The afternoon was spent getting to Mt. Tom Price, a big iron ore-mining town. This town contrasts dramatically with Goldsworthy. Goldsworthy, built in a different era, was cramped and Spartan, lacking most of the comforts of civilization, and most of the housing was metal-walled rows of units for single men. Mt. Tom Price, on the other hand, is designed for families. It is well landscaped, has nice houses, schools, a community center, several shops, and is really quite pleasant.

The town and nearby mountain were named after Tom Price, the American engineer who explored the Hamersley Range for iron ore. Our campsite this evening is at a clean but uninteresting camping park a few miles out of town, in the shadow of the great, iron-rich mountains.

Monday, October 3

This morning, we were scheduled to tour the Hamersley Iron Mines. There was a strike last week, but we were told that the miners were going back to work, so we could have our tour. They did go back to work this morning—for one hour—then called another strike. (Striking is, by most accounts, a popular pastime in Australia.)

We sat on the coach outside the compound, looking through the locked gates, while an employee of the company told us about the operation. She was enthusiastic about the size and scope of the mine's work, but was embarrassed by the current situation. She opened her talk by saying, "The Hamersley Iron Mine operates—please don't laugh—24 hours a day." She told us that Mt. Tom Price holds the richest deposits of iron ore in the world; it is, in fact, a four-mile-long mountain of ore. About 130,000 tons of ore are mined each day. She detailed the blasting, moving, and refining involved in preparing the ore for shipment, by train, to the mine's seaport in Dampier.

Though we could not see the mine from where we were, we could see the mammoth ore trucks. Each one has a capacity of more than 170 tons. These vehicles are so immense that their tires are eleven feet in diameter. The few mechanics we saw wandering around the trucks were dwarfed by the towering machines. Our guide told us that Hamersley, like other big companies mining in the region, works hard to preserve the ecology of the area. As soon as mining is completed at a location, the site is recovered and replanted, so there is as little adverse effect as possible.

Because we didn't get our tour, Stuart thought he'd make it up to us by getting us to our next campsite early—by lunch, in fact. It was a great idea. We're staying at Millstream National Park, and it is a glorious place. Our tents are pitched in the midst of a forest of paperbark trees. Scattered among the paperbarks are fan palms, gum trees, acacias, and wildflowers. Just a few yards away is a beautiful, clear, blue river.

Jo, Jill, Nikki, Gay, Angela, and I swam and played for hours in the cool, reed-fringed river. We dove from the trees that over-hung the water, had races, splashed, laughed, and enjoyed our surroundings. When we finally began to feel waterlogged, Jo, Jill, and I went for a long walk. We followed the river for miles, through the beautiful, pale, sun-dappled forest, down to where the red cliffs rise above the treetops. Black swans swam among the reeds on the far side of the river. We saw sulphur-crested cockatoos, finches, butterflies, and flowers everywhere.

We had another swim before dinner, and another walk afterward, then darkness and the forest closed around us, filled with warmth, peace, and whispering stillness, and we crept off to our tents.

Tuesday, October 4

Morning dawned bright and fair. And early. We really hated leaving Millstream, as it's the most beautiful place we've camped on this tour. But before long, we were packed and back on the coach.

Soon after leaving Millstream, we entered Chichester Range National Park. The Chichester Range is a product of millions of years of volcanic activity, all of which ended so many millions of years ago that no traces remain of the craters or vents. While they lasted, the awesome eruptions completely buried this area with basaltic lava and showered the landscape with a dense blanket of volcanic ash and rock fragments. Hundreds of millions of years of erosion have created a rolling sea of stone broken by low mesas, oddly shaped hills, and tumbles of boulders. It is an eerie place, with little vegetation other than the occasional tuft of golden spinifex—just miles and miles of weird, desolate, undulating red landscape, more reminiscent of the moon than anything else.

We drove to Roebourne, the oldest town in the northwest, then detoured north to Cossack. Cossack was once an important pearling town, with a port that handled shipping for 50 years until the inlet silted up. Now it is a picturesque ghost town. The handsome old courthouse—built of dark, local stone accented with the white of its cornerstones, chimney, and square veranda columns—has been renovated as a museum. Nearby, the two-story post office, police barracks and school, all completed between 1869 and 1890, still stand, though blind and mute. The town's other few buildings are in disrepair, some roofless, some with crumbling walls. The town occupies a bright, palm-fringed stretch of sand on the edge of the deep-blue Indian Ocean, which makes the whole place quite charming, if a bit lonely.

From Cossack we drove to Dampier, a small, bustling port town. This is the seaport from which the Hamersley Iron Mine ships all its ore, and across the bay we could see mountains of ore and the extensive loading operation.

We were dropped off in town with an hour free. I stopped to buy a pair of thongs (often called flip-flops in the US, this footwear is an essential part of Australian national dress, though I was buying them as protection against the things that grow in the shared showering facilities at the campsites), then Jo, Jill, Nikki, and I headed for the beach. Although there are miles of beaches, you are limited in your choices of where to swim—you have to stay inside the shark cage. We were more than glad to go along with this restriction because, aside from any considerations about sharks, the ocean was rough, and we felt safer knowing the outer cage walls would keep us from being swept out to sea.

After a good swim, followed by a quick, open-air, freshwater shower, Jo and I walked up the beach to dry out. We found staggering numbers of seashells along the shore. I could have collected thousands, but settled on a few handfuls.

We walked back to where Nikki and Jill were lying in the sun. Nearby, on the rocks beside the shark cage, there were several people fishing. There was a large, official sign posted at the site that read: "Cleaning of fish in this area is PROHIBITED—offenders will be eaten."

A long afternoon haul brought us to Ashburton River just before sunset. The approach to the river was unpromising—dust, desolation, and a big gas station/road-house at the turnoff—but then we topped a rise, and there below us was a calm, clear stream flowing gently among large trees and strangely worn rocks. The sunset made the location appear even lovelier.

Because we weren't near any towns, and because there was so much open space, the stars were particularly easy to see—and spectacular. I want to visit a planetarium while I'm over here, to learn more about southern skies. But even without that, I've enjoyed stargazing. The Southern Cross has been pointed out to me, and I found Orion, though he's upside down in this hemisphere. Cutting across it all is the dazzling white blanket of the Milky Way. I saw a shooting star flashing through the sky, and, though I'm told they're fairly common here, I was delighted beyond words. What a glorious night.

Wednesday, October 5

The opening of my tent faced the river, so I awoke to a vision of crystal dawn reflected in the tranquil water. The sun was not up quite as early as we were, but appeared before too long. It was another beautiful day.

Soon we were on the road again, making our way south toward Carnarvon. After driving a little more than a hundred miles, we crossed the Tropic of Capricorn. The spot is distinguishable only because of a sign that announces you have arrived at the line, but it is remarkable how quickly things begin to cool off once you've crossed it.

In another few hours, we reached Carnarvon. Our first stop was at a banana plantation, where we were taken on a tour by the proprietor.

The banana tree is not actually a tree, but rather a very tall herb. Despite its solid appearance, it is mostly water. The plant grows astonishingly quickly, then produces one giant purple flower which, when pollinated, produces a huge bunch of bananas. The plant then dies, and a new one starts up from its roots soon afterwards. We saw the graceful, almost palm-like herbs in all stages of growth—sprouts, adults, with flowers, and with bunches of green bananas. The plantation was quite beautiful, in the opulent greenness of its tight rows of banana plants.

We crossed the Gascoyne River on our way into town. The 500-mile-long Gascoyne is Western Australia's longest river. Heavy rains can turn it into a roaring torrent, but for most of the year it is dry. The wide stretch of wavy sand below us looked inauspicious, but the riverbed conceals immense underground reservoirs, from which Carnarvon pumps all its water.

Carnarvon sits on the east shore of Shark Bay, at the mouth of the Gascoyne River. This stretch of coast offers some of the best fishing in Australia, as Shark Bay attracts large numbers of fish, especially whiting (and yes, sharks, too). We passed broad, flat, pale, ocean beaches and inlets filled with fishing boats. We saw prawn trawlers and the town's scallop processing plant. Sadly, the scallop season just ended, so we shan't be dining on them this evening.

We drove down Carnarvon's wide main street. The main street is 120 feet across, to accommodate the camel trains that supplied this area until the early 1920s. Actually, tremendously wide main streets are common in small Australian towns, because so many of the towns grew up along the routes of the great cattle drives or the camel trains, and the streets had to allow for the passage of large numbers of animals.

Stuart dropped everyone in town for two hours of shopping. Jo, Jill, and I had seen a public swimming pool just as we entered town. We always have our swimsuits handy, so we grabbed them and headed off for a couple of hours of swimming. It was a glorious pool, 50 meters long. This was especially good for Jo, because at home she swims competitively, and she was worrying about getting out of shape. We had the place all to ourselves, too. Jill and I swam several lengths, then floated about and talked for a while, before doing a few more lengths. Jo did an hour solid of fast laps.

We dried ourselves in the still warm sun of a rapidly cooling afternoon, then walked the few blocks back to the center of town. We looked in a few shop windows and wondered how everyone else spent the two free hours. We found out when, at the appointed departure time, the rest of our group emerged from pubs and coffee shops. We boarded the coach and headed for our evening campsite.

Thursday, October 6

This morning, we collapsed camp with our usual dispatch, finishing at least 20 minutes ahead of another group camping at the site (no competitive spirit, here). Then we were on the road again, heading south.

The North West Coastal Highway skirted Shark Bay for a hundred miles, but then we lost sight of the sea. The tires sang their now-familiar song, and time was blurred by the sound, and by the sight of the changeless land spreading away from us, flat and ageless. In another hundred, timeless miles, we turned into Kalbarri National Park. We stopped near Murchison Gorge, where the Murchison River has carved down through 450 feet of red sandstone. The broad, winding Murchison River flowed peacefully through the valley below us, disappearing into a landscape that was greener than any we had seen for some time.

Murchison Gorge is deeper and wider than the gorges we saw up north, though not as startlingly sculpted. The drama here is softened by the veil of green over everything. The rocks—the more muted red with tan of sandstone—are still wonderful and worn. The tops of the rock walls are sheer, though shattered in places, making climbing possible. The incline becomes gentler as it gets nearer the water.

Gum trees line the watercourse. In the middle of the river, perched on a single, wide pedestal of stone, there is a tilted rock "table," which looked so solid, yet, at the same time, so precarious. Greenery climbs the broken, red walls. Among the upper cliffs and crags are gnarled, twisted little trees and shrubs, all showing the effects of growing against the wind. And everywhere we turned there were wildflowers.

Jo set the auto-timer on her camera and got a picture of herself, Jill, and me together, standing on a huge, beak-like overhang of rock that overlooks the gorge. It was such a lovely spot that Jo and I brought our lunches back, rather than sit around the coach, which we reckoned we'd seen enough of.

We had a few more hours of exploration, then it was on the road again. By late afternoon, great, dark clouds began to gather. It seemed strange, as I have seen almost no clouds in the last month. I guess endless days of blue skies are behind me now.

This evening's campsite, just outside Geraldton, has the advantage of being only a stone's throw from the beach. Though the water was too cold and rough for swimming, the beach was perfect for a nice, long walk, to which end Jo and I took off as soon as camp was set up.

We waded in the water, then strolled barefoot on the incredibly soft sand. It was a glorious evening, with the lowering sun breaking through the clouds from time to time in great beams of gold that danced on the dark ocean before us. The evening breeze rose, and the pure white sand shifted and slid along the ground, drifting in places, looking very much like a light, blowing snow. Dark green sea plants clustered on the sand cliffs beside us. Jo and I walked for nearly an hour, turning back only because we realized that before long the incoming tide would cut off our retreat.

After dinner, Jo, Jill, Nikki, Angela, and I set off on our nightly stroll. We stuck to the roads, as the beach had by now been reclaimed by the tide. Every now and then a shadow flickered across the edge of the light from our one flashlight. We finally caught one of the culprits in the full beam—it was a large crab. It reared up to challenge us, then decided scuttling off was a better idea. We saw dozens of crabs before we finally got back to camp.

Friday, October 7

As we traveled south, we were suddenly in the midst of an awesomely green landscape. Within an hour's time we traded the red desert and spinifex for rolling green hills and large shade trees. Sheep roamed in the fields, grazing in an area that looked more like England than Australia. The occasional palm tree now seemed strangely out of place. It was refreshing, familiar, cool, green, beautiful— yet almost instantly I missed the strangeness and grandeur of the red land I was leaving behind.

Before long, the wildflowers began to increase in number and variety, until the whole world seemed to be an intoxicating riot of color and delicate shapes. I wished we had time to stop and look at them all, but I soothed myself with the knowledge that I'll see lots of flowers on my next tour.

We stopped for morning break in a little town called Moora. Nikki, Jo, and I bought soft drinks, then headed off for a stroll around town. Nikki and Jo feel like old friends by now. Though both are British, only Nikki seems obviously so. She is tall, fair, with long, wavy, light brown hair. She is smart, ladylike, laughs easily, but has a no-nonsense air that hints at the depth of her thoughts. Jo is a golden sprite. She is an impish athlete with a shining halo of golden hair and a glowing tan. She is always in motion and is passionate about the out-of-doors. Both are readers and thinkers, and both share my love for beauty and Australia. It is these two, from all in this group, with whom I shall stay in contact.

When we came to the broad, open village green, Jo took off, running across the grass, stopping to pick flowers, playfully jostling us when she returned, dashing off again. It's hard sometimes to imagine her as a policewoman. Then it was back on the coach, and onward to New Norcia.

New Norcia is reminiscent of a small, rural village in southern Europe. Olive groves and bell towers spring from the red dust. White-trimmed, red stone walls surround large, stately, old buildings of reddish field stone outlined in white. Multitudes of arched windows bespeak a Spanish-Moorish heritage. New Norcia was founded as a Spanish Benedictine monastery in 1846. The monastery is still there, complete with serene, white-robed monks, but the complex now includes an orphanage, boarding school, library, museum, and art gallery.

Jo, Nikki, and I explored New Norcia for more than an hour. As we passed the bell tower, Jo shared her experience of having been a bell ringer back home when she was younger ("you have to be careful, or the ropes will pull you right off your feet"). We took photographs of the handsome buildings, apple orchards, stone walls, and each other, enjoying both the Old World charm and the strangeness of finding it here.

Perth is only 80 miles from New Norcia, so it was not long before we rolled into town. Stuart reminded us that we were no longer "out bush," and we'd have to watch out for cars and such (I haven't "looked both ways before crossing" in a month). Then he dropped us in the center of town with a few hours free. Jo, Nikki, and I sauntered off to run errands and see some of the sights. Perth is a bright, delightful town, and I look forward to seeing more of it when my next tour is finished.

Tonight we are staying in a real motel, with real beds. After receiving our room assignments and settling in, Roberta, Jill, Nikki, Jo, and I wandered out into the streets of Perth in search of a suitable place for dinner. We found a nice Chinese restaurant about three blocks from our motel. As this was going to be our last meal together, we dragged the event out for a considerable length of time, toasting each other's health and happiness, and trying to figure out how we can get back together again.

We topped off the evening with coffee in Jo and Jill's room, talking late into the night, no one really wanting to break up the party, though we all knew we needed the sleep.

Saturday, October 8

My alarm didn't go off until 7 a.m.—relatively late for our normal schedule. If we'd gone to bed at a decent time, it would have been a good night's sleep.

Before I was half dressed, Jo was at the door. Roberta was moving to the Jewell House (the very hotel to which I shall return at the end of my next tour), and had offered to take my excess baggage with her, to leave in storage there till I arrive. Jo had volunteered to give her a hand. Hence, I was blissfully unencumbered as I checked out.

Jo and I talked in the courtyard as we waited for my taxi, which arrived at 8:25. I tossed my duffel in the cab, waved good-bye to Jo, and was off.

I arrived at the East Perth Passenger Terminal 15 minutes later, for the commencement of my six-day Westrail

Wildflower Study Tour. This is a slightly fancier tour than the others I've been on, so there are a few extras, like a hostess, a botanist, flower-pressing books, hotels, and beds.

Stephanie (Steph), our hostess, is married, in her 40s, has dark, curly hair, and is intelligent and pleasant. She is, of all on the tour, closest to my age. Ray, our driver, is in his 50s, has gorgeous, thick white hair, a good tan, great smile, and seems mischievous. He says I have fascinating eyes. Jean, our botanist, is attractive, with salt and pepper hair, is in her 50s, and is enthusiastic and informative. The next youngest member of the group is 65, and the ages are more heavily weighted on the 75-plus end of the scale. Steph told me that last week they had a younger group, which she felt certain I would have enjoyed. I might have. However, I am perfectly contented to travel in this present company.

Everyone thinks it's charming and fun to have a "youngster" along on the trip, and they are all delightfully friendly. The men are chivalrous, the women, motherly, and everyone is looking out for me, making sure I don't feel left out. They really are a dear group of people. Many of those on the tour really love botany. Several of them were just on the northern wildflower tour (this one is heading south), and some are here for their third or fourth year. They say you see something new every time you come.

Once we were under way, Jean explained the procedures for the coming days. Only she, as a botanist, is allowed to pick flowers. She will supply us with specimens, which we can put in our pressing books. Each evening, she'll label the books with each flower's Latin name. Even she can't pick flowers in National Parks, however, and orchids can't be picked anywhere. (Of the 600 varieties of orchid in Australia, 140 occur in this region.)

The southwest of Western Australia is considered to have one of the most dazzling spring floral displays in the world. There are approximately 8,000 species of wildflower here, and before long, we were in the middle of them. It was mind-boggling. We stopped at a promising spot and swarmed off the bus, going into the botanist's version of a feeding frenzy—flying in all directions, trying to photograph and identify as many of the glorious flowers as possible. This tour is going to use up a lot of film, I can tell already.

Most of my compatriots are quite knowledgeable and eager to share any good finds with everyone else. The *delecta* this morning included five different orchids: donkey orchid, giant white spider orchid, red spider orchid, purple enamel orchid, and the yellow, star-like cowslip orchid. The orchids of this region differ from those of the tropics, being smaller, of somewhat different shape, and generally growing closer to the ground.

Many of the gum trees are in bloom. Their fragrant blossoms are as diverse as the eucalypts themselves, ranging from tiny, delicate white to large, shaggy red flowers.

Back on the bus, Jean gave us our specimens—verticordia, dampiera, grevillea, melaleuka, dryandra—and we tried to tape them in our pressing books as we bounced along the road.

We had a picnic lunch at Australind, a small town planned in the 1840s as the site for a dreamed-of Australia-India trading company. The splendid, white beaches were lined with magnificent, twisted sandalwood trees. Nearby, we saw St. Nicholas's Church, the smallest church in Australia, which was built in the 1800s as a one-room, worker's hut.

Then we were off, climbing up through the Darling Ranges. Flowers grew on trees, vines, bushes, and in clusters on every available inch of open ground. In places, the ground was completely blanketed with the reddish-orange flowers of the coral vine.

During one of our rambles I saw a stick insect. I've read that one rarely sees these in their natural habitats, mainly because they're so hard to see. Apparently, someone or something had dislodged this one from its perch, and there it was, a six-inch stick with legs ambling slowly back towards its bush. Wonderful.

About 5 p.m., we rolled into Bunbury, a little port town perched on the edge of the sea. We drove along the beautiful coastline, which is ragged with basalt pillars. Fishermen stood among the uneven, black columns of rock, casting their long lines into the waves that pawed the shore. We had a quick spin through town, and then headed for the Clifton Beach Motel, our overnight stop for this evening.

Sunday, October 9

The day started merrily. At around 7 o'clock, the kookaburras started to wake up, an event signaled by peals of insane, giddy, laughter. I love these birds. One can't help but chuckle along with them.

Not long after rising, we were on the road. Winding through the narrow streets and up the gentle, green hills of Bunbury, we came to a lookout. The little town, with its white-walled, red tile-roofed houses and abundant gardens, spread below us, rolling down toward the sparkling sea. We stayed a few minutes, enjoying the view and the fresh ocean breeze, then continued on, turning southwest, toward Busselton.

There was a morning flower break, and far more specimens were added to our growing collections. By now I have several varieties of feather flower (Verticordia); pink and white pimelea; delicate, red, insect-trapping sundew flowers (Drosera); a number of different grevilleas; yellow woolly flowers (Conostylis); smoke bush (Conospermum); freesia; hibbertia: yellow-flowered acacia; delicate, mauve Tetratheca; many of the awesomely diverse pea-family flowers that seem to grow everywhere; and numerous other strange and beautiful blooms.

I was pleased to happen upon a large patch of kangaroo paws. Kangaroo paws, Western Australia's state flower, have soft, fuzzy, red stems and curving, green blossoms. (Where else but Australia would you find a plant with red stems and green flowers?)

We paid a visit to a place named the Bunyip Pool. A bunyip is a mythical spirit/monster that inhabited pools and scared away the natives, on which it liked to dine. It also kept many early settlers at bay, as they had no reason to doubt the existence of such a creature in a land that had so many other strange animals.

The once-scary pool now attracts visitors. There is an abundance of glorious flora and a little souvenir shop just bulging with goodies. I bought one book on W.A. wild-flowers, another on local birds, and a cassette recording of Australian bird calls. Now I won't have to try to explain to everyone back home the kookaburra's crazy laugh, the singing snap of the whip bird, the sweet sound of the golden whistler.

My shopping done, I went outside to enjoy the flowers that grow in such profusion at this location. There were black and gold kangaroo paws, as well as the more famil-iar red and green variety; gorgeous flowering gums; broad, purple cascades of native wisteria; densely flowered, pink Swan River myrtle; delicate, lavender fringed lilies; and more. Nearby stood 10-foot-high bushes of yellow Banksia. Banksias, named for Joseph Banks, the botanist on Captain Cook's voyage to Australia, are odd but attrac-tive, with stiff, serrated leaves and flowers that are like spiny, floral pinecones.

Continuing on, we passed through Yoongarillup, Jarrahwood, Nannup, Glenoran, and Manjimup. The *-up* ending so many town names in this area is the word for water hole or meeting place in the local Aboriginal dialect.

The shady coolness of the Karri forest closed in around us. We stopped near the Four Aces, four perfectly aligned

Karri trees, the tallest of which stands more than 250 feet high. Karri trees, which are members of the eucalypt family, rival North America's redwoods in size and value. They grow as tall as 250 to 285 feet, often rising more than 150 feet before the first branch interrupts the straight sweep of their silver-gray trunks.

All around the densely wooded area, the trees were festooned with garlands of white clematis and purple hardenbergia. A flower-bordered path through the forest led us from the Four Aces to the nearby one-tree bridge. Here, one giant tree was dropped across a stream, then planks and railings were nailed on top to form a bridge.

Around 5 p.m., we reached Pemberton and the Gloucester Motel, our place of rest for this evening. After dinner, Ray whisked away most of our merry band to a nearby arts and crafts gallery. I decided to stay in the room and write. When the group returned, I heard about the beautiful wood carvings and saw some of the souvenirs they had purchased, but I needed to write more than I needed to shop, and was happy with my choice.

Monday, October 10

Today's driving took us through beautiful forests of giant Karri and sweet-smelling Jarrah trees. Conservation groups are trying to enlarge W.A.'s national parks, to ensure the preservation of magnificent forests like these. I hope they succeed. It would be heartbreaking to lose the fragrant, green glory of these wild, wooded places.

Our first stop was at the Gloucester Tree, named for the Duke of Gloucester, who hammered in the first peg back in the 1940s. The peg was the first rung of a spiral "staircase" fixed in the tree's trunk and running all the way to the top, where a fire lookout station is perched. This particular Karri is 200 feet tall, making it the highest fire lookout tree in the world. But the station is no longer in use, having been replaced by helicopters.

You can still climb the tree, but only three people can go up at a time. Two young men were just coming down from the stiff climb when we arrived. They told us that the view was great, but the ascent was pretty scary. "The nearer to the top you get," one of the young men explained, "the tighter the spiral gets. It's hard climbing, and the tree keeps swaying in the breeze. All you can do is hold on like grim death, and don't look down."

What fascinated me most about the tree was how it has reacted to the pegs—its efforts to protect and heal itself. Where each rung entered the tree, a thick bump of bark has grown outward, enfolding the base of the peg, enclosing the irritant, oyster-like, in a woody pearl.

We had an early collection stop, but most of the day was spent in national parks, so we didn't add much to our pressing books, just took lots of photographs. We drove down Rainbow Trail, cutting through the dense, green forest, and arriving before long at a wide, clear stream. I wandered along the sparkling watercourse, reveling in the place's beauty, stopping to photograph the plants and flowers surrounding me. Clematis draped much of the undergrowth with bright, white clusters and runners of star-shaped flowers. Tassel bush decorated the shore. Small, brilliant orchids peeked out through the foliage everywhere: pink enamel orchids, sun orchids, silky blue orchids, and blue lady orchids.

Jean called us together and led us to a few small shrubs she'd found several yards off the road. They were covered with exquisite white flowers. The flower was a *Xanthosia rotundifolia,* better known as a Southern Cross. Out of a central bloom extend four "arms" of equal length, each of which ends in another delicate blossom, forming a perfect cross. It is almost luminescent.

We continued on to Warren National Park, where we had

lunch in a spot as suited to botanical exploration as any we had seen thus far. Nearby was a stand of blackboys (*Xanthorrhoea*), strange, short (up to 16 feet, but most are only two to six feet tall), shaggy-topped, palm-trunked trees with tall, bulrush-like central spikes covered with tiny white flowers. I also spotted numerous red bottlebrushes, yellow hibbertia and purple hovea. I encountered many of the orchids I've seen elsewhere and saw my first tall leek orchid (an exceptionally fine example, Jean says), which stands about three feet tall, with inch-high green and purple-black flowers covering a dark stalk. I must have photographed a dozen flowers I couldn't identify for every one I could. There are just too many to keep track of them all.

As we drove on, we startled flocks of kelly green, yellow, and black parrots—Port Lincoln parrots, I was told. Everyone dismissed them as being fairly common, but I was quite wide-eyed with delight.

The highlight of my day came after we reached Albany. The tour I just departed was supposed to be in town, too, and Nikki and Jo had said they'd try to get to the hotel or call. There was no message, so I scanned the district map to see if I could find their campsite. I was still searching the map when the two of them waltzed in. We dined together in the hotel's dining room, talking about what we've done since we were last together. After dinner, we asked the receptionist if she could recommend someplace we could go for a quiet drink. The nearest spot was almost half a mile away, but we're pretty accustomed to walking by now, so we set off.

The three of us talked for hours. Jo and Nikki both said they were glad we could get together one more time. We tried to figure out where else our paths could cross before we leave Australia, but they'll be turning eastward tomorrow, and I'm not heading that way for at least a week. Jo said she's already planning a trip to Chicago, and I promised to try to get to England.

Finally we strolled back to the hotel and called a cab for Jo and Nikki. We all promised to write, then bid each other fond farewells. I waved good-bye, and wondered when I'd see them again.

Tuesday, October 11

Albany is the oldest town in Western Australia. It was founded 2-1/2 years earlier than Perth. Today, exploring this sun-drenched, Victorian, coastal village and its surroundings was our objective.

We drove to the top of Mt. Melville, a high, green hill, where wildflowers crowded between great outcrops and boulders of lichen-stained granite. The lookout on Mt. Melville afforded us a panoramic view of Albany, King George Sound, Princess Royal and Oyster Harbours, lush, green farmland, and, in the distance, the Porongurup and Stirling Ranges.

Descending from Mt. Melville, we turned toward King George Sound—the vast, enclosed waterway that first attracted settlers to this spot—then continued out to Cheynes Beach, where a former whaling station is being converted into a whaling museum. One of the old whaling ships is docked there, and you can see the vats in which whale blubber was rendered into oil.

Whaling came late to Western Australia; a group of Norwegians founded the Western Australia Whaling Company in 1912. With interruptions for two World Wars, whaling continued in this region into the 1970s. This station was for many years the only operational one left in Australia, but in 1978 whale oil was usurped by jojoba oil, and the station closed down.

As the other members of the group wandered through the souvenir shop, buying postcards and carved whale teeth, I walked down to the beach. It was a spectacularly beautiful spot, with the gently sloping crescent of pearly white sand running from the surrounding green hills down to the clear, vividly blue water. I took off my shoes and strolled along the beach, then waded in the water, trying to hold my skirt up far enough to keep it away from the waves, but usually failing. It was a glorious day and a mesmerizing location. All too soon, a horn blast from the coach broke into my reverie and—still barefooted, covered in sand, and partially soaked in seawater—I climbed back up the hill and rejoined the group.

We headed out of town, following the ribbon of road that skirts the sea. We stopped at Jimmy Newhills Inlet, a beautiful, needle-thin inlet in the otherwise forbiddingly rugged coast. The Jimmy Newhills from whom the inlet received its name was out one day in a sailboat, alone, when a sudden windstorm (for which this area is apparently notorious) arose, blowing him swiftly toward the towering granite cliffs of shore—and certain death. But instead of smashing against the rocks, Jimmy Newhills was, providentially, driven by the wind into this narrow inlet. Three days after he had been assumed dead, he walked back into Albany.

We continued along this fabulous piece of coastline, with its high, craggy cliffs of worn, gray stone. Even here, along the stony, storm-beaten edge of the continent, there are abundant wildflowers, many of them unlike anything I've ever seen before: big, spiky, golden balls (dryandra); swirls and spirals of rigid greenery; strange star-bursts of purple with almost pine-like "needles"; halos of odd, triangular leaves around weird, frosty, gray-white balls that might be flowers or seed pods, and look like both. Closer to the massive, granite cliffs there are twisted, wind-tortured trees and shrubs growing almost parallel to the ground.

A little farther along, we reached The Gap and Natural Bridge, impressive formations that stand side by side. As we approached these wonders, we were greeted by a sign that read: "Gap-Natural Bridge—Dangerous Coast—You

Have Been Warned." The scolding-mother tone, while reminding us that this wild place demands respect, also elicited a chuckle or two.

The Gap is a great "crease" in the cliff face that captures the breakers and causes them to swirl and crash against the granite wall with even greater fury than elsewhere. It was awesome and beautiful, with the dark, glittering blue, foam-topped waves clawing wildly at the gray cliffs, sending spray high into the air before dropping back into the crystalline vortex at the base of the rocks.

The Natural Bridge is, naturally, a stone bridge. The dark granite is grooved and split, so the water-eroded bridge looks almost as though it was built from giant boulders. The bridge and the stone around it have been wonderfully sculpted by wind and sea. The granite bridge is nearly flat on top, so, braced against the stiff breeze, I ventured out on its broad back and stood above the pounding surf, surveying the stark, glorious, dramatic coast.

We returned to Albany for lunch, and then had a few hours on our own to wander around the charming, old buildings of this lovely little town. Albany was settled in 1826 as a safeguard against French colonization of the West Coast. Originally called Frederickstown, after Frederick, Duke of York and Albany, the new settlement was known as Albany by 1832. Western Australia's first church and first post office still stand here. Victorian shop fronts line Main Street, and the cornerstones of many buildings bear dates from Albany's early days.

We all met again down near the harbor, where we toured the Old Gaol Folk Museum. The Old Gaol (jail), which was built in 1851 as a convict depot, houses one of those kinds of collections peculiar to small-town museums. There are relics from when the building did serve as a jail—murderer's row, the "black hole" for intense solitary confinement, manacles, stocks, etc. There are also souvenirs of every war Australia has fought in and mementos of every visit to Albany by any member of the Royal Family. There are whale bones and jaws, seashells, rocks, dolls, and an early salon hair-permanenting machine. The building itself was the best part of the visit. The thick, whitewashed walls are wonderfully substantial looking. The brick floors are worn, and the doorjambs sag slightly. The old kitchen, with its brick oven, the walled exercise yard, the Great Hall, the storage rooms and Warders' Quarters are clean, solid, and austere.

Departing the harbor, we turned toward Mt. Clarence, driving down the Avenue of Honor. On both sides of the Avenue, there are trees planted, one for each Albany boy killed in W.W.I, each with a small brass plaque at its base identifying the soldier for whom the tree stands as a memorial.

Near the top of the hill stands the Australia and New Zealand Light Horse Memorial, a massive stone plinth surmounted by two huge bronze horses, one rearing and one struggling to its feet, and their riders, one still mounted and one downed. On the wall around the monument is inscribed: "Erected by their comrades & the Governments of Australia and New Zealand in memory of the members of the Australian Light Horse, the New Zealand Mounted Rifles, the Imperial Camel Corps & the Australian Flying Corps who lost their lives in Egypt, Palestine & Syria, 1916-1918." The memorial originally stood in Port Said, Egypt. However, in the ensuing years, increasing amounts of damage were being done to it by vandals and political malcontents, so finally Australia dismantled it and brought it to Albany, the port from which so many soldiers departed for North Africa.

Wednesday, October 12

Today we headed north, to Porongurup National Park and the Stirling Range. We had morning tea in Cranbrook,

"Gateway to the Stirlings," with a group of current and retired Park Rangers who served us scones with locally collected white gum honey. They took us through displays of wildflowers they had cultivated, then showed us a movie on flowers indigenous to the district. Nearly 1,000 species of wildflower can be found in the Stirlings, of which more than a hundred are unique to the range. Most interesting are the *Darwinias*, or Stirling Bells. Not only do they grow nowhere else in the world except the Stirling Range, but each of the seven varieties of *Darwinia* has its own mountain, growing nowhere else in the range,

Two park rangers came with us as guides through the mountains, to make certain we saw the best of the area's wildflowers. And the area's flowers were glorious, and riotously abundant. I finally saw scarlet Banksia in the wild—and there were miles of it. This astonishing flower looks something like a bright red and lavender electric resistor coil. Golden, spiky dryandra; bright-pink rose coneflower; and soft, fuzzy, blue-gray smoke bush grew with luxuriant exuberance. The landscape was covered with wildflowers as far as the eye could see in all directions—pink and blue, yellow and white, silver and red and purple.

It was raining lightly, but I was out there, camera wrapped in a plastic bag with only an opening for the lens hood, shooting away as usual. I waded along, waist deep in flowers, my mind reeling, overwhelmed by the sheer numbers of bright blossoms surrounding me. Lost in the joyous beauty of the place, I was totally unaware of how far I had wandered until the horn sounded, and I turned to see the coach more than a mile down the valley from me. I started back at a run, losing sight of the coach as I descended into the dense forest of flowers. As I sped over the soft earth, the wind in my face, the colors crowding in around me, I felt fleeter and freer than I can ever remember. Such is the liberating quality of joy.

We drove through the jagged mountains, which looked

dramatically beautiful, if ominous—black against the soft gray sky, wreathed in low-hanging clouds. The rain let up just long enough for us to have lunch, then run around taking pictures of the rabbit orchids and sun orchids, blue fringed lilies and orangey-yellow cats paws around our picnic site.

The rangers left us just before we got out of the park, and we turned up Chester Pass Road heading for Gnowangerup. Moments after exiting the park we looked back to see a rainbow arching across the range.

After a couple more flower stops, we spent the rest of the afternoon driving to Katanning, which is in the center of wheat and sheep-raising country. The gray, drizzly day and the monotony of farm after green-and-gold farm had me feeling rather nostalgic about the cloudless, blazing blue skies and red earth I've left behind.

After dinner, I went for a walk. One of the men from our group, Bill, a recently retired electrical engineer, was out strolling, too, and asked if he could join me. We wandered all over town, discussing the current state of world affairs, business practices in the U.S. and Australia, electronics and the technology explosion, wildflowers, and how charming the town is. Katanning is a typical, rural Australian town, with lots of open space, picturesque buildings with pillared verandas, and very friendly people. Everyone we passed spoke to us: children, teens, and adults. Bill, being from a small town in Western Australia, was not nearly as amazed at this as I was. We walked for about two hours before finally heading back toward this evening's lodgings.

Thursday, October 13

We were off quite early for a big day of collecting (we kept Jean very busy) and driving (nearly 200 miles). We headed north, passing through Dumbleyung before swinging west.

We drove into an area where the soil was pale gold and sandy, where the flowers grew in dazzling, almost overwhelming profusion. Fields of clustered flowers stretched away from us on all sides. The blossoms here were not as strange or as large as those in the Stirling Range, but were more beautiful and in even greater numbers. Dense bunches of lavender, yellow, white, and variegated feather flowers *(Verticordia)* grew everywhere. Brilliant red candle flowers sprung from deep, green carpets of almost moss-like leaves. Bright pink Geraldton wax, deep purple flag iris and dampiera, blue leshenaultia, white myrtle, silver adananthos, tall, bell-flowered foxglove, red and gold grevillea, like bright, plastic brushes, smoke bush, yellow acacia, red bottle brush, and infinitely more in every color of the rainbow seemed to blanket the whole world.

More miles and more flowers, and on past Harrismith. We stopped in a forest of jam trees, trees with sap that smells like raspberry jam. Then we continued on. Now we were driving through farm country, where the narrow roads and broad, rolling fields were bordered with tall, graceful gum trees, their leaves gathered near the tops of curving, upswept branches, looking so much, in silhouette, like the pines of Rome.

Flocks of Port Lincoln parrots burst from thickets as we passed. These birds are also known as 28s, because that is what their calls sound like.

There were more stops for collecting, and more taping and labeling as our pressing books got fatter and fatter. At final count, I had more than 150 different flower species in my book. I saw five times that many that we couldn't collect. Even then, I've only scratched the surface.

We rolled into Perth at 6:15. After saying farewell to Ray, Jean, Steph, and the gang, I taxied over to the Jewell House, where a small, pleasant room and my extra luggage awaited me.

Friday, October 14

I hiked around Perth today, getting my bearings and seeing some of the sights. Perth is a beautiful little city. I was delighted by its charm and surprised by its sophistication. I was also amazed by the unusually large number of places to eat. Every other shop is a café, restaurant, or pastry shop, and the arcades are lined with snack bars and exotic food stalls.

I wandered down Hay Street Mall, admiring the great, white-trimmed, red brick clock tower, with its ornate faces; the dazzling, elegant, chrome and glass Carillon Centre; the beautiful, Tudor-style shops lining London Court; and the general bright, chic ambiance of Perth's city center.

I stopped at the Western Australia Government Tourist Centre, to research local tours and to find accommodations for my next destination, Adelaide. When all was arranged, I headed back down Hay St., through London Court and over to St. George Terrace, stopping to photograph St. George Cathedral. Manicured gardens and lovely, old buildings lined my way as I turned my steps in the direction of the Tasmania and Victoria Tourist Bureaus, where I picked up information for farther down the track.

Finally, I walked back to city center, arriving at Cinema City in plenty of time to catch the 5:40 show of *Phar Lap: Hero to a Nation.* It's the true story of the great, record-breaking, Australian racehorse who won the Melbourne Cup in 1930, then died under mysterious circumstances when he came to the United States to race in 1932. (In the U.S. during the '30s, mob-dominated racing had little room for an unbeatable, unbuyable horse. Threats had been made, so foul play was suspected, though never proven.)

It was a glorious movie. It was a lousy audience. I'm accustomed to the kind of crowd that cheers wildly as the hero wins against all odds. The audience here was very polite and absolutely silent. As the magnificent Phar Lap, bleeding profusely from a split hoof, pounded down the turf in the movie's final race, sweeping past all other contenders, I had to sit on my hands and bite my lip, I wanted so badly to cheer and applaud. Everyone was quiet, even when leaving the theatre.* How can they do that?

The movie didn't mention the fact that, even though Phar Lap is dead, one can still see him. He has been preserved (that sounds nicer than "stuffed") and is now housed in the National History Museum in Melbourne. I intend to look in on him when I'm there. Also, everyone said Phar Lap won because he had a great heart—he wanted to win. They didn't know, of course, until after the autopsy, that they were quite literally correct. Phar Lap's heart was about 1-1/2 times the size of a normal thoroughbred's heart.

Saturday, October 15

Perth is built entirely on sand, on the shores of Perth Water, where the Swan River widens into a broad bay. Captain James Stirling selected the site when he explored the Swan River (named for the myriad black swans that glide upon its waters) in 1827. The first settlers arrived here in 1829.

Perth was founded as a colony of free men, but after 20 hard years, a severe labor shortage forced the region's settlers to actually request convicts. Still, it was not until the discovery of gold in the 1890s that Stirling's colonial dream became a thriving reality.

Perth is often called the most isolated major city in the world, as far from Sydney as it is from Singapore. It is also said to be the sunniest state capital in Australia, with an average of almost eight hours of sunshine per day all year 'round.

---

* I have since heard two possible explanations for the silence: one, that many Australians still feel a real sense of grief over the death of Phar Lap, and the other, that, while Australian audiences on the whole are notorious for their enthusiasm, folks in Perth are just quieter.

I started my day with a bus tour of Perth. The city is only one mile square, but has 350 suburbs within a 20-mile radius. Every suburb has its own yacht club, and almost every family in the area has its own boat. According to our guide, traffic is often greater on the water than on the roads.

We drove through the city, along the river, and over the Narrows Bridge to Mill Point, location of the old windmill, built by settlers in 1835 for grinding wheat. We drove by Perth's zoo, around the beautiful University of Western Australia, and past the Royal Perth Yacht Club (home of the Australian yacht that won the America's Cup).

As we passed through the suburbs, our guide pointed out the large amount of scrub left, even at on-going building sites. He explained that one is allowed to clear only as much land as is necessary for putting up a building, and a certain percentage of land must always be left with its natural trees and flowers. Very smart, but also very picturesque, with houses snuggled into beautiful settings of abundant flora.

Next we headed up to Kings Park, a 1,000-acre reserve atop cliffs that border the city and Swan River. Much of the park is undisturbed bush, though parts are cleared for picnicking, playgrounds, a botanical garden, and the occasional memorial. Palisades at the park's edge afforded us a glorious view of Perth and the river.

We wound up our tour with another pass through town to see Government House, the Supreme Court gardens, and the new buildings along St. George Terrace. The buildings in Perth are a fascinating blend of old, historical edifices and bright, modern structures. There seems to be no in-between, just 1880s and 1980s. It is curious, but most attractive.

We were dropped off in town at lunchtime, and I wandered down Hay Street Mall in search of a place to eat. In some ways, Perth is more cosmopolitan than Chicago, due to the fact that it is the port to which all European,

English, Indian, and most "Near North" (what Americans call the Far East) ships come first. This is most evident in the local eating habits. Whereas in Chicago, there is a wide variety of foods in restaurants which can be sought out by the cognoscenti, in Perth, at the fast food stalls in the shopping malls, octopus and hot goat curry are as common as fish and chips. So I browsed among the stalls of Vietnamese, Malaysian, Chinese, Lebanese, French, Swedish, Greek, Italian, and Polish foods, finally settling on an Indonesian meal of curried vegetables and beef satay.

Back on the street, I ran into a couple from the Wildflower Tour, and we stopped to chat. As sophisticated as Perth is, you tend to forget that it's still a fairly small town—if you know anyone here, you're bound to bump into them from time to time.

I hopped on another bus and headed south, toward Armadale. The bus climbed into the hills along the leading edge of the Darling Range. We wound through groves of lemon-scented gums, sugar gums, and weaving gums, finally stopping at the Elizabethan Village.

The Elizabethan Village is a cluster of faithful, full-size reproductions of places in Stratford-on-Avon, including Shakespeare's birthplace, Anne Hathaway's cottage, and the White Swan Inn. Having seen the original buildings in their bustling, market-town settings in England, I found it a bit odd, though pleasant, seeing these handsome clones clustered together, alone on a hillside covered with eucalypts.

The village houses an impressive collection of original 13th- to 17th-century furniture, tapestries, paintings, books, maps, kitchenware, armor, and weapons. I browsed happily among the wonderful antiques, while listening to tales of Elizabethan life recounted by the knowledgeable guides.

Onward, through more fragrant scrub, I soon reached Cohuna Wildlife Sanctuary. Here, the wilderness was just slightly modified, with kangaroos, wallabies, and emus strolling among the trees, and among the visitors. I never tire of seeing these creatures, and though there is a special joy in encountering them in the wild, I am happy to see them wherever I can. Before heading into the sanctuary, I filled my pockets with animal treats from a steel drum near the entrance.

Inside Cohuna, I passed a large pond where regal black swans and beautiful black, brown, and white mountain ducks swam and preened. A pair of wedge-tailed eagles watched me from their perch in a dead tree. Emus strutted and kangaroos lounged in the sun. A few of the kangaroos had joeys in their pouches, and it was usually these nursing mothers that sought the food pellets I carried.

At the far side of the reserve, I came to the huge, walk-through aviary, a noisy, open-air, two-story enclosure filled with galahs, cockatoos, parrots, cockatiels, lorikeets, and budgerigars. Galahs—nonchalant almost to the point of being a nuisance—kept strolling between my feet. A bird I wanted to photograph was facing the wrong way, so I reached over and tapped it on the shoulder, and it calmly turned to face my camera. One glorious pink cockatoo was obviously annoyed that I was taking so much time photographing a pair of galahs, so it chased the other birds away, then stood, proudly posing for me, fanning its head feathers, turning from side to side. What a ham.

Not far from the aviary, I entered a dark room carved into a low hill. When my eyes adjusted to the dim light, I could see into the nests of two separate families of wombats. The underground burrows of the wonderful, pudgy, woodchuck-like marsupials each had one wall of sound-proof glass, so the sleepy, nocturnal creatures could be observed without being disturbed. I stood for some time, watching the funny, adorable wombats fidget, snuffle about, and sleep, with baby snuggled up against mama. I've read that wombats are quite gentle and can make good pets, if you can overlook their love of tunneling.

I wandered for hours, amid the fragrant bush and friendly animals, delighting in the warm sun that filtered through the gum leaves and the almost-wildness of my surroundings. Then it was back to town.

My plans for the evening took me again into the Darling Ranges. I had made reservations for dinner and the horse show at El Caballo Blanco, an Andalusian riding academy and resort. The horses were glorious, and the riders skilled beyond imagining—so I enjoyed myself thoroughly.

In the gift shop, where I stopped to buy postcards picturing the magnificent Andalusian stallions I'd just seen, I got talking to the resort's manager. He has lived all over Australia, first as a miner, then, after additional schooling, as a caterer and finally as a resort manager. He told me a bit about his current work, but the stories he liked telling best were about the hard but exciting life in the big ore-mining communities up North and back East, where heat is intense, dirt is all-pervasive, and mateship and gameness thrive.

During the drive back to town, as I was alone, the bus driver invited me to sit in the co-pilot's seat. As we sped along, he joyously pointed out parks, buildings and, when the mountain road broke free of the trees, spectacular views of Perth, sparkling in the darkness below us. He told me about Western Australia, and about his travels elsewhere in the country. He said that, of all the things he's done, his favorite job is that of bus driver, because you meet so many good people every day.

Sunday, October 16

This morning, I started slow and stayed slow, lazing out of bed, then sitting in my bathrobe, writing for a few hours. I watched the changing weather outside my window, and it was lovely and strange. At one point, fleecy, white clouds dotted the sky, and each little cloud was pouring down torrents of rain, but between the clouds there were broad stretches of blue sky and sunshine.

I spent a good deal of time looking through pamphlets and brochures for Victoria and Tasmania. The problem, as always, is deciding how to schedule my time, trying to work in all the sights and adventures I want to fit in for both states. What a frustrating but delightful dilemma. If I were to think at all of the future, I might wish that all my problems would be this agreeable. But today, I think only of Australia, and of getting back to the bush.

At 3 o'clock, I ventured forth for the first time. It was breezy out, so I was pleasantly surprised to find it very warm. I strolled down Hay Street Mall, where I was astonished by the sweet sound of bells: the carillon at Carillon Centre. How odd I've never heard it before. Perhaps it only plays on Sunday, or perhaps it's too noisy on business days to hear it. Whatever, it was an exquisite moment, walking alone down Hay Street in the warm, silken breeze, listening to the bells play in the gentle, Sunday afternoon stillness.

After a leisurely meal within reach of the sound of the bells, I strolled back toward the hotel along a silent, nearly deserted Murray Street. A rain began, so gentle that it barely made a sound. I opened my umbrella and slowed my pace. There is something very special and intimate about sharing the sidewalk with nothing but the rain.

The shower made the cathedral and other fine, old buildings near the Jewell House shimmer, the edges slightly blurring. The sky was pale gray and quite bright. Even in the rain, there was a beautiful rainbow stretched across the clouds.

My heart leaps up when I behold
A rainbow in the sky;
So was it when my life began;
So is it now I am a man;
So be it when I shall grow old,
Or let me die!

To me, a rainbow always seems to be a visible reaffirmation of the presence of God. "I have set my rainbow in the clouds, and it will be the sign of the covenant between me and the earth."

Monday, October 17

It's hard to believe, but today is my two-month anniversary—two months ago, August 17, I arrived in Australia. It has been one of those time periods peculiar to traveling—both amazingly short and infinitely long. And what a glorious time it has been. Today was no exception.

The tour to Wave Rock involves a 430-mile round trip—the longest one-day tour in Australia—so we started early. We had a good group: one Canadian boy, three girls from Singapore, a gentleman from London, me representing the U.S., and the remaining eight from all over Australia. Our driver/guide for the tour, Greg, was intelligent and funny, and regaled us with information and stories as we rolled along.

We drove up into the Darling Ranges, which, Greg informed us, are not really mountains, but the leading edge of a massive, granite escarpment. We passed orchards where the fruit trees were so heavy laden that supports and braces were needed, to keep the branches from breaking off. Then we passed from the cultivated areas into the eucalypt forest.

Eucalyptus seeds are germinated by fire, so when a forest fire sweeps through a stand of gums, it automatically triggers new growth. Greg told us that this area was once covered by rainforest. However, local Aboriginal tribes burned off the rainforest for centuries, to make hunting easier, and this changed the indigenous vegetation, destroying the rainforest and encouraging the fire-germinated eucalypts. The practice also wiped out the koala population on this coast, because the slow-moving koalas could not escape the fires.

Wild bushland alternated with tidy farms, and hills rolled smoothly into plains. Fragrant forests gave way to golden, sandy stretches lushly adorned with wildflowers. We stopped whenever the flowers were so dense or the vistas so inspiring that Greg could almost hear our camera fingers twitching.

Rolling into the Avon Valley, we were greeted by an astonishing sight: broad, stark, white fields dotted with lace-edged, brown pools, dead trees standing black against the glistening backdrop. Greg said it is called salt erosion. Before farmers cleared the fields, there were vast forests in this valley. The huge red gums, white gums, and jarrahs each use up to 1,000 gallons of water per day. This kept the water table under the land stable. When all the trees were cut down, the water wasn't being used and the water table began to rise, getting closer and closer to the surface.

Millions of years ago, this area was under water—salt water—and much of the salt was left deep in the earth. As the water table rose, it dissolved the salt and brought it along. Now it is surfacing in many places, the strongly saline water destroying fields and forests wherever it emerges, creating a ghostly, crystallized landscape. Possible solutions to the problem are still in the experimental stage, but farmers are spending a lot of money trying various methods of drainage and reclamation. Even if these efforts are effective, they won't show results for 30 years.

A truck crowded with sheep passed us, and Greg explained why the crowding is not cruel, but rather the contrary. Sheep are clumsy, and not very good at standing up even when they are not on moving vehicles. They are packed tightly together on the trucks so they can support each other.

A signpost prompted Greg to tell us that the *-ing* and *-in* suffixes on local town names (Quairading, Kondinin, Kellerberrin, Bendering, etc.) means "place of" in this region's Aboriginal dialect.

So the hours passed, and eventually we arrived at Wave Rock. This formation is a wall of granite that has been shaped by millions of years of rain into what looks like an immense (47 feet high), cresting wave. The Wave is striped black and white from centuries of mineral-bearing water trickling down its reddish surface. Wave Rock, which is more than 300 feet long, is actually the northern edge of a granite outcrop called Hyden Rock.

I climbed up the far edge of the Wave, onto the broad back of the massive outcrop. The top of Hyden Rock is covered with strangely eroded boulders. The ancient granite dips and folds and rolls. It is patchy with green lichens and black moss. Hyden Rock rises, in levels, another 90 feet higher than the Wave, affording an almost limitless view of the surrounding countryside.

We had lunch at the base of Wave Rock, in a green glade fringed by graceful casuarinas and blanketed in yellow flowers. Then we headed off to a nearby spot called the Hippo's Yawn, a cave that, amazingly enough, looks just like the mouth of a great, stone hippo, yawning.

Next stop was Bate's Cave at The Humps. According to Aboriginal legend, this was once the home of Mulka the Terrible. Born with the mark of the devil—crossed eyes—Mulka escaped from his tribe, where he would have been put to death, and came to live in this cave.

Mulka spent many happy days here, killing and eating passersby, until one day the tribe decided to hunt him down. Mulka ran, but the tribe caught up with him and killed him. To dishonor him, they did not bury his body, leaving it for the ants and crows. However, Mulka's spirit escaped his uncovered body and returned to the cave. To this day, we were told, Aborigines will not go near the area.

We went into the cave to look at the paintings of kangaroos and other animals, done presumably before Mulka's time. There are also numerous stencil-paintings of hands on the walls, which are said to be the handprints of Mulka and his victims.

We hiked a short way farther to see a Gnamma hole, a water hole "dug" into the stone by early Aborigines. First, a fire was built on the rock and stoked till it was red hot, then cold water was poured on it, which cracked the rock. The broken rock was cleared away, then another fire was built on the same spot, and the whole operation was repeated—as often as necessary to make the hole adequately deep, usually five or six feet.

Back on the bus for the trip home, we were treated to a taped interview with King Wally, a once widely known Aborigine, who died in 1979. King Wally talked about the didgeridoo and how his father taught him the breath control needed for playing it. He sang a few songs, but most of the tape was taken up by the wonderful, undulating drone of the didgeridoo, interspersed with occasional unearthly sounds (also created with the didgeridoo) that King Wally said represented the cries of animals.

Then Greg told us the story of folk hero/scoundrel Moondyne Joe, who made his name in the late 1800s as something of an escape artist. Transported from England for stealing food (he was the eldest of eleven children), he was pardoned in Western Australia, but was later arrested after (depending on the source of the tale) borrowing or stealing a horse. He immediately escaped and disappeared. He was found six months later and imprisoned, but he escaped again—and again, and again.

Between stints in jail, Moondyne Joe supported himself with robbery, so he increasingly deserved his arrests. Finally, a new prison governor told him that, if he behaved himself and didn't escape for a while, charges against him would be dropped. Moondyne did behave himself, and after two years he was released.

While in prison, Moondyne Joe had fallen in love with a 26-year-old widow, Louisa, who came to the prison to teach reading and writing. Upon his release, they were married, and they spent many happy years together. When the gold rush came, they tried their hands at prospecting. Unfortunately, conditions in the gold camps were not wholesome, and Louisa caught typhus and died. The disconsolate Moondyne, now in his 70s, went into town to get drunk, and he was (you guessed it) arrested.

From force of habit, Moondyne had escaped within hours. The delighted press reprinted a once frequent headline that they had thought they'd never use again: "Moondyne is Away."

The police decided he should be sent back to Perth, to live out his last days with friends, but the communication got botched, and Moondyne was thrown in prison when he arrived in Perth. After four months, he escaped again. This time, when the authorities caught up with him, he was beginning to show signs of dementia, so they put him in a lunatic asylum, where he died three months later.

Greg then played a tape of songs about Moondyne Joe, his exploits, and his romance with Louisa.

Soon we arrived in Babakin, population 17, where we were welcomed at the Country Women's Association (CWA) Hall for a late afternoon tea. The ladies, mostly from nearby stations, were all charming and most hospitable.

Babakin does have one claim to fame—it is the home of the rare underground orchid. (Seriously—there really is such a thing as an underground orchid.) There are only two species of underground orchid in the world, and, as they are small and fairly delicate—not to mention the fact that they're underground—they are not easy to locate. A bulletin board at the CWA Hall was filled with photographs of and magazine articles about this strange flower,

which is surprisingly beautiful. It is almost all white—
stems, leaves, petals, everything—because underground, it
doesn't need chlorophyll for photosynthesis, it just absorbs
the nutrients it needs from the soil. The only color is the
deep red-purple interior of the white flower.

Our drive home was filled with the delights I have come
to expect from country rambles: clouds of galahs rising at
our approach, stops to admire wildflowers, a spectacular
sunset over open fields, and a beautiful view of Perth's
lights as we came over the edge of the Darling Range. I
was finally dropped off back at the hotel a little after 8 p.m.

This evening, I called Sue (from the Red Centre tour) in
Melbourne. I wanted to know when our "reunion" was
scheduled so I could time my arrival appropriately. Sue
has insisted that I stay with her when I get to Melbourne,
which will be fun, and also removes the worry of trying to
find suitable housing for that part of my trip.

Anyway, life is a dream. I continue my journey; I continue to write.

And speaking of dreams, it's late, so good night.

Tuesday, October 18

This morning, I wandered around town for a long
while, taking photographs of things I've seen and want to
remember: the railway station, Hay Street Mall, Carillon
Centre, London Court, the river, old buildings on Murray
Street and William Street, Government House, the Mint. I
crossed parks and squares where sea gulls squawked and
scrounged, filling the scrap-hunting niche reserved for
pigeons in other parts of the world. I saw people I know
from the wildflower tour and stopped to chat each time.

At 1 o'clock, I stood waiting once again for a bus.
Waiting with me was Carol, a Canadian, who is also staying at the Jewell House. Soon we were on our way, cover-

ing the 34 miles northward to Yanchep National Park.

As we drove into the 7,000-acre reserve, through the trees and into a clearing by the lake, we could see much of the beauty and wildlife for which this park is known. We spilled out of the bus and headed off to explore.

Yanchep offers, among other delights, limestone caverns, where an underground spring feeds a series of unbelievably clear pools. The Crystal Cave, as the caverns have been named, is a veritable fairyland of delicate forms, sparkling crystals and shimmering reflections. The vaulted, cream-colored "rooms" are filled with flow stone shawls, calcite straws, stalactites, stalagmites, and columns. In the section known as the Jewel City, lights shine through a chaos of limestone lace and crystalline fringe that encrusts a series of arches, all of which is reflected in the pool below.

After an hour in the caves, Carol and I reemerged into the daylight. We wandered past the park offices and souvenir kiosk, over to the new koala colony. (Koalas are being reintroduced to this area from the East.) Then we headed down to the lake for a walk along the shore.

The water was fringed with reeds, and large numbers of water birds swooped, swam, or perched wherever we went. Big, old trees, including many jarrahs, shaded the shoreline and bordered broad lawns. Kangaroos dashed through the bush. Wildflowers splashed the open fields with color. It was a beautiful day and a wonderful spot.

"Yanchep," the bus driver told us when we boarded the bus for home, is the Aboriginal word for "bulrushes," of which there were many along the lake shore. The plant's starchy root was a major source of nourishment for area natives.

When we got back to Perth, Carol and I strolled back toward the hotel, stopping along the way for cappuccino. Then we parted company for a while, to organize our laundry. Now, laundry is usually a pretty uninteresting pastime, so little did I suspect what a truly trans-cultural experience it could be in a place like this.

When I first arrived at the laundry room, there was a couple there ahead of me. He was from Canada, but was currently a resident of New Zealand, along with his Kiwi wife. The two of them are on holiday, spending a month in Australia. Then Carol joined us, followed by a lad from Holland, who is here on a working visa for three years. After the New Zealand couple departed, a man from Fiji came in. He was nearing the end of a five-year, around-the-world wander. Then a lady from Sydney joined us. We all spent a lot of time exchanging information—cheapest travel, best food, reasonable hotels, exciting destinations. It was a fascinating evening—and amazingly enough, all my clothes were clean when it was over.

Wednesday, October 19

I had originally thought that I'd get to Fremantle, the old port of Perth. The day, however, turned out a little differently than planned.

The weather was hot, which was a bit of a change. The sun was out, and so were the sunbathers and street musicians. Flower and fresh fruit stalls lined Murray Street near the Forrest Place Mall. It was all delightfully cheerful and colorful, and I spent a lot of time enjoying everything.

I went to the City Arcade for an early lunch. While I ate in the crowded seating area, I fell into conversing with a young woman eating there with her little boy. Sue is an expatriate American, and she was pleased to find an American to talk to. For years, she was a wanderer, traveling and living in Europe and Asia before settling in Perth eleven years ago. She was married then, but was divorced two years ago, shortly after her son's birth. (Ben is 2-1/2.) While she may not run into a lot of Americans, she doesn't appear to see much of anyone, at least socially, because she works nights (geriatrics nurse) so she can spend her days with Ben.

We talked for nearly two hours, then Sue invited me to her place for afternoon tea. I could tell she was lonely, so I decided I could spare the afternoon—Fremantle will still be there next time I come to Perth.

Not far from the bus stop, we stopped outside London Court so Ben could see the clock tower at 1 o'clock: Saint George comes out and slays the dragon on the hour.

Sue's townhouse is in a fascinatingly mixed, multi-cultural neighborhood. On the corner there is a mosque, and within a block of her place there are a dozen Chinese stores, a Greek restaurant, Mexican, Armenian, French, Italian, and Turkish take-away shops, and a variety of other strange and wonderful things. (There are also two brothels—but then, this is a port town. They're not legal, they're just ignored, Sue explained.)

We had tea, watched Ben play, and talked for another two hours. I rinsed the teacups and watched Sue get Ben ready for his nap. We talked a while longer, but soon Sue had to prepare for her departure for work. I wished her all the best, thanked her for her hospitality, then headed to the bus stop to wait for the next bus back to Hay Street.

I wandered around town for a few more hours, stopping for coffee and doing some last minute shopping. Then I walked back to the hotel.

At the hotel, I ran into one of the people I met in the laundry room last night—the lady from Sydney. She'd spent the day in Fremantle, had enjoyed it, and was dying to relate her adventure. She had searched out the Fremantle Gaol, assuming the century-plus-old, convict-built edifice must now be a museum. With a bit of hunting, she located a door marked "Visitors" and went in. She said it took a few minutes of puzzled exchange with an officer there before it sank in that this was a real prison, still in use, at which point, with mixed feelings of embarrassment and amusement, she left.

Thursday, October 20

This morning I checked out of my room and struggled to the corner to catch the airport bus. With my purse, camera bag, canvas carry-on bag with canteen strapped to its side, green duffel bag, sleeping bag, and suitcase, I didn't feel I was projecting exactly a suave, globetrotter image.

The bus arrived, and the inevitably knee-socks-and-shorts-clad driver helped me aboard with my road show. As I drove away from Perth, I didn't feel like I really knew her. Maybe it's the amount of time I gave her. Maybe it's because there's still so much more I wanted to see. I think part of the problem is that it was my first real city after all that time in the wilderness. (Who'd have ever imagined that I could have trouble adjusting to a city?) Still, I had a wonderful time; Perth is a beautiful place.

WALTZING SOUTH AUSTRALIA

It was bright and sunny when I departed Perth—a perfect day for flying. Flight time from Perth to Adelaide: three hours and five minutes. Below me: the great, flat, unrelieved Nullarbor Plain, then out over the Great Australian Bight.

It has occurred to me on several occasions, and occupied my thoughts during much of the flight, that it is going to be difficult—maybe impossible—to return to what I was before. I have come to love this wandering life. Sue (New York divorcée in Perth) assured me that you do get tired of traveling—why, after eight years of it she was ready to settle down. Small comfort.

Of course, there's not much point in having come if I go right back to where I was, to what I was. I'm just not sure yet what I'm becoming. There is this strange dichotomy that I can see in my mind's eye: a well-dressed, civilized, suburban woman with a comfortable apartment and season tickets for the theatre; and a somewhat rougher version of that same woman, with a notebook, an open road, and a sleeping bag rolled out under the stars. Both images are pleasing to me, yet difficult to reconcile. At present, though, I am happier in the second role.

I'm glad I still have more than three months to work this out. I'm hoping by then I'll actually be looking forward to getting back to the "real world"—or that I'll have a stronger sense of how to keep the dream alive. As it is now, the only strong sense directing me is the longing to get back to the wilderness. I hope to spend 14 days camping in Tasmania and at least nine days on a horse trek in Victoria. Beauty and serenity continue to grow in importance for me, and they are no longer simply desirable, but seem absolutely necessary. I love the sensory input. I rejoice in the stimulation of doing and learning new things every day. There is pleasure, too, in having the time to write—and having so much to write about. My hand speeds over the page, pouring words onto the paper. My heart rejoices at the very act of writing.

Back to details.

It was cold, gray, and windy when we landed. I stood by the curb for nearly an hour before the next city-bound bus arrived and whisked me into Adelaide. The bus stopped in front of an impressive hotel on North Terrace, which, fortunately, had a taxi stand nearby.

I had a few misgivings as I approached my hotel's location. The neighborhood looked unpromising, and there was no sign at the address I'd been given. An unmarked entrance opened into a small room with a desk marked "reception." The receptionist (the manager's wife, I learned) slipped in through a side door, drying her hands on her apron. She anxiously apologized for not having a sign or any other identification up, then called her daughter to come and help me with my luggage. They both seem very nice, so I decided to give the place a try.

The rooms are clean and quite comfortable, if a bit faded and worn. The ceilings are high, and the moldings are handsome, though cracked in spots. The whole place has that rather sad air of past glory.

As I settled into my room, I found that my window doesn't close, the sink doesn't drain, and the TV has no picture (though this last item doesn't bother me, as I didn't expect a TV). However, within an hour of my arrival, the manager was at the door, with two other, smaller daughters in tow, to see if he could fix the TV. He couldn't, so he carried one in from another room. He was charming, and terribly apologetic about the broken TV. His little girls were adorable.

Good things about the hotel: It's inexpensive. It's close to downtown. It has a very friendly family running it. It has tea-making facilities in the room (my last hotel didn't). It has large, fluffy, white towels—nicer than those in most places I've stayed—and awesomely white sheets. The pluses seem to outweigh the negatives, but we'll see.

Friday, October 21

I arose to a bright, warm, sunny day—a real change from the bleak, gray chilliness of yesterday. The weatherman on TV said the sudden change was a surprise, but now it looks like we'll have good weather for the rest of the week.

I walked to the center of town and headed for the South Australia Tourist Bureau. I made arrangements to visit the Barossa Valley, the major wine-growing district of S.A., and historic Hahndorf, a small German settlement, which I've been told is a "must see" when you're in this area. I also scanned the literature of other offerings they had—fascinating tours to strange and wild places, if one but had the time.

I wandered around Rundle Mall (the central shopping area of almost all Australian cities is a delightful pedestrian mall, but Adelaide's was the first). Then I headed over to Westpac Travel, to arrange my horse-riding journey and my camping trip in Tasmania, as well as various necessary buses and planes. Sadly, both the riding trip and the Tassie camping tour have been shortened, to six days and nine days respectively, so I shan't be spending quite as much time out bush as I had hoped. Still, I have a lot to look forward to.

I strolled over to Opal Field Gems, a place that has opal-cutting demonstrations, movies on opal mining and grading, and a large collection of opals on display, as well as for sale. I was dazzled by some of the incredible gems they had there—colors, shapes and sizes unlike anything I'd ever seen before. In response to my exclamations, the sales manager explained that the reason I'd never seen such fabulous stones before is because demand for opals has always exceeded supply, so not many of the really spectacular, premium stones are sent out of the country.

They had several "pseudomorphs." A pseudomorph occurs when a bone (say, from a dinosaur) or a seashell has been buried for a million or so years. Water eventually dissolves the bone or shell, and the perfect mold left behind fills with water and silica, which, given enough time, becomes an opal. They had a few "bones" on display and, what interested me even more, a few "cockle shells"—perfect shell shapes but solid opal. If only I had $7,000. . .

I spent a good bit of time taking notes, studying around, listening to everything that was being said. The sales manager brought out several exquisite opals she thought I might like. I told her that I didn't feel sufficiently knowledgeable to make any decisions yet but asked if I might photograph some of the bright stones. She obligingly spread a handful of the most spectacular opals across a piece of black velvet so I could capture them on film, if not in reality.

I walked back down Rundle Mall, stopping at the fresh

fruit stands to buy strawberries, pears, and loquats. Then I browsed through a couple of nearby arcades, where I found a little German delicatessen and purchased cheese and black bread for my dinner. Around 7 p.m., I headed back toward the hotel. I've decided to stay here. It's not perfect, but it's not bad.

Saturday, October 22

Up bright and early this morning to catch my bus for today's visit to the Barossa Valley, the most famous of South Australia's wine districts. We exited the city on King William Street, which is 137 feet wide from gutter to gutter, making it the widest main street of any capital city in Australia. We crossed through broad gardens, over the River Torrens, and headed north.

We drove through Adelaide's northern suburbs—first, wonderful, quaint, old buildings, then miles of modern sprawl. We passed through the suburbs swiftly and rolled out into the glorious countryside. Around us now were pastures dotted with grazing sheep, tree-lined streams, occasional vineyards, which became increasingly frequent as we got into the Barossa Valley, quaint old homesteads, stores and outposts, and beautiful fields filled with Paterson's Curse.

Paterson's Curse, also known as Salvation Jane, was introduced to Australia by a well-intentioned Mr. Paterson, who hoped that the fast-spreading plant would produce a rich food-source for cattle and sheep. There was only one problem—the beasts wouldn't eat it, so it went a bit out of control. Unfortunately, like all successful weeds, it crowds out the things you do want growing, so there is a constant battle to control it on land currently under cultivation. Elsewhere, the plant runs riot across fields, up hills, by the roadside, its tall, graceful stalks of purple flowers forming undulating blankets of color across the landscape. It is, like most effective curses, astonishingly beautiful to those of us not afflicted by it.

We drove through Gawler, then north to Shea Oak Log. By this time, we were well into the Barossa Valley. The Barossa region was named by Colonel William Light, Adelaide's founder, in memory of the 1811 British victory over Napoleonic forces at the Battle of Barossa in Spain, a battle in which Light had fought.

The influence of the region's many German settlers is reflected in the names of some of the Barossa's prominent wineries—Kaiser Stuhl, Krondorf, Seppeltsfield, Hardy's Siegersdorf—and in the preponderance of Riesling grapes. The wineries of the Barossa produce a large number of German-style Rhines and Moselles, but also turn out some fine red varieties, especially Cabernet Sauvignon and Shiraz (Australian Burgundy-style red).

A long, gravel road bordered by tall, slender date palms led us into Seppeltsfield, home of the large, 130-year-old Seppelt winery. The old buildings are imposing, but still delightfully Australian: rough, solid bluestone with an abundance of elegant, peachy-cream, Victorian trim; the agreeable incongruity of delicate gingerbread edging corrugated iron roofs.

Australia produces a lot of great wines, wines that have shown well at, and even won, wine competitions in the U.S. and Europe. But, as do most of the world's wine producing countries, Australia also cranks out a lot of average to mediocre wine for the mass markets. This latter is, unfortunately (though understandably, given the sizes of the many tour groups), the wine to which we were most exposed today.

A delightful young woman showed us through the crushing rooms and on to the giant, stainless steel vats, where millions of gallons of grape juice are turned into wine. Our guide explained the procedure; "We add a special yeast to hurry along the fermentation process. It takes about three days to produce wine (I cringed) and four to five days for port and sherry. Then we add a spirit to kill the yeast. This also raises the alcohol content. That is why these are called fortified wines."

They also produce some excellent vintage port, which is aged in dark, oak casks imported from France. We walked through one of the huge storage facilities and saw the great, wooden casks in long rows, stacked to the roof. Seppelt has one port available that is 105 years old and $1500 a bottle. Needless to say, none of this was offered for sampling to the herds of tourists.

After our tour, we crossed the broad, garden-fringed courtyard to the sales and tasting rooms. I found a few wines that were pleasant, if not dazzling. The prices, at least, show that they don't take these lesser wines too seriously—most ranged around $5. The really exceptional wines are shown to serious buyers, I was told, by appointment only. On this trip, I can't afford to be too much of a wine snob; I purchased (quite happily) an inexpensive but refreshing little Moselle.

After lunch, we headed off on a driving tour of the valley. The area is filled with tidy houses, solidly built stone walls, pretty, slender-steepled churches, and lovingly tended gardens, all showing the German heritage of the Lutheran refugees who settled here in the 1840s. We drove through Nuriootpa and Angaston, then under the decorated arch, surmounted by a wine barrel, that marks the entrance to Tanunda. The town is picturesque, with its hedgerows and shade trees, its shops and small houses, white or gray, half hidden by shrubs and gardens.

Our p.m. stop was at Orlando Winery, where the bushes are trimmed in the shapes of wine glasses. I've heard that some of this winery's offerings are quite excellent. In fact, they are said to produce some of the district's finest Rhine Riesling. However, one gentleman on the tour told me that the winery was built around Barossa Pearl, a "champagne" that sold for $1.50 when introduced. He described it as "rather rough and ready." The wines served to the mob crowding the tasting room (ours was not the only group there at the time) were somewhere between the extremes—nice, but unexceptional.

On the road again, we wound through the mountains and down Torrens Gorge. We were surrounded by craggy cliffs, deep ravines, and rolling pastures filled with beautiful horses. We turned down a short side road that cut through the trees and stopped at the Barossa Reservoir Dam, better known as the Whispering Wall.

Due to its curvature, the dam is acoustically perfect, carrying sound clearly across its 472-foot-long surface. This unusual trait was first noticed during construction; a worker on one side of the dam was sent for tools and found them ready and waiting when he arrived on the opposite side. Several members of our group crossed the dam, and conversations were held back and forth. It was quite astonishing. Even when you know what's supposed to happen, it's still a surprise that it works.

We continued on through the mountains, then suburbs, then into the city once more. I walked around for a while, then, after dinner, I strolled down Hindley Street,

Adelaide's nightlife district, and, finally, back to the hotel.

When I got to my room, I found that the manager was working on the sluggish drain and had gotten the window to close. We are making headway here.

Sunday, October 23

I rose, again, to glorious sunshine—another beautiful "day in my life in Australia." My tour didn't start till after lunch, so I had time to enjoy sun and city before I was due at the S.A. Tourist Bureau. Then, once more, I was winding along a road out of Adelaide.

We drove along Mt. Barker Road, ascending into the Mt. Lofty Ranges. Our semi-steep climb took us around a sheer-sided hairpin turn called the Devil's Elbow, then up through the town of Eagle-on-the-Hill. The town is named after its hotel, which was built in the mid-1800s by a man who had a pet eagle. During operating hours, the eagle was tethered near the bar, but after hours, the bird was given the run of the establishment. There were never any robberies or break-ins while the eagle was around.

In about an hour we reached Hahndorf. Captain Hahn was the pilot of a ship full of Lutheran refugees who settled here 150 years ago, and the grateful refugees named the town to honor him.

We were dropped off in the middle of town with a few hours free to putter and browse. Hahndorf is a charming old town, with most of the original buildings intact. The architecture is predominantly early Australian, but the town still retains a distinctly German air. There are shops for Tortes, Wursts, and Kaeses, and Sauerkraut abounds. The horse-drawn wagons on the main street boast decidedly Teutonic paint motifs. The balcony of the Hahndorf Inn is lined with flower boxes full of pink and red geraniums. An oompah band played in market square, and many of those browsing through the shops spoke German. One place I saw that was an amusing hybrid of the two cultures was a restaurant named "Guten Tucker" (tucker is Aussie slang for food).

Small, tidy stores had wonderful things to buy. Mostly I just looked, but I did succumb to the temptations of one shop, where I bought three very fine seashells. The rest of the time I spent wandering around town, admiring and photographing the lovely, solid old buildings, whether half-timbered rural German or iron-roofed, stone-walled colonial Australian. I walked down to the Old Mill, once a flourmill, now a restaurant, and back around to the former Hahndorf Academy, which is now an art gallery, then continued along the main street through market square.

When we left Hahndorf, we descended through the Adelaide Hills, through the town of Stirling, then stopped at Windy Point. The point is the only lookout in Australia, we were told, from which an entire city and all its suburbs can be seen. The view was spectacular, with the mountains rising behind us, Adelaide at our feet, and the ocean, blazing in the late afternoon sunlight, stretching to the horizon.

Monday, October 24

I think a lot these days, mostly about what I'm seeing and doing, or about what I'm going to see and do. But now I have the time to indulge in the luxury of just sitting and letting my mind run where it will. I sat this morning in the sunlight flooding through my window, sipping tea, staring out at the street, my head filled with the turmoil of joy and expectations that my current freedom has created. Perhaps it is an indication of how right my course is that fear has no place in any of my thoughts. Right now is so perfect that, though the future often crosses my mind, there is no real worry about what my life will be. Dreaming my dream, and watching it unfold, is all the occupation I need now.

Rousing from my reverie, I realized that I was running late, so I fairly flew the half mile into town to catch a 9:15 bus for the tour of Adelaide.

Adelaide, the capital of South Australia, was named for Queen Adelaide, consort of the British King William IV. The city sits at the foot of the Mt. Lofty Ranges, on slightly rising ground along the River Torrens. The site was chosen in 1836 by explorer Charles Sturt and British Army engineer Colonel William Light.

Colonel Light, who became Adelaide's first surveyor general, founded and designed the city. Light stipulated that avenues be wide, crossing at right angles, and that the five city squares be made into gardens. He surrounded the one-square-mile city with 1,700 acres of gardens and parks. Light determined the width of the parks by putting a cannon at each corner of the city, firing it, then setting the outer perimeter of the park where the cannonball landed.

We drove down Currie Street and around Light Square, then over to Grote Street, where we passed the Central Market. We crossed Victoria Square, where statues, trees and an impressive, modern fountain ornament a park surrounded by beautiful buildings—most notably St. Francis Xavier Cathedral and the ornate, clock-towered General Post Office. At the square's edge, we passed the only trams left in South Australia. They run several times each day down to the beachfront town of Glenelg.

Our first stop was Veale Gardens. The beautifully mani-cured gardens—named after an early city clerk—are plant-ed with 3,000 rose bushes, which made the walk through a fairly intoxicating one.

Continuing on, we wound through the streets of Adelaide, circling the squares—Whitmore, Hurtle, Hindmarsh. Then we drove down North Terrace, Adelaide's most impressive boulevard. Flanking the wide, tree-lined street is a dazzling array of grand buildings—the Constitutional Museum, Grecian-columned Parliament House, the shining Festival Centre, the governor's resi-dence, the Adelaide Railway Station.

Along the eastern end of North Terrace is the University of Adelaide (founded in 1874), which, with its spires and ivy-covered walls, could have been transplanted from England. The South Australian Museum, Art Gallery, and Public Library line the north side of the street, and directly opposite is Ayers House. Ayers House, an elegant, 40-room, bluestone mansion dating back to 1846, was once the home of Henry Ayers (for whom Ayers Rock was named), seven-term (an Australian record) premier of South Australia toward the end of the 19th century. Cathedrals, monuments, and a few lovely hotels and office buildings fill out the rest of North Terrace, which ends at the Botanic Gardens.

We crossed the River Torrens, which separates the south-ern business district from the northern residential section, and headed up to Montefiore Hill to see Light's Vision, a statue erected in honor of William Light. The statue shows him, hand outstretched toward Adelaide, showing passers-by how his plan turned out. A plaque on the statue's base carries a quote from Light's writings stating that, in deriding him, his detractors had fixed on him the responsibility for Adelaide's layout. He would accept that responsibility, but not their judgment—that he left to future generations. Those future generations have praised Light, for the city is a work of brilliant planning and foresight.

We drove through several of the old neighborhoods, where we were shown various types of building materials and architectural styles, from the quaint to the grandiose. Our guide explained that all the iron lace-work decorating homes around Adelaide was brought over as ballast in the first ships to arrive in South Australia.

When the tour ended, I headed for the Festival Centre, to take their tour. Newer than the Sydney Opera House, the Centre boasts many technical and acoustical advances not found in what locals refer to as "that other place." It is strikingly beautiful, all dramatic angles and soaring, white planes. There is a great deal of art inside and out, from massive sculptures in stone or steel to great tapestries and paintings. I especially liked Sidney Nolan's *Rainbow Serpent*, a colorful, evocative, 324-panel mural that seemed at once both primitive and modern.

As we crossed from the main Festival Centre to the adjacent theatre building, someone stated that she disliked the colorful South Plaza, created by West German sculptor O.H. Hajek, because it "stuck out." Our thoroughly delightful guide related that a theatre patron had also once remarked, to the artist, that she didn't like it because it didn't blend in with its surroundings. Hajek replied, "I don't want it to blend in. I want you to look at it." I smiled and thought of Darch (my younger brother, a gifted artist) and his own trials and tribulations with a sometimes unappreciative, or uncomprehending, public.

After leaving the Festival Centre, I wandered over to

the Constitutional Museum, which is housed in the former parliament building. This museum involves a 100-minute "tour" called Bound for South Australia (which is also the title of a well-known sailors' song from the 1800s). I was ushered into the first room and instructed to follow the "guide's" directions.

I found myself in a cave filled with Aboriginal artifacts. The voice of the pre-recorded guide explained what the implements were, as programmed lights spotlighted whatever was under discussion. From there, I moved to shipboard on the *H.M.S. Buffalo,* the first ship from England to South Australia, where the rigors of the journey were detailed, just as the surroundings were recreated. I passed into the office of one of the first crown governors of S.A., where I listened to debates on whether the new colony should have a constitution, what sort of legislative body they should have, and who should vote. Leaving the office, I ascended a picture-lined staircase, accompanied by the cheers of the newly enfranchised colonists.

Upstairs, I entered the parliamentary chamber. This room and its furnishings were actually used by legislators during South Australia's earlier days. I sat in one of the old, dark-wood chairs; leaned on the heavy, wooden table before me; and gazed at the paintings on the dark walls of the large, dimly lit room. A gavel pounded, and the assembly was called to order by the Speaker. Then, lights illuminating where the various legislators would have been seated, voices transmitted from the appropriate locations, the debates that shaped South Australia whirled around me.

Occasionally, the voice of the guide broke in to explain what was happening, who was involved, and what the outcome was. Some of the discussions became heated, and enthralling enough that I found myself spinning to face a speaker, even though it was only a light on an empty chair. By the time I left the chamber, South Australia had a constitution, Australia had become a federation, women had the vote, and S.A. had moved well into the 20th century.

The last room was a theatre, where a 28-projector, multi-screen presentation brought South Australia through two World Wars, depression, growth, wealth, modern social turbulence, and up to the present day. I left feeling very much involved in Australian history.

Tuesday, October 25

With the need to be someplace wild again pressing down on me, I headed this morning for the Kangaroo Island booking office to arrange a visit to that wild, wind-swept island, with its awesome rock formations and abundant wildlife. Within less than an hour, flights and accommodations were arranged, and I headed back out into the day.

I wandered off through town, going to several of the spots I was whisked past on my tours: Victoria Square, the Glenelg trams, Grote Street, King William Street. As I wandered, I stopped often in opal stores, building up my knowledge and admiring the stones. Each store offers different shapes, sizes, and settings, but, in the nicer shops, the mix of gem grades is similar. There is very little of the common white, or milk, opal—the least valuable grade of the gem, and the one most frequently shipped overseas. The most valuable stones, the fabulous black opals, are fairly abundant, though more so in larger showrooms. These dark, colorful stones, some of which look like molten sapphires and emeralds swirled together, are dazzling, but way out of my price range. Most plentiful of all are the precious crystal opals, which are less pricey than black opals, but are still incredibly lovely.

I eventually found a pair of very simple but beautiful earrings set with sky-blue crystal opal cabochons. I loved them, and I decided that simply being in Australia was sufficient justification for buying them. However, it's back to living on a shoestring now—at least till I see how the money is holding out.

Keeping with that budget-mindedness, I headed for the Central Market, a large hall to which farmers, butchers, wholesalers, and other food purveyors come three days a week to sell their wares at better-than-store prices. Seafood, cheeses, fruit, vegetables, nuts, and more were heaped in dazzling array. I love these kinds of markets, so I had great fun. Plus, for considerably less than the cost of one restaurant meal, I obtained provisions for three days.

Well after dark, I returned to my lodgings. I was surprised to see that the hotel is now identified: Kiwi Lodge. I suspect that the current manager took over only shortly before I arrived.

Wednesday, October 26

Up early and off for a day of sun and organizing. At the New South Wales Department of Tourism, I collected information on Canberra and Sydney. Back in King William Street, I stopped to pick up my tickets for Victoria and Tasmania. Then it was on to the Kangaroo Island booking office, to get my tickets for tomorrow's journey. At the travel agent's, there was a huge, wall-sized map of the world, with Australia in the center. It really brought home to me how far away from Chicago I am—half a world away! It still amazes me.

I headed up to North Terrace and strolled along the lovely boulevard, stopping frequently to admire and photograph the museums, monuments, galleries, parks, hotels, and other delights overlooking the river. Eventually, I reached the Botanic Gardens. I followed paths through dense stands of tall, graceful casuarinas, where sunlight shimmered magically through their needle-like leaves. I circled ponds filled with the broad leaves of lotus flowers. I found delicate orchids in patches of sunlight amid the dancing shadows of swaying branches. I watched tiny, bright birds flit among the flowering shrubs, and a snowstorm of white butterflies weave deliriously through the fragrant bushes.

I wandered back through Rundle Mall, down Pulteney Street, then crossed over to Victoria Square on Wakefield Street. For a while, I watched people and birds, the fountain and trams, then turned my steps down King William Street for a last spin through town. By this time, it was well past 5 o'clock, and I decided it was as good a time as any to head back to the hotel, to get ready for tomorrow.

I packed and took my big suitcase downstairs, along with my sleeping bag, canteen, and other extraneous baggage, to go into the luggage room. They'll keep my luggage here for me till I return Saturday. Then the manager ordered my taxi for the morning. The people here really have been nice, and most helpful. It has added considerably to my stay.

Thursday, October 27

The taxi was at the door when I descended at 6:25 a.m., and I was whisked off to the Adelaide Airport Light

Aircraft Terminal, where I was to rendezvous with Emu.

This is as small an operation as you'd expect anything called Emu Airways to be. The small, metal-roofed, one-room Emu terminal (which is shared with O'Conner Air Service) holds an office area, with one desk surrounded by partitions, a Coke machine, five chairs, and a scale. There are apparently only two people involved, at least for the 7:30 flight: a woman who handles ticketing, baggage check-in and weighing, does the office work, and makes the coffee; and a man who checks the mail bags and news-papers, fuels the plane, drives the baggage "truck," loads the plane, and is pilot. This was the first run of the day, so we were transporting all the morning papers for the island.

I was traveling light—I thought. My green nylon duffel and canvas flight bag were all I was carrying, but the woman looked concerned and weighed them both. I under-stood why when I walked out to the plane. Smaller planes exist, but I have not flown in them. It was really a spiffy little machine, though, clean, bright, and shiny. It was a Cessna, with two props and nine seats—the front two for the pilot and (when there is one) co-pilot, and the last three taken up by mail. The other passengers were regu-lars, and chatted with the pilot as we prepared for take-off.

Half an hour later, we landed at American River "air-port." Actually, it was just an open paddock on private property. However, its not being a real airport seems fit-ting, since American River is neither American nor a river. It's an arm of the sea that almost separates the Dudley Peninsula from the rest of the island. It got its name from the American sealers of the brig Union, who built a boat here in 1803.

My flight was met by Des, owner of the small, comfort-able American River Motel. At the motel, Des dropped my

bag on the bed in my bright, airy room, then guided me
upstairs into the dining room, where his wife, Joan, had
coffee and toast waiting for me. Other guests were gathered around the communal table, and I was introduced
before being seated. Because there never seems to be any
"ice" to break in this part of the world, we were all talking
and laughing like old friends in a matter of minutes. Pat
and Lou, two girls from Adelaide, even suggested that we
might do a little exploring together.

I asked Des if he knew anyone who offered a good tour
of the island. He grinned and said, "Absolutely." Only
minutes later, he was pulling his minivan out of the drive,
with Pat, Lou, and me loaded in the back.

It was a chilly but very dramatic day: huge clouds, black
and white, dappling the sky; ragged shreds of blue showing here and there; sunshine suddenly bursting brilliantly
through, streaming down in great, silvery pillars of light; a
crisp breeze; waves crashing on the jagged coastline—a
perfect day for seeing natural wonders.

Kangaroo Island is a fairly large island, nearly 100 miles
long and 30 miles wide. The terrain is a combination of
lush, rolling, sheep-dotted pasture land; dense scrub; serene
forests; wild, rugged, sea-lashed cliffs; and long, peaceful
beaches. Because of its isolation from the mainland, as
well as the very low population level, Kangaroo Island is
rich with native wildlife, some of it unique to the island.

We drove through the thick bush-land, where openings
in the sea of green were filled with masses of wildflowers.
The road was unsealed, and the long, straight slash of reddish dirt looked like a fresh cut in an otherwise unbroken
mass of plant life. Waves of greenery hung over the edges,
seemingly ready to engulf the road at any moment.

As we approached the sea, the dense brush gave way to

low coastal vegetation springing out of pure, white sand, dotted with small flowers that hugged the ground, trying to escape the wind. We had arrived at Seal Bay.

At the edge of the large dunes that rolled down toward the beach, a flash, like a bright gem, caught my eye. A dazzling little bird, in blues from deep sapphire to robin's egg blue, flitted from branch to branch of a low shrub. It looked like a Fabergé jewel. "Splendid Blue wren," Des said. "It's the mating season, that's why he's so colorful. Showing off for the ladies."

We walked out onto the hills of drifted sand and clambered down their steep, shifting sides, descending to the beach, where we were surrounded by Australian sea lions. The colony here is made up of nearly 500 sea lions, and they were ranged all along the bay, as far as the rock-sheltered white sand stretched in either direction.

These sea lions are beautiful creatures, with glossy coats and huge, innocent-looking, dark eyes. They are large, but quick. Many of them were sleeping, but several of the youngsters dashed into the surf to play. They splashed joyously, then raced back onto the beach. After a bit of exercise, they would suddenly stop, and just crash to the ground, going from playtime to nap time in a split second.

Some of the bulls showed off for our benefit, stretching their necks skyward and assuming regal poses. Because the pups are getting quite large, now, we could get relatively close—their massive fathers feel that the children can fend for themselves, and they aren't as jumpy as when the pups are younger. However, one makes a point of staying a respectful distance from the very territorial males. Besides, the mothers with their babies are more adorable, even if the pups are nearly full grown.

Some of the pups were still nursing, and the smaller

ones hid behind their mamas when we approached. But most of them were very nonchalant and allowed us to sit only a few feet away, watching them, photographing them.

I could have stayed all day, just sitting there on the beach, watching those delightful creatures so astonishingly close at hand. But after an hour, it was time to move on.

Our next stop was Flinders Chase National Park, at the far end of the island. Our entrance was heralded by bursts of startled birds; galahs, cockatoos, magpies (with striking black and white markings), and wattlebirds (yellow breasted and fan-tailed beauties). There were a few birds we didn't startle, as well—the ever-curious emus, the seemingly unconscious Cape Barren geese, and the too-proud-to-be-bothered peacocks.

There were kangaroos everywhere, lying in the sun, scratching, playing, grazing, bounding across the fields. The Kangaroo Island kangaroos are unique to the island; since it was separated from the mainland thousands of years ago, the island's 'roos developed independently. They are small, about 3 feet high, with soft, brown coats and dark faces. Before long, a few of the gentle creatures had come over to see what we were up to.

The only enclosures in the park are around the picnic tables. While the kangaroos will beg for food, the emus will walk in and take it, so it is from the latter that diners are protected. Des unloaded the lunch things and, at the first sign of food, an emu was at the gate, trying to figure out how to get in.

When we had finished eating, the emu still stood at the gate, watching us. One little 'roo had hopped over, and was straining to peek over the stone wall, which was as tall as he was. Des produced a bag of bread, and we gave pieces to our two beggars. The emu swallowed his piece whole, then grabbed the kangaroo's piece right out of its paws.

We left the enclosure and went down to the field, where we were soon surrounded by kangaroos. We were, of course, still hotly pursued by the emu, who didn't want to miss out on any free food. The poor bird did look rather frantic and confused over the situation—couldn't understand why we would give food to the 'roos when he wanted it all.

We strolled down through the gum trees, which were filled with magpies, wattlebirds and, higher up, sleeping koalas. The kangaroos followed us, nuzzling our hands for food. They were infinitely curious about the strange, black box I kept holding in front of my face, and they peered into my lens, trying to see what was clicking. Des says they make wonderful, faithful, loving pets. Don't I wish.

The peacocks came over at this point to see what was going on, but didn't get too close. They're showy, but not as bold as the emus. We walked past the Cape Barren geese, which were busily searching the grass for food. They neither shied away nor showed curiosity, giving no indication of even noticing that we were there.

This was another spot where I would have liked to have stayed a lot longer, just watching the wonderful birds and animals, especially the kangaroos. The emus are great, too. What bizarrely prehistoric-looking things they are. Des said all these creatures can be found everywhere on the island, this is just one of the larger concentrations of them.

Back in the van, we were off to see the aptly named Remarkable Rocks. The Rocks, immense granite boulders that have been shattered and sculpted by salt spray and the relentless wind, stand alone on a barren granite hill. From a distance, they reminded me of Stonehenge—stark, brooding, mysterious, dark stones outlined against a dark sky. As we walked among the Rocks, with the wind whipping around us and the waves crashing below, the dramatic effect was not lessened. The towering Rocks have been tortured into the most incredible shapes—twisted, hollowed out, fanged, eggshell thin in places, jagged, smooth, round, bizarre, balancing against one another, stained, awesome, beautiful. Remarkable.

We headed next to Cape Du Couëdic, to see Admiral's Arch, a natural arch created by centuries of crashing waves. Beneath the granite arch, slabs of basalt jut out of the water. The surrounding limestone has been turned into sharp, ragged rock lace.

Pat, Lou, and I crossed over the top of the great arch and climbed down the steep, rugged cliffs on its seaward side. We stood on the exposed pillars of basalt beneath the arch, watching the sea. The dark blue water beat against the rocks, throwing white spray high into the air. Not far from shore we could see the Casuarina Islets—small, steep, rugged tracts that have been designated as bird sanctuaries. The rocky islets were aflutter with the numberless sea birds that nest there, and the air was filled with their cries.

High on the hill above the arch, across acres of unbroken heath, stands a lighthouse. It is no longer manned, being operated electronically. Knowing that made it seem even more stark and lonely, standing there between the now-angry sky and the fury of the sea.

There are several lighthouses on the island now. The first was built at Cape Willoughby in 1852. They are very necessary, as the coast of Kangaroo Island is treacherous. It is not known how many ships were lost before the first recorded disaster in August 1847, but since then more than 40 ships have been wrecked and sunk off the island's coast.

We finally departed the arch, continuing on to Kelly Hill

Caves. These caves are very extensive and richly orna-
mented with spectacular formations. Stalagmites, stalactites, shawl formations, and the strange, unexplained helictites sparkle white, with stains of red, yellow, and blue
from iron, tannin (from tree roots), and manganese. The
floor is crystal, and the light spread through it when the
cave guide put her lamp against it. Room after room of
dripping, shimmering shapes greeted us, dazzled us. It
really is beautiful down there.

The caves were named for a horse. A stockman riding
through the area long ago accidentally discovered the
caves when he and his mount disappeared suddenly into a
sinkhole. The stockman managed to climb out and went
for help. He brought several men back to the spot but,
though the hole was still there, there was no sign of the
horse. In fact, even though the caves have, since that time,
been extensively (though by no means entirely) explored,
no trace of the horse was ever found. The hill and its caves
were named after the poor, lost beast, which was called
Ned Kelly, after the famous bushranger*.

We spent nearly an hour in the caves, and by the time
we emerged it was past 4:30 and time to head for home.
Des had picked up four girls who were hitchhiking across
the island, and we dropped them off at a spot where they'd
be able to catch the bus into Kingscote.

We finally rolled into the motel at a little after 6 o'clock,
just in time for a supper of incredibly fresh, locally caught
whiting. (That's one of the definite advantages to visiting a
country with a lot of coastline: fabulous seafood anywhere
you're near water—and you're almost always near water.)

*See appendix

Friday, October 28

After a refreshing night's sleep, I arose to a bright but chilly morning. Donning the only warm clothing I'd thought to bring, I met Des by the minivan for a drive into Kingscote. Kingscote, with a population of 1,100, is the largest town on the island (K.I.'s total population is 3,000). Joining Lou, Pat, and me were Roy and Jeanette, a delightful couple from Adelaide who are also staying at the motel. Des dropped us off, and the five of us wandered about the little town by the sea.

We saw the hitchhikers Des picked up yesterday, as they sat repacking their backpacks on the lawn of the post office. We stopped in a few shops, browsing through the knickknacks, buying postcards, looking at books. After a couple of brisk, windy hours, we stopped at a little bakery for hot tea and muffins.

Warmed and filled after our break, we headed back into the stiff sea breeze. We walked down to the jetty and out to where the cray boats were docked. The crayfishing season begins in three days, so there was a flurry of preparation around the small, sleek fishing vessels. Cray pots were stacked high on the docks and on the boats' decks. (What Australians call crayfish are what we call rock lobsters. The freshwater crustaceans we call crayfish, they call yabbies.) We chatted with the fishermen and explored the mechanical wonders of the ferry docks, then walked back toward shore.

The shore is lined with the kind of wonderful, bent and twisted trees you only find by the edges of wind-swept seas. Sea gulls floated and swooped in the wind, circling the boats, trying to see if anything had been caught yet. We crossed the park and strolled along the grass and among the rocks, watching the waves lap the shore. There is something about the rhythmic slap, slap of the water and the freshness of a sea breeze that make it possible to feel both tranquil and invigorated at the same time.

The weather began to turn against us, and soon it was too cold and gray to consider further outdoor activities. We returned to American River, where we had lunch, then turned to the video player for further amusement. A couple of movies, interspersed liberally with conversation and laughter, made the afternoon pass quickly.

After dinner, we sat in the lounge, chatting. Roy and Jeanette were leaving by the late ferry, so before long, they had to say good-bye. Lou, Pat, and I made plans for tomorrow night, when all of us will be back in Adelaide. They're leaving early in the morning, but they'll meet my plane when I arrive, and I'll spend an evening seeing part of their Adelaide.

Saturday, October 29

It was a cool day, with clouds scudding across the sky and a refreshing breeze: perfect weather for walking. So I set off for a long walk down the Scenic Walkway. The walkway, a narrow path beaten through the bush, skirts the beach, goes up and down several hills, winds inland a bit through trees and brush, then comes over a rise for a marvelous view of the sea from the tip of the island.

The forest is dense with a wonderful variety of gums—tall and smooth or short, shaggy and twisted—and casuarinas, the same family of narrow-leafed trees that includes the lovely desert oaks. It was beautiful and peaceful, with the only sounds the creaking of limbs, whispering breeze, and waves on the shore below. I wandered for hours.

At one spot, a separate path forks off and runs down to the beach. I went down it and broke out of the woods onto a beautiful scene of white sand, blue surf, and dozens of black swans. A few sea gulls squawked their annoyance at my presence, but the swans paid me no notice and continued to fish or glide about as I crouched nearby watching.

As the afternoon wore on, I turned my steps once more in the direction of the hotel. Just before the path ends, the brush is cleared back a little and you can see the large numbers of rocks and pebbles that are normally hidden by the undergrowth. There is granite, limestone, and lots of brightly colored, sparkling quartz. I collected some beautiful pieces of quartz—gold, red, and white—with something very close to the same delight I felt the first time I learned what it was (around age 9, I think).

I got back to the hotel in time to have a cup of coffee before heading for the "airport." On this run, there were no mailbags, and the plane held its full complement of eight passengers (one in the co-pilot's seat). The sea sparkled beneath us, and the island's green dimmed to blue as it dwindled on the horizon.

When I landed in Adelaide at 6 p.m., Lou and Pat were waiting for me. We headed out of town and along the coast to Lou's house. Lou's parents had invited me to dinner on Lou's recommendation. We had a lot of fun together, talking and looking at photographs of their trips to many of the places around Australia that I also have visited. They're actually hoping to take a year off, just to tour Australia.

Pat arrived saying she'd been given orders to bring me to her house, because her parents wanted to meet me, too. Pat's parents were having a dinner party, so I got to meet the whole neighborhood. We chatted and laughed for half an hour. Everyone was thoroughly delightful.

Finally, we headed for a party with Lou and Pat's friends from the sailing club. It was a young, tan, vigorous, and very friendly crowd. As the only American there, I was soon surrounded by people wanting to know a.) all about America, b.) what I've been doing in Australia and what I think of it, and c.) would I like to go on their boats. Parts a. and b. I was more than glad to go into, but I was really sorry to tell them I'd be gone before they were out on the water again. They were disappointed, but said that if I were ever back in Adelaide, I'd be welcome on any of their boats.

It was a wonderful evening, and everyone treated me like a long-lost friend. I hated to drag myself away at 12:30, but it was a half hour drive back to the hotel, there was a time change to consider (onto daylight savings time, so we lost an hour), and I have to rise by 6 a.m. to catch my bus.

Sunday, October 30

As the bus pulled out of the Adelaide depot, the sky began to clear and the sun poured down on us. As always, I stayed glued to the window, enjoying the changing scenery, as we rolled out of the city and into the surrounding farms and grazing land, through verdant hills and rural towns.

I feel that I've given South Australia short shrift. There is so much more I want to see. But that's nothing new— I've felt that way everywhere. Still, I'm pleased to be on my way, toward Melbourne and new adventures.

WALTZING VICTORIA

We had a rest stop near the border, in a small town appropriately named Bordertown. Then it was back on the bus and on into Victoria. The terrain became hillier, with the Grampians rising in the hazy distance. The greenness intensified, and there were fields of grazing sheep and yellow flowers. The sky was dotted with puffy white clouds. It was a glorious day, and the twelve hours of the bus trip flew by.

As we neared Ballarat, we passed along the Avenue of Honor, which is lined with more than 4,000 trees planted in memory of each citizen of Ballarat who died in W.W.I. The road leads up to and through a monumental memorial arch.

Few people outside Australia realize how much this country contributed to every major war effort in the last 100 years, so the Aussies themselves are keen on keeping the memory alive. (Australia has remained largely unacknowledged because Australian troops were often lumped in with "British forces"—but only by her allies; her enemies always knew when they were fighting Aussies.)

During World War I, Australia had the highest casualty rate of any country fighting—around 70 percent—due to the fact that they were always at the front. Australian soldiers were, however (especially at Gallipoli) greatly admired by their Turkish opponents, who referred to them as the new Spartans.

In World War II, Aussies had already distinguished

themselves in North Africa for more than a year before the U.S. entered the war. The famous "Rats of Tobruk" were Australians who held out for eight months against a ferocious siege by Rommel and his troops. Also, Aussie military units backed up and fought with the American soldiers in Vietnam and Iraq. Anyway, suffice it to say, there is a considerable amount of honoring those who died.

Sue (from the Red Centre tour) was waiting for me when my bus pulled in to the Melbourne terminal. After packing my gear in her car, she took me on a whirlwind tour of town, showing me all the top museums, shopping areas, and night spots. Then we headed out to the suburb of Essendon, to her flat (apartment), where she immediately made me feel very much at home.

Monday, October 31

This morning, I headed into town to make some arrangements for my stay here—tours mostly. I took the tram (streetcar) into the city. Melbourne still has an active and extensive fleet of electric trams, which is a delightful way to get about. Because Sue showed me the highlights of Melbourne last night, I had some idea of the city's layout, which made finding my way around much easier.

I got my business out of the way, then just explored. Melbourne is a beautiful city, full of wonderful old buildings, charming shops and cafés, narrow lanes and broad streets. It has a decidedly Old World flavor to it.

I puttered through some of Melbourne's many arcades. Like London, Australian cities have arcades of little shops running through buildings between main streets. Block Arcade was particularly lovely, with imposing stone arches, high glass ceiling, and beautiful mosaic floors.

I bought flowers from one of the many street vendors, then, at 5:30, I caught the tram back to Essendon. I found Sue sitting on the front step—she'd locked herself out. She'd given me a spare key, and so found herself rescued by her own generosity.

We had dinner, then headed for the library, where Sue taught (she's a volunteer tutor in an adult literacy program), and I wrote. When the lesson was finished, we drove to Sue's grandparents' house, where we enjoyed an amiable chat over cocoa and bickies (biscuits, i.e., cookies). Then it was home and to bed. (Actually, to sleeping bag. I'm occupying a section of floor here—but Sue has a lilo, so it's still quite comfortable.)

Tuesday, November 1

Today, as it is the first Tuesday in November, is Melbourne Cup Day. This horse race, which has been run annually since 1861, is one of the most important events on the Australian calendar. In the words of Mark Twain, "It overshadows all other holidays. I might say it almost blots them out." Twain also amusingly describes the weeklong festivities preceding the big event, and concludes that the entire balance of the year is simply spent marking time till the next Melbourne Cup.

The Cup race is run on a two-mile, turf track. The race has long been dominated by New Zealand-bred horses. Even Australia's most famous racehorse, Phar Lap, who won the cup in 1930, came from New Zealand. In honor of the Cup, all business in Melbourne is closed today, so Sue didn't have to go to work. The weather was clear and sunny, so we decided to head for the Royal Melbourne Zoo.

Melbourne's zoo is wonderful—well laid out and beautifully planted. It has many "walk-through" areas, where we strolled among the kangaroos, wallabies, and tremendously diverse birdlife. They have the most extensive aviary I've ever seen, planted to look like the areas of the country from which the numerous birds come. Then, for me, we went to see echidnas, wombats, and platypuses. For Sue, we visited hippopotami, seals, and American bison.

When we left the zoo, we drove to the home of friends, Bobby and Pam. Sue's beau, John, was already there. We watched several horse races on TV, waiting for the running of the Melbourne Cup. Then, at 2:40, for a few heart-pounding minutes, all Australia came to a stop, as a field of glorious horses thundered around the two-mile track.

We munched on chips and chicken that Pam had put out for the gathering, and talked about horses. Pam, especially, made every effort to make me feel welcome, urging me to come back anytime, inviting me to see the trots (harness racing) with them sometime. She really was a doll.

It amazes me how often people we genuinely like, could possibly really care for in time, touch the edges of our lives, then disappear. It's sad, sometimes, but good, too, because it renews my faith in mankind. There are a lot of wonderful people in this world.

Wednesday, November 2

It seemed fitting that I should visit Australia's greatest-ever race horse the day after the country's greatest race, so, after stepping off the tram, I walked to Russell Street and up to the National Museum.

Phar Lap died in the U.S. in 1932, after his stunning victory at Agua Caliente, Mexico, but his remains are beautifully preserved here, in the National Museum. What a glorious animal he was. The "Red Terror," as he was known, stood 17 hands high—tall, even for a thoroughbred. He is (was?) the most gorgeous, bright chestnut, and impressively built. It must have been exciting to see him run.

After seeing Phar Lap (name is Thai for "Wink of the Sky," or "Lightning"), I wandered through exhibits on Australian minerals, wildlife, prehistory (5 million years ago, kangaroos were more than 10 feet tall, and there was a species of wombat as large as a rhinoceros), Aboriginal culture, coins, military history, gold mining, cars, and timepieces.

Just before 2 o'clock, I headed back through the museum to the planetarium for the sky show. I have been most eager, ever since seeing the unobstructed Australian night sky while in the Centre, to get to a planetarium.

The show pointed out the constellations that can be seen from this hemisphere. Named by navigators and explorers, rather than by astrologers, poets, or priests, many southern constellations have names that are both nautical and relatively modern: Antlia, the Air Pump; Vela, the Sail; Carina, the Keel; Sextans, the Sextant; Fornax, the Furnace; and Telescopium, the Telescope. I was surprised to learn that Alpha Centauri, the star nearest to our Sun, is one of the Pointers, two stars used to locate the Southern Cross.

The Southern Hemisphere faces directly toward the center of the Milky Way, 30,000 light-years away. From this vantage point, the great, spiraling form of our galaxy is discernible. Also visible from this hemisphere are the Magellanic Clouds, two companion galaxies.

After the sky show, I headed up the road to the Old

Melbourne Gaol. Only one cellblock of the gaol remains, and it has been turned into a grim but interesting museum. It's an enormous, solidly built structure, with foot-thick stone walls. There are rows of cells, with heavy timber doors and great iron bolts, lining the walls of each of the building's three stories.

The cells on the ground floor contain death masks and case histories of most of the people who died at the gaol. All were executed (by hanging) except one. The exception was a man who had been assigned to hang a woman for murder. He was having trouble dealing with the idea of executing a woman, and family and friends taunted him mercilessly. Finally, the day before the scheduled hanging, he drank several shots of whiskey, then went into his room and cut his throat. I thought that was terribly sad.

Judging by the histories, everyone else deserved to come to a bad end—a real chronicle of misspent lives, greed, bloodshed, and ruthlessness. One thing that was interesting, if a bit gruesome, was that even on the death masks you could tell they'd been hanged, with the strange puffiness around their necks.

Among the other displays were the flogging triangle, leather belts and collars worn during flogging to protect prisoners' kidneys and necks, irons, whips, and the canvas masks that convicts were required to wear whenever they left their cells. Upstairs, there were letters written by prisoners, and stories about lesser offenders, who were not executed.

It was at this gaol that the notorious bushranger/folk hero Ned Kelly* was imprisoned and hanged. The home-made armor he and his gang wore when they faced police in a final gun battle is on display. The armor weighed more than 90 pounds, so it didn't take many wounds to

*See appendix

weaken Kelly to the point where he couldn't support it.
Ned Kelly is seen by many as sort of a cross between
Robin Hood and Butch Cassidy—a definitely romantic
figure. (Some just see him as a murdering bank robber.)
He was only 25 when he died.

Well, on that happy note. . .

I continued my wandering, heading back to Bourke
Street, and through the Royal Arcade, which is famous for
its statues of Gog and Magog. These effigies represent the
two survivors of a mythical race of giants destroyed by
Brutus the Trojan, legendary founder of London. Statues
of these giants have existed in London from at least the
time of Henry V. The two in the Royal Arcade are copies
of wooden effigies that stand in the Guildhall in London,
near the site where it is said that Brutus made the giants
serve him. Now, the impressive red and gold colossi serve
to strike the hour, and remind visitors how closely
Melbourne is tied to the Old World.

Thursday, November 3

Melbourne's National Gallery of Art is said to house the
most important art collection in the Southern Hemisphere.
This is easy to believe. I was waiting on its gray, granite
doorstep when the gallery opened at 10 a.m. I didn't leave
until it closed at 5 o'clock, and I could have stayed longer.

I wandered through rooms that were simple, uncluttered,
and well-lighted, enjoying the fine collections of porce-
lain, silver, antique furniture, Oriental art, European art,
primitive artifacts, and historical costumes. The Great
Hall, with its splendid, stained-glass ceiling, and the gray
granite courtyard, with its greenery and odd fountains,

were impressive, refreshing interruptions in the chain of art-filled rooms.

Eventually I headed to the Australian galleries on the second floor. I was delighted to see an exhibit of photographs taken all over the country, especially the Outback. I was most interested, however, in seeing the works of Australian painters, and it was with these that I spent the most time.

About the first artists who tried to depict Australia so it didn't just look like England with kangaroos were Eugène von Guérard and John Glover. Both men were enamored of the brightness of the Pacific sun and the beauty and strangeness of Australia's trees. Painting at about this same time (early to mid-1800s) were Nicholas Chevalier, Louis Buvelot, and William Charles Piguenit. They also were attempting landscapes, but they were not quite as successful as von Guérard and Glover at capturing the elusive quality of the Australian countryside.

Conrad Martens was another important, early painter. Working mostly in washes and watercolors, he concentrated mainly on romantic views in and around Sydney, especially of the harbor. Yet he too (except when depicting the tropical north) failed to capture the true spirit of the country he painted.

It was not until the late 1800s that Australia's first school of painting, the Heidelberg School, emerged. This group, now often called the Australian Impressionists, was founded by four men: Frederick McCubbin, Tom Roberts, Arthur Streeton, and Charles Conder. They liked to paint outdoors and would spend weekends camping in the country, especially in the Heidelberg district near Melbourne.

It was the mystique of Australia they wanted to capture—the light, the muted colors, the magic, the strange, haunting beauty—and they did so admirably. Here, at last, was the real Australia: the graceful gums, the browns, gray-greens and golds, the space, the heat, the drama and tragedies, the life, the wonder.

The Heidelberg School was influenced more by James Whistler than by the French Impressionists, but was influenced still more by the country itself. Soon, other artists were attracted to this style of painting—David Davies, John Longstaff, Walter Withers. Australian art flourished. These are the paintings I loved best.

Of the more recent artists, I liked Hans Heysen, whose beautiful landscapes, with their imposing white gums, are reminiscent of the Australian Impressionist influence, and Russell Drysdale, whose hot, rugged, red-dominated works are brooding, evocative, and vibrantly Australian.

I enjoyed this day, not just because I love beautiful things and handsome paintings. I enjoyed it especially because I felt a closeness of spirit to these works, because of the love for the subject that I share with their creators. I almost feel like I spent the day away from the city.

Friday, November 4

Melbourne was founded by free men. A group of enterprising settlers from Tasmania, needing land to graze their livestock, decided to strike out for the mainland. They chose one of their number to go prospecting for them, and, in 1835, John Batman sailed across Bass Strait and entered Port Phillip. Making his way up the Yarra River, he found a spot that he thought looked like a nice place for a village. Batman, who got along well with the local tribes, was enthusiastic about the land and offered to buy it from the Aborigines. Blankets, axes and food were exchanged for the property on which Melbourne now sits.

Melbourne, named for Lord Melbourne, the Prime Minister of England, was designed two years later by Robert Hoddle. It was a while before Hoddle's grand metropolitan vision would be realized, but his forward-looking plans were responsible for all the wide, tree-lined avenues radiating out from the city.

Today I was scheduled to see Mr. Batman's village, so I headed early for the Ansett office, to catch my tour of Melbourne's city sights.

Heading first into the inner-city suburb of Carlton, we approached Melbourne University up an avenue lined with palm trees brought from the Middle East by ANZAC troops returning from the first World War. Winding through the grounds of the 15,000-student university, we passed the handsome Tudor quadrangle, built in 1854.

We walked through Carlton Gardens, where paths and sweeping, tree-lined lawns all lead to the Exhibition Building. An impressive, domed edifice of classic design, it was opened in 1880 for the World's Fair. It was used next as a temporary location for the Federal Parliament, until that was moved to Canberra in 1927. Today it is once again employed for exhibitions.

Cruising through the city, we passed the imposing Town Hall, which was begun in 1856, then turned up Russell Street and passed the National Museum and Old Melbourne Gaol. We swung south past St. Patrick's Cathedral, a marvelously Gothic structure surmounted by a 340-foot, three-and-a-half-ton, bronze spire. We saw State Parliament, with its graceful, Grecian-style columns; the Royal Mint, alongside the palm-lined Treasury Gardens; the stately, 19th-century Windsor Hotel; and the elegant old Princess Theatre.

We stopped to explore splendid, formal Fitzroy Gardens. Here, we also viewed "Captain Cook's cottage," which actually belonged to Cook's parents later in life. The small, stone cottage was dismantled and brought over from Yorkshire, England, as a memorial to the man who first charted Australia's coast.

We drove through many of Melbourne's neighborhoods: the beautiful, old, 19th-century enclaves, with their iron lace-adorned terrace houses, as well as the multitude of ethnic neighborhoods. Every nation on earth seems to be represented in this city, from Italy to India, with a particularly large contingent from Greece. In fact, Melbourne has the third largest Greek-speaking community in the world, after Athens and Thessalonica. There is also a chic, slightly understated Chinatown in Little Bourke Street, with tiled arches at each corner and elegantly stylized glass lamps overhead.

As we continued, we crossed and recrossed the Yarra River. The Yarra is something of a sore point with Melbournians. They love the river and think it incomparable for beauty. It is beautiful, a broad ribbon of water winding between rows of trees and green parks. It is also usually a bit muddy, which has given rise to derisive remarks from some quarters. I've been told that this is the river of which it was first said, "It's too thick to drink and too thin to plow," though I've heard that applied elsewhere, too. Our guide told us that an acquaintance of his (not from Melbourne) sends postcards of clear, blue streams from wherever he travels, with the note, "This is what a river is supposed to look like." My favorite comment came from a Sydney-sider who remarked, "Good old Yarra—she's the only river in the world that flows upside down." "Yarra" is Aborigine for "flowing," and it is the water's speed that keeps it churned up.

At the Shrine of Remembrance, we stopped again. We crossed the spacious gardens, passing the obelisk and eternal flame for W.W.II casualties, and climbed the stairs of the great, white stone memorial to the W.W.I dead. A "digger," an Australian soldier in the familiar slouch hat, guarded the entrance.

The main chamber is imposing and hushed, with an echoing stone silence. Wreaths and flags decorate the floors and walls. In the center of the room there is a marble slab inscribed with part of John 15:13—"Greater Love Hath No Man." Inaudibly, almost involuntarily, I completed the verse: "Greater love hath no man than this, that a man lay down his life for his friends."

Leaving the memorial, we followed the garden-bordered sweep of St. Kilda Road back toward city center. As we crossed Princes Bridge, the dome of Flinders Street Station came into view. We passed St. Paul's Cathedral and City Square, then turned west on Collins Street, heading into the city's financial district. Here I was delighted by the baroque-style Commonwealth Banking Association building and the fabulous, Gothic ANZ Bank headquarters, with its high, pointed arches, stone griffins and leaded, diamond-paned windows.

We were dropped off in town, left to our own devices for lunch. I walked to the City Baths, because the café there had been recommended. The City Baths are beautiful—a huge, elaborate, white marble-trimmed, red brick building that was, in the days before everyone had indoor plumbing, where the general populace retired of an evening to bathe. Now it houses public swimming pools, as well as the excellent little café.

At 1:45, we were off to the Dandenongs, the mountains

that border Melbourne on the east. In spite of the basically
gray day, it was a spectacular drive. We climbed up into
the mountains, through the cool greenness of Sherbrooke
Forest. Immense gum trees closed in around us. These
giant gums, also known as Australian mountain ash, attain
heights of 300 feet and have circumferences of nearly 25
feet. I love these trees, with their tall, straight trunks,
smooth and pale, some of them loosely draped with
strands of newly shed outer bark, all of them crowned with
wonderfully clean-smelling leaves. Beneath the trees, the
terrain is crowded with magnificent giant ferns and
umbrella ferns.

At teatime, the tour stopped at a little tea room in the
forest, but I chose to wander off into the woods. It was
beautiful, cool, green, and awesomely peaceful. The trees
and ferns towered over me as I descended toward a stream
not far away. A crimson rosella flew past me, and I could
hear the calls of the whipbird and bellbirds, as well as
other sweet songs I could not identify. I crossed the stream
and headed up the hill on the opposite side, winding
between the umbrella ferns, shaded by the gums. The
moss and dead leaves were thick underfoot and muffled
my steps. Only the stream and the birds sang in the otherwise unbroken silence of the forest.

I wandered happily for 45 minutes, then it was time to
return to the bus. We continued our climb up Mt.
Dandenong, winding up the forested slopes. The peak
afforded us a gorgeous view of the valley and the surrounding mountains. One thing that amused me was seeing
a mountainside road named Bonza View. ("Bonza" is
Australian slang for "terrific.")

Eventually, we turned our wheels homeward, wending
our way down the tree-clad mountains, then through the

suburbs and into Melbourne.

Sue is away for the weekend (a pharmacists' convention in Adelaide), and Steve, Sue's flatmate, is hardly ever around, so I have the place pretty much to myself tonight. It's nice to have a little time alone.

Miscellany

The elegance of Melbourne has reminded me that, though one tends to think of Australia in terms of frontiers and wilderness, by percentage, Australia has more big-city dwellers than any other country on earth—85 percent of the population resides in cities or towns, and most are within an hour's drive of an ocean.

Saturday, November 5

I boarded the bus for Phillip Island around noon. We headed across town and turned into William Street, passing the Supreme Court at Lonsdale Street. Then we exited the city. As we drove, the driver kept up the usual delightful patter that adds so much to one's store of information, both important and anecdotal. We learned that:

- In Melbourne's early days, cement was expensive, because it had to be brought from England, so most houses were built on foundations of basalt blocks. This proved to be extremely successful, as well as very attractive.

- By law, in Victoria, there are no private beaches—all water must be accessible to everyone.

- St. Kilda is the nightlife and rather understated "racy" section of town. However, it is equally famous for its cafés and cake shops, with the influences of Vienna, Warsaw, Prague, Budapest, and Tel Aviv much in evidence.

- Herbert Hoover, who once managed a gold mine in Australia, was the man most responsible for stopping the wholesale slaughter of the koala. When he was elected President of the U.S., he placed a ban on the importation of koala pelts, thereby destroying the market for the fur.

- The towns on Phillip Island are named after towns on the Isle of Wight (England), as both islands are almost the same size and shape.

- Koalas have soft, flexible rib cages, so they can scrunch comfortably into the tree forks where they are usually seen snoozing. This is why they are held with an arm under their bottoms, not around their waists. Grabbing a koala around the middle squeezes the air out of its lungs, the poor beast panics, and you end up getting pretty badly clawed.

We skirted Port Phillip Bay, passing through St. Kilda and the beautiful, old, seaside suburb of Brighton. As we followed the shoreline, our guide pointed out some of the unusual things used as breakwaters. The first we saw was a W.W.II submarine, which was purchased from the U.S., towed to its present site, then filled with cement, so it would stay in place. The next was the *Cerebus*, a Melbourne-built, ironclad warship from the last century, similar to our Civil War's *Monitor*, only much bigger, with two gun turrets. It has now come to this inglorious end, protecting the beach, not from invaders, but from waves.

We passed an Ampol roadhouse, and I thought back to the one in Katherine, N.T., and thought how much place and circumstance determine how you feel about things. Now that I'm back in "civilization," it would again seem strange to shower and change at a roadhouse, whereas it seemed so natural in the outback. I don't think it's so much because I feel constrained by society's expectations here, but rather because I felt so much safer, so much less exposed out there.

We crossed the top of the Mornington Peninsula to Tooradin. The town is named for a mythical creature (unfriendly) believed by Aborigines to inhabit the adjacent Kooweerup Swamps. The swamps have been, for the most part, drained, though it's a constant struggle, as the land is only a few feet above sea level. The area, now used for farming, is crisscrossed with wide, mangrove-lined drainage ditches (though I did not learn what, other than mosquitos, is raised on these swamp-farms).

We circled Western Port Bay, following the Bass Highway. In another hour we left the highway, turning west toward the fishing community of San Remo, where we crossed the causeway onto Phillip Island. We drove slowly on the island, heeding the many warning signs for koala and kangaroo crossings. As we rolled down the rough, narrow roads, all eyes were focused on the branches of the beautiful Manna gums lining both sides. The trees were full of galahs, wattlebirds and rosellas. Higher up, koalas munched calmly or slept among the top leaves. What a beautiful place. I loved the wonderful, twisted trees as much as I loved the little bundles of gray fur that clung to their branches.

We stopped frequently to enjoy and photograph our surroundings. We spent almost an hour wandering among the trees, looking for koalas and bright birds, before heading into Cowes, the island's main town, for supper. After eating, I wandered up the nearly deserted beach, photographing the fishing boats beside the pier and the tall greenery that crowded the edge of the golden sand. Then it was time to be back at the bus.

We drove out to a spot called the Nobbies, a gnarled, offshore rock formation that is home to a large group of seals. Then we headed for our real destination—the thing for which people flock to Phillip Island: the beach where the penguins come ashore every night.

As we neared the spot, we saw road signs that advised "CAUTION—Penguins on Road After Dusk." The penguins that come ashore here are fairy penguins, which, at 13 inches in height, are the smallest variety of penguin. Every night of the year, at sunset, hundreds of these adorable little birds emerge from Bass Strait to return to their nests.

Shortly after the sun sets the first group of penguins "lands." There is a shimmer at the edge of the water, a little extra white on a wave, a flip-flash of silver, then a penguin stands up. If there are no other penguins around, it again disappears into the foam. Soon, others arrive. They do not come ashore alone, always in groups—there is safety in numbers. Still, the sea gulls harass the small band trooping up the beach, trying to get them to give up the food they've brought for their mates.

If a wave comes along, the penguins drop on their stomachs and ride it in. They are undaunted by the crowd that has come to watch them—until someone disobeys the rules and takes a flash picture. The penguins flee for the safety of the water. (And the offender's camera is confiscated.) In a few minutes, when it appears that the danger is gone, they start back up the beach.

By this time, farther down the shore, another group has gathered and is waddling solemnly towards home, and the flash and shimmer of another approaching group can be seen on the crest of a breaking wave. Soon, hundreds of penguins are on the beach—600, it is estimated. There are approximately 1,200 in the colony, but this is the mating and breeding season, so someone has to stay at home and sit on the egg. This job is traded off, with the male and female staying behind on alternate days. As a result, there is a tremendous "social hour" when the penguins return home, and we could hear them chattering and whirring as each related the day's activities to its mate. Some eggs had already hatched, and we could see the downy chicks in the nests, waiting anxiously for dinner.

After an hour we started to wander back up the beach, but we had to be careful, because there was always the possibility that a penguin would be underfoot. All around us, there were nests full of chattering penguins, grooming their young and feeding mates and chicks. I saw one little crisis in progress—one of the penguins had apparently forgotten which nest it belonged in, and I watched as it wandered into, and got chased out of, nest after nest. I hope the poor little creature found its way home before too long.

I walked along as slowly as possible, lingering over each little scene of penguin domesticity. It was wonderful, incredible. I could hardly believe the adorable creatures were so close, and so unperturbed by our presence.

We arrived back in Melbourne at 11:40 p.m., and I was dropped off at the tram stop near Flinders Station. Though I'd been assured that it was quite safe, I was still a bit nervous standing alone on the deserted downtown street corner waiting for the midnight tram. Almost no one was about at that hour, and the silence was broken only by the wind and the bell of an approaching streetcar. By 12:30, I was in Essendon, and I strolled homeward through darkness and quiet so intense that they seemed almost palpable.

Sunday, November 6
Today's tour got off to an early start, rolling westward

through the beautiful, Victorian countryside. Horses and sheep grazed in fields yellow with Cape weed, and great flocks of white cockatoos burst into the air at our approach.

About 70 miles out of Melbourne we came to Ballarat. Gold was discovered here in 1851, and the town became one of the centers of the greatest gold rush the world has ever seen. More than 600,000 fortune seekers had arrived in Victoria by 1860, doubling the country's population.

It is not known exactly how much gold was mined in this area during the rush, but 121 million ounces found here were sold to the government mint in Melbourne. A tremendous amount was carried out of the country, though it was impossible to determine how much. Almost all of the 40,000 Chinese miners who flocked to Victoria's gold fields between 1854 and 1858 took their gold with them when they returned home.

Miners' cottages, all still in use, are dotted around the town. They are nice, sturdy little houses, occasionally amusing due to numerous room additions in styles and materials differing from the original structure, but always charming.

Ballarat is probably best known as the site of the Eureka Stockade. When gold mining was the biggest business in Victoria, it was still the law that only landowners could vote. Few miners owned land, so they were unrepresented in government. Landowners resented the huge influx of vagrants and fortune seekers who went traipsing all over the countryside, digging everything up, occasionally trespassing on the great pastoral estates. Narrow-minded politicians, over-zealous officials of various sorts, and numerous others of less-than-adventurous mettle wanted to get as much of the gold as possible without risking their lives to get it (the life expectancy of miners in those days was between 30 and 35 years). So they taxed the miners heavily and imposed a monthly license fee, collectable whether gold was struck or not. Those who couldn't pay were hunted down and fined or imprisoned.

Part of the problem, where treatment of the miners was concerned, resulted from the quality of the police force. There was a severe labor shortage, so recruiters had to accept anyone who could be persuaded to put on a uniform. This produced a less-than-ideal collection of men who ranged from the young and inexperienced to the brutal and corrupt. Many were ex-convicts from Tasmania. Enforcing the license fee became great sport and was financially rewarding for the pursuers, who collected, in addition to the fee, half the fine on every defaulter.

The majority of miners were not revolutionaries or troublemakers, but were simple, hard-working men who were angered by the treatment they received at the hands of the uniformed bullies and by the injustice of the exorbitant license fees. So in 1854, the diggers issued a proclamation of "Right and Justice," pledged their loyalty to each other, and resolved to stand together and fight for their rights and liberties. Peter Lalor, who was about 25-years-old at the time, was elected leader of the united diggers. They hastily constructed a simple stockade in the Eureka gold field, and raised over it a new flag—the Southern Cross on a field of blue.

The diggers were vastly outnumbered by the soldiers and police that silently surrounded the stockade on December 3, 1854. The diggers also had the disadvantage of being poorly armed—mostly picks and shovels, with only a few rifles. The entire uprising lasted 15 minutes, with 34 diggers killed, and many wounded. Peter Lalor was wounded so severely that he lost an arm. He barely escaped the skirmish, and did so with a price on his head.

However, popular opinion and many honorable politicians took the side of the miners, realizing how unjustly they had been treated. Laws were reformed, justice was done, and eventually Peter Lalor, no longer, a fugitive, became Speaker of the Victoria Legislative Assembly.

The Eureka Stockade incident was by no means the sole cause of legal reform, though it did speed things up. Its greater significance lay in its embodiment of the spirit of Australia, a spirit of mateship, liberty, courage, and honor.

We drove along Eureka Street, passing the location and a replica of the Eureka Stockade. In the town's center, wide streets led us past a wealth of verandas and white, iron lace. Scattered among the Victorian Australian buildings were other architectural styles—Gothic, Renaissance, or anything considered grand enough to display the town's golden promise.

The town is honey-combed with abandoned mine shafts. Our guide related to us that, a few years ago, when there had been a period of very wet weather, a young couple who had just moved into a new house found that the floor boards in the family room were exceptionally springy. They pulled up a few boards and discovered that beneath the house there was a hole 90 feet deep, where several mines had subsided. (It was not a hopeless case—the hole was filled in, with a lot of dirt, the floorboards were replaced, and they lived happily ever after.)

We stopped at the city gardens, where poppies, mums and other flowers, blazing orange, yellow and crimson, lined the walkways, and broad lawns were bordered by trees and glass houses filled with more exotic blooms. Nearby, black swans were gliding gracefully back and forth on the clear, still water of tree-fringed Lake Wendouree. "Ballarat" is the Aboriginal word for "camp-

ing site" or "resting place," and I must agree that this
would be an ideal spot for an extended stay.

I strolled across the grass to a small, glassed-in pavilion
filled with Italian marble sculpture, then along the brilliant
banks of flowers, through the fern grotto and beyond, to
the little, iron-roofed cottage of Australian poet and horseman Adam Lindsay Gordon. Inside the cottage there is a
collection of items that belonged to Gordon, plus paintings
of the poet and some of his exploits, including the famous
"Gordon's Leap," among the most notable and daring feats
of horsemanship ever recorded.*

Then we reboarded the bus for the ride to Sovereign Hill.
What a delight. Sovereign Hill is a re-creation of Ballarat
of the 1850s, during the height of the gold rush. Here, the
Cobb & Co.* stagecoach still rumbles through town. The
streets—Main Street, Golden Point, Penny Weight, Red
Hill—are lined with buildings from the period.

At the Victoria Theatre, where the notorious Lola
Montez (who arrived from San Francisco in 1855)
danced her famous *El Olle* and Spider Dance, musicians
still perform. The ancient presses at the office of the
Ballarat Times clatter noisily, turning out "news" for
visitors. The Gold Office, miners' chapel, Chinese Joss
House, and United States Hotel stand nearby. The bakery,
confectioner, apothecary, woodturning shop, tin smith,
and post office are all going concerns, catering to the
needs of the community and its many guests. There is
even a gold mine to explore.

There are more than 100 full-time "citizens" and shop-
keepers, all in period dress, but a lot of people from
Ballarat, also authentically costumed, work as volunteers
at Sovereign Hill. When I stopped for lunch, one of these
volunteers, an older gentleman attired in top hat and frock

*See appendix

coat, asked if he might share my table and a bit of conversation. He wanted to know where I'd been, what I'd been doing, and how I liked Australia. Then he told me about his visit to America and Europe, and described in enthusiastic detail what it's like living in Ballarat and volunteering at Sovereign Hill. He loves the sense of history it gives you and enjoys sharing what he knows.

I wandered again into the bustle of the gold-rush town. In the schoolhouse, the schoolmaster was teaching penmanship, with ink wells and quill pens, to a room full of tourist/pupils. In the wagonwright's shop there were antique wagons, new replicas, and skilled craftsmen building, rebuilding, or repairing the wagons. Red-coated soldiers stood in the streets. Musicians played on the porches and in the theatre. The smithy worked at his anvil and shoed horses. Prospectors panned for gold and showed visitors how it's done. There were even suitably dressed children, playing with old rag dolls, writing on small slate boards, climbing through the wagons, feeding the chickens, sewing with their mothers in the bark huts.

After several hours of wide-eyed wandering, I headed across the parking lot to the Gold Museum, where I learned enough about the chemistry, legends, and uses of gold, as well as Australian history as it relates to gold, to fill a book. Hmmm—maybe that could be my next project.

Monday, November 7

This morning the sky looked like the Glory of God, dappled with clouds, sunbeams flooding downward, dazzling but irresistible to watch. It was a spectacular beginning to another busy day. There was a chill in the air and a fresh breeze blowing as I made my way to the Ansett office for today's tour—Lorne and the Great Ocean Road.

On our way out of town, our guide noted that the parks through which we were passing are among nearly 2,000 acres of parks and gardens in Melbourne. We drove toward Geelong (the second largest city in Victoria) along the Princes Highway, which is a section of Australia's Highway 1, the longest highway in the world. It extends 7,500 miles, running from Cairns all the way around Australia (clockwise) to Darwin.

Geelong is a beautiful, bustling port (Australia's fifth busiest). Typical of larger towns in this region, Geelong has wide, tree-lined streets, ornate Victorian buildings, quaint residential areas, and extensive parks and gardens. We crossed through the city, down the handsome main thoroughfare, then turned south, toward the coast and the Great Ocean Road.

Along this stretch of coast, the rugged hills of the Otway Range drop directly to the sea. The Great Ocean Road is a narrow ribbon that clings to the land's edge, rising and falling as it winds among hills or skirts quiet coves. In spots, white-capped waves crashed against great cliffs, and elsewhere, deep blue rollers washed up on gentle beaches. Nasturtiums were growing wild beside the road, in colorful profusion.

After our long drive, we arrived in Lorne for a less-than-stimulating time. The town is a popular resort, nestled between low mountains and a long arch of sheltered, tree-lined beach. During the summer, especially on weekends, it is crowded with surfers, swimmers, hikers, and other fun-seekers. On Mondays, particularly if they're chilly, gray Mondays, they roll up the streets and go home. Even the souvenir shops were closed. We looked in the windows of charming restaurants and cafés, and peered into darkened shops, then strolled on.

I took photos of the beach and of the beautiful golden cypress trees along the shore. I walked along the sand, then walked up and down the main street, where I was joined by another tour member, a girl from Brisbane. We found a take-away shop and bought roasted chicken, then sat on the curb and ate lunch, watching the beach and the silent street, and talking till it was time to leave. (In the summer, this much time is spent in Lorne so tourists can frolic in the waves, but today's weather precluded such activities.)

We returned along the craggy, magnificent shoreline. Our guide explained that they usually take the road through the mountains for the return trip, to enjoy the beautiful forests (the forests, parks and bush tracks around Lorne are among the area's foremost attractions). But, due to recent fires, the forests aren't there right now, and what's left is less than beautiful. I didn't mind, as the Great Ocean Road is worth seeing more than once. In fact, I'd like to return someday and follow this highway even farther—at least to Port Campbell, where the coast, dotted with pinnacles, spires and arches, is even more remarkable. (Add it to the list.)

Tuesday, November 8

It was dark and rainy today, and the wind whistled around the house. It was a good day to stay in and catch up. It has been ages since I last wrote to anyone, so I churned out about a score of letters and post cards.

Jenny, Sue's little sister, is here studying for her final

exams (she's a student at the University of Melbourne).
Whenever she needs a break, I get to see the latest in
Australian game shows, including local versions of some
U.S. programs. I also saw a commercial for McDonald's
that advertised kiwi fruit sundaes and passion fruit
shakes—hard to imagine them in Chicago.

The people from Walhalla Mountain Saddle Safaris had
given me the name of someone to contact regarding transportation to the start of the ride. I got in touch with Colin,
who goes on these trips regularly, and just as regularly ferries those of us who are without cars up into the hills. I'm
supposed to be at his house by 7 a.m. a week from this
Saturday. Colin invited me to meet him and two other sad-
dle-safari regulars at the Southern Cross Hotel the
Wednesday before the trip. They'll bring photos from previous rides, so I'll have some idea what I'm in for. I
appreciate his thoughtfulness.

Reading back over part of my journal, I have again been
impressed with the wonder of this trip. I've seen so many
of my dreams come true here. I've spent my nights once
more beneath the stars. I've waded into the flowers by the
road. I've watched the clouds, and filled my days with
dripping ferns and towering trees. I've had the time to
write. I've retrieved so much of the simplicity and freedom that I'd thought were lost with my youth. I've soaked
myself in beauty, though I have not yet (and perhaps never
will) reached the saturation point.

It will be hard to leave this dream behind. But I am glad
to know that dreams come true, and knowing that makes
the future shine.

Wednesday, November 9

Another chilly, cloudy day—but at least the wind has died down and the rain has stopped. I was at the Ansett office bright and early for a tour heading north and west, to the Central Goldfields.

The sun started to come out around 10 o'clock, but remained indecisive. However, as we moved farther north, the weather slowly improved. Our drive took us through some really beautiful areas. We traversed the Black Forest and passed Hanging Rock (of *Picnic at Hanging Rock* fame). The road climbed up into the mountains, then descended into Kyneton, where we stopped for morning tea.

I walked up the main street, past fine, old, bluestone buildings, heading for the Post Office, to find a phone so I could call Judy (English Judy from the Red Centre). This is a long tour, and doesn't get back into Melbourne till 6:30. Not realizing this, I'd made plans to meet Judy for dinner at 5:30.

As I looked up the phone number of the Royal Melbourne Hospital (where Judy works), I overheard a man standing near me tell the clerk that he'd been out shearing for nine weeks. A real shearer! Not someone who does it for tourists, but someone who does it for a living. From behind the phone book I looked him over—tan, lean, powerfully built, a bit rough—exactly what I'd want a sheep shearer to look like. I was delighted. (I'm easily amused.)

As we left town, our guide pointed out several pumps near the road. There is a great deal of spa-type mineral water in this area, and at these pumps, you can fill your own bottles. Then we were out in the country again.

Everywhere we looked, the beautiful, green fields were dotted with old mills, homesteads, and churches set in clumps of wonderful, gnarled, old gum trees. Soon we began to see mullock heaps, now nearly grown over, left behind by the gold miners.

Before long we arrived in Castlemaine, one of the many historic towns that grew up during the gold rush. The center of town has changed little since the 1860s. There are still hitching posts in front of the town hall. Castlemaine was one of the stops on the famous Cobb & Co.* stage-coach routes, and was the home of Robert O'Hara Burke (to whom there is a monument), former police inspector and leader of the ill-fated Burke and Wills expedition.*

After a quick spin around Castlemaine, we headed for Maldon. Maldon, a relic from the heyday of the goldfields, was selected as the National Trust's first "notable town in Australia" for its wonderfully preserved gold rush-era streetscapes. Fine, old buildings constructed of local stone line the streets, and it would seem perfectly natural to see horses and gold miners there. As always, I would like to stay longer than we can, just to sit and look at it.

As we got nearer to Bendigo, one of the centers of gold mining in Australia, we saw more and more pieces of mar-velous, old mining equipment littering the countryside. It didn't really detract, but rather gave me the feeling of being in sort of a living, outdoor museum, seeing the equipment where it was used and as it was left by the min-ers who abandoned the fields. It had a poignancy that the same equipment, polished and repaired and inside a real museum, could not possess.

When at last we arrived in Bendigo, our first stop was at Sacred Heart Cathedral, the only Gothic cathedral built in the Southern Hemisphere in the last 50 years. It is huge and impressive, with glorious, vaulted ceilings, stained-glass windows, a mighty pipe organ, and all the other trap-pings of your standard immense Gothic cathedral.

*See appendix

Bendigo was very quiet, because it was Bendigo Cup Day, and most of the population was at the race. We made our way down a nearly deserted McRae Street, admiring the monuments and fine old buildings on either side, among them, the Shamrock Hotel. This huge, ornate hotel was built in the late 1800s, the third hotel of this name on the site. It was one of the few places open, so we repaired there for lunch, gathering at one end of the long, carved-wood bar in the large, light dining hall.

Dame Nellie Melba, the great, Australian operatic sopra-no, on a tour around the country, once stayed at the Shamrock Hotel. However, she didn't like the chiming of the clock on the Post Office's tower, directly across the street. They stopped the clock.

Our destination after lunch was the Central Deborah Gold Mine, which is one of Bendigo's major gold-mining sites. Begun in 1851, it operated until 1954—the last of the old mines to close.

The shaft of the mine is more than 1,600 feet deep, with 17 different working levels. The shaft is divided into four sections: one for air hoses, both for breathing and for the compression hoses for driving the rock drills; one for men and ore; one for bailing water, seepage being the biggest obstacle to mining this area; and the last one for an emer-gency exit ladder.

The lift that carried men and ore up and down the shaft was operated by a cable that extended into the engine room. The lift had room for only four men. When carrying men, it moved at a rate of 500 feet per minute. With a load of ore, the lift's speed was 800 feet per minute. Another cable running from the engine room operated the bailer. Towards the end of her run, 300,000 gallons of water were being bailed out of the mine each day. Part of the problem was that, as other mines closed, there were fewer and fewer bailers operating in the area, and the water table kept rising. Today, the water is only a few feet from the mine's entrance.

One of the things I found interesting was that the lifts had an emergency braking system. The cable that carried the lift was connected to a powerful spring. If the cable broke, the spring activated a set of steel jaws on each side of the platform that bit into the wooden skids. The stop was fast and jarring, but better than plummeting to the bottom of the shaft.

The only means of communication with the surface was a long cord attached to a bell in the engine room. There was a whole system of signals, from one ring for stop the car and two rings for bring load up, to 10 rings for an accident, 15 rings if it was serious.

Next we saw the gold treatment rooms. It was here that the ore, which was predominantly quartz, was crushed to separate out the gold. Great stamper batteries crushed the quartz to powder. This piece of equipment was operated for our benefit, not only to show how it worked, but also to demonstrate the terrible noise levels involved.

After the crushing, water washed the lighter minerals away and sluiced the remainder over mercury-coated pans. Mercury binds quickly and strongly with gold, so if gold was present, it was stopped by the mercury. This formed an amalgam, which was rolled into large balls and put into retorts for heating. Mercury vaporizes before gold is completely melted, and the special retorts captured the mercury vapor and cooled it back to its liquid state for reuse. (One had to be very careful during this part of the processing; inhaling mercury vapor can be fatal, and a few people did die.) What was left in the retort was mostly gold, and was ready to be taken away for further purification and processing into its final form.

After a day in the mines, workers would retire to the changing rooms, where the then rare luxury of a hot shower awaited them. There was a little hitch, though. After the men showered, they could pass from the changing room to the drying room, but couldn't take any clothes. Their street clothes would be in the drying room, but their work clothes were not returned until the "rag pickers" had had an opportunity to check for possible smuggling of gold out of the mine.

Next door to the changing room was the first aid room. The room was small, with one bed, a large medicine cabinet, and several stretchers. Because the lift was so narrow, if a miner was injured, the stretcher had to be suspended under the lift. They told us that an injured miner brought up this way from the lowest levels would probably be in even worse shape when he reached the top, as the stretcher would begin to swing from side to side, and swung more violently the longer it was in motion.

Leaving the mine, we crossed the street to the beginning of the Talking Tram ride. The tram, a beautiful old thing of wood, brass and leather, "talks" by means of a tape recording, supplemented by an informative guide dressed in a uniform befitting the age of the tram. Our ride took us through Bendigo, which is a splendid town. This was once one of the richest gold-mining towns in Australia. The main street is flanked by gardens, statues, and gloriously ornate buildings—the kind that only the combination of the Victorian Era and a gold rush's wealth could produce. The town's aspirations to greatness are evident, with the central square called Charing Cross and the main street dubbed Pall Mall.

Our run through town brought us to the Tram Museum, where antique trams from all over Australia are restored, both for display and for use as part of the Talking Tram program. We wandered around and through the old tram-cars, admiring their parquet floors, brass fixtures, and leather upholstery. They certainly used to build them for more than just utility. The main reason the Tram Museum ended up in Bendigo is that this was one of the first towns to have electric trams—even before Melbourne—and it's one of the last to still use them.

After showing us around the museum, the enthusiastic tram driver/docent led us back to the marvelous old vehicle for the ride back to the mine and our waiting bus.

As we left town, Rod (our guide) pointed out a small pine tree on top of a building under construction. He said it is traditional to put the tree there to denote that the structure has reached its maximum height without any loss of life.

Even though the day grew darker as we traveled home, it did not detract from the beauty of the area through which we passed. The distant mountains rose in undulating ranks, dark blue-gray against the paler gray of the clouds. The green, rolling pastures were dotted with fat sheep. There were, as always, the magnificent, twisted gums. We passed old, weather-worn windmills and meandering streams, and startled sulphur-crested cockatoos, emus, and flocks of galahs.

As we passed through Wallan and headed for Beveridge, Rod informed us that we were in Kelly country. Though the majority of Ned Kelly's exploits occurred a bit east of here, this was where, in 1855, the famous bushranger* was born.

We drove back to Melbourne via the Hume Highway, which follows almost exactly the route taken by explorer

*See appendix

Hamilton Hume, for whom it is named.

Because the bus's route took it directly past the Royal Melbourne Hospital, I asked Rod if I could be dropped off there. So, at 6:30, I stepped off the bus into what had become a full-fledged downpour. I was pretty wet by the time I reached the hospital entrance, and both Judy and I were soaked through when we finally got to her car.

We went first to a little pub for a glass of wine and a chance to look at Judy's photos of our trips to the Red Centre and Kakadu. It often seems to be true that the heart takes better pictures than a camera. Of course, the camera is limited to what it can "see," and cannot record what we heard, felt, smelled, experienced. However, the pictures were sufficiently impressive to reassure me that my passion for the Territory is justified. Its glory has not been exaggerated by my mind through its distance. It really is that spectacular, that strangely beautiful.

Looking at the photos got both of us pretty geared up for next Thursday's reunion. Judy's pictures of Katherine Gorge and Mataranka didn't turn out, so I promised to send her copies of mine when I get home (assuming my pictures turn out).

We went to a delightful Indian restaurant, Shahnai, where Judy treated me to dinner. We chatted late into the night, then Judy drove me home.

Great day. Wonderful evening. Good friend.

Thursday, November 10

Today, I got mending, washing, and ironing done. I wrote for a while, getting caught up on my journal (a lot happened yesterday), and I read a lot.

The things I continue to learn about Australia always fascinate and often amuse me. For example: Australia is the flattest, driest country in the world, yet it has the second longest mountain range and fourth most extensive river system in the world. (I love a touch of irony in a country.)

Paging through the collected works of Adam Lindsay Gordon,* I came across a poem that took me back to those beautiful mornings in the Centre, when I awoke to flowering wattles and infinite blue sky.

> *In the Spring, when the wattle gold trembles*
> *'Twixt shadow and shine,*
> *When each dew-laden air draught resembles*
> *A long draught of wine:*
> *When the sky-line's blue burnish'd resistance*
> *Makes deeper the dreamiest distance,*
> *Some song in all hearts hath existence,—*
> *Such songs have been mine.*
>
> -from "A Dedication"

Indeed, such songs have been mine, as well and shall be mine again.

Friday, November 11

This morning, I caught the tram into town. A Greyhound bus passed us, and I wanted to be on it. Melbourne's nice, but life here is becoming too settled. I long to be on the move again.

I stopped at the Telecom center, to find a phone, and called home to see how my family is faring (all well and happy, I was pleased to hear). Next, I called Joyce, the

*See appendix

surgeon I met in Cooktown back in September, and made plans to meet her for lunch tomorrow.

Then I headed out into the day. I walked all over town, retracing the routes of several of my bus tours in order to examine and photograph the numerous spots we'd passed. I walked through Chinatown, up to Parliament, by the Mint, and around St. Patrick's Cathedral. Then I continued on to the Exhibition Building and Carlton Gardens, then down Latrobe Street and past the law courts. I crossed over to Queen Street and headed back down into the financial district for a shot of the beautiful, old ANZ Bank headquarters.

All that accomplished, I turned into Little Collins Street, for a visit to Lightning Ridge Opals, a place I'd seen advertised as having large collections of opals and deadly Australian fauna (a fairly odd combination, but I guess they're both things for which Australia is well known).

I watched a movie on opal mining that explained some of the attraction mining has, despite the harsh conditions. You're your own boss, you can start up with almost no working capital, and everything in the mining towns is extremely uncomplicated, if not exactly easy. Anyone can get a mining license, for a small fee. Then you are allowed to peg a claim (known as staking a claim in the U.S.) of approximately 100 square feet in opal country, and you can keep whatever you find.

The film included interviews with several miners, who noted that only about 10 percent of those who come out to dig really get fabulously wealthy. About 70 percent don't do too well and end up going home. The balance make a decent living—just enough to make it worth staying.

I perused the collection of crawlies, which included snakes, spiders, scorpions, a blue-ringed octopus, and some cone snails—all highly venomous denizens of various parts of Australia's land or sea. One instinctively avoids the first three, but the octopus was so small and the cone snails so lovely that one would not steer clear of them based on appearances alone.

After studying the critters, I moved on to the rocks. I looked at the opals for a short time, browsed through the seashells and butterflies also on display, then headed back out into the streets.

I wandered for a while longer, looking at and photographing places of interest. I had late tea at a sidewalk café in the "Paris end" of Collins Street, where some of Melbourne's more fashionable shops are located, then I continued on, enjoying the clear evening and the passing parade. It doesn't get dark until after 8 p.m., so it's especially nice to be out in the evening.

There are numerous street musicians in the malls and arcades. Most of them are youngsters with delusions of rock and roll grandeur. Some of them are poor souls who nearly break your heart, with their sad, innocent faces and air of loneliness, usually playing something like "Waltzing Matilda" on an accordion. One girl standing in the Block Arcade was playing Bach chamber music on a violin—and she was quite good. All this music added to the music of the city itself, as everyone took advantage of the warm, spring night.

Saturday, November 12

I got off the tram near Flinders Street Station and walked across Prince's Bridge to my 10:30 rendezvous at the Victoria Arts Centre. Gwinny soon arrived on the scene, and Joyce strolled up a few minutes later. We stopped first for a cup of coffee and a chance to catch up on what everyone has been doing since we were last together. Then we walked over to Symphony Hall, which is part of the Arts Centre complex, just in time to catch the tour.

Melbourne's Symphony Hall is designed around the concept of reflecting the state's natural wealth. The carpets represent the mineral rhodonite, a rich, deep rose-colored stone that gets darker as you dig deeper. Hence, the carpets on the upper floors are paler rose, and the color deepens as you descend to each consecutive level. The ceilings are covered in gold leaf, the walls, in soft, beige leather. Everything else is brass or glass or pink marble. A massive sculpture/light fixture rises nearly four stories through the center of the building. Made of brass, glass, and highly polished steel, it represents the magnified structure of a quartz crystal. In the main auditorium, there is extensive use of native woods, and the walls and seats are all colored to match the red to rose to brown hues of the rock formations in the area.

When the tour was finished, the three of us retired to the little, riverside restaurant at the Arts Centre. We enjoyed a leisurely lunch and much good conversation, then Joyce had to leave for a late afternoon appointment. I was sorry to say good-bye, but was glad I'd had the chance to see them again. I headed back to Flinders Street Station and caught a tram out to Essendon.

During the evening, Judy called to make sure Sue and I knew what the plans are for our Red Centre Reunion next week. She also invited me over to spend the day with her out in her garden tomorrow. It should be lovely.

Sunday, November 13

I stopped at the Queen Victoria Market to buy flowers for Judy. The market, begun more than 100 years ago, covers more than 16 acres, and alternates between glorious, fresh-air food market and, on Sundays, astonishing flea market. Fortunately, in both transformations, there are lots of flowers, so I had no trouble locating an armful. It was the one good thing that happened this morning.

Maybe it is indicative of my having been in the city for too long, but I found something of my old intolerance to delays rising in me as I found my efforts to reach Judy's house nearly foiled by the Metropolitan Transportation System. They had a whole new ticketing system being implemented today, with apparently endless fare changes and new rules. In their efforts to deal with the complexities of the new system, the conductors all seemed to have given up announcing streets or approaching transfer points. (The trams don't stop unless someone pulls the stop cord—charmingly old-fashioned, but vastly frustrating if you have no idea where you are.)

I spent 2-1/2 hours riding around, backtracking, asking befuddled conductors to make announcements that never came. My enjoyment of the tidy, tree-shaded suburbs through which we were passing began to dim. Finally, on my third tram, another passenger, realizing that the conductor had not announced the desired stop, pointed out the window and said, "Excuse me, Miss, but I think that's the tram you wanted." I thanked him, pulled the stop cord, and jumped off just in time to miss the other tram.

I think the conductor on the next tram could tell—was it my voice, my eyes, my clenched teeth—that it would be a good idea to make sure I didn't miss another stop. He was cheerful, sympathetic, and even stopped the tram right at

Judy's street, though it's not a regular tram stop. So, by the time I finally arrived at Judy's, my mood had improved considerably.

Judy and her housemate, Janice, were in the garden when I arrived. They had long since given me up as lost or not coming. As I related my tale of woe, Janice poured me a glass of wine, figuring I probably needed it.

Judy shares a large, beautiful, old, five-bedroom, Victorian house with four other people. It's a wonderful place, with lots of beveled and stained glass, amazingly high ceilings, marvelous bays and window seats, and shelves and niches everywhere.

After the house tour, we returned to the garden. We enjoyed wine, sunlight, and each other's company until 5 o'clock, at which time Judy had to go to work. Judy dropped me at the tram stop nearest the Royal Melbourne Hospital, and I headed home.

Monday, November 14

I've held seven different positions in four divisions of two major, international corporations, all in less than ten years. But that time has given me something much more important than a lengthy résumé—it has given me friends. One friend, Peter, the Australian representative at Kraft's U.S. headquarters, had introduced me to Ian, president of Kraft Australia. This morning I phoned Ian, to see if I could arrange to visit the Port Melbourne office, to see what the Australian operation is like.

Perhaps it seems that I am walking back into a world I fled, but this is not quite true. I did not flee business, I simply walked away. I do not hate it. On the contrary.

Business is like chess: a fascinating, complex game played with often-beautiful pieces. I am intrigued by it, love its trappings and its sideshows, admire the skill of the players and the beauty of the pieces and the playing board. But I don't play chess—I play Scrabble. I like words.

I remember seeing an ad on TV in which an attractive, white-haired man sat in an impressive office, behind a huge desk, and asked viewers, "Do you want to be where I am when you're my age?" The shudder that ran through my body let me know what I had denied for so long—I was in the wrong game. So now I go back as an outsider, to view a game I can love because my life no longer depends on the outcome.

Ian asked if I would be free tomorrow, then said he'd call me back. I got ready to face the day, then awaited Ian's call, which was soon in coming. The Kraft driver will pick me up at 9:30 tomorrow morning, and Ian will arrange a full day of meetings for me, so I can learn all about big business in Australia.

I headed into town to run some errands. At the foreign currency department of the ANZ Bank, I cashed my Christmas check from Mom and Dad. Then I wandered about, doing a little necessary shopping, and a lot of unnecessary browsing. I bought a basket of strawberries at a fresh-fruit stand near the Post Office, then hopped on the tram and headed back out to Essendon.

Tuesday, November 15

Climbing out of a sleeping bag and digging a navy blue business suit out of a heap of camping gear struck me as being wonderfully skewed—like a delightful game of

"What's wrong with this picture?"

The Kraft driver, Geoff, was at the door at 9:30, as promised. I followed him to the car and was whisked off to Kraft headquarters.

When I arrived, I was ushered into Ian's office, where tea was served. Ian's secretary brought me a copy of the official "Visit of Cynthia Clampitt" memo that had gone out to all the people I'd be meeting and outlined what I'd see.

After tea, I was introduced to Roger, who took me on a tour of the production facilities and the Physical Distribution Centre. The many different locations we visited necessitated a variety of protective clothing changes: lab coats, production room jackets, hair nets, hard hats, ear protectors, depending on the environment we were in (I've always liked playing "dress up"). I witnessed the production and packaging (which happens at astonishing speeds) of a tremendous range of products. I even saw Vegemite being made, in vats two stories high. I always love seeing the processes behind products.

One of the things that fascinated me was seeing the labels going on products—so many in foreign languages. Many different Oriental alphabets were in evidence, and a large percentage of processed cheese in tins was labeled in Arabic. Of course, because Australia's population is only around 16 million, larger companies must seek markets outside the country if they are to grow. Export trade is very important to Australian business.

Several members of the marketing staff, the editor of the employee paper, and some of the food scientists from research and development joined us at lunchtime and, over a pleasant meal, I heard about advertising, employee benefits (Australians generally get four weeks of vacation!), and the latest in nutrition science.

After lunch, I headed off with Rod, one of the marketing executives, to his office, where we discussed the amazing popularity within Australia of Vegemite (a savory, concentrated yeast extract used by virtually everyone for everything from spreading on bread to flavoring a stew). Rod got me a Vegemite T-shirt and a terrific Vegemite poster, which pleased me tremendously, as I really like Vegemite.

We talked about the difficulties of marketing products in a country of vast distances and small population. Heat, distance, and the fact that 70 percent of the country's milk is produced in only three months of the year, have made the ultra-high-temperature, long-life processing of milk more popular here than it is in the U.S. However, there is not as much regionalism as in the U.S., so marketing campaigns can usually be national.

At 3 o'clock, Geoff picked me up and drove me to the St. Kilda Road offices, where the finance and export divisions are located. I was greeted by (another) Ian, Director of Export Operations. Kraft Australia exports products to more than a hundred countries, and Ian showed me maps, ads, and brochures that underlined the extent of the operation. India, Japan, and the rest of the Orient are important markets for nearly all of Australia's large companies. The Middle East—another area where heat and distance present problems—represents another huge market segment. Throughout the Arab world, special packaging is used that incorporates information needed to satisfy Muslim law.

Next, I met with Bill, manager of sales for Victoria. We discussed the differences between selling in the U.S. and in Australia, the major difference being that, because of low population densities, a sales representative must cover a much larger territory. Hence, some reps are also private pilots.

I found the day immensely entertaining, but also very

informative. Knowing about a country's business puts the country in some sort of perspective. I've read a huge amount about Australian history, and experienced a lot of her wild, free present, but today I saw something of the practical side of Australia, the underlying gears and mechanisms. However, as delightful as it was, I was glad that I was an outside observer, glad that I could leave the underpinnings, the nuts and bolts, and escape back to the non-practical side of legends and Outback and wild, beautiful places—at least for the time being.

Wednesday, November 16

A basically uneventful day, cold and rainy, filled with little domesticities. The evening, however, was interesting. I took the tram downtown at about 6 o'clock, then walked over to the Southern Cross Hotel, where I met Colin, the gentleman who will be transporting me to the beginning of our ride this Saturday.

We were joined by Bradley, a business associate of Colin's, and Beth, Colin's lady fair. All three have been on these saddle safaris before and had brought along photographs of previous trips.

We ordered coffee. Then they talked about the mountains and horseback riding, while I perused their photos. The scenery looks spectacular, and the horses are impressive. My joy was not entirely undiluted, however, as they touched briefly on the subject of difficulty. It seems very likely that I'm getting in over my head. But, still, Colin and company were very enthusiastic about the upcoming trip. And the pictures were beautiful.

Thursday, November 17

I received a Christmas check from my brother, Darch, yesterday, and I stopped at the bank to cash it. Then I settled into serious hunting. I wanted to find something that will keep me warm and dry on the safari if the rain and cold keep up.

After a long search, I found a saddlery shop in Flinders Lane that carries riding gear. They had just what I wanted—oilskins. That is the generic name for traditional, oiled-cotton riding raincoats. In Australia, the two best-known brands are Drizabone and Claybourn, both of which names have become almost synonymous with the garment itself.

My coat, a Claybourn, is a wonderful, long thing, with a snapping rear vent that opens to go over, and protect, the saddle, and inside straps that snap around your legs, so your legs stay dry while you're riding. It's an amazing piece of clothing, and I simply adore the way it looks. It's not cheap, but well worth it if the weather remains inclement.

So now, at least I look ready for the riding trip. Since most of my "experience" is vicarious, rather than practical, I'm certain that there is much for which I'm unequipped. With boots called riding boots only by Lord & Taylor, and a hat and coat that I discovered through Australian movies, I've acquired the obvious externals. Fortunately (?), I'm determined (crazy) enough not to let my dreams, my passion for beauty, and my excitement over the nearly mythic connection between Australia and horses be overridden by the minor fact that my lack of experience probably disqualifies me for what I'm about to attempt.

I rushed home to change and get ready for the Red Centre Reunion. We met at 5:30 at the Southern Cross Hotel, for drinks and photo swapping. It was fabulous seeing the gang again. Besides Sue, Judy and me, Marge, John and Robyn were also on hand. Jeff couldn't make it because he's out in Perth, looking for a job.

It was wonderful seeing everyone's pictures. Some had gotten their photos developed at dealers offering two-for-one prices on prints, so we could take the duplicates of any shots we liked. This was particularly good for me, because I haven't seen any of my slides yet and am pleased to have some tangible evidence that everything really was as wonderful as I remember.

Dinner was at the Italian Waiters' Club. It was fun and noisy. We talked until about 10:30, trying to figure out how we'd get together again before the world ends. I invited everyone to visit me in Chicago, which they promised to do if they get to the States. Judy gave me a book titled *Dreamtime Heritage: Australian Aboriginal Myths* as a memento of our trip and friendship.

What a wonderful evening. What great people. What a life I lead.

Friday, November 18

I spent much of the day preparing for my trip. I ran into town to buy a birthday present for Sue, as it's her birthday today. I wrote a bit, packed, and planned to go to bed early, because I'll be up at 4:30 tomorrow morning. However, Steve, Sue's flatmate, turned on Spartacus at 10:30, and I got hooked. Oh, well—I'll be shot tomorrow, but it's a great film. And tomorrow—back into the wilderness.

Saturday, November 19–Thursday, November 24

I have done the most amazing things—beyond what I ever imagined myself doing. Traveling across Victoria's legendary High Country on horseback was harder than I had dreamed, and more wonderful. The mountains were glorious, and the riding, exciting, though I suspect I ran through about a two years' supply of adrenaline

On Saturday, I rose at 4:30 a.m. Fortunately, Sue had gone home for the weekend, so I didn't have to worry about waking her. I got dressed, finished packing, grabbed my hat, Claybourn, green duffel, and sleeping bag, and headed out the door. The walk to the tram stop was incredibly quiet—only the birds and I were up at that hour.

I caught the 5:30 tram into town, then caught a taxi, arriving at Colin's house in Cheltenham by 6:45. After (thank goodness) a cup of coffee, Colin and I packed our gear in the car, then went the rounds, picking up first Beth, then Bradley.

A three hour drive took us through the rolling, green Victorian countryside, then up into the hills and forests at the feet of the Great Dividing Range. Our group for the safari gathered at Licola, a tiny "town" that seems to exist only in a sort of "last chance" capacity—food and petrol for those about to disappear into the wilderness.

There were eleven riders in all, with a wide variety of backgrounds, and ages running from 19 to about 45. I was the only American and the least experienced rider of the group. My three months of lessons, which culminated in the rib-breaking fall just prior to my departure for Australia, were ranged against people who own horses, train horses, and even ride daily as part of their work. I was definitely out-classed here. This was not a bunch of weekend hacks out for a romp in the woods. This was a

bunch of hardcore riders out for the thrill of a lifetime.
Almost everyone had been on one or more of these adventures before. Of course, it added tremendously to my sense
of security and well-being when Judy, a veteran of many
saddle safaris, donned a crash helmet, noting cheerfully,
"My doctor said if I get injured again as badly as I did last
time—well, it would be the last time." (Despite this dis-
heartening introduction, Judy turned out to be both a good
friend and the source of most of the botanical information
I garnered on this trip.)

The eleven riders include Colin, who is the kind of rider
who can pick a flower at a dead gallop; Bradley and Beth,
both accomplished equestrians; Jenny and Lisa, sisters
from Melbourne, whose only difficulty was adjusting to a
saddle, as they usually ride bareback; Mary and Bob,
horse owners from near Melbourne; Judy of the white
crash helmet, also a local horse owner; Les, a rancher
from New South Wales; Carol, one of the few newcomers,
but still an experienced rider; and me. We were accompanied by trail boss Malcolm (Mal), who is blond, rugged,
handsome, and looks like he belongs here; and Mal's
young but skilled assistant trail bosses, Andrew and Marie.
Meeting us most nights with the truck was Debbie, Mal's
wife, a petite, vivacious, pretty brunette.

The only other group members were Rex and Huon.
Rex is a shelty and belongs to Mal and Debbie. He traveled with Debbie in the truck. Huon, a probable German
shepherd/labrador cross, belongs to Andrew and Marie.
He came with us, dashing madly back-and-forth all day
long, making sure everything was all right and that no
one got lost.

Soon after we arrived in Licola, an enormous trailer
bearing our horses passed us. We followed it about a mile

up the road, then helped unload and walk the horses. I grabbed my camera, and started shooting pictures of the horses, the clearing where they were tethered, and everything around us. It was a glorious day, and the surrounding mountains and trees sparkled with sunlight and promises.

Debbie soon arrived in the four-wheel-drive truck. She fed us a hearty lunch before stowing the last of our gear. I decided to let my camera equipment go in the truck, at least until I saw what kind of riding we'd be doing. It was a wise decision, and one I was forced to stay with for the duration of the trip. As much as I would have loved photos of this adventure, neither camera nor rider would have survived the experience.

After lunch, I was introduced to Ginger, a powerful, dark coppery-red gelding, who'd be my mount for the next six days. Ginger is a beautiful, good-natured animal, but spirited and very competitive. It was going to be a challenging relationship.

We were soon mounted and on our way. We walked our horses for a while, so we could get used to them, and vice versa. The Australian stock saddle took a little getting used to, too. It's built to keep you from sliding backward or forward when going up or down steep inclines. This is useful—vital, in fact—but it's a good deal different from anything I've ridden on before.

Mal explained, for the benefit of the newcomers, how to handle mountains. Going uphill, you stand in the stirrups, but crouching, with knees bent, so you're still close to the horse, you grab a handful of mane and hold yourself as far forward over the horse's neck as possible (not all that easy, especially if it's a long climb). Going downhill, you lie back in the saddle as far as you can, gripping the back of the saddle if necessary for balance. You don't want to

interfere with the horse's ability to climb or descend at
what it feels is the easiest pace and on the surest footing.
However, these are spirited animals, and they are excited
by the freedom of the mountains, so you need to maintain
some control, so your horse doesn't descend too quickly.

The mountains rose around us, craggy and dramatic.
Eucalypts of all sizes crowded the lower slopes. The air
was fragrant and clean. Snow-fed streams of incredible
clarity splashed and sang, and tumbled over cliffs.

We ascended the Bennison Spur, climbing over 4,000
feet, through the trees and up the steep, rocky side of the
mountain. It was a bit arduous, but the higher we climbed,
the more glorious the views became. We circled the top of
the Spur, clinging to narrow, rocky ledges, with the mountain dropping sheerly away inches from our horses'
hooves. The horses picked their ways carefully among the
boulders and trees.

We stopped momentarily at Bennison Lookout, to
admire the forests and the green and blue mountains below
and around us, stretching into the distance on all sides.
Then we climbed on.

Suddenly the trees parted, and before us lay an undulating field filled with thick tufts of snow grass, ground-hug-
ging bushes, and beautiful wildflowers. Open fields meant
mad canters. It was here I first discovered Ginger's competitive streak. If everyone is going fast, Ginger tries to go
faster. That first day, I was not strong enough to really
enjoy Ginger's tremendous power, so I merely hung on
like grim death as he swept past the other horses, his great
strides eating up the ground beneath us. But, as insecure as
I felt, I could still sense Ginger's pleasure in his own
speed, in the freedom of flying across that open field.

The pace slowed again as we got back into the trees.

The red tinge of new growth on the eucalypts gave an almost autumnal look to the forest. The air was perfumed with the wonderful, heady scent of flowering wattles, as well as other mountain flowers, mixed with the crisp fragrance of the eucalypts, and freshened by the breezes coming off the snow fields above us. My pleasure in all this natural beauty was immeasurably enhanced by the sheer romance of traversing this splendid country on horseback.

After four hours of riding, we topped a high crest that looked down on a narrow, green valley surrounded by rocky, scrub-covered hills and dark, fragrant forest. This was where we would camp for the night. Debbie had arrived ahead of us and already had a fire blazing and the billy boiling.

The drop down into the valley was fairly steep. I laid flat back in the saddle and gripped the cantle as firmly as possible, for balance. Riding is largely a matter of balance. However, I have an imbalance in the inner ear—i.e., no balance at all. I had learned to compensate by increasing my leg strength, but three months out of the saddle had seriously reduced that strength. About the only thing keeping me on that horse was stubbornness.

At the bottom of the hill we forded Shaw Creek, a clear, ice-cold mountain stream that runs across the plain. The horses were a bit skittish here. Normally, a horse prefers not to leap into a swiftly flowing stream unless it trusts its rider. Our horses didn't know us that well yet, but we managed to coax them over the bank, into the cold water, and up the other side—though it was, in my case anyway, more the promise of dinner than my skill as a rider that got Ginger to make the crossing. On the other side, the horses broke joyfully into a canter, heading without guidance straight for camp.

First thing to be done was tend to the horses. We took off their saddles, bridles, and blankets, hung the blankets out to dry, put on their rope halters, and took them down to the stream for a quick wash-down and a long, cool drink. Then we tethered them around the campsite and got them their well-deserved feedbags. After that, we grabbed our own gear and headed for our tents. I was billeted with Carol and Judy.

The dinner Debbie prepared was excellent, as were all the meals on the trip. It's amazing what you can turn out over an open fire with just a few buckets, a skillet, and a bit of imagination. After we finished eating, we all huddled around the campfire, wrapped warmly in our oilskins, talking, listening to Mal's tales of previous rides, as the temperature plummeted. We all hated to pull ourselves away from the fire to head for our freezing tents, but eventually we did. My nice little sleeping bag, which was perfect for the burning deserts and steaming Top End, was no match for the high-altitude evening chill. I didn't sleep much—but I did shiver a lot.

Sunday morning, we rose to find our surroundings white with frost. Our breath formed icy plumes in the crisp mountain air, as we clutched our cups of hot tea and coffee. My breakfast consisted of three heaping teaspoons of instant coffee and one teaspoon of drinking chocolate in a cup of hot water. This does not taste really terrific, but it sure wakes you up fast. Most of us were in varying degrees of pain, as even those who ride regularly rarely ride so strenuously.

After breakfast, I brushed down Ginger, then Colin showed me how to saddle and bridle him. The kind of riding we were doing necessitated numerous straps, which had to be wrapped around or secured to various parts of the saddle, horse, and cinch, to keep the saddle from sliding around when climbing or descending mountains or jumping. Ginger was acting coy, as he still wasn't sure who I was, but I managed to get him ready despite his dancing. Soon, we were on our way.

We rode for three hours, crossing fields and winding through dense thickets of slender, graceful sallee gums. We passed through increasingly glorious scenery, and a fair bit of snow, as we climbed to nearly 5,000 feet on Mt. Raymond.

As we rode, I acquired a new skill—jumping. Ginger loves to jump over things, will even go out of his way to jump over a tree or shrub. I got better at it as the days passed, but even then there were good jumps and bad jumps. If they took you by surprise, or were tricky, they could be unnerving. But a good, clean jump while cantering down the track became a real pleasure. That first time, however, I didn't think I'd make it. I'm certain I left nail marks in the saddle.

Just before lunch, after jumping a stream, Blondie, a big, feisty palomino mare, got annoyed at Barrister and Ginger for being so close behind her, and she lashed out with her rear hooves. Barrister (Marie's mount) jumped sideways, and Ginger reared. I had never been on a rearing horse before, and I was not on the rearing horse for long. I fell hard, landing on my left shoulder. It took me a second or two to catch my breath—about as long as it took Andrew to catch my horse. I was pleased that my ribs had held up—but I don't even want to think about what I've done to my shoulder.

Speaking of Blondie's feistiness, it was interesting, as days passed, to learn each horse's quirks and mannerisms—each one has such a distinct personality. All the horses are pretty spunky, but some are more aggressive than others. Dollar and Ginger don't get along well. Blondie is always annoyed with someone, but it changes from day to day. Flash, Judy's mount, wants to run all the time. He's one of the fastest horses in the group—probably second only to Malcolm's mount. Samboe, Buck, and Ginger like to jump, but Bobby hates jumping. Tex is the most laid-back of the horses—almost nothing bothers him.

Ginger will not tolerate being passed on the left. I can always tell if another horse is moving up on our left, because Ginger's ears flatten back, he pulls at the reins, snorts, starts dancing, his front hooves pawing the air, as he prepares to defend his flank. (It makes you wonder what dark secrets are hidden in his past.) When walking, Ginger will follow, but trotting or cantering, he wants to get out in front. And Ginger loves to eat. Offer him a handful of oats and he'll follow you anywhere.

We had our picnic lunch on a hillside bordering the Mt. Raymond snow plain, a rolling expanse of lush, green snow grass bisected by a clear, blue stream. We sat among the snow gums and yellow mountain flowers. The snow-capped peak of Mt. Howitt rose serenely in the distance. The sky was cloudless and blue. The fragrance of wattle filled the air. The only sounds were the breeze coming across the plain, the cries of birds, and the horses cropping the thick grass around the trees where they were tethered.

The afternoon held another four hours of riding. We continued to alternate rambles through the woods with canters across open fields. About half way through the afternoon, at Mal's urging, I attempted and successfully cleared a fairly high jump (middle of Ginger's chest, so I'm guessing 3 to 3-1/2 feet). It was a good, clean jump. Mal talked

me through it, and I was quite pleased that I made it.
When I looked back, I saw some of the more experienced
riders going around the jump—too tough, especially on a
narrow, mountain track. Oh, well, ignorance is bliss.
Besides, I don't believe Mal would lead me astray. I think
he just likes to see riders push themselves a little. Mal
playfully taunted the abstainers with the fact that I, a mere
novice, had made the jump. It may have added nothing to
my skill as a rider, but it built my confidence a bit.

By late afternoon, we reached Bryce Gorge, a rugged
gash in the mountains, where trees and scrub cling to
steep, broken, almost perpendicular stone walls. A waterfall poured over one shattered cliff, a silver stream dropping hundreds of feet to another ledge, plummeting again,
then disappearing into the shadows. We stopped at the
edge of a sheer cliff, and stood, facing the waterfall,
enjoying the beauty of the spot.

We rode back out of the trees, then cantered the length
of a narrow, green valley, pulling up at last near Guy's
Hut, one of the famous, High Country cattlemen's huts
built near the turn of the century. The quaintly rustic hut
sat at the base of a forested hill, on the edge of a velvety,
green field, which was cut in half by a clear but rocky
stream. On the far side of that stream, Debbie waited once
more, with the billy already on the fire.

I peeled myself, painfully, off Ginger's back, and soon
had him unsaddled and down at the stream for a wash. We
then enjoyed another cordial evening around the fire
before heading once more for our freezing tents. If I ever
do this again, I'm buying one of those alpine, down-filled
sleeping bags. The one I have now just isn't designed to
deal with this much cold, and neither am I.

Monday dawned clear and bright, and the sun pouring down on the tent warmed it quickly. As we started to get ourselves organized for the day, Mal came over and announced that everyone would be coming back to Guy's Hut for lunch, so those of us who'd like to could stay in camp. Five of us opted for this, using the warm, sunny morning as the perfect opportunity to run downstream and wash hair, persons, and items of clothing. The water was too cold to use straight, so I took half a billy of boiling water and mixed it 50/50 with the icy stream water. Not wanting to get any soap in the crystalline creek, we stayed well away from the stream edge as we washed.

I took a long walk, trying to stretch out my legs. I saw two brilliant, red parrots—crimson rosellas, I would imagine—which surprised me. I would not expect to see parrots in this chilly a climate. As I continued walking I was struck, again, with the incredible beauty and profusion of flowers. Their honeyed scent, noticeable even when we were riding, filled the air. I have become particularly fond of the fragrance of wattle, a beautiful member of the acacia family.

After a while, I just lay down in the sun and rested, having not gotten much sleep the three preceding nights.

Everyone returned at 1 o'clock for lunch, after which I saddled up Ginger in preparation for the afternoon's ride. Mal went with Debbie in the truck, so Andrew led our intrepid band. Being somewhat younger and more exuberant (and less experienced) than Mal, Andrew conducted a rather gung-ho ride.

Actually, there wasn't any problem until we came to a long, wide, hilly, open area and everyone took off in sort of generally, but not quite the same direction, but with no one in particular leading. Ginger took the signal and took off like a bullet. We were headed downhill, so I was slightly off balance. One of the horses in front of us wheeled sharply to the right, and another wheeled to the left. Ginger started going to the right, then suddenly swerved to the left, but I kept going to the right. It was a beautiful fall, though. I hit the ground, did a forward roll, and came up on my feet—didn't even lose my hat. The only pain I was feeling was in my right hand. The cloth reins sizzling through my fingers on my way down had stripped the skin and a good deal of what lay under it from the bottom of a couple of fingers. (I was glad I had a pair of leather gloves in my duffel—by the next morning my hand was so sore I couldn't close my right fist. The leather gripped the reins better than I could.)

I got up on Ginger, and Andrew teased me about having gotten my once-a-day fall out of the way. I jammed my feet forward in the stirrups, and determined that, even if it killed me, I would not come off my horse again. (I had a few close calls, with tricky jumps and unyielding tree limbs, but I did manage to stay mounted for the rest of the trip.)

We took off on another mad canter. The scenery remained glorious, though clouds had begun to gather. Despite my discomfort, my love for horses and the romance of riding was undiminished. As we flew across the open fields, I could hear the theme from the film *The Man From Snowy River* playing in my head. I was beginning to feel at home in the saddle. My strength was still minimal, but I was no longer saddle sore.

A little after 5:30, we came roaring into camp, about a mile from Kelly's Hut, another famous, High Country locale. It was pouring rain, but we were safe and dry in our oilskins, which you always carry tied to the front of your saddle, because the weather in the mountains is unpredictable.

We were again camped in beautiful surroundings, by the side of a crystal-clear stream. Although it was raining, we still had to wash down the horses, then, because there is a cattle fence running around the valley, we let the horses go. A little more work, and soon the feedbags were ready. Mal stood at the edge of camp and let out a yell that echoed through the surrounding hills. In a few minutes we heard the thundering of hooves, growing louder and nearer, until suddenly our horses all topped the ridge of the hill, manes flowing in the breeze, heads tossing, pounding down the paddock toward dinner. It was one of the most beautiful things I've ever seen.

When the horses were cared for, we went about getting ourselves settled in. My boots were pinching slightly, so I exchanged them for thongs. As I approached the huddle of figures around the campfire, Bradley looked up, grinned and declared, "There stands a dinkum Aussie—wearing a Snowy River hat, oilskins, and thongs!" Though I was fully aware of the fact that the combination looked more absurd than authentic, I believe that Bradley somehow understood how pleased I was by the remark.

Tuesday morning, to my infinite joy, the scene from the previous evening was repeated, as the horses came in for their morning feed. They were, in fact, even more breathtaking than the night before, as they flew across the fields in the morning light, their coats glistening in the sun.

We dressed and got ready quite judiciously, as the truck would not be meeting us that night. We loaded Tex with the packs for food, matches, horseshoes, nails, and various other necessities. Then we strapped our bedrolls to the backs of our saddles, tied our oilskins to the fronts, clipped our tin cups to the sides, and set off.

We rode for three hours through the forest and across luxuriant, green alpine fields bordered by snow gums. Snow gums are wonderful trees, with broad, smooth, twisting trunks. Streaked in muted shades of green, brown, cream, rust, gold, and tan, they look almost like Impressionist paintings.

We stopped for lunch near the entrance of a state park. A large sign nearby proclaimed, "Snow Year 'Round— Blizzards March through November." That was encouraging. After eating, I went for a stroll through the wildflowers. I was knee deep in buttercups, alpine daisies, purple eyebright, and golden billy buttons as I wound between the twisting trees and flowering wattles. It was wonderful. Then it was time to get under way.

Several more hours of riding brought us to the peak of Mt. Wellington, which is about 5,500 feet high. One runs out of superlatives when trying to describe the scene that lay before us. In one direction, there were billowing white clouds and blue sky, with silvery shafts of sunlight pouring down on the mountains below. In the opposite direction, the clouds were black and heavy, and we could see the rain pouring down like dark, shimmering curtains, and the lightning flashing and dancing across the face of the storm. Below us and in front of us, white mist drifted in the valleys between blue and purple mountains. It was awesome, majestic, glorious.

Around us, on the treeless peak, jagged, lichen-covered outcrops of gray stone stuck out at sharp angles, like ancient tombstones or crumbling fortress walls. Low shrubs grew between the jutting rocks. The vegetation became denser along the mountain's flanks, sweeping away from us on all sides in an all-engulfing torrent of green.

All too soon, we had to leave our inspiring perch, to avoid being caught so exposed by the approaching storm. Within half an hour, we were being pelted with cold rain and hail. The fields became white with hailstones. I was surprised that the horses took the storm so calmly, but I guess they're accustomed to the fluctuations of weather in the mountains.

It was almost another hour before we got to Miller's Hut (yet another cattleman's hut). Miller's Hut is an ancient, drop-log style cabin, with a ramshackle fireplace that's almost half the size of the hut. Logs have been braced against one side of the hut, to keep it from sliding downhill. There is a mud floor, with a gutter running down the center to carry water through and out of the hut. The location is beautiful, with huge, old gum trees, saw grass, wildflowers. Thorny vines covered with pink blossoms, which looked like some sort of wild, climbing rose, festooned many of the trees and shrubs. Nearby, there were numerous wombat holes, though the shy, chubby creatures stayed out of sight.

We tethered our horses along the wooden rails of the rustic corral in front of the hut. We quickly got the saddles off the horses and under cover, safe from the rain. Then we all went in search of firewood. Once a substantial pile was accumulated, and a fire was blazing, I wandered back outdoors to see how Ginger was doing. There was almost no grass near the horses, so, because Ginger is so fond of eating, I gathered an arm-load of the tall, shiny, dark green, jagged-edged saw grass that Ginger likes so much, then headed back to the corral. Ginger snorted a greeting when I approached and nuzzled my arm before happily gobbling down all the greenery. It wasn't a lot of food—but I felt better.

The rain began to let up, so we got a fire going outdoors, escaping the smoky hut. We ate around the cheerful blaze, and talked until well after dark.

I was in a lot of pain from my earlier fall, and having trouble moving my arm. Beth kindly volunteered to put some horse liniment on my shoulder. For what it smelled like, it should have helped a lot more than it did.

Malcolm mentioned that he thought I'd be having an easier time if I had kept up my riding while traveling around Australia. I explained that this had been impossible due to my broken ribs. Marie asked how I'd broken them, and I replied that it had been in a horse riding accident. This elicited a low whistle and the comment, "Boy, you're game." (That's a different word than my mother used.) I had suddenly acquired a new and more respectable status—I was a battler, a diehard, not just some ill-equipped tourist. Mal and Andrew launched into a litany of further challenges I could tackle—skiing, mountain climbing, other riding trips—because obviously I was crazy enough to not quit while I was ahead.

When it was time to bed down for the night, Judy and I decided to sleep indoors. We rolled out our swags, and I threw four big logs on the fire, trying to get the hut's single room warm. Before much longer, bodies were spread all over the floor of the tiny hut—only those with magnificent, high-altitude bags slept outside, under the trees and finally clearing sky.

Wednesday morning dawned bright and cold. We all stood around the fire, waiting till the sun had climbed high enough to thaw us out. By the time we were all saddled up and ready to go, my oilskins were rolled up and tied onto my saddle, as the sun poured down on us, warming us despite the coolness of the mountain breeze.

It was to be a day of truly wild riding. After about four hours of rambling up and down, winding through glorious, dense woods, trotting down stony tracks, cantering across open fields, we came to the top of the descent to Lake Tarli Karng. It was a very steep drop, and before long Mal told us to dismount and lead our horses. The sleeping bags strapped to the backs of our saddles made a standard dismount difficult, so I thought I'd try (as had several other riders) the slightly flashier leg-over-the-horse's-head-and-jump dismount. It is not wise to attempt this for the first time if you are on the side of a mountain. I hit a stone at a strange angle, it gave way, and my knee slammed into the rocks. I tied up Ginger's reins and just let him walk/slide down on his own, because I couldn't keep up with him. All things considered, I made pretty good time on the descent, though I was the last one down and remounted.

We were not far from the lake, so we rode only a little longer, right to the edge of the deep, beautiful tarn. It was lunchtime, so we dismounted, tethered the horses, and loosened their girths. One of the horses had lost a shoe, so Mal reshoed him during the break. Meanwhile, I soaked my swelling knee in the icy water of the lake.

Tarli Karng is a magnificent spot. The sheer, densely wooded cliffs rise up dramatically, almost perpendicularly, on all sides. The red, pale green, and gold of fresh, new, spring leaves splashed the forest with color. The water of the lake, which is extremely deep, is so dark a blue as to appear almost black. Flowering shrubs fringed the clearing where we stopped to boil our billy and crowded between the wonderful, huge, old trees that surrounded us. Overhead, above the tree tops, shimmered a cloudless, blue sky, and sunshine poured into the deep valley.

The ascent was more exciting than the descent had been—stand in the stirrups, grab a handful of mane, and hit the wall at a dead canter. We went straight up. It was great. It's amazing how strong and sure-footed those horses are, surging over rocks, powering up inclines you'd hardly tackle on foot.

After another hour of riding we had to dismount again (more carefully this time), because the track was again too steep for the horses to descend with a mounted rider. It was a bit arduous, trying to keep pace with the horses without falling down the mountain.

We forded a stream and found ourselves in the middle of a group of campers. We chatted with them as we remounted. They thought the horses looked like a great way to travel. Then Mal, who has a great sense of the dramatic, kicked his horse, and with a loud "Hyah," took us straight up the steep, rugged wall facing the camp. Talk about impressing the poor pedestrians.

When we got to level ground, we began our usual mad canter. This time, however, the bush was dense, and we were being lashed by tree branches. Fortunately, Colin and Bradley had made a chinstrap for my hat from a piece of bailing twine, or I would have lost it in the trees. I almost lost my face.

I tried to keep my head down as far on Ginger's neck as possible, but I kept looking up, because I was afraid he would try to jump something, or strike off down an even worse path in an effort to pass the lead horses. I took a fairly bad beating, but I didn't pull Ginger up till I saw the lead horses stop. We paused for a moment, to wait for stragglers and count the wounded. I was one of three with slashed noses. I'd accumulated numerous other cuts and bruises, as well (fortunately, most of them hidden by my clothing). Everyone had some scratches or bumps, but the better the rider, the fewer the abrasions. Malcolm was almost totally unscathed.

We plunged merrily onward, meandering through the wonderful forest, following narrow paths along the mountains' sides, trotting down winding tracks. The day continued to be beautiful and bright, and beams of sunlight filtered through the trees and danced along the streams. We rarely spoke, just rode and listened to the sounds of the forest and our horses' hooves.

We had a few more mad canters, forded a few rivers, and finally descended a steep track and crossed the Wellington River. Nearby, Debbie and the truck were waiting for us. There was a fenced paddock, so, after unsaddling and washing down the horses, we could turn them loose. I loved watching them playing in the green grass, running, dodging, tossing their heads, then dashing toward the fence nearest camp to see if their feed bags were ready.

After the horses were cared for, we pulled off our boots and ran down to and into the river. The wide, clear, rock-strewn stream was flanked with great, flowering bushes on one side, and rugged stone walls on the other. The mountains rose up all around us, beautiful, green, protective.

The water was cold, but delightfully refreshing. Rex and Huon joined joyously in the splashing. Rex, particularly, likes swimming. He can spend any amount of time in the water, walk out and, even as he shakes off the wetness, have someone say, "Hey, Rex, let's go in the water, boy," and the beautiful shelty leaps up, looks around with an expression of "What a great idea—why didn't I think of it?" and sprints back into the stream. This happened about a dozen times before Rex decided that sleeping by the fire sounded better than swimming again.

Much invigorated by the chilly water, we all bustled about with renewed energy as we collected firewood and got a fire started. Then we gathered around the blaze for the evening meal. Bradley was greeted by a mixture of hoots and applause when he emerged from his tent in clean, white slacks. The contrast was pretty dramatic between his pristine attire and the grubby clothing the rest of us were wearing. His efforts were greatly appreciated by all, however.

It was a glorious evening, crisp and clear, but not so cold, as we were at a much lower altitude than on previous nights. Between the towering gum trees I could see a great expanse of sky brilliant with innumerable stars. The air was remarkably fresh—makes you wish you could breathe more up there and stockpile it for later when you're back in civilization. In the starlight, I could see the horses moving in the paddock. The sound of water running over rocks drifted up to us as we sat around the fire. Late in the evening, Debbie made damper, and we sat and talked, ate damper and drank billy tea until nearly midnight.

Thursday morning, I found it difficult to rouse myself. The combination of a relatively warm night, a lot of fresh air, and my being rather tired produced a deep, sweet slumber from which I did not entirely wish to wake. But a cup of strong coffee, combined with the bright, clear crispness of the morning, brought me around.

When I went to catch Ginger, he saw me coming and waited patiently for me. He nuzzled me as I untangled his bit and bridle, and accepted it easily when I slipped it on him. He was really beautiful, standing there in the morning sun. He's a wonderful horse. I shall miss him terribly.

I could hardly believe that I was tying my oilskins onto

my saddle for the last time. Though I had enough cuts and bruises to testify to the fact that I had been through a lot, it seemed as if the week had evaporated like water on a hot iron.

Malcolm was determined to make the last day the most memorable one. After walking just long enough to warm up the horses, we were off on a wild dash up and down the mountains and valleys.

We descended a slope through a thick tangle of trees and brush. This time the trees were a blessing, as the incline was so steep that the branches pressing in on all sides helped the horses keep their footing, and kept me in my saddle. At the bottom of this descent, Mal made a spectacular leap into the river below. At least it sounded spectacular. We were still pretty well tangled in the foliage. The next rider over the cliff was not so fortunate. I didn't see that, either, but I heard the yell, splash, and ensuing sounds of rider swimming back to horse. Another rider tried the jump, with the same results. Mal decided that it was time to try another launch point, so he directed the remaining horses a few yards up stream, where the bank was a little closer to the water level, giving us a fair chance of making the jump and retaining our mounts.

We crossed streams frequently, once getting in well over our stirrups. Cantering and jumping made up a major portion of the morning's ride. Once, when the group broke into a canter, Ginger and I got stuck behind Blondie, who was not keeping up with the rest. When the trail widened momentarily, Ginger swept past the palomino as if she were standing still. Ginger's hooves thundered on the ground, as his powerful stride quickly closed the gap between us and the lead horses. I think it was the first time I took as much pleasure in Ginger's speed as he did.

Our surroundings continued to be glorious. Far different from the rocky grandeur of the higher peaks, the beauty at this lower altitude was attributable to the many streams, the greater diversity of trees and flowering shrubs, and the masses of ferns that closed in on all sides, cool and green and lush.

Around noon we stopped at the MacAlister River, where we swam or waded, depending on our degree of abandon. It was a perfect day: warm, sunny, silken. We dried ourselves in the sun before mounting up once again.

We raced through the trees and across fields of stirrup-deep grass and Scottish thistles. Ginger easily cleared the fallen trees that often lay across our path and leapt unhesitatingly into the streams we crossed. His long mane whipped in the wind as we flew across the rolling, green hills.

We cantered into our lunch site at 3 o'clock. As we were only 40 minutes out of Licola, the truck was there to meet us. We were also joined by Judy's and Carol's husbands, who had spent the day fishing while waiting to collect their wives. The spot where we stopped was at the edge of an open field lush with tall grass and wildflowers. A clear stream gurgled merrily close by. We were surrounded by old, gnarled gum trees, and nearby stood an ancient, weatherworn windmill.

We cantered most of the way to Licola, at which place we arrived much too soon. We yarded the horses, loosened their girths, and bid a sad, fond farewell to them before walking into town.

It was a while before Debbie and the ute arrived with our gear. We traded addresses as we waited. Judy, who had brought along a marvelously unobtrusive little camera that fit into shirt pocket or saddlebag, promised to send me photos of the many places I'd been without my own camera. Many members of the group were already making plans for return trips.

Mal came over and congratulated me on having made it to the end—he never thought I'd finish the ride. He told me that last year a group of six New York journalists, all men, had arranged a similar trip, and had called a halt to it only two hours into the ride. He'd been certain I'd do the same. Now, he said he reckoned I was the only American writer he knew who'd successfully taken on the High Country.

By 5 o'clock, I and my gear were packed into Jenny and Lisa's car (I discovered they live near Essendon) and we were ready to leave. Great, white clouds rose up behind the mountains around us, billowing against the brilliant sky. The sun poured down in wide, golden shafts that danced across the blue and green mountains.

It was a beautiful drive, down from the forested mountains, through the rolling foothills, and across miles of lush grazing land—although we all felt a little strange (and a little uncomfortable) sitting in a car. I missed Ginger already, and the three of us wanted to turn around and go back.

As we saw more and more cars and got closer to civilization, I found it difficult to accept the traffic and noise and buildings. Everything had been so serene in the mountains, so uncomplicated, so beautiful. I shall, of course, readjust to the city again. But I shall never stop longing for the beauty and joy of the wild places.

Friday, November 25

When I got home last night, Steve, an Aussie Rules football player, actually paled at the sight of me and said I looked like a social services poster for abused children.

Sue was upset about how extensive the bruising was. One massive bruise, where a branch slammed point first into my upper arm, not breaking off till it hit bone, is particularly frightful looking. Sue gave me a tube of cream for serious bruises and blood clots, which did a remarkable job overnight on some of the lesser bumps, though it will take a while to heal the bigger injuries. It's good to have a friend who's a pharmacist, to help things along.

I slept late this morning, in an attempt to recover from this adventure before I start my next one (I leave for Tasmania tomorrow). I have never been so tired and so hurt before. I'm glad I did it, though. I have gained much in strength and confidence.

I miss the mountains, the horses, the beauty, and to these I wish to return. I dreamed of crossing the mountains on horseback, and I've done it—and I still love the dream. But success always has a price. This time, pain was part of the process, part of proving I could do it, part of the cost.

I have discovered that there is a certain honesty to physical danger that is lacking in more civilized threats. There were moments on the trip when I actually feared for my life—and it was easier to deal with than fearing for my job during the last corporate realignment I underwent. Things are real out there, and I think the taste of reality has become as important to me as the beauty of my surroundings. No "attitude adjustment hour," no stress management or escapist behavior. As soon as the dangerous cliff is behind you, it is forgotten, and there is only the trail ahead.

I was awakened this morning by a long-distance call from Mom, Dad, Darch, and Margaret (my sister-in-law), wishing me a Happy Thanksgiving and checking to see if I'm still having a good time. I said I was. Darch immediately picked up on the change. He said my voice sounded strong, more confident (I thought I just sounded tired), and he demanded details. Darch, as an artist, stays pretty close to the edge, so he's a great cheerleader when that's where you're living. Mom and Dad are very supportive, but they are parents, and they worry about their "little girl," so I spared them a lot of details from this last jaunt.

It was hard doing much today besides sleeping. I addressed a few Christmas cards, worked on my journal, but mostly just drifted in and out of sleep.

Fortunately, I was well enough rested by evening to accept Sue's invitation to go to the trots (harness racing) with her and John. John got me an Honorary Membership at the track, so I could get into the members' lounge. We were joined by Bobby and Pam (John's friends), whom I was glad to see again.

We had dinner in the lounge, adjourning to the stands whenever a race was being run. The horses were heart-breakingly beautiful, and it made me want to be riding again. But it was enough to watch, which we did till the last race at 11 p.m. Then we headed home.

WALTZING
TASMANIA

Saturday, November 26

My first impression of Tasmania, as I flew over her this morning, was GREEN. Below me were green fields and forests, verdant grazing land and prosperous farms. There were also purple mountains and blue lakes, but mostly it was green.

Tasmania, Australia's island state, was discovered in 1642 by Abel Janszoon Tasman, greatest of the Dutch navigators and explorers. Physically, the island is actually part of the Great Dividing Range, the mountains that run along the entire eastern coast of the mainland. In it's earliest days, until the name was changed in 1856, Tasmania was known as Van Diemen's Land, after the governor of the East Indies who had sent Tasman on his voyage of exploration.

I was met at the airport by Blue, the latest of my camping safari coach captains. We picked up the balance of our group in town (eleven in the group), then went on a tour of Launceston.

Launceston, named for the Cornish birthplace of Philip King, governor of New South Wales, was settled in 1804. The city lies in a green valley where the North and South Esk Rivers meet to form the River Tamar. Today, with 65,000 inhabitants, it is Tasmania's second largest city.

Though proclaimed a city in 1888, Launceston still has the feel of a quaint village, with its numerous parks, old

churches, and rows of sensible, 19th-century, stone buildings, so solid and English. The town has an air of timelessness to it, a charming antiquity that makes you feel as
though you've entered another era.

Despite its antiquity and smallness, Launceston was the
first city in the Southern Hemisphere, and one of the first
in the world, to have a hydroelectric power station. The
station here was opened in 1895.

Outside Launceston, we were immediately surrounded
by farming and grazing land more reminiscent of rural
England than an island in the South Pacific. The rolling,
green hills and fields were dotted with woolly cream-puff
Merino sheep. Rows of hawthorn bushes outlined fields
and roadways everywhere. The dense, prickly hawthorns
were planted during Tassie's convict days, as natural
restraining barriers.

Our first stop was at nearby Cataract Gorge, a deep,
rugged gorge cut by the South Esk River. Wildflowers
crowded between the boulders and showered down the
steep cliff faces of the gorge. Far below, the river foamed
over tumbled rock, then emptied into a broad basin. The
wide lawns around the basin were, like the water, filled
with people enjoying the location and the splendid weather.

A few members of our group stretched out on the lawn.
Others boarded the Launceston Basin Chairlift, billed as
the longest single chairlift span in the world, 1500 feet of
cable suspended above the gorge. I wandered alone up the
footpath, climbing along the edge of the gorge, among the
dark boulders with their floral crowns and cascades. I took
photos with great abandon, no doubt venting some of my
pent-up frustration over having been without my camera
for most of the horse-riding trip.

Departing the gorge, we headed for Entally House at

Hadspen. Built in 1820, this was one of the area's earliest grand estates. Originally situated on a more than 3,000-acre property, the house now sits in the midst of the last remaining 10 acres, the rest having been sold to neighboring farms.

Entally House has the wide verandas and sloping roofs typical of Australian colonial homes. The large, handsome, main house looks out over wide lawns, with a view toward the nearby hills. Everything necessary for a country gentleman's comfort was included in the estate compound: English gardens, greenhouse, stables, carriage house, chapel, blacksmith shop, servants' quarters, and an ivy-covered stone wall surrounding the great, cobbled yard behind the owner's residence.

Much of the original furniture remains. The children's room is filled with old dolls and toys. The music room, drawing room, and dining room are elegantly furnished, mostly with fine English pieces. In the drawing room, a guide showed us a wonderful chest of drawers that contains several secret compartments. It works like a puzzle box, to make breaking in difficult—necessary, because most of the servants were convicts.

The estate's long, tree-lined drive led us out to a narrow country road, and we continued on our way. As the sun at last began to dip toward the ragged, green horizon, we pulled into our evening's campsite. This camping trip will be a bit more civilized than others I've been on. We'll be sleeping in tents, but we'll be at a campground every night, with showers, toilets, cooking facilities. I guess I can tolerate a little convenience.

The group is mixed. Our guide, Blue, is Tasmanian to the core. ("Blue," by the way, is a very traditional Aussie nickname, normally given to men with red hair.) Joe and

Frieda are of Austrian birth, but have been Australians for 25 years. Beryl, from Sydney, is traveling with her 11-year-old (as of this Friday) son, Paul. Kay and Mary are both 19 and are Melbournians. Huntley and Jill, from Canberra, are traveling with Chrissy, 17, who is the youngest of their four daughters. Stephanie is a slightly flaky but very chic 20-year-old. It is a congenial crowd.

Sunday, November 27

We rolled across the verdant Tasmanian countryside, passing through the quaint, old, coach-stop town of Carrick, where rustic, stone buildings line the rough, narrow main street. As we drove, green fields gave way to hills.

Climbing upward, through increasingly dense forest, we came before long to the Tasmanian Wildlife Sanctuary. The grounds of the sanctuary were teeming with cockatoos, kangaroos, and wallabies. Animal treats were on sale there, so again I filled my pockets and walked out among the animals.

Most of the wallabies had joeys. The wallabies are only two to three feet high, so the babies peeking out of mamas' pouches are tiny. The gentle, beautiful, little creatures approached eagerly, snuffling toward my pockets, grasping my fingers with their tiny front paws as they ate out of my hand.

I entered the broad, grassy enclosure where the wombats wandered. (They have their own area to limit their excavating.) These delightful, funny little animals have short, thick, muscular necks, which make it impossible for them to look up, so when they beg for food, they simply trot up and stare at your ankles, and wait for you to bend down to their level. They don't look quite real—sort of a cross between a woodchuck, a bear cub, and a footstool. I've seen stuffed, acrylic-plush wombats that looked as realistic as the actual creatures.

I headed for the nocturnal house, where, in the dim, artificial twilight, I could see animals that are normally active only at night. As I entered, I could hear the Tasmanian devils screaming, snarling, and making noises worthy of their names. They weren't fighting or upset—the horrible shrieking and roaring is just normal "conversation."

The animals are housed in settings as close to natural as possible—mostly forest or scrubland surroundings. However, the "natural habitat" of the brush-tail possum was a group of garbage cans behind a house porch. That's real adaptation. I saw ring-tail possums, Eastern bettongs (rat kangaroos, which, though only about one foot tall, can jump more than seven feet in the air), sugar gliders (gliding possums—like flying squirrels), a pair of tawny frog-mouths (I love the name—they're broad-beaked, gray-brown birds of prey that look like dead branches when they stretch out their necks and assume their defensive "disappearing" pose), an Eastern quoll (native "cat"—a marsupial that looks a bit like a spotted possum—has up to 26 young per litter, but has only six teats in its pouch, so only the strongest survive), Tasmanian pygmy possums (really tiny—you could get several in one hand), long-tailed marsupial rats, and a baby barred bandicoot. All are native to Tasmania; some occur nowhere else.

Outdoors again, I wandered among the tall trees that surround and are part of the sanctuary. Below, green fields spread away from the bottom of the hill on which the sanctuary perches, and in the distance, the forest-clad mountains rose up toward the cloudless blue sky. Wrens and finches, some of them as bright as jewels, flitted through the trees.

I sat on a low, wooden bench, just to enjoy the view, but was soon interrupted by the gentle pressure of a wallaby's nose on my shoulder. Two wallabies stood, watching expectantly, batting their long eyelashes, as I dug into my pockets for more treats.

I photographed echidnas (spiny anteaters—funny, little, hedgehog-like creatures that look like their hind feet are on backwards), potoroos (diminutive, rodent-faced, kangaroo-legged marsupials), wombats, and the ubiquitous cockatoos.

A dozen Tasmanian devils occupied a large enclosure at the sanctuary's center. Because this was outdoors, in full daylight, the nocturnal devils were asleep, draped across rocks, curled under bushes, nestled together in small clusters.

Tasmanian devils are small, about the size of a terrier, but have long teeth and powerful, locking jaws. They are basically scavengers, as they are not remarkably swift of foot, but they do hunt, sometimes catching animals as big as wallabies. However, they really owe their names and reputations to the insanely wild screaming/choking/snarling/roaring sounds they make, which, on a dark night, if you didn't know what they were, would leave no doubt in your mind that the very gates of Hell had been opened.

A member of the sanctuary staff climbed over the stone wall and dropped into the enclosure. Whether it was her presence or the bucket of food she carried that caught their attention, eyes began to open slowly, and little black noses began to sniff the air. The devils were fed cut-up rabbit, skin, bones and all, plus a special "pet food," to round out their diets and keep them healthy. The little devils all tumbled together, pawing at the feeder's knees, hopping up and down and begging, looking for all the world like silly puppies, growling softly with pleasure as they gulped down their food and went back for seconds. Actually, they are not unappealing. They look a little like a cross between a very small bear cub and a fox, with their shiny, black fur, pointed noses and little, round ears.

I hated to leave, because I adore all those wonderful animals, but eventually we reboarded the coach and started off for our next destination. We passed huge fields white with poppies, which are grown for the production of codeine.

We continued to pass through lush, green countryside and quaint, small towns filled with lovely, old buildings. This is real step-back-in-time territory. The forests began to get more dense as we drove into increasingly mountainous terrain. We drove along Mole Creek, an important honey-gathering area, famous for Tasmanian leatherwood honey, which is unique to this locale. The place was inundated with flowers.

We soon arrived at King Solomon's Cave—one of 199 caves in this region. A guide met us at the entrance, and we descended into the resplendent, subterranean world. We wandered through magnificent caverns with names like the Temple, Angels' Paradise, and the Bridal Chamber, all of which were festooned and decorated with sparkling crystal. In addition to all the calcite forms I've seen in other caves, there were curving rimstone dams enclosing clear pools, where the stone looked like shimmering, overlapping water lily pads, as well as clusters of aragonite crystals. Aragonite is the mineral normally found in pearls, a form of calcium carbonate. In several places, it clung to the cave walls in sparkling, jagged "bouquets" of pure white.

Tall, moss-covered trees, dense, bright-green ferns, and red-flowered Tasmanian waratah bushes surrounded us as we walked back to our coach. There, lunch awaited us, as did Jan, Blue's wife, who is to be our cook and hostess for the duration of the trip. (Up to this point, Lynette, Jan and Blue's daughter, had been filling in, as Jan was finishing up another tour. A real family operation, this.)

We turned north, heading for the coast. Within a few hours, we reached Tiagarra. Tiagarra is on a point of land surrounded by brilliant azure water, on which the sunlight danced and sparkled. The hills are covered with low shrubs that are a thousand shades of green, and wonderful, old, wind-sculpted trees dot the lawns of the museum there.

Tiagarra means "Keep," and this is the keeping place of artifacts from the now extinct Tasmanian Aborigines. (There are still mixed-blood descendants of the Tassie Aborigines around, but all the full-blooded natives are gone.)

The rocks near Tiagarra are decorated with rare Tassie rock art, which we studied as we strolled around the grounds. Brush and moss have been cleared from slabs and outcrops, and we could see the signs and symbols that had been painstakingly scraped into the rocks. Most of the art consisted of circles and coils, but occasionally the outline of a fish or emu could be discerned.

The people who once occupied Tasmania almost certainly lived first on the mainland, until the better-armed ancestors of today's Aborigines arrived and pushed them south. The short (5'4", on average), stocky Tasmanian Aborigines were very probably a different race from the mainland Aborigines—apparently of Negritoid and/or Melanesian stock.

Though they shared practices such as ritual scarification, burning forests, and a division of labor not particularly

favorable to women, cultural difference between mainland
and Tasmanian Aborigines were numerous. The Tasmanian
Aborigines had a less complex language, fewer tools, and
they "captured" fire from lightning strikes. They did not
draw and had a less developed mythology. Hunting and
war with other tribes seemed to be the men's main occupa-
tions. However, though more primitive, they lived better
than mainlanders because of the abundance of food—lobsters, oysters, scallops, ducks, swans, seals, kangaroos,
and mutton birds. (For reasons unknown, they banned the
eating of scaled fish.)

The first white men to appear were sealers. They liked
the native women because they were good at tracking and
catching seals. And, because Tasmanian women were
badly treated within their own society, many readily
attached themselves to white protectors.

Soon, settlers and convicts began to arrive. Convicts and
their guards frequently mistreated the Aborigines with
whom they came in contact, and armed, escaped convicts,
the early "bushrangers," sometimes hunted them for sport.
Hobart developed even more rapidly as a whaling base
than as a convict settlement, and the whalers, on the
whole, were not much kinder than the convicts.

Tasmanian Aborigines mounted frustrated attacks on
those who settled their hunting grounds. The Europeans
lost approximately 200 men in conflicts with the natives.
Retaliatory raids were sometimes brutal, but often were
ineffective, because the natives could "disappear" in the
bush. But over time, the casualties mounted. The estimated
1200 Aborigines in Tasmania when white men first arrived
were reduced to less than 300 in 30 years.

Some settlers made an effort to protect the natives. In particular, the English missionary George Augustus Robinson

befriended these people, his close relations with them giving us our only real insight into Tasmania's Aborigines.

The remaining natives were convinced to settle on a reserve on Flinders Island. They were clothed, fed, and educated. European diseases took some toll of the natives, but the biggest problem was that, deprived of their traditional pursuits, they simply pined away. Only 47 remained by 1845. They were transferred back to the Tasmanian mainland, where they quickly deteriorated due to contact with white civilization and alcohol. In 1874, the last full-blooded male died in a tavern in Hobart. Truganini, the last full-blooded Tasmanian Aborigine, died in 1876.

Monday, November 28

A long drive this morning took us through forests of fragrant sassafras, myrtle, wattle, native peppercorn, and flowering dogwood. Clematis blossoms festooned many of the trees. We crossed the Hellyer River in Hellyer Gorge and passed into the cool darkness of a myrtle forest, which is a temperate rainforest. Tasmanian myrtle is not the same as European myrtle. A lovely tree with rough-barked, black trunk, spreading branches and dark green leaves, Tasmanian myrtle is an evergreen. Also known as "Antarctic beech," it grows to a height of more than 100 feet. New spring growth, which we saw everywhere, is bronze and chestnut, and beautiful.

We climbed high into the mountains, stopping at Round Mountain Lookout for a spectacular view of the surrounding countryside. The clouds were close above us and trailed streamers along some of the farther peaks. Tall trees swept away from us in great tides of green down the sides of the mountains. Immense stone outcrops were dappled with pale lichens. The sun spilled between the clouds and played across the peaks and valleys, changing the greens and blues, sparking off great boulders, drawing the entire landscape into the dance.

The road wound between cliffs and peaks before descending to the coast on the far side of the mountain range. Here, tall, rolling dunes of white sand paralleled our route and blocked our view of the sea.

By noon we were in Strahan (pronounced "Straun"), a tiny center for crayfishing and tourism, best known for being the only town on Tasmania's formidable west coast. We had a picnic lunch at the town's edge, then strolled over to the landing at Macquarie Harbour for the beginning of a four-hour cruise up the Gordon River. The Gordon, which extends for 135 miles, is the longest river in Tasmania.

As we left the harbor, it seemed as if the entire day had turned blue and white. The sky and water were intensely blue, and the great mountains that surround the area shimmered a paler blue in the distance. There were great, billowing, white clouds, which seemed reflected by the glistening white of the mountains' peaks and the narrow strips of white sand that border the water.

For the first few miles out of Macquarie Harbour, the river is paralleled by mountains, the most prominent of which is Frenchman's Cap. The mountain is so called because it resembles the Phrygian caps commonly worn by French revolutionaries of the 18th century. This peak, along with the others in the range, appears to be covered by snow, but the gleaming mountaintops are, in reality, capped with pure-white quartzite.

As we moved farther inland, the forests on either side of

the river became more and more dense. This is said to be the thickest, most impenetrable forest in the world. It is almost totally unexplored. It was because of this forest, and the surrounding, virtually impassable mountains, that this spot was used as a penal colony. There was no way out overland.

Much of the region is covered by myrtle rainforest, with patches of huon pine, blackwood, and celery top pine. The greatest impediment to traversing this area, however, was, and is, the "horizontal forest." The horizontal tree (*Anodopetalum biglandulosum*) grows 15 to 30 feet tall, then bends under its own weight to a horizontal position. New branches also bend, and intertwine, until, in time, there is an impenetrable wall as much as 90 feet high. The only way across is literally to climb up and walk on top of the tangled mass. But if you fall through, you may not get out again.

As we returned down river, we saw a cluster of uneven, rocky humps rising out of the water to our left. This was once the most feared place in Tassie's penal system. We passed Grummet Island, where defiant prisoners were incarcerated, and the ironically named Holiday Island, a cemetery named for the first convict buried there, and pulled in at Sarah, or Settlement, Island, the largest of the three. From 1821-1833, the worst, most unruly prisoners were sent to these isolated rock piles. Of 85 deaths on the islands during this time only 35 were of natural causes. More than a hundred convicts did escape, but 62 died in the bush and nine were murdered by their comrades. Now, the past is only hinted at; buildings of hand-made brick and island stone stand in ruins, almost reclaimed by the island's lush foliage.

We cruised out to Hell's Gates, the entrance to

Macquarie Harbour, a narrow channel bordered on one side by jagged rocks, on the other by a long sand bar. Tides rip through this opening, creating eddies and fierce surf. In addition, the west coast of Tasmania faces the Southern Ocean, with nothing between it and South America. Terrific storms sweep across thousands of miles of uninterrupted ocean to break on this shore. Twin lighthouses stand like sentries on either side of the wild passage, where many ships have been lost. We were told of one early lighthouse keeper who watched helplessly as the ship bearing his wife and children foundered on the rocks only a few dozen yards away.

Today the spot was serene and beautiful, giving no indication of its treacherous nature. A sleek, white fishing vessel passed us, though not under sail—it is not wise to trust the wind to carry you through such an inlet. The boat and the clean, white lighthouses stood out starkly against the deep blue of the water and sky. The only contrast to the pervasive blue and white was a swath of bright, green foliage running along the white-sand beaches and up to the lighthouses.

Reg Morrison, owner and pilot of the vessel on which we were cruising, was full of stories about the area. He and his brothers are among only a dozen or so people who have tried to traverse this wild region. In the late 1930s they went on expeditions to find and cut the rare stands of Tasmania's valuable huon pine. Speed of travel was measured in miles per month, as they struggled through the rainforest and horizontal forest. They carved a path through the trees, but the trees seemed to close behind them. So dense was the foliage that there wasn't even a break in the mass of green when they came to tributaries of the river—branches wove together in a solid wall over the water, hiding any changes in the terrain.

Macquarie Harbour is tinged a golden-brown hue, from the tannic acid produced by the rainforest that crowds around it. Once more, we crossed the tea-colored water, pulling into the boat mooring at Strahan at 5 p.m.

Our campsite was less than a mile out of Strahan, on a splendid, tree-bordered beach of the broad, serene harbor. After dinner, Kay, Mary, Chrissy, and I took off on a long walk, passing back through Strahan and all the way around to the far side of the harbor. Strahan is a charming little town with clean, white buildings that are reflected in the water at the town's edge. Low cliffs crowned with trees, shrubs, and flowers rise up directly behind the shops that line Strahan's one street. The fleet of boats riding at their moorings is small and tidy. Picturesque in full light, the town took on an almost dream-like air as the lowering sun tinted walls, clouds, and water a pale mauve.

When we got back to camp, Kay and I sat on the beach and watched the spectacular sunset over the water. The sky was a rich, fiery orange, paling upward to silver. The water looked like deep blue satin. The colors went through infinite variations as the sun disappeared behind the horizon. Just after it set, the sky became gold and the water, a serene lavender. It was a beautiful ending to an excellent day.

Tuesday, November 29

We were up early again and off for Queenstown, a wildly rugged and barren area where the mountains were stripped of all vegetation and topsoil by early mining operations nearly a century ago. Trees were cut to fuel the copper smelter, and the rising sulphur fumes from the smelting operation killed the rest of the vegetation. Then the rain took away the topsoil. Some of the early settlements were buried by the resultant, unexpected landslides, often with great loss of life.

The mountains are now beginning to recover, but they still present a pretty dramatic scene: craggy white cliffs stained green and orange by the rich copper deposits, large outcrops of other rocks and minerals, black slag heaps from smelting days.

First stop was the Mt. Lyell Mine. Originally opened to find gold, the mine now brings up only copper ore. Tunnels go two miles down under the mountain. High above, in the internal reaches of the range, there is a huge, open-cut mine. We stopped at the edge of this massive, tiered hole, which is 800 feet deep, 3,000 feet wide and 6,000 feet long.

Other minerals besides gold and copper are found in this area. Peacock ore is a pyrite—iridescent copper iron sulphide—fool's gold family. It's useless but dazzling: shimmering blue, purple, green, and gold. Another is the mauve and green stichtite, which is interesting because its existence was hypothesized (based on the region's mineral profile) before the stone was actually discovered. Bright orange crocoite, silvery galena, tourmaline, serpentine, magnetite, and many other charming stones abound. I collected a few pieces of copper ore and bought samples of all the other rocks.

At the mining museum, we saw displays on the area's history and how the mines were developed. An exhibit of the local flora also offered pictures of what the area would have looked like if the mountains had not been stripped—your typical lush, heavily wooded, Tasmanian coastal region.

In Queenstown, we stopped in the main square to view

the monument to the miners who settled the area. We had a little time free to shop for souvenirs and stroll through the town. It is a pleasant little village, nestled among the mountains, at the head of the narrow valley.

Next we drove inland, up onto the Central Plateau, skirting the lovely Derwent River, headed for Lake St. Clair, a magnificent, glacier-carved spot surrounded by mountains and forest. The lake, the deepest natural lake in Australia, is more than 600 feet deep. Mt. Olympus rises in the distance, towering above the trees on the far side of the lake and reflected in its clear, blue water.

Crowding the shores are forests full of wonderful, gentle, inquisitive creatures. We saw several Tasmanian native hens, the state bird, a funny, chubby, brown-feathered thing that, if it can fly, doesn't, but rather darts in and out among the trees, running along the ground, stopping to look for food. There were also numerous currawongs, black birds, about the size of crows, with bright yellow eyes, white flashes on their tails, and tremendous appetites for picnics.

The most numerous, and most delightful, creatures on hand were the wallabies. The ones here are primarily the diminutive Bennett's wallabies and rufous wallabies. Only about 2 to 2-1/2 feet in height, these adorable creatures have beautiful faces, a bit like a faun's, with large, dark, thickly lashed eyes. It is spring, so most of the females have joeys in their pouches. We offered them bread, lettuce, and apples, and they gently placed forepaws on our arms to steady themselves as they ate out of our hands. They would occasionally place their paws on our knees and lean across our laps to see what another wallaby was eating. They watched everything we did, followed us around, let us stroke their incredibly soft fur, and generally behaved like the family pet. (And these are non-captive animals—this is a national park, not an animal reserve.)

Paul, one of the brightest little boys I've ever had the pleasure to meet, is much in awe of my camera, so, after setting the controls for him and showing him how to focus, I let him use it—to take a picture of me feeding the wallabies. He was very excited about trying the camera, but a bit nervous. I think he was as relieved when I took it back as he was pleased that I'd given it to him. Then I took a picture of him feeding the wallabies.

At 3 p.m. we reached Mt. Field National Park. The sun was still high enough to peek over the mountains and reach into the emerald depths of the rainforest, and in the flickering, filtered half-light, we headed off to find Russell Falls.

The paths leading through the forest are like tunnels, roofed with gum branches, walled in by an astonishing variety of ferns. Clear streams with thickly padded banks of moss parallel the footpaths, weaving between the myrtle, sassafras trees, soft tree-ferns, and towering, 200-foot eucalypts.

The dense vegetation that surrounds Russell Falls holds it like a secret, like a diamond wrapped in green velvet, which is only seen by those willing to search through the folds. We wandered through the green twilight, the sound of the many, rushing streams echoing around us, and we wondered how far the falls might be. Then suddenly, it was before us, the water descending like a shimmering gossamer veil.

The 150-foot cascade is broken into two tiers. A path beside the falls leads to the middle level, where the narrower upper tier spreads into clear pools before again rushing over the edge of the rocks. The ledge is wide and the water serene. I picked my way carefully across the smooth stones protruding from the pools. Standing in the center of that ledge, with the shimmering waterfall before and behind me, and the lush forest spreading at my feet, I felt almost intoxicated by the wildness and beauty of the place.

I climbed farther up the path, to where the stream that feeds the cascade descends a series of stone "steps" before plunging over into the top tier of the waterfall. The music of the water, and the view of the great, undulating blanket of forest covering the mountains and valley, mesmerized me. I lingered as long as I could; everyone else returned to camp long before I was able to tear myself away and walk back through the cool, dark rainforest to where our tents were to be pitched.

By the time I got back to camp, Paul had almost finished putting up my tent for me, as a surprise. So now we add chivalry to the list of his virtues. I must remember to tell his mother what an exceptional job I think she's doing.

The damp chill of the rainforest had frozen up my injured shoulder (the one I fell on), so I had a long, hot shower in the coin-operated facility at the park. Then Jill, who is a nurse, kindly massaged it for me. The massage was painful, but by the time Jill was done, I could at least move my arm again.

After bedding down for the night, I had company in the tent. A brush-tail possum strolled in through the partially open flap, certain that anyone inside would be glad to see him. I shooed him away, and he looked at me like he couldn't believe I'd ask him to go, then he slowly trundled back outside. Within half an hour he was back, to see if I'd changed my mind. When he left this time (at my insistence) I got up to secure the tent flap more tightly. I glanced outside and saw the charming creature sitting, watching me, waiting for an invitation to come in. I love this, though, being surrounded by animals I've only seen in books or zoos before. (The Australian brush-tail possum, by the way, bears no resemblance to the homely, rat-tailed opossum found in the U.S. This attractive, furry, dark-eyed marsupial looks more like a very large squirrel.)

Wednesday, November 30

It was gray and drizzly this morning, after a night of gentle rain. On the way to the facilities block first thing, I encountered the ever-cheerful Paul, who greeted me with an excited, "Wouldn't you love to see Russell Falls now, since it's been raining?" Remarkable boy.

Once on the road, we made our way through more of Tasmania's beautiful wilderness on our way to Strathgordon to see Lake Pedder and Lake Gordon. One percent of Tasmania lies under these lakes. Both bodies of water have been made considerably larger than their original sizes by the building of hydroelectric dams. The Lake Gordon Dam is the largest dam in the Southern Hemisphere. One nice thing they've done, to avoid cluttering up the landscape, is build the power stations entirely underground.

Electricity is one of Tasmania's most important products. Even though Tassie represents only three percent of Australia's population, and less than one percent of her land, she produces more than ten percent of the country's electricity.

The area is wonderful, though it was a bit obscured today by drifting mist and low-hanging clouds that cloaked the mountains that rise directly up out of the lakes. The green-clad hills and islands and the extensive lakes were still beautifully impressive.

We made a short stop at the Visitors' Centre at the edge of the massive Lake Gordon Dam. The dam is more than 450 feet high and, at the top, 650 feet across. I bought some post cards of the area, a bottle of Tasmanian leatherwood honey (fabulous, with a scent reminiscent of caraway), and a piece of huon pine. The scarcity of the huon pine tree is compounded by the fact that it takes about 800 years to grow (some huons have been dated as being 2–3,000 years old), so reforestation is not a viable option. The wood is beautiful, fine-grained, satiny, delicately fragrant, and golden.

The general dampness of the day made a break for tea sound appealing, so we stopped at the Lake Pedder Chalet. I was delighted with the spot as soon as I looked into the back yard. Dozens of green rosellas were on the lawn, crunching on seeds that had been left out for them.

As we continued south and east, through the lovely Derwent Valley, we drove by fields of hops. Tasmania's hop production meets almost all the requirements of Australia's many breweries, and this is the biggest and most successful hop-growing region in Tasmania.

At New Norfolk, we stopped to see St. Matthew's Church of England. Built in 1823, it is the oldest church in Tasmania, though only the walls and floor of the nave survive from the original design. New Norfolk is one of the oldest towns in Tasmania. Governor Lachlan Macquarie* chose the site in 1811 as a home for refugees from Norfolk Island.

By 4:30, we reached Hobart, the largest city, chief port, and capital of Tasmania. Hobart, a bright, charming, little city, population 167,000, sits on the west bank of the Derwent River approximately 12 miles from its mouth, and rolls up across the green foothills of Mt. Wellington, which rises 4,165 feet in the near background.

*See appendix

Hobart was first explored by George Bass in 1798. Five years later, Philip King, governor of New South Wales, sent a party to establish a settlement in this general area. In 1804, the settlement was moved to the city's present site, Sullivan Cove, and named for Robert Hobart, then Secretary of State for the Colonies.

In more recent history, Hobart was the birthplace of the most notorious and dashing Tasmanian devil of all—swashbuckler Errol Flynn, who was the son of a distinguished Australian marine biologist and zoologist. It is hard to imagine the outrageous Flynn growing up in this quiet, conservative little town. (It is, however, easier to imagine him as an Australian if you read Beam Ends, which Flynn wrote well before fame had swept him away. Written with enthusiasm and intelligence, it describes a sailing adventure, undertaken by Flynn and three friends, from Sydney to New Guinea, along the Great Barrier Reef.)

One of the big attractions in Hobart is the Wrest Point Casino, to which place many of our number hurried after dinner. I've been coming down with something for a couple of days now. I've developed a cough that sounds like I'm dying of TB, and tonight my temperature went through the roof, so I decided to stay behind for a more restful evening of tea and writing.

After a while, Jan and Blue joined me in the small, dimly lit, shed-like cooking shelter. Warm, open, and comfortable people, they settled easily into talking about their lives. Jan and Blue grew up near Launceston and have lived in Tasmania their entire lives. They love this state and are terribly proud of it. They met when he was 17 and she was 12. Blue had to wait for Jan to grow up enough to marry him, but he knew she was the girl for him right from the start. They've been married for 25 years now.

By the time I was heading for my tent, I had chills, so I put on about three layers of clothing, then crawled into my sleeping bag. I hope I just have bad bronchitis and not pneumonia, though I don't have time for either.

Thursday, December 1

It's the first day of summer here, though it's still rather cool, because we're so far south. But the sun is shining and the clouds have disappeared.

Our first stop of the day was at Hobart's historic Shot Tower, which was constructed in 1870. The handsome, solid, hewn-stone building—a tall, tapering cylinder, which looks rather like a lighthouse, with a cottage of the same rough stone hugging its base—sits high on a hill overlooking the city, surrounded by tidy, well-tended gardens, green hedges, and old trees. We climbed the tight spiral of stairs inside the tower to the top for a splendid view of Hobart, the Derwent River, and the surrounding hills and grazing land, as well as for an explanation of how shot was produced.

The process of producing shot at the tower fascinated me. I don't know who first thought of pouring molten, arsenic-treated lead into a colander and letting it drip 200 feet down into a bucket of water, but, in light of the physics involved it makes perfect sense. The size of the holes in the colander would determine the size of the droplets. The liquid metal would become spherical as it descended, and would harden in that shape when it hit the water.

The rambling, uneven streets of Hobart's Battery Point

provided our next diversion. Most of the houses in this area were built when the city was first settled, and it is said to be Australia's most complete colonial village. Rows of laborers' cottages are interspersed between the large, elegant domiciles of wealthy merchants. The entire area is crowded with trees and flowers. We passed St. George's Church, a handsome, spired edifice, which was once also used as a poor school. The successful merchants of years past contributed substantial amounts of money to subsidize the educations of the children of their less fortunate neighbors.

Blue dropped us off at Salamanca Place, the handsome, old, restored harbor front. The solid, pale sandstone warehouses, all built between 1835 and 1860, have been converted into arcades of fascinating shops. We had two hours free, so I browsed through Salamanca Place, then headed back to Battery Point, to get photographs of the spots we'd passed. I looked about Hobart, checking out the spotless, white, Japanese merchant ships, inspecting Parliament House, a sprawling, Georgian-style, sandstone edifice, and generally playing tourist. Then I wandered in the direction of the shopping district.

I stopped in to see a chemist (who said I sound like I have pneumonia), and bought everything he could sell me without a prescription: three kinds of cold tablets, air-sickness medicine (the only non-prescription medication I could get that contains antihistamines), vitamin C, cough syrup, and cough lozenges. I downed some of everything, then headed off for more sightseeing before hitting the road again.

Lunchtime found us in Richmond, site of the oldest bridge and oldest Roman Catholic church in Australia. Set on a river, surrounded by rolling, green, sheep-dotted countryside, Richmond, like so many small, Tasmanian towns, has an almost rural English feel to it, though it is still noticeably colonial.

The small, sturdy, old town looks like a museum piece. Solid buildings, natural stone or immaculately white-washed plaster, line the short main street, down which I wandered. I came across one charming old home that had a handsome, highly polished, carved wood door. The stone steps leading up to the veranda were concave, and a sign on the veranda post warned, "Beware—time worn step."

Wooden wagon wheels leaned against a low stone wall. Masses of yellow-flowered acacias clustered around a small, clean, white cottage at the town's edge. The loveliest spot in town was the old Richmond Gaol, which was built in 1825. It is a substantial, pale-gold, stone-block building with gorgeous gardens and broad lawns.

By the main entrance of St. John's, the small, sandstone, Roman Catholic church, we saw the tiny grave of the four-month-old son of transported Irish rebel Thomas Francis Meagher. Meagher escaped from Tasmania before the birth of his son and went to America. His wife was supposed to join him after the child's birth, but she never made it. In America, Meagher became a Union officer during the U.S. Civil War, and afterwards became secretary of the Montana Territory.

We walked down to the Richmond Bridge, a handsome, convict-built, stone structure begun in 1823. There is a slight "wave" in the sturdy, immovable-looking bridge, from where the ground shifted beneath its supports during construction.

The terrain became wilder again, as we continued on. At Pirates Cove, the unrestrained greenery dropped sharply down toward the sea and a long, curving, steep-sided, white-sand beach. Now we could see water ahead of us, as well as beside us. The cove marks the beginning of the Tasman Peninsula. Only a narrow slip of land, called Eaglehawk Neck, connects the peninsula with the rest of Tasmania.

Just before crossing Eaglehawk Neck we stopped to see the Tessellated Pavement. The Tessellated Pavement is a phenomenon where volcanic rock, worn smooth by the ocean, has been fractured by earth movements along lines and perpendiculars so straight, so nearly perfect that the area looks like it has been paved. Looking at it, it is hard to believe that this giant mosaic of smooth, evenly broken, dark, stone blocks is not the work of masons.

On the peninsula, we drove through Doo Town, where every one of the residents has an appropriately named home: Love me Doo, Much a-Doo, Didgeri-Doo, Doo Bist, She'll Doo, etc. We had a lot of fun driving slowly through town, reading all the names.

Our next stop was at Tasman Arch, a high, sea-carved arch in the rugged coast of the peninsula. We stood on a cliff, parallel with the top of the arch, looking down on the blue water that swirled about its base, 150 feet below. The pale, water-chiseled stone walls were bare, but the top of the arch was crowned with crowds of green and silver scrub. We could see the high cliffs of the crenellated coast stretching away from us, in one direction sweeping up into the green hills, and in the other direction disappearing into the blue mist of the sea.

We walked farther out on the craggy point of land, to the Devil's Kitchen. Here, tall, broken stone walls rise from a chaos of rocks where an arch collapsed. Nearby, a dull thundering issued from the Blow Hole, where waves captured in an underground cave break free and shoot into the air. The spot was beautiful and wild, with the drama of water interacting violently with the shoreline, the irresistible force meeting the immovable object.

We finally arrived at our campsite—a magnificent spot on Garden Point, surrounded on three sides by water, with stands of towering gum trees and a view of the mountains. It was delightful, if chilly.

Because my health was questionable and my cough getting worse, I headed for my tent shortly after dinner, hoping a little extra sleep would help things along. I did wake up once during the night, and went stumbling off to the facilities block. Dotted across the lawn and perched on every garbage can were brush-tail possums. They glanced up and watched me walk past, curious, but unimpressed with my presence. Then they went back to nibbling whatever it was they'd found to nibble. Funny little creatures.

Friday, December 2
Today—Port Arthur!

In 1830, the Lieutenant Governor of Van Diemen's Land (as Tassie was then called), Colonel George Arthur, decided to consolidate all the colony's penal establishments into one at the port that came to bear his name. The location was easily guarded, as Eaglehawk Neck, the only connection with the rest of the island, is just a few hundred yards across, so it could be completely closed off. It was spanned by a row of savage guard dogs and watched by soldiers. The sea was hardly an easy alternative, as the coast is fairly rough here, and almost no one knew how to swim in those days. Of the 12,500 convicts that went through Port Arthur, only 11 ever escaped.

The treatment prisoners received at Port Arthur sometimes sounds harsh by modern standards, but was considered enlightened in its day—and it was a major improvement over what some other establishments had been meting out to convicts. Rules were as strict for guards as for prisoners, and though punishment could be severe, torture was not allowed. In fact, flogging was abolished here before it was abolished in the British Navy and Army. Also, an attempt was made to rehabilitate convicts.

The biggest impediment to reforming convicts was usually their proximity to other convicts. As Charles Darwin noted, when visiting Tasmania, "A man who should try to improve, could not while living with other [convicts]—his life would be one of intolerable misery and persecution." However, as Darwin continued, though "as a place of punishment, the object is scarcely gained; but as a means of making men outwardly honest—of converting vagabonds, most useless in one hemisphere, into active citizens of another, and thus giving birth to a new and splendid country—it has succeeded to a degree perhaps unparalleled in history."

The ruins of the settlement are extensive, poignant, and beautiful. Some of the staff and officers' quarters are still intact—some are even still used as private homes. Probably the most frequently photographed building is the convict church. Designed by a convict named Mason, the church is a many-spired, golden-stoned, 19th-century Gothic Revival structure, the roof of which disappeared ages ago.

The asylum has been restored and is used as a museum. There are numerous artifacts from convict days—manacles and leg irons, clothes, letters, drawings of and by prisoners (including a post-mortem sketch of Alexander Pearce, the

infamous Macquarie Harbour Man-Eater, so called
because on two separate escape attempts he managed to
kill and eat all his companions), and other items—and a
scale model of what the entire complex looked like when
in use. I saw an audio-visual presentation covering the settlement's history and giving opinions from prisoners' letters of life at Port Arthur. Of course, nobody was really
happy to be here, and the letters were filled with longing
for freedom.

Adjacent to the asylum is the Model Prison—considered
so advanced for its time that it was a model for other prisons. The lash was replaced by isolation, and attempts were
made to teach the more incorrigible criminals the value of
work (tools and instruction for various trades were supplied), while keeping them separate from other criminals,
with the hope that, in the ensuing silence, they would have
the opportunity to reflect on their crimes and repent.
Although you hear stories about people transported for
stealing bread (and that did happen), the convicts incarcerated in the Model Prison were the really hardened ones,
the multiple offenders and the criminally insane.

The Model Prison is constructed of heavy, gray stone. It
was built in a cross shape, so all four corridors could be
watched from a central point. Stone-paved exercise yards
radiate out from the prison. It is magnificently geometri-
cal, and beautiful in its strength and simplicity of design.

From the Model Prison, I wandered over to the imposing
ruins of the hospital, government offices, guard towers,
and massive penitentiary. Stone steps are bowed beneath
the weight of years. Flowers sprout from shattered cor-
nices. The large, pale, brick and stone buildings are hauntingly lovely in their current state of disrepair.

A few of the smaller structures, including the farm overseer's cottage and dairy, have been restored. Sheep graze in the broad, green paddocks of the old prison farm. Wide lawns and neat English-style gardens surround the senior officers' houses and skeletal remains of Government Cottage, and large shade trees line the roads. All the buildings overlook the beautiful harbor and nearby islands.

After hours in the ruins, I rejoined our group at the harbor dock, where we boarded a motor launch for a cruise. The boat took us out around Point Puer. This is where convict boys aged 10-18 were sent. ("Puer" is Latin for "boy.") Aside from the isolation, it was more like a boarding school than a prison. The boys were educated and taught a trade, which put them well ahead of most of the impoverished youngsters still in England. As soon as they were adequately educated and competent at their trades, they were released. Many of them became quite successful, supplying the needs of the young colony. There were still some problems, mostly because even at so tender an age some of the boys had become fairly nasty individuals. But on the whole, it was a real chance for a clean start and a new life.

Next we cruised out to the Isle of the Dead, where we landed and disembarked. It was on this island that Port Arthur's dead were buried, to prevent the spread of disease. Free men and women buried on the island received headstones, while convicts were interred in unmarked, multiple graves. Of the former there are 180, of the latter, 1,768 buried here. Only 76 of the headstones remain—vandals have smashed or stolen the rest—but those that still stand are interesting. Of the soldiers, sailors, preachers, teachers, officials, wives, and children buried there, many bore names that are still prominent in Australia. Our guide pointed out the forebears of well-known athletes, business magnates, and other eminent citizens, and told us that one of the early chaplains at the prison, Rev. Eastman, who died at the age of 51 and was buried here, was a relative of the man who founded the Eastman Kodak Company.

The headstones are marvelous to read. They were carved by convicts, many of whom were learning their language as they learned their trade. The spelling is often original, the spacing and breaking of words occasionally baffling, the punctuation either non-existent or after every word. Many convicts put their names or initials on their work, to make certain they got credit for it; those who produced goods or provided services beneficial to the settlement got points toward early release.

Departing the surprisingly beautiful, flower-covered, little island, we headed for shore, where, in sight of the penitentiary and guard towers, Jan and Blue had lunch waiting. After eating, I walked back up into the ruins, enjoying a final wander around the site where so many lives began or ended at the beginning of Australia's history.

We skirted the coast as we made our way north. We made only one stop during our drive—to see the Spiky Bridge. Built in 1843 by convicts from a nearby probation station, the bridge is topped by jagged rows of sharp, spiky rocks. It is said that the prisoners, tired of seeing their supervisors sitting comfortably on the bridge they were building, decided to top off the sides of the structure in this fashion so there'd be no place for the guards to perch. There are other explanations for this peculiar construction, but they are more practical, and therefore less interesting.

We reached camp, which is just outside Orford, on Prosser Bay, by about 4 p.m. It took us a while to pound our tent pegs into the rock-hard soil, but we eventually got camp set up, and settled in. Then we stood on the shore, inspecting the coastline and sea with Blue's high-powered binoculars. Across the bay, a ship was being loaded from a mountain of wood chips. (Wood chips are an important export item for Tasmania.) Still farther out we could see the coast of Maria Island. This island, which is now a wildlife sanctuary, was named by Abel Tasman in honor of Maria Van Diemen, wife of the governor of the East Indies. Tasman said he named it for the lady because it was so beautiful. Sadly, a visit to the island is one of the things that got eliminated when they reduced this trip from 14 to nine days. Pity. Maybe next time.

After dinner, we retired to the nearby pub for a nightcap. The patrons gathered there were a pretty strange combination of types, ranging from our band of scruffy campers to the over-chic, semi-punk, local teens. (There is something almost sad about trying to be painfully chic when your destination is the pub at a campground on the edge of a tiny, Tasmanian coastal village.) Then there was a median group—the "just folks" types—who bridged the gap between the two more disparate bands.

It was a jolly evening, as we stretched out around the fire, chatting, enjoying a few drinks, and watching the incoming patrons. Chrissy and Stephanie played (sort of) a game of what was intended to be pool. Their lack of expertise turned it into a hilarious, entertaining, and almost unending match. They were a picture of youthful exuberance—especially Chrissy, who, with her masses of curly, golden hair and rosy cheeks, looks as though she should have wings and a little bow and arrow.

Before it got too late, I headed back to camp, to try for another good night's sleep.

Saturday, December 3

Traveling up the eastern seaboard today, we passed through a great deal of much tamer scenery than we witnessed in the West. Still beautiful, and constantly changing, most of this area was rural farming or stock-raising land interspersed with charming fishing villages.

I noted, sadly, that this busier, more-populated coast has one unfortunate similarity to Chicago—most of the wildlife we saw (predominantly Tasmanian devils) was flattened onto the road. Being scavengers, the little devils come down to dine on the edible garbage tossed out by motorists, as well as anything dead on the road. Being fierce and tenacious scavengers, they protect their finds jealously and challenge anything that looks like it's headed for the same meal—including cars. That, and their night-dark coats, contribute to a rather high mortality rate among on-street devils.

Our first stop of the day was in the fishing village of Bicheno. We left the handful of small, tidy buildings behind us and walked to Whaler's Lookout, a high, rugged hill of enormous, lichen-stained granite boulders covered in part by stands of gum trees, casuarinas, wattle and wildflowers. From this and similar lookouts along the ocean front, watchers could see the spouts of approaching schools of whales and alert the whaling fleet in the cove below.

A narrow path wound up and around the lookout, affording us glorious and varied views of this stretch of coast. In one direction, trees and flowers covered a hilly, green landscape. In another, ragged outcrops of gray granite met the sea in a line of white foam. Below us, white-sand beaches outlined the bright, clear, blue waters of the cove.

Across town, we stopped near the shore for lunch. I,

however, opted to explore the nearby Sea Life World, which offers the weird and rare combination of marine life zoo and seafood restaurant.

Inside, there were tanks full of local fish, mollusks, eels, and crustaceans, some of which are found only in the waters around Tasmania. Some of the fish were the more common table varieties—salmon, tuna, bass. There were some peculiar looking specimens, too, like the Long Snout Boarfish and the Red Latchet. There was a whole herd of sea horses and displays of the number one local delicacy —crayfish, also known as rock lobster.

The most astonishing things were the indigenous giant crabs and giant crayfish—truly the stuff of which nightmares are made. The giant crabs stand about two feet high, have very stocky legs and a body that is close to a foot across. These monsters weigh up to 30 pounds. The giant crayfish are closer to the ground, but have greater body mass—running about 1-1/2 feet in length and five inches in diameter. Bigger than your average crustaceans.

I continued on to the outdoor area, where the *Enterprise,* the first scow in Tasmania, is on display. I wandered around the deck, then went below to examine artifacts from her sailing days. A recording made by the boat's last owner and skipper, Bill Price, described the vessel's history, from its building in 1902 to retirement in 1980. Price detailed the glories and difficulties of life at sea, as well as problems he'd had with the boat during the 61 years he'd worked on and with her. He recalled the indignities inflicted by the economy, when hauling lumber died down, and you had to haul manure if you wanted to work.

By the time I finally reemerged into the parking lot, everyone else had eaten lunch. I grabbed a sandwich, then joined the others in the sublime pursuits of drinking tea and feeding sea gulls.

It was an amusing group of gulls—not your usual gang of look-alikes. There was one that looked like a cross between Ebenezer Scrooge and Quasimodo. Large, dark, wild-eyed, back hunched and head down, he bullied and chased the other gulls. He really looked fiendish. There was one poor bird that looked like an old drunk who'd been beaten up on the way home. He was ruffled and disheveled, had one slightly droopy eyelid and a real totter to his walk. That one and another poor soul with half a leg missing were the two we tried to get bread to, because they weren't as fast as the other gulls. Every once in a while, old Scrooge would barrel in, scattering the other birds, then stare at us, waiting for his share. Here were drama, pathos, a villain—what more could we ask for in an afternoon's entertainment?

Back on the coach, we continued north, alternating lonely beaches with lovely farms, all the while drawing closer to the green mountains. Turning inland for a while, we began a steady climb. A narrow, twisting road carried us up into the mountains, through Elephant Pass. The road led through St. Mary's, a small town at the head of the Esk River, and then into the winding descent of St. Mary's Pass. On the other side, we drove through St. Helen's and headed down to Binalong Bay.

The bay was spectacular, with rugged stone outcrops and tumbles of boulders interspersed between long, curving stretches of white sand. The shore was lush, with bright, mauve-flowered succulent creepers clinging to the rocks, and dense native brush rising from the sand's edge and intensifying before sweeping into stands of gum trees. There were broad, open spaces filled with small boys playing rudimentary forms of cricket. The water was as blue and clear as jewels. This is where Blue and Jan spent their honeymoon.

After a long break for wading, walking, or just sitting in the sun, we were off again, this time only the short distance to our campsite near St. Helen's. It's not the most picturesque place we've stayed, but it has a fireplace and a pile of wood, so we can have at least one campfire on this trip.

We put up our tents, then Jill, Frieda, Chrissy, Mary, and I busied ourselves with wrapping the thank you gifts we'd gotten for Jan and Blue. We all signed a card, and obtained the signatures of everyone else without being detected. We had everything ready before dinner.

Dinner was something of an event. We dined on the local specialty, rock lobster, which Jan served with a sparkling wine. Then we presented our gifts. Finally, we just let Blue build up the fire, and we sat around it, sipping coffee and chatting.

Sunday, December 4

After breakfast, we bid farewell to Jan, who was being picked up to cook for another tour. Then we packed up camp for the last time and boarded the coach for the final leg of our journey. We continued to pass through a lush, green landscape, alternating between rich agricultural districts, temperate rainforests, and glorious, gum tree-covered mountains.

We stopped to explore a bit of the rainforest. Handsome Tasmanian myrtle trees closed around us. Scattered among the myrtles were sassafras trees, fragrant and smooth-barked, and numerous soft tree-ferns, commonly known as "man-ferns" because of the soft mass of gingery, hair-like fibers at the top of their tall trunks.

The temperate rainforest is as dark and intensely green as the tropical rainforest, but cooler, and not so root and vine oriented. It was awesomely quiet, with the dense carpet of moss muffling our footsteps. It would have been pleasant to linger there, but we had to continue on our way.

We were now driving through an area that flourished during Tasmania's tin mining and Chinese gambling days. Little of the wealth or activity from this period remains, and ghost towns are not uncommon. But some of the pubs have hung on. A large sign in front of the Weldborough Hotel proclaims, "Worst Pub on the Coast." Another warns, "Don't-Stop—Food Shocking—Warm Beer." We examined a "sample menu" displayed at the entrance, which advertises such delicacies as gum leaf soup, maggot mornay, wombat stew, blow fly sponge, and leeches and cream. I was sorry they weren't open.

A bit farther down the road, Blue picked some trigger plants—beautiful, pale purple flowers I've seen growing in fields and by the road. There are several blooms on each slender stalk, each with four petals and a tiny "hammer." Blue demonstrated how, when the center of the delicate little blossom is touched, the hammer slams shut, covering any visiting insect with pollen.

We stopped several more times, to see Chinese memorials and to enjoy mountaintop views of sweeping forest and dramatic cliffs. We passed through fertile valleys filled with thriving farms. The soil here is rich. Tasmania supplies nearly 25 percent of Australia's potatoes and more than half of the country's frozen vegetables. Apples are another important Tassie product, though not to the extent they once were. Interestingly, the first apple trees in Tasmania were planted by Captain William Bligh in 1788, when the *Bounty* docked here en route to Tahiti.

Arriving in Launceston around noon, we headed straight for the airport. We quickly spread our picnic beneath the trees, on one of the airport's surrounding lawns, for one last lunch together. Beryl and Paul were the first to leave us. They had a 1:50 flight to catch, so after lunch, we all went to see them off. Jill, Huntley, and Chrissy were spending the night in Launceston, and the rest of us weren't taking off till 5:10, so Blue herded us back onto the coach for a last few snatches of sightseeing.

We drove along the River Tamar, stopping to climb to the top of Brady's Lookout (named for bushranger Matthew Brady), where we had a magnificent view of the entire river valley. The hill was topped by wonderful, twisted trees and tall, weird, orange flowers that looked something like a wine bottle that's been used as a candle holder for too long. The thick grass that carpeted the hillside was dotted with hundreds of small, yellow flowers and bordered by tall, purple thistles. The gentle, blue river below us wound off into the hilly, luxuriant, green landscape.

We descended the hill and continued along the banks of the river. Blue pointed out a corn mill built by his forebears and a boat dock that has been in Jan's family for several generations. We passed Jan and Blue's orchard and the site where they're building a new house. Both their families have been in Tasmania for more than 100 years. It's nice to have guides who are an integral part of the place you've come to see.

We rested for a while by the river's edge, at the base of a one-of-a-kind bridge with tilted, A-frame suspension. It

was fascinating, and looked as much like a work of art as
a product of engineering. Then it was time to head back
toward the airport.

We touched down in Melbourne at 6:10, and then I really had to fly. I raced over to the International terminal, to
cash a traveller's cheque, dashed back to domestic to
claim my luggage, then headed down to the taxi stand and
grabbed a cab. I had the driver take me first to Essendon.
Sue wasn't home, so I wrote a note thanking her again for
her hospitality, and left the spare key with it. Then I struggled downstairs with all the baggage I'd left behind (leave
it to me to find a cabbie with a torn Achilles tendon), got it
loaded, and headed straight into the city to the Greyhound
station.

My bus departed at 8:15 p.m. It was a beautiful, clear night, and in the deepening violets and pinks of twilight I watched the lovely silhouette of Victoria's landscape disappear from my view. Around 11 p.m., my seatmate disembarked, and I had a few precious hours to stretch out, sleeping fitfully until the next refreshment stop,

as Sunday

faded into—

Monday, December 5

I had reentered the slightly surreal world of nighttime coach travel, where solitary, darkened buses emerge from the blackness of a deserted, country night into the pool of light surrounding a lone roadhouse. Zombie-like passengers stumble off the bus and head for the take-away counter to order their 2 a.m. suppers. After eating, everyone just stands around, at varying distances from the bus, silently waiting for the trip to resume. It lacked the awesome eeriness of the Outback nighttime stops, but it was strange enough.

We rolled into Canberra at 6:50 a.m. The Hotel Civic is within walking distance of the Greyhound depot, which, unfortunately, means you have to walk. I made it in two trips, retired to the ladies' room to repair myself after a day and night of traveling, then announced myself to the receptionist. She told me a room wouldn't be ready until 10 o'clock. I was too tired to drop dead at her feet, so I wandered into the breakfast room for coffee and toast.

When I reemerged, the receptionist rushed over to tell me that she had found that a room was vacant, if I'd like it. I breathed a quick prayer of thanks and took the room. I hauled my gear up the broad, wood stairway, to the large, clean, pleasant room. It was 8:15 when I collapsed into bed. It was my first time in a bed in five weeks, and I couldn't believe how good it felt. It was 2 p.m. when I regained consciousness. The two camping trips right on top of each other, followed by an all-nighter on the coach, combined with the fact that I was still awfully ill, had fairly worn me out.

Now that I was awake and somewhat rested, I decided to go for a walk to see what Canberra is like. Words like "mausoleum," "cemetery," and "monument" come to mind. The hotel is fabulously well located, right near the city's artificial heart. I'm probably being a little too hard on Canberra. It's really quite lovely, but it's so obvious that it was, as it boasts, "totally planned."

People work here, but they don't live here, so during business hours the streets and malls are nearly deserted. (When I say people don't live here, I'm not being metaphorical. There are no living quarters, other than embassies, in the central part of the city. People live in the surrounding suburbs.)

I had the unreasonable but still unsettling feeling that I was no longer in Australia. The streets and gardens are planted with a dazzling array of ornamental and shade trees from all over the world, but I couldn't find any eucalypts. I kept thinking, "Where are the gum trees? This is

Australia—there *have* to be gum trees."

I walked down Northbourne Avenue and around City Hill, then down Commonwealth Avenue to the shore of Lake Burley Griffin, a man-made lake named after Chicago architect Walter Burley Griffin, who designed Canberra. There, I stopped to inspect the Captain Cook Globe, an immense, bronze model of the world, on which are outlined all the routes taken and countries visited or discovered by the great navigator and explorer. I watched the nearby Captain Cook Memorial Water Jet go off, its silvery pillar of water traveling 425 feet into the air, arching gracefully in the breeze and cascading into the lake.

Out on Regatta Point, I visited the Canberra Planning Exhibition. This facility offers photographs, models and displays that detail the development of Canberra. *Canberra* is an Aboriginal word meaning "meeting place." The site for the federal capital, a broad plain bordered on the south by the Australian Alps, was selected in 1908. Walter Burley Griffin won a contest for designing the city in 1912; the prize was £1,000 and a chance to work for the government. Burley Griffin got a few streets laid out, planted lots of trees, and began to get things under way, when he had a disagreement with some of the politicos, and they fired him. Today, his plans for the city's layout are being followed fairly faithfully, but after getting the sack, Burley Griffin went to India, where he died without ever seeing his plans realized.

After Burley Griffin's departure, Canberra went on hold for almost 50 years, during the Depression and two World Wars, so it has really been built almost entirely in the last 20 years. Ironically, the only building in the entire Australian Capital Territory that was designed by Walter Burley Griffin is an incinerator he did early in his career that was built in

one of Canberra's outlying suburbs. (The Australian Capital
Territory is comparable to the District of Columbia—a parcel of land separated from the states, where the federal government is located.)

After a stroll along the edge of the lake and a long look at
some of the bright, white edifices lining the far shore, I
started to walk back toward the hotel. Again, I would like to
say on Canberra's behalf, it really is quite lovely here. It's
just that the only other places I've ever been that are this
eerily quiet, this perfectly laid out, this totally manicured,
with this many flowers and trees in neat rows, and buildings
that are balanced and symmetrical and all the same color
stone, have been cemeteries. And as beautiful as it is, after
having spent so much time in real places, it feels lifeless.

Anyway, back on Northbourne Avenue, I headed for the
Visitors Information Centre, to get maps and arrange to see
some of the sights. Then, having not eaten anything since
my 7 a.m. toast, I made my way through the attractive,
nearly empty City Walk shopping area, to find a spot for an
early dinner. I chose Cuu Long, a charming little
Vietnamese restaurant, because I'd never had Vietnamese
food before. I had prawn and squid soup, followed by
marinated chicken grilled with garlic. It was fabulous.

Fatigue compounded my feeling of separation from the
"real" Australia, as I walked back through quiet malls and
down the empty street toward my hotel. I began to unpack
and settle in. In a fit of nostalgia, I put on my Snowy River
hat and oilskins and stood wistfully in front of the full-
length mirror. I have owned few pieces of clothing that
were so evocative, that pleased me so completely as these.
I love this look and what it represents. I took my riding
gear off, put it in the closet, and, still smiling, went to bed.

Tuesday, December 6

I was up bright and early and over to Jolimont Centre in time to catch the first Canberra Explorer of the day. The Explorer is a bus that runs around town every 45 minutes, with 14 stops, and you can buy a day pass that allows you to get on and off the bus as often as you like.

The first leg of the run took us through the grounds of the Australian National University. We passed the futuristic, UFO-shaped Academy of Science, which is sometimes referred to by locals as the Martian Embassy. Then we climbed to the summit of Black Mountain (where there are lots of gum trees, I was happy to see). The mountain is topped by the tall, white, receiver-ringed needle of the Telecommunications Tower, the upper platforms of which offer panoramic views of Canberra. It was a rather cloudy day, but the view was still excellent. Then it was down the hill and into the city.

The bus passed Commonwealth Gardens, the Captain Cook Memorial Water Jet, the National Library (a squared-off, modernistic Parthenon faced in white marble), and the High Court and National Gallery, which is where I alighted first. The two buildings, which are connected by an elevated walkway, are extremely modern, complex, multi-angular, and stunning. I inspected first the steel and glass-faced High Court building, with its long ceremonial ramp and waterfall. Then I retired to the National Gallery—a dazzling white building designed by another contest winner.

I took a guided tour through the halls of Australian painting and decorative arts, then spent time on my own, examining more Australian art (they have Sidney Nolan's series on Ned Kelly here—unusual, rather primitive, but interesting work) and looking at some international pieces.

The collection is not as extensive as the one in Melbourne, but is still pretty impressive.

I caught the 1 o'clock Explorer bus and toured more of the city. We passed behind Parliament House, because there were pickets passing in front of it, then drove around "Embassy Circuit." Many embassies are in office buildings or suburban houses, but some countries have impressive embassy buildings and residences, often designed in the styles of the countries they represent.

I felt a flush of national pride as we passed the extensive complex of red-brick, American colonial-style buildings that serve as the U.S. Embassy, ambassador's residence, and various offices. It is the largest embassy complex in Canberra.

I enjoyed seeing the elegant Belgian and South African Embassies, the tea gardens of the Japanese Embassy, and the imposing entrance to the Indonesian Embassy, with its wealth of Balinese statues. I admired the airy, exotic, pillared Indian High Commission; the sweeping roof of Papua New Guinea's High Commission, styled after a "haus tambaran" cult house; and the pointed, tiled roof of the temple-like Royal Thai Embassy.

We drove by the Prime Minister's Lodge and past a beautiful Serbian church. Then we turned down Kings Avenue and crossed the bridge, from which we could see, standing alone on an island in Lake Burley Griffin, the sleek, tall, 53-bell Carillon given to Australia by Britain to mark Canberra's Silver Jubilee. On the far shore, we passed the Australian American Memorial—a gleaming, 200-foot needle surmounted by a huge, stylized eagle erected by public subscription to commemorate the contribution made by the people of the United States to the defense of Australia during World War II.

We swung onto Anzac Parade. This broad avenue, dedicated to the Australia New Zealand Army Corps, is flanked by Australian blue gums, with New Zealand flowering shrubs planted down the center. It was completed in 1965, to mark the 50th anniversary of the landing at Gallipoli.

Anzac Parade leads from Lake Burley Griffin up to the impressive Australian War Memorial. This is where I alighted from the coach for the second and final time.

The Australian War Memorial is a vast, stylized Byzantine edifice of gray sandstone. The memorial is also an art gallery, with 12,000 paintings; a library, with hundreds of thousands of military history books, war records, unit histories, war diaries, and other documents; and a museum, with 40,000 relics (including fighter planes, artillery pieces, tanks, and a Japanese midget submarine that was sunk in Sydney Harbour) from the wars in which Australia has participated, from the first Sudan war of 1885, through the World Wars and Southeast Asian conflicts, and up to today. It is estimated that it would take at least three days to see everything there.

I crossed the courtyard and entered the great, domed Hall of Memory, where I was surrounded by magnificent, 70-foot-tall mosaics and tall, stained-glass windows depicting the three fighting services and women's services. Passing into the cloisters, I viewed the huge, bronze Roll of Honour, which bears the names (without rank or distinction) of the 102,000 Australians killed in World War I and World War II.

Then I headed inside, where I toured 100 years of war. In addition to paintings and relics, the memorial offers 68 large, detailed, three-dimensional battle dioramas (a medium pioneered by the memorial), maps of battles and strategies, films and newsreels made on the fronts of more recent battles, numerous histories of individual heroes and heroines, and the world's largest collection of Victoria Crosses (28).

I knew Australia sustained tremendous casualties during World War I, but I had not realized what a beating the country took during World War II. The Japanese did immense damage in the North and along the eastern seaboard, bombing towns and sinking ships, even as far south as Tasmania.

The population of Australia at the outset of World War II was less than seven million. Before Japan entered the war, Australia's fighting forces were in Europe and North Africa, fighting on England's behalf, so Australia was vulnerable. The Japanese saw Australia as the "plum" of the Pacific and conquered Java mainly as a center of operations for attacking Australia. Australia could not hold off invasion alone, but American and British forces came to Australia's aid, with America in particular supplying heavy military and naval reinforcements.

The Battle of the Coral Sea was fought against the massive Japanese invasion fleet on its way to Sydney and Melbourne. The Battle of Guadalcanal stopped the second major Japanese offensive against Australia. Bombing of Darwin began in February 1942 and escalated, often involving 100 or more bombers, as Japan's invasion efforts were frustrated.

The exhibits manage to give a glimpse of the glory and honor that have always attracted individuals to battle without detracting in the slightest from the representation of the tragedy, pain, and horror of war. It was tremendously moving. It is hard to believe that the human spirit, or even the human body, could endure so much. War produces a considerable amount of misery, but it also produces the most astonishing acts of heroism and bravery, self-sacrifice and honor.

Of all the innumerable stories, a few stick most tenaciously in the front of the mind. It is, of course, the individuals that stand out in one's memory, brave soldiers, sailors, nurses, doctors, and civilians whose gallantry, ingenuity, stamina, and heroism seem almost unimaginable.

The story that stays with me the strongest, the one that moved me to tears then and still does now, is the tale of a gun loader on one of the many ships Australia lost during W.W.II. The "abandon ship" order had come, but the sailor was shot twice as he headed for the rail. Instead of jumping, he went back to his gun, strapped himself to it, and continued to fire at the Japanese fighter planes as the ship sank, making it easier for everyone else to escape. The hundreds of sailors in the water, those who reported the incident, watched the gunner bring down one last Japanese plane as the waves closed over his body, then he was gone.

The trip to Canberra was worth it for the War Memorial alone, even if there were nothing else to see.

Wednesday, December 7

I'd planned to visit Tidbinbilla Space Tracking Station, but last night's rain made things there a bit muddy, I was told, so I was asked if I'd mind switching to a tour that was just leaving for a sheep station. I didn't mind at all.

We drove out of Canberra, and even out of the A.C.T., crossing into New South Wales. The pleasure, the relief with which I viewed the countryside we had entered was almost unbounded. We were back in Australia. We passed through the small, livable, unplanned town of Queanbeyan, and then out into undulating grazing-land dotted with massive gum trees and wonderful old homesteads.

When we turned in at Burbong Station, one of the owners, Rhuben Colverwell, was waiting at the gate. Wearing oilskins, as the day was still damp, and a stockman's hat, mounted on a magnificent black horse, he cantered alongside the coach as we headed for the homestead, where Ray Colverwell, Rhuben's brother and the other owner of the station, awaited our arrival. I was in heaven—horses, dogs, sheep, gum trees, wonderful old buildings—it was glorious.

Ray and Rhuben are the third generation of Colverwells on this property, which was settled in 1871 by their forebears. Somewhat diminished from its original size, 2,000-acre Burbong is still a working sheep station, with 2,000 sheep, 10 horses, and nine sheep dogs. Ray and Rhuben work the station themselves, only hiring extra help at shearing time.

Ray escorted us to the shearing shed, where he sheared a big Merino ewe of her masses of valuable wool. (One Merino sheep yields about 16 pounds of wool.) He showed us how the wool is graded—this was extra fine—and gave us handfuls as souvenirs. The dense, lanolin-rich wool has a marvelous texture.

Then we headed toward the paddock, where Rhuben, mounted on his work horse, guided, with whistles and voice commands, two dear sheep dogs, who rounded up a mob of sheep, herded them in toward us, cut out a few, brought them back, then moved the lot through the gate and brought them to a standstill right in front of us. It was wonderful to watch the dogs work. Then we all spent a few minutes inspecting sheep, petting dogs, talking to Ray and Rhuben, and photographing nearly everything in sight. I asked Ray and Rhuben if they'd take me on as a hand, and they just chuckled. I guess they thought I was kidding.

While Rhuben and the dogs got the sheep back into the paddock, Ray led us over to the original homestead built in 1871. The two-room house was rustically charming, with a huge fireplace and much hand-made furniture. It is not, of course, where the current generations live, but it is good that they have preserved it.

By this time, the typical Aussie barbecue of steak and sausages was ready, and we gathered around the grill. After lunch, the billy was boiled for tea and, after we'd had ours, we took a cup of tea, with lots of milk and sugar, out to the kangaroos that hang around waiting for just this treat. As many as I've seen, I still never cease to be delighted by these wonderful creatures. I personally think koalas are highly over-rated—kangaroos, and of course wallabies, too, are by far the more affecting animals. Galahs and cockatoos shrieked and cackled nearby, as the 'roos slurped down their tea.

Before it was time to leave, our bus driver offered to teach anyone who was interested how to throw a boomerang. I watched while a few people tried but didn't quite learn, then I decided I might as well give it a go. As I walked over to where the driver stood, I was half way between certain I could do it and positive I'd bury the thing in the dirt. I listened carefully (something I've learned is useful in most situations), then let her rip. I did exactly as I was told, but was still a little surprised to see how perfectly it worked. Its almost flawless flight elicited a burst of applause from those watching. I was not quite game enough to try catching it when it returned to me, but a second successful throw had me sufficiently hooked to get me to buy my own boomerang (just as the driver had hoped). I'm not certain where in Chicago I'll be able to use it, but should the occasion arise, I'm now ready.

My eyes feasted hungrily on the sight of that beautiful countryside as we drove back toward Canberra, and I returned to my hotel happy and refreshed.

Thursday, December 8

Today was pretty much a non-day. I slept late, then arose to packing and writing. A lot of the writing was on Christmas cards. I've never had such an international mailing before. I love it. At this rate, by the end of my trip I should know someone from just about everywhere. Then I finished up a package of things to send home and, around three o'clock, strolled over to the post office.

A brief wander down by Lake Burley Griffin and then in search of dinner made me appreciate more the elegant organization of Canberra. It may not be charming, but it's easy.

The day now ends as it began, with writing, which will soon be followed by sleep.

Friday, December 9

I was at the Greyhound station by 7:15 a.m.. As the bus pulled away from Canberra, I realized I hadn't been quite fair to her, had not seen everything I might have. But I still couldn't quite care. I was too sick and too tired to do much more than I did. And the city didn't feel real to me. Simply, Canberra found no real hold on my heart. Perhaps, under different circumstances, I'd feel differently. And if, someday, I pass through again, there are things I'd still like to see, but no deep longing ties me to Canberra, I am not drawn to it, as I have been drawn to so many other places. Sorry, Canberra. Sorry, Walter.

The bus trip to Sydney was as spectacular and euphoria-inducing as any I've enjoyed here. We passed by undulating fields of golden grass with grazing sheep and saw green, hillside paddocks filled with beautiful horses. Mountains rose up beside us and in front of us. At one spot, the trees were filled with hundreds of white birds, mostly corellas (small, white cockatoos). Deep purple and bright yellow wildflowers bloomed on all sides. Wattle bushes clung to the rocky sides of mountains, and everywhere there were magnificent gum trees. Soon we caught sight of the ocean, with the early morning sunlight dancing on the waves.

WALTZING NEW SOUTH WALES

Sydney sprawls a bit, so we were still more than an hour from downtown when we entered the first of her suburbs. But most of the suburbs are fairly buried in trees, and there are few tall buildings, so you don't feel like you're in a big city until you actually get downtown.

From the Greyhound station, I caught a taxi for the short trip to the C.B. Hotel. This place is an experience! A small entrance belies the size of the 200-plus room hostelry. It's clean, with a friendly staff, but is very minimal. The small rooms offer bed, bureau, and towel; there are no tea making facilities, hand basins, electric outlets, or mirrors. The communal bathroom is clean, adequately large, and has brick floors. The rooms have uncarpeted linoleum floors. But then, what do you expect for $60 a week. On the positive side, there is a laundry facility (thank goodness), a TV room, and a couple of vending machines in the lobby.

The clientele is mixed: pensioners who didn't save quite enough for a comfortable retirement; young travelers (leaning heavily toward non-English-speaking countries—lots of Swedes and Germans); a few briefcase-toting, three piece-suited Asian business men (obviously not representing high-budget corporations); and young locals getting away for the weekend (here the accent is on teenage couples). The hotel is, however, very well located for touring the city, and is adequate for my needs.

After checking in, I headed off to explore the neighborhood. This area is tremendously diverse, but with the population weighted toward Asian, as we border on Chinatown. Great, curly maned Fou lions guard tall, imperial gates. Façades fluctuate between Asian and European. Import shops bulge with exotic gifts, and foreign eateries abound. Within a one-block radius of the hotel there are two Vietnamese, four Indonesian, one Lebanese, one Indian, one Mexican, and nearly a dozen Chinese restaurants.

I stopped by the Ansett office, to see what was available in the way of orientation and sightseeing (a day tour being both easier and less expensive than renting a car). Then, after four hours of wandering, I decided it was time for dinner, as I'd had no breakfast or lunch.

I settled on the Java Indonesian Restaurant, a little place a half block from the hotel, and one that opens at the relatively early hour of 5:30. The meal was delightful—lamb cooked in coconut milk with chillis.

The hostess/waitress was a lovely girl from Djakarta who is studying accounting here. When she has her degree, she will return to Indonesia. There are many other Indonesian students at the school, so she doesn't get enough chances to practice her English, she told me. She was pleased to have someone to talk to, and we chatted for about an hour, at which time other customers started coming in.

Saturday, December 10

Clouds were rolling in threateningly as I walked to the Ansett office in Oxford Square, but my tour headed out on time, undeterred by the shift in weather. When the storm did break, it was as if we were under a waterfall. Water was running down gutters like raging rivers. Intersections were soon flooded, and cars were swamped. We saw numerous truly pathetic motorcyclists looking very wet and uncomfortable. I felt particularly bad for them because of why they were out and about. Each year around Christmas time, nearly 5,000 bikers from all over New South Wales gather in Sydney for a "parade" that transports gifts to underprivileged children—and this was the big day. Fortunately, the rain stopped before the event started, but there were a lot of soggy bikers out there.

As sudden and violent as the storm was, it ended relatively quickly. Within little more than an hour, the sun was out and the sky was clearing.

An hour out of the city, we came to El Caballo Blanco, showplace for beautiful horses, especially the magnificent, white Andalusians. I wandered around the extensive grounds, past small shops and lavish gardens, then down to the broad, green paddocks to see the horses. Everywhere, handsome, aristocratic mares were followed, nuzzled, or danced around by their jesterish foals.

A huge arena inside the spacious, Spanish-style central building was the site for a lavish horse show. There were a dozen skilled riders, and at least 20 of the glorious "dancing" stallions, as well as other horses, from tiny Welsh ponies to massive draft horses. The stables were open after the show, and I went back to see the horses. I walked slowly, stopping to admire a graceful head or to stroke a velvety muzzle. I even love the smell of horses and all the leather, so I was happy.

Driving back toward Sydney, we saw hundreds of jacaranda trees. They are past their prime, we were told, but the great, purple clouds of flowers filling their branches still delighted me.

Sunday, December 11

I was up bright and early for a tour of the city, its beaches (there are 36 ocean beaches within the city limits), and outlying areas. This would be my first sight of Sydney Harbour, the Harbour Bridge, and the Opera House since I flew over them four months ago. I have come full circle.

Sydney, the capital of New South Wales and one of the most important ports in the South Pacific, is the oldest city in Australia. It was founded in 1788, with the arrival of the First Fleet,* commanded by Captain Arthur Phillip, who was pleased to have found "the finest harbour in the world, in which a thousand sail of the line may ride in the most perfect security." The harbor, which is 150 miles in circumference, has become the centerpiece of the city.

Sydney is built on the low hills surrounding the splendid harbor, with its innumerable bays and inlets. The city radiates outward from the harbor, sprawling over 670 square miles. But Sydney's size does not detract from the glory of its surroundings. In fact, as Mark Twain observed, "[The harbor] would be beautiful without Sydney, but not above half as beautiful as it is now, with Sydney added."

As we drove down Macquarie Street toward Circular Quay (pronounced "key"), the first harbor feature to come into view was the Harbour Bridge. I had not expected it to be so impressive. It towers above the surrounding buildings. Soon the Opera House was in view, its familiar "sails" glittering in the sunlight. Sydney's harbor now lay before me. I was dazzled, entranced. That curving, sparkling, blue expanse stretched between the city's gentle, green hills is one of the most spectacular sights I've ever seen.

We crossed the Harbour Bridge (affectionately called the Coat Hanger) on our way to the northern suburbs. The

*See appendix

bridge, which was opened in 1932, is one of the largest single-span bridges in the world—1,650 feet long and 160 feet wide.

Clean, white houses with red tile roofs climb the green hills facing the harbor. Flowering trees and shrubs seem to overflow the gardens. Everywhere, the views of harbor and hills are magnificent. It is hard to imagine not enjoying any day that begins with this kind of scenery.

We drove through Manly, one of Sydney's oldest beachfront suburbs. Captain Arthur Phillip, who visited the site in 1788, called it Manly because of the proud bearing of its Aborigines. The charming, old town offers 17 miles of good surfing and swimming beaches.

We continued north past more of Sydney's excellent surf beaches—Queenscliff, North Steyne, Dee Why—stopping often to take pictures of the dramatic seascape, the craggy cliffs and gentle coves, the interaction of water and rocks, the merging of ocean and sky in the infinite blue distance. Then we headed up into the mountainous and heavily forested Kuring-Gai Chase National Park. Soon we were in the midst of kangaroos, wallabies, koalas, and emus at the Waratah Park Wildlife Sanctuary.

The sanctuary grounds, typical of all the preserves I've seen over here, were lovely. The vegetation is largely undisturbed, and the rolling fields, beautiful trees, and flowers of the natural bushland surroundings made it especially pleasant, in addition to providing a good home for the animals.

We watched Tasmanian devils, wombats, parrots, and cockatoos, petted koalas and kangaroos, and photographed everything that moved. Emus, some followed by awkward, foot-tall chicks, pursued us in search of handouts. I had almost forgotten the strange drumming noise that is the emu's call, but heard it a lot today. A pair of wedge-tailed eagles watched us from their perch. Sulphur-crested cockatoos strolled about, stopping beneath the trees to crunch on gum nuts. I fell in love with a Major Mitchell cockatoo, also known as a Leadbeater's cockatoo. This exquisite bird is rose and white, with a bright orange, yellow, pink, and white crest. Wow.

One sad, homely little roo stood off to the side, alone, staring at the ground, obviously aware of the fact that he was not as popular as the adorable wallabies. He looked so dejected—he reminded me of Eeyore. I went over and fed and petted him, and he happily followed me around till it was time for us to leave. I was sorry I couldn't take him with me.

Heading back through the beautiful forests of Kuring-Gai Chase, down the coast, we arrived at Circular Quay at noon. We were on our own for lunch, so I wandered off into The Rocks, the wonderful, historic spot where the First Fleet landed in 1788 and began building the new colony. Many of the solid, old, convict-built, stone structures from this period are still in use. It is a remarkably picturesque location and houses several of Sydney's nicer restaurants and a wide range of delightful shops and galleries.

I explored the Argyle Arts Centre, a massive stone edifice built as a bond store in 1826, now converted into a marvelous arcade of unusual, purely Australian shops and art and artifact dealers. I found one tiny shop, the Argyle Alchemist, which sells Australian perfumes. I tried several lovely fragrances, but only the golden wattle perfume made my pulse quicken, its wild sweetness closely capturing the way the flowering wattles smelled in the mountains. It was wonderful. Fortunately, it was also reasonably priced, as I absolutely had to have some.

For lunch, I had the Australian national foodstuff—a meat pie with sauce. Then it was time to meander back through the narrow streets of The Rocks toward Circular Quay, to reboard the bus for the afternoon portion of the tour.

We stopped outside the Opera House, then turned up Macquarie Street, passing State Parliament, the old Sydney Hospital, and the Mint. As we approached Hyde Park, we could see St. James Church and the Hyde Park Barracks, both designed by convict architect Francis Greenway, who, under the patronage of Governor Lachlan Macquarie,* designed and built quite a bit around early Sydney. Continuing along College Street, we saw St. Mary's Cathedral and the Australian Museum. I must return to these places later, on foot, to enjoy them fully.

We crossed the Domain, a broad, green park where Sydney's "Speakers' Corner," much like the one in London's Hyde Park, is located. Because it is Sunday, several speakers were out on their soapboxes, all drawing varying sizes of groups, from one to a few dozen. We drove along the Botanic Gardens and out to Mrs. Macquarie's Point, which Mrs. Macquarie (wife of Governor Lachlan Macquarie) loved for its splendid vistas of the harbor and surrounding hills (and I had to agree with her—amazing view).

Following the road back along the far side of the green finger of the point, we passed through the old, harborside area of Woolloomooloo. Then, driving through Kings Cross, Sydney's Soho/Greenwich Village/nightlife area, we headed out through the southern suburbs, which are as beautiful as the northern ones, with houses nestled in rolling hills overlooking the harbor. We passed along Rushcutters Bay, through the very fashionable neighborhoods of Double Bay (appropriately nicknamed Double

*See appendix

Pay), and up into the hills of Vaucluse, on the shores of Rose Bay.

We stopped high on a cliff in Vaucluse and looked back toward the city. The harbor stretched before us. Across the water, Sydney's skyline was silhouetted against a backdrop of towering, black and white clouds. Great shafts of light spilled through the clouds; the silver beams sparkled on the water, danced among the sailboats and islands, caught on the Harbour Bridge and Opera House in the distance, outlining them against the sky.

At The Gap, where Sydney Harbour meets the Pacific Ocean, we climbed a hill, to a spot where we could see the waters' joining. The hill ends abruptly and plunges directly into the sea, turning a face of ragged sandstone toward the incoming waves. The high stone wall of Inner North Head forms the far boundary of the passage. The land around us was green, with myriad bright, fragrant flowers. The sky over the ocean was dazzlingly blue, dotted with fleecy clouds that were vaguely reflected in the equally dazzling blue of the water.

Following the road along South Head, we came to the port's first lighthouse, which was designed by Francis Greenway. It is a graceful, classically styled, stark white building, its central tower beautiful against the brilliant blue sky. It is said that Governor Macquarie was so impressed with the structure that he granted Greenway a pardon. (Greenway contributed so extensively to early Sydney's architecture, a late Georgian style of design that later became known as Macquarie style, that it was eventually deemed fit that he should appear on Australia's $10 note—rather ironic, when you consider he was transported for forgery.)

Continuing south, we came to famous Bondi Beach

(pronounced Bon-dye), where we stopped for afternoon tea and a walk in the sun. The beach and water were adorned with hundreds of bronzed bodies and a rainbow of bright surfboards.

With a run past a few other beautiful beaches, we headed back through the city. Our return trip took us through now fashionable Paddington, also known as Paddo. The iron lace-fronted terrace houses that climb the steeply sloping streets in this part of town were built between 1850 and 1900. The handsome, Victorian buildings are now being snatched up and renovated by chic Sydneysiders.

Then it was back into the city center, for one last spin around downtown. Sydney really is quite splendid.

Monday, December 12

This morning, my tour du jour exited the city through the western suburbs, heading for "the magical range of the Blue Mountains," as D.H. Lawrence described them. Not much more than an hour out of the city, we could see the mountains in the distance, a shimmering blue wall on the far side of green fields. The mountains rise with startling abruptness from the flat coastal plain.

The Blue Mountains get their color, and hence their name, from the eucalyptus-oil haze rising from the gum trees that cover the area. Sunlight is diffused by this fragrant aura and makes the mountains look, from a distance, intensely blue. However, once you're in the mountains, the effect is no longer visible.

We climbed steadily, steeply, to the top of the range, where the road leveled out. These mountains are actually the remnants of a massive plateau. The walls are precipitous, but the top is flat. The canyon-like valleys were created by waterfalls and rivers carving down through the sandstone. Because of this, the valleys dead-end at stone walls, and there are no passes, which made the initial crossing of the range difficult. But the cliffs and gorges of this ancient, eroded landscape have a strange, primeval beauty that is entirely different from the beauty of younger mountains. As Charles Darwin noted in his Geological Observations, "It is not easy to conceive of a more magnificent spectacle than is presented to a person walking on the summit plains, when without any notice he arrives at the brink of one of the cliffs."

We paused often to admire the broad vistas, steep cliffs, and dense forests. New growth on the gums is yellow or red or frosty celadon, depending on the variety. This time of year, there is a lot of new growth, which gives the spring forest an almost autumnal hue.

We stopped at Echo Point, a jutting ledge that affords an excellent view of the rock formation the Three Sisters and a major portion of the Jamison Valley. The view was amazing: the forests more than 2,000 feet below, lapping at the mountains' feet, mottled by shadows of passing clouds; sudden, vertical up-thrusts of stone, tall, pale rock walls emerging from and topped with dark, green foliage. The wind coming through the valley below sounded lonely and haunting. It was glorious.

The Three Sisters, three rugged pinnacles of rock, derive their name from Aboriginal mythology. The sisters, back in the time of legend, went into the forest to forage with the local witch doctor. The three girls got tired and decided to stay behind while the doctor headed farther into the woods. They idly threw stones over the cliff as they waited for the magician's return. Unfortunately, this woke up a bunyip, a (mythical) creature that was fond of dining on humans. Hearing the girls' cries of distress, the witch doctor came running, magic stick in hand, but he was too far away to actually intervene, so he turned the three sisters into the three stone pillars that still stand in the mountains. At this point, the bunyip turned his attentions to the good doctor, who, after a lengthy chase, was cornered at the base of the mountains. So the magician turned himself into a lyrebird. Even today, you can see the lyrebird scratching around at the base of the mountains, looking for his magic stick so he can change himself and the three sisters back to their original forms.

Not far from Echo Point, we stopped at the depot for the Katoomba scenic railway and skyway. I opted for the railway, which is, I learned upon reaching the bottom, the steepest in the world. It was, by then, easy to believe. The incline is 52 degrees, though it felt like the 750-foot drop was straight down.

The little railway was built in the 1880s by the Katoomba Coal Mine Company. The small, cage-like "cars" descend through a natural chimney of stone, all dripping with water and ferns, then burst out into the verdant splendor of the mountainside forest.

The bottom of the track is about a third of the way down the mountain. I wanted to wander about the bush for a while, so I scrambled out of my little, metal cage, and soon I was ambling happily along the narrow bush track that clings to the high stone wall.

The view at that level was dazzling, with the bare, sandstone cliffs rising straight up overhead, dense foliage robing the pathway, tree tops below, with the forest marching down to the valley floor. Stringybarks, peppermint gums, and red bloodwoods make up much of the forest at this high level. The spaces between the trees were crowded with ferns, some of which looked like giant whirlpools of green, and flowering shrubs—boronia, waratah, mountain devils. There were as many shades of green as there were different plants.

I hadn't gone very far before I heard falling water, and I followed the sound. Just below the level of the shaded mountain track, the bright, clear water of an underground river bursts from a crack in the cliff face and disappears down the mountainside. About a quarter mile beyond the underground river is Katoomba Falls. It is from these and similar streams and falls that the area derives its name—"Katoomba" comes from an Aboriginal word that means "falling waters" or "the falling together of many streams."

I would have loved to have spent ages longer there, but after two hours I had to make the return trip to the cliff's top. I shall return to this place, to these mountains. This was hardly even an appetizer of a visit. These mountains deserve days.

I still had a little time before the bus departed, so I wandered off into some nearby trees. I saw a crimson rosella, then another, and began to quietly follow them. The rosellas soon led me to an even greater "find"—a king parrot. The bird, with its brilliant orange head and breast and emerald green wings, sat on a branch not more than 20 feet from me. I would have gotten closer had I not run out of cliff. I took a few photos, then waited to see if he'd turn around, which he did a few minutes later. I wrapped an arm around a tree, leaned out as far as I dared, and tried not to breathe. The glorious parrot dropped to a lower branch on a tree nearer to me. I stayed there until the last possible moment, so enjoying the sight of that wonderful, bright bird.

Tuesday, December 13

Today I was destined for the famous Hunter Valley wine region, with visits to two of the area's many fine wineries. Whereas South Australia's wineries turn out mostly German-style wines, this region produces predominantly French Burgundy types, although they do make some fine "German" wines, too. The grapes grown here are mostly Sémillon, Chardonnay, Cabernet Sauvignon, and Pinot Noir.

My bus crossed the Harbour Bridge and headed north out of the city. Mountains and forests, fields and paddocks, small towns and large stations flashed past my window. As we drove through the dense mountain bush, our driver pointed out the incredible gymea lilies. Also known as an Illawarra lily, this flower stands ten feet tall and has a bloom the size of a dinner plate. It is late in the season, and the huge, red flowers were well past their primes, but were still impressive.

I saw gum trees unlike any I had seen before. Some had wonderful chamois/cream-colored trunks, others were a bright rust hue. They stood out strikingly among the numerous gray- and brown-trunked trees. There were many familiar trees as well. The small, celadon-leafed, hedge-like, wildly fragrant spinning gums clustered about the bases of taller trees. Stringybarks and blue gums towered over an under story dense with flowering shrubs.

We crossed a gentle, verdant valley full of horse-raising properties, then continued past Cessnock and east to Hungerford Hill Wine Village. This is an obviously tourist-oriented winery, which offers shops, picnic grounds, and nice restaurants. The tasting room is in a large cellar, half underground and with a sod roof. At the long, wooden counter we were treated to several agreeable wines. We browsed through the bottles and bins that filled the huge room, then headed outside to choose a place to dine.

After lunch, we traveled north, toward the Hunter River and our next winery—Hermitage. Here, we viewed the broad, lush vineyards and had a guided tour of the large production facility. Although much harvesting is done mechanically these days, Hermitage still has all their grapes picked by hand to protect the quality of the grapes and, therefore, of the wine. The biggest problem in producing wine in this region is the heat (temperatures usually range between 90 and 120 degrees in the summer, when the wine is being made), so a great deal of attention is paid to properly insulating the buildings and cooling the vats, so the grapes don't cook.

The German varieties of wines are made to be drunk fairly young. They're fermented in stainless steel containers, then bottled. The French-style wines are treated a little more traditionally. Fermentation is begun in the stainless steel vats, then completed in imported wooden barrels. Maturation starts in the wooden barrels, but is finished in the bottle.

The tasting room was a real treat. These were the best wines I've had so far in Australia. The Fumé Blanc was light, dry, elegant. The Chardonnay had a fuller body and deeper color, and was exceptionally smooth. The Traminer Riesling was delicate, slightly sweet, sheer heaven. A two-year-old Sauternes was lush, succulent, sweet but not heavy. Chateau d'Yquem is not threatened, but this reasonably priced delight would be within the reach of more impoverished connoisseurs.

Wednesday, December 14

It was another bright, warm day, and I enjoyed the sunshine and sea breeze as I walked to Oxford Square to catch another bus. Again, we headed north, along the coast, toward Gosford. We passed through Kuring-Gai Chase and crossed the splendid, mountain-cradled Hawkesbury River, then swung east, toward Old Sydney Town.

Old Sydney Town is a recreation of what The Rocks— the original part of Sydney—looked like 200 years ago. Life, as it was lived during the terms of the first five governors of New South Wales, is portrayed by the many "citizens" of the town—soldiers, sailors, craftsmen, convicts, musicians, settlers, etc. They even go by the names of people who actually lived in the area during Sydney's early days.

Once inside Old Sydney Town, I perused my map of the 50-acre site, then headed off, past Miller's hut and the windmill, along Rocks Row to Middlesex Lane. I passed the large, handsome, sandstone Court House/Gaol, and strolled onto the Parade Ground, where troops of the New South Wales Corps* were gathering for drilling, cannon firing, and musket practice.

The arms the soldiers of the N.S.W. Corps used were the Brown Bess muskets. These guns, which were in service for 150 years, were best known for their lack of accuracy. We saw them loaded and fired, then one of the soldiers showed us the mechanism of these flintlock firearms, explained the loading and firing procedures, outlined a bit of their history, and told us some expressions engendered by this gun that would continue into current usage. The gun was pretty much made up of the flintlock, the stock, and a barrel, so lock, stock, and barrel came to mean the entirety of something.

*See appendix

When the musket was fully and properly loaded, a small amount of gunpowder would trickle out a hole at the side into the pan that receives the spark. When the flint hit the metal, it ignited the powder, which burned back through the hole and set off the charge inside. Sometimes, however, although the powder in the pan burned, it failed to set off the internal charge—it was just a flash in the pan.

The safety position on the musket was with the hammer half way between closed and fully cocked. With the hammer locked in this position, a soldier could safely load his weapon. However, in older guns, this locking mechanism could wear out and the musket would then go off half-cocked.

I spent a blissful three hours strolling around town, talking to the "villagers," all of whom were well informed about the individuals they portrayed, as well as whatever surrounded or affected that person at the time he or she lived in the colony. I learned how split-wood shingles were made and affixed to roofs with wooden dowels and watched bullocks load tree trunks onto a dray. I sat in on a few frustrating, cruel, one-sided trials, which were actually taken from court records of the time. I witnessed a flogging, and found out how "volunteers" were enlisted in the N.S.W. Corps.

I visited the Observatory, the first built in the antipodes, but its builder, Lieutenant William Dawes, was not in. However, his assistant filled me in on some of the primitive utensils Dawes had to work with; showed how the Observatory, built on solid rock to avoid vibrations, had its roof mounted on cannonballs, so it could rotate; and explained some of the observations Dawes made and how they contributed to safe navigation south of the equator.

From the Observatory, I headed down to the waterfront,

where I boarded the merchant brig Perseverance, a replica of the trim, two-masted vessel built in Sydney in 1807. Then I strolled up past the coach house, blacksmith, printery, and naval dockyard, and down to the pottery. The huge, brick kiln in front of the pottery is a deep brownish-red rust in hue, and its color is almost perfectly matched by a tall gum tree growing beside the pottery building.

Musicians had gathered outside the Market Place when I returned down Sergeant Majors Row, and the town's "citizens" and visitors alike gathered to listen to their rousing sea shanties and Irish dance tunes. A few of the soldiers lounged nearby, cleaning their muskets and chatting.

I listened for a while, then wandered on, along the dirt streets, among the rows and clusters of whitewashed cottages. The life of the new colony went on around me: horse-drawn carriages clattered by, convicts worked on buildings, merchants went about their businesses, skilled tradesman—stone masons, metal workers, smithies, leather workers, potters—demonstrated their expertise and hawked their wares.

One of the local laborers, a shingle splitter, detailed the way in which the British government supplied the new colony with these tradesmen. Those in charge of providing the needed workers would hire beautiful young women who were to visit various taverns. Each of these lovely creatures would buy drinks for a wealthy man, then pick his pockets. When a man with the required skills came in, she'd buy him drinks until he was unaware of what was happening, then she'd plant on him whatever she had lifted from the first gent. There was, of course, always a constable or soldier near this sort of establishment, and our shady lady would inform him that she thought she'd witnessed a robbery. The official would step in, catch the "villain" red-handed, and soon he was bound for Botany Bay. Nasty, but effective.

One of the interesting things about the map of Old Sydney Town is that, not only are the original names of the colony's streets given, but the current names (when they differ) also appear. Now, when walking through The Rocks, I can see where these events occurred, where these buildings stood, and where some remain to this day.

Thursday, December 15

After a nice, relaxing morning, I made my way toward the center of town to meet Stephen (another Red Centre veteran) for lunch. We talked for more than an hour, catching up on all our news. I have been invited to come and stay with his family and spend Christmas with them. This kindness will make the holiday away from home far more pleasant than it would be if spent alone. I shall spend another week in town before accepting their hospitality, though, to avoid wearing out my welcome before the holidays even begin.

After walking back to Stephen's office with him, I set out for the Australian Museum. I perused the displays on marsupials, of which there are around 170 species that occur nowhere but Australia. There is a Thylacine among the animals on display. This is the famous Tasmanian tiger, in reality a striped, marsupial wolf, which is feared to be extinct, though recent tentative sightings offer hope that survivors exist in Tasmania's unexplored regions.

I saw a fascinating film on kangaroos. Kangaroos range in size from the tiny rat kangaroo to the powerful, seven-foot-tall gray and red kangaroos. There is a kangaroo for every terrain—desert, forest, swamp, mountain, scrub. There are even tree kangaroos. Possibly the most astonishing of the kangaroo's traits is the ability of the female to hold a spare embryo in a suspended state. If a nursing joey dies, the reserve embryo is jolted into continued development.

I browsed slowly through the extensive gem and mineral exhibit, then headed for the hall of Australian birds. This took up half a floor. An aspect of this section that I particularly enjoyed was the buttons you can push to play recordings of many species' calls or songs. So often I have heard the birds without seeing them, and it was nice to be able to connect the voices with the singers.

At 5 p.m., the museum closed, and I strolled back toward the hotel. I decided to dine again at the Java Indonesian Restaurant. Yanti, the hostess/waitress/university student with whom I talked on my previous visit, recommended a spicy fish dish, which I ordered, then the two of us talked until other customers came in.

Among those other customers was a charming retired couple: Ron, an Australian, and Norma, his Filipina wife. They invited me to join them for dessert and coffee. Norma recommended an odd, refreshing dessert called Cendol—green ribbons of agar-agar with coconut milk, palm sugar, and shaved ice. The three of us talked for a couple of hours.

Ron and Norma don't get into Sydney often, preferring their home on the coast about two hours north of the city, but had come down for a big stamp sale for collectors. They asked if I'd had a chance to take advantage of any of the fine local beaches, and I replied that I hadn't. They told me their home overlooks the water and, if I'd like, I could come home with them, spend the night, then spend tomorrow playing on the beach and swimming with

Norma (Ron can't stay in the sun too much). After that, I could catch a train back to Sydney. I dashed back to the C.B., threw a nightgown, toothbrush, and swim suit into my canvas flight bag, and met Ron and Norma back at the restaurant in record time.

It was dark, so I didn't see much of the countryside through which we passed, but I could tell when we finally got out of suburban Sydney and into the country. Ron played a Fats Waller tape as we sped along, and detailed for me what I would be seeing if it weren't dark. In a little over two hours we were in the seaside village of Terrigal, just east of Gosford.

Ron and Norma's house is perched on the side of a hill, surrounded by trees and gardens, with the back terrace facing the ocean. The night was clear, and even in the dark I could tell that the view was exceptional.

Norma made coffee, and we all chatted for a while longer. There were scratching and scurrying sounds out on the terrace. Norma looked out, then called me to the window to watch the brush-tail possums feeding on the bread that she always leaves out for them. The wonderful, furry, little creatures gazed up at us with their large, dark eyes, then decided we were harmless and went back to their munching.

It was nearly midnight when I finally went down to the room that had been designated as mine, and I was soon asleep.

Friday, December 16
I was awakened, as I was warned I would be, by dozens of rainbow lorikeets that always come to breakfast

on the terrace—at 5:30 a.m. These brilliant, multi-colored little parrots are as noisy as they are beautiful, so no one sleeps through their arrival. When, after dressing and making up the bed, I ascended to the breakfast room, Norma had coffee and tomatoes on toast waiting, and we sat and watched the birds dine as we enjoyed our own meal. It was a bright, cloudless day, and the view of the beach and ocean was as impressive as I had imagined from the previous night's evidence.

After eating, we watched a tennis match on TV. Then Norma and I changed into our swimsuits, and Ron dropped us off at the beach. The flowering trees at the beach's edge smelled heavenly, and the blossoms dripped nectar when I picked one. The sun was warm, and there was a soft breeze.

We dropped our towels on the sand and headed straight for the water. In contrast to the sun and sand, the water felt chilly at first, but we adjusted to it quickly. Norma and I swam and dove, and tried to body surf on the larger waves. The view from the water of the land was glorious: the tree-lined beach, with the green hills rising up behind; the land's arms reaching out on either side of the bay to protect the spot.

After swimming for about an hour we went for a long walk up the beach. Norma pointed out the homes of people she and Ron know. We stopped often, to watch surfers cutting across the waves or children playing in the water and on the sand.

When we got back to where we'd left our towels, we sat in the sun for a while, but soon headed into the water again. The waves rolled by in an easy rhythm. The water was like silk. It was easy to pass our remaining hours enjoying the surf.

We had a late lunch—mostly things Ron had picked from their large garden—then spent a long, leisurely, companionable time chatting over tea. Ron and Norma are as intelligent as they are charming, and I enjoyed the lively discussions of everything from nature conservation to world politics. Then, with exchange of addresses and an invitation for a return visit, it was time for me to catch the train back to Sydney. Ron and Norma dropped me at the Gosford depot, and I waved farewell to my two newest Australian friends.

As the train sped southward, the mountains rose around us, then fell away to the sea. We crossed the Hawkesbury River at Broken Bay, and, nearby, I could see the sprawling commercial oyster beds and the attendant, wharf-side Fresh Oyster shops. I leaned back in my seat, breathed deeply, and smiled my contentment with the beauty around me and the kindness and generosity of the people I've met.

Saturday, December 17

I stayed in for part of the day, reading, writing, and rehashing my trip. I calculated today that, so far, I've traveled more than 14,000 miles within Australia.

In the afternoon I went for a long walk to get some fresh air and sunshine. As I wandered through town, through city streets which pleased me but which were, like other city streets, no longer the sole focus of my delight, I thought of how I've changed. I am learning to need less, getting down to basics. Not since I was a student would I have stayed in a place like the C.B. Hotel, and even earlier in this trip, such minimalism would have been almost unthinkable. Now, it is enough.

"I've pared myself down to essentials," I told myself, as I strolled down Castlereagh Street, looking in the windows of the elegant antique shops. "All I need is my hat, my knife, my sleeping bag. . . and that sterling silver candelabrum."

Ah, well—not everything has changed.

I turned my steps toward Hyde Park, where I wandered down shaded paths, past eucalypts and massive fig trees. I sat on one of the park's broad lawns for a while, enjoying the greenery and the bright gardens. I was surprised when a large ibis strolled past me. It's not a bird I expect to see in a central city park.

After a few hours, I headed back to the hotel, where I settled into an evening of laundry and reading.

Sunday, December 18

It was a gray day, though pleasantly warm. I walked through the city, which is fairly quiet on Sundays, then headed down to Circular Quay. I strolled along the harborfront and finally wandered over to the Argyle Arts Centre, where I purchased a ticket for the 12:45 walking tour of The Rocks.

I puttered through galleries and shops until it was time for my tour, then joined the small group assembled at the starting point. Our guide, Roz, was very enthusiastic about the work being done to preserve this area, and she gave us a quick rundown of restoration efforts before we headed out.

We walked first to Cadman's Cottage. Built in 1816, this is the oldest dwelling still standing in Sydney. John Cadman, for whom it was built, was superintendent of government boats, so the cottage includes space for storing boating equipment.

Roz explained that the peculiar, orangey color of the exterior is quite authentic. The way it was produced when the house was first built was by mixing glue, flour, and vegetable peelings together in a wheelbarrow and allowing it to ferment for several days. Then it was painted on the outside of buildings. When they'd finished the job, the convicts working on the project usually licked the wheelbarrow clean, because the fermented glue was an effective intoxicant. (Bleh!)

Ascending the well-worn stone steps that run alongside Cadman's Cottage, we turned into George Street. Once called Sergeant Majors Row, this is the oldest street in Sydney. In places where the asphalt has worn thin, we could still see the street's original wooden cobbles.

Across the street was the first Bank of N.S.W., established in 1817 by Governor Lachlan Macquarie.* We passed Union Bond (1841) and the Counting House (1848), and along the Sergeant Majors Row Terrace (1881). Under the Harbour Bridge, Dawes Point offered an unobstructed view of the harbor, city and Opera House. The point was named for Lieutenant William Dawes, who built Sydney's earliest observatory.

We proceeded down Lower Fort Street, past the elegant Georgian terrace houses of early Sydney's upper classes. On the corners of Windmill Street and Lower Fort are the Hero of Waterloo and former Whalers Arms, two 1840s hostelries. The Hero of Waterloo was once notorious as the spot where men were "recruited" for whaling ships and merchant ships. There were trap doors in the bar, which led to subterranean cells serviced by a secret tunnel. When a likely candidate had drunk far beyond his capacity, he would be dropped into the cell below, from which he was

*See appendix

collected by those needing crew. When he regained consciousness, he would be well out to sea.

A little farther along we came to Argyle Place, Sydney's only village green. The tidy, little park is lined with cottages, all built between 1830 and 1880, all employing great quantities of the lovely ironwork known as Sydney lace. These were once the homes of the city's early successful merchants. On the far side of the green is the Lord Nelson Hotel, which is the oldest licensed hotel in Australia.

At the near end of Argyle Place is the Garrison Church. The church's real name is Holy Trinity Church, but, as the first Official Garrison Church of the colony, attended largely by redcoats stationed at the nearby Dawes Point Battery, it became known almost exclusively as Garrison Church. Started in 1840, it is the second oldest church in Sydney and the earliest existing example of Australian Gothic architecture.

Turning down Argyle Street, we entered the Argyle Cut, a tunnel cut through the solid sandstone that makes up the city's foundation. It was designed to give the genteel folk and wealthy merchants living in the Millers Point area direct access to Circular Quay. It was begun in 1843 using convict labor, picks and shovels, but the job of carving the 300-foot tunnel out of the rock was more of an effort than could be handled this way. Eventually, free men and dynamite were brought in, and the job was completed.

The narrow, dark Argyle Cut proved to be the downfall of the area as a home for the wealthier classes. It was a perfect place to catch and rob anyone trying to get into town, and the gangs that started to gather at the spot virtually held the entire Millers Point area hostage. Soon, anyone with any money, sense, or desire to live moved out, and the area became fairly slummy for many years.

The biggest and most powerful gang of this era was the Rocks Push. With 2,500 members at its peak, the Push far outnumbered the area's residents. The gangs were finally dispersed when plague broke out in Sydney in the late 1800s, and the government used it as an excuse to really clean up the area, hunting rats, leveling and burning infested slums, and arresting or chasing out the often murderous gang members.

Continuing through the Cut and down Argyle Street, we found ourselves once more in front of the Argyle Stores, which were begun in 1826. The solid, old, convict-built, sandstone structure now houses the Argyle Arts Centre and Argyle Tavern. Here, the tour ended.

I headed next to the No. 6 Jetty at Circular Quay, where I bought a ticket for the Captain Cook Harbour Cruise. I was just in time for the 2 p.m. departure of the 2-1/2 hour tour.

Leaving Sydney Cove and rounding Bennelong Point and the Opera House, we could see the city's skyline across the broad lawns and brilliant flower beds of the Botanic Gardens. Boats of various types and sizes were everywhere, many moored and multitudes plying the bright water. This is a city of more than 50,000 pleasure craft.

We passed Fort Denison, an island originally fortified against Russian invasion. The old stone tower, cannons, and cannonballs are still there, though today the island is used as a maritime observation station. During Sydney's convict days, the island was known as Pinchgut, because the problem prisoners once confined there were put on bread and water diets to subdue them.

Cruising along the convoluted harbor shore, around points and across bays, we could see, among the cliffs and hills that leapt or rolled upward and away from the water's edge, churches, offices, and hundreds of houses, some small, some grand, their white walls and red roofs contrasting with the lush greenery that surrounds and overlaps them. And everywhere, the water reflects the hills, the buildings, the sky.

Incoming ocean waves ruffled the calm water as we passed the harbor's entrance. The cliffs of Middle Head face the opening to the sea, and there we saw the concrete gun emplacements built into the stone wall—and fairly well camouflaged by it—designed to protect Sydney Harbour during W.W.II.

We cruised into Middle Harbour. Much of this large section of the vast, sprawling waterway is lined with elegant homes, but there are also large tracts of bush, craggy cliffs, parkland, and historic sites. Bougainvillea cascaded down the rock walls, and small, sheltered coves were dotted with sunbathers.

At The Spit, a sharp needle of land that juts into the water, we had to wait for the drawbridge to be raised. Boats were queued up on both sides of the bridge, waiting till all the cars were off it, then one side could pass at a time, as the narrow passage can't handle two-way traffic.

Eventually, we turned back toward Sydney Cove. We skirted the opposite shore on our return, passing the landing for Taronga Park Zoo, then cut straight across the broad, blue expanse, and pulled into Circular Quay.

Monday, December 19

Today, I walked a lot, admired much, and photographed a fair bit. Leaving the hotel, I headed along Goulburn, then swung down Elizabeth Street to Hyde Park. I wandered through the gardens, down the broad, tree-lined walkway and around the great Archibald Memorial Fountain. Reaching St. James Road, I walked past the bronze statue of Queen Victoria and over to Greenway's charming, little St. James Church, a well-proportioned, classically designed edifice of golden stone, with columns, porches and a slender, copper-sheathed spire.

I crossed the street to see the Hyde Park Barracks, another impressive Greenway creation, then turned down Macquarie Street. I stopped to admire the beautiful, pale peach, white-pillared Mint building; the substantial, copper-domed Sydney Hospital, with its many tall windows and gracefully arched entryways; and the elegant, white, veranda'd Parliament House.

Continuing on, I passed the strangely medieval Conservatory of Music (another Greenway contribution) and turned into the Royal Botanic Gardens. I ambled happily across the broad, flower-bordered lawns, which stretch down to the low stone wall that runs along the water's edge then sweep up a hill where the crenellated walls of the Gothic-Revival Government House can be seen over the treetops. I lingered a while, enjoying the trees, flowers, and birds around me, the sunshine's warmth, the light dancing on the water.

A fence of wrought iron spears, in places almost obscured by the riot of cascading flowers, marks the far boundary of the gardens. From this edge of the garden, I had a wonderful view of the Opera House and Harbour Bridge. I descended to the Opera House, then headed around Circular Quay and up Pitt Street into town.

Christmas shoppers were out in full force, and mounted police were on hand for crowd control. In Martin Place, the ornaments on the giant Christmas tree sparkled in the blazing summer sun. Everyone was dressed in summer clothes and sandals, yet everywhere I went they were playing "I'm Dreaming of a White Christmas," which I doubt any of those around me had ever experienced.

I made my way through the happy crowds in Martin Place, stopping to watch roller-skaters and carolers. Martin Place, 90 feet wide and five blocks long, is Sydney's grand pedestrian thoroughfare. The broad plaza is graced with sculpture, fountains, and a memorial to Australia's war dead, and is usually filled with fruit and flower vendors, street musicians, and people just enjoying sun and surroundings. At one end of Martin Place, the sweep of offices and shops gives way to the impressive General Post Office. This handsome building has a colonnaded frontage that stretches for 320 feet, and a 210-foot-high tower that was once the highest building in Sydney.

I turned down George Street and headed back toward the Harbour Bridge. After again admiring the view from Dawes Point, I wandered down through the Rocks, and then headed back across town toward my hotel.

Appeals are almost as common as shoppers this time of year, and most are for worthy causes, so I keep my pockets filled with change. Widows, orphans, old soldiers, the poor, the blind, the lame must be remembered. A gift to feed the hungry got me an "I Love Sydney" button. A dear, seriously challenged but cherub-faced Santa in a wheelchair handed me a pen printed with "God is Love—Barry's Friendly Corner." Nearby was a sign that read, "May God bless you this Christmas."

He has.

Tuesday, December 20

I disposed of another entire day with wandering, exploring Sydney's colorful, crowded Chinatown, the bustling ship yards, business and shopping districts, parks, arcades and side streets.

Making my way down toward The Rocks, I stumbled upon a celebration at the Rocks Police Station. There was a large contingent of mounted police in early colonial uniforms and an excellent brass band playing Christmas carols.

I wandered through The Rocks, then back into town. As I have done most days since the streets began to blossom with fruit stalls, I bought a mango. The mangoes I've eaten here in Sydney are definitely the most delicious I've ever had—and the juiciest. (I learned after the first attempt that this is not something you want to eat while you're walking down the street.) Today was no exception, and I picked up my daily mango before heading back to the hotel, well after dark.

Wednesday, December 21

I rose relatively early, to try and get a few things out of the way before the major event of the day began. Then, just after noon, I headed down Pitt Street in the direction of the Theatre Royal and *Nicholas Nickleby*, my Christmas present to myself.

I've heard only good things about theatre in Australia, and I was eager to test the reports. I was not disappointed. *The Life and Adventures of Nicholas Nickleby* was wonderful. The cast of 36 actors plays 150 roles in 91 scenes during the 8-1/2-hour production. There is sorrow, evil, honor, laughter, courage, and love. It is magical, and utterly Dickens. I never even noticed the time. Actually, the great pleasure of it is, like so many plays and good books, after four hours you think, "Gee, I wish this would go on longer." Only in this case, it does. It's thoroughly satisfying.

There was a break at 5 o'clock, but by 7, I was back in my seat, ready for the final 4-1/2 hours of the play. Soon, we were off again, into the frantic action and swirling emotions of Dickensian England, rapt, transported, until the final moments, the happy ending, the triumph of love, virtue, and justice. (Sigh.)

I fairly floated home on the residual euphoria.

Thursday, December 22

On one of my many wanders through The Rocks, I had discovered the Geological and Mining Museum, which was closed at the time. I promised myself that I'd return, and to that end I headed once more across town.

I like rocks almost as much as I like seashells, so I was thoroughly delighted with the displays: great slabs of pink granite and black marble, clusters of crystals, countless gems, strange formations, fossils, amazing and beautiful things, some familiar, many I'd never heard of before.

I made my way through the museum's recreated gold mine, reading about—and seeing—the history of mining techniques in Australia. In the mocked-up assay office, the processes of refining gold ore and determining the value and purity of gold nuggets were explained. Numerous dioramas and models showed mining and smelting or refining operations, both historic and current, for silver, copper, lead, gold, diamonds, aluminum, and many more of the numerous minerals found in Australia.

Australia has been blessed with astonishing quantities of minerals. The country's reserves of iron ore and bauxite (aluminum) are among the world's largest. Also large by world standards are Australia's deposits of copper, lead, zinc, and the rare minerals rutile, zircon and ilmenite. The country's resources also include coal, manganese, nickel, wolfram (tungsten), tin, titanium, uranium, mica, dolomite, talc, asbestos, and phosphates. Precious metals—gold, silver, platinum—are also mined in Australia.

Gem stones and semiprecious stones are numerous and abundant: agate, topaz, sapphire (the largest sapphire in the world, a 2,302-carat stone, was found in Queensland), diamond, tourmaline, serpentine, zircon, ruby, opal (not only does Australia produce the most opal, but it has also produced the largest—a 34,215-carat stone was unearthed at Andamooka, S.A., though the largest gem-quality stone is a 17,700-carat opal, the Olympic Australis, found at Coober Pedy), blue kyanite, amethyst, chrysoprase, red jasper, garnet, aragonite, tigers eye, calcite, ribbon stone, and prehnite.

I wandered happily through the geodes and jewels, browsed among the fossils, and finally cruised into the exhibition on 100 years of Broken Hill's history. Broken Hill, also known as Silver City (with the main street named Argent), as well as Broken Hill Proprietary (BHP), one of Australia's largest companies, grew up around the largest silver-lead-zinc ore body in the world—a jagged, broken-looking mountain of metal that made its discoverer, Charles Rasp, a very wealthy man. After 100 years of intensive mining, it is still producing prodigiously.

The historical retrospective included not only the stories of the mine's great wealth and rapid growth, but also detailed many of the problems that resulted from early mining techniques. One of the things that still occasionally causes problems is "mine creep": the subsidence of ancient mine shafts causing problems on the surface—especially when the subsidence occurs under buildings or roads. There were photographs of buckled roads and many structures in various stages of collapse as the ground gave way beneath them.

Aside from cave-ins, the biggest danger in the mines was from fire. Miles of timber were used to support the mine workings—miles of dry firewood waiting for the spark.

In July 1895, a fire started in the BHP mine. Fighting the fire proved ineffectual, so part of the mine was sealed off—where the fire continued to burn for years. In February 1906, a fire broke out in the Junction mine. It was battled for two months by combined forces from the Junction, Junction North and North mines. As the fire was still burning out of control at the end of two months, the mine was flooded to the 500-foot level. Unfortunately, this also flooded the Junction North and North mines, parts of which collapsed during dewatering. It's hard to conceive of dealing with fires on that scale, within those sorts of time frames.

The city and mines still thrive, but it's hard to imagine how anyone got past some of those early obstacles. Just living there was something of a challenge during those early days. Hot, dry, and treeless, Broken Hill of the 1880s was nobody's idea of the perfect home.

Before I could believe it, it was 4 p.m. and closing time for the museum. I stepped back out into the daylight and George Street. I hadn't gone very far when I chanced upon a shop named Marine Specimens. I really almost overloaded my circuits in this place. They have the most stupendous collection of seashells I've ever seen. Not even the Australian Museum has as many shells as this place. Unbelievable shells. Baskets and baskets of more common shells, and glass cases lining the wall filled with rarer and more valuable specimens. One special cabinet near the owner's office holds the real mind-blowers—the $300-and-up shells.

Like a kid in a candy store, I ricocheted around the room, trying to make some sort of decision about where to start, what to select. I've never seen a place with so many shells I don't have. After an hour I stumbled out, slightly starry-eyed, having finally come to the conclusion that I mustn't buy anything until I got away and thought about it in a cool and detached manner. But I shall return!

I wandered across town, window shopping and gift buying, as I made my way slowly back toward the C.B. At 9 p.m., Stephen and his brother, Thomas, met me at the hotel. Thomas had the car in town for the day, so, to save an extra trip in tomorrow, they just took my suitcase, sleeping bag, and duffel bag tonight—everything else I can carry on the train tomorrow.

When Stephen and Thomas were gone, I reascended to my room, where I spent the remainder of the evening wrapping the gifts I picked up today—wine, chocolates, fancy mixed nuts. No worries about the right color or size. Then I wrote until I was tired enough to sleep.

Friday, December 23
I spent much of the day perusing bookstores and

browsing through shopping arcades. I think my favorite arcade is the Strand. Its gracious, wood-paneled shops, wrought-iron balconies, and turn-of-the-century, "gas" lamps delight the historian/romantic in me.

I ambled slowly through Hyde Park before turning my steps towards Stephen's office. Stephen and I headed to the C.B. to get my gear, then walked to Central Station, where we caught the train to Sefton. Stephen is a train buff, so I got a run-down on the history and uses of most of the trains and engines we saw in the train yard.

The pleasant, half-hour ride to Sefton took us through a sea of suburbs, all red-tiled roofs and tidy gardens, and past Sydney's largest cemetery (so vast it used to have its own train service—with three stops within the grounds). It was only a short walk from the depot to Stephen's home, where I was introduced to Anne, Stephen's mother. Anne is dear, and said she is particularly happy to welcome a wanderer into her home because she has another son, Damien, who has been on the road for three years, and who has spent much time depending on the kindness of strangers.

Anne has been a widow for many years. Of her four children, only Stephen and Thomas are still home. Mary is married, has three children of her own, and lives nearby. Damien is, as noted, seeing the world. Thomas is getting married in March, and Bernadette, his fiancée, arrived at the house moments after he did. In July or August, after playing father figure to the younger children for 23 years, Stephen will move to a townhouse he owns across town.

These are nice people, educated and kind. I believe I shall enjoy my stay here.

Saturday, December 24

Today, Stephen and I headed off for a bit of exploring among some of Sydney's older neighborhoods. We drove to Balmain, then parked the car and continued on foot. We climbed the hilly streets among rows of terrace houses decked in Sydney lace ironwork, wandered past old churches and new parks, then hiked down to the wharf and through the gardens along the shore.

Stephen pointed out the old, wooden ferry boats plying the harbor's waters, and I photographed one as it pulled into the pier. In the near distance, the Harbour Bridge arched against the sky, like a huge clasp linking the clusters of buildings on both sides of the blue water. A lone wind-surfer sped away from the shore toward the dockyard, where he was dwarfed by the massive ships that lined the opposite side of the bay.

Continuing on, we wound through the narrow avenues and alleys of the old suburb, enjoying the sunshine, fresh air, and attractive, sometimes odd, buildings. Sydney is built entirely on sandstone, but in some places it is more obvious than others. We passed one cottage, built on a massive outcrop, where the white picket fence around the yard was bolted to the rock.

When we got back to the car, we headed onward to Long Nose Point, where the narrow road winds between trees, gardens, and large, old homes. Near the tip of the point, we again parked, and descended to the little wharf, which was made charming by the surrounding gardens, with graceful casuarinas fringing broad lawns. Again, we were afforded spectacular views of the harbor and city as we hiked along the shoreline.

We got back to the house just after 6 o'clock. When dinner was finished and all the dishes were washed and put away, we put up the Christmas tree and decorated it. I brought out my gifts and placed them under the tree. It almost looks as though it might really be Christmas, even if it is the middle of the summer.

Sunday, December 25

Merry Christmas!

Today was one of the hottest Christmases in Sydney's history. The top temperature was over 100 degrees in the shade. The thing that made it seem more amazing was that Mom, Dad, Darch, and Margaret called and announced that the Midwest is having one of the coldest Christmases in its history—17 degrees below zero, with a wind-chill factor of 70 below. I'd rather be here.

After wishing everyone back home a Merry Christmas, I joined my "Sydney family" in the living room for gift opening. Anne had thoughtfully picked out a lovely linen handkerchief for me. I was surprised and delighted, not having expected anything. Since this is a family that enjoys snacking, my offerings were well received.

For the main portion of the day we were whisked away to Mary's (married daughter), where we were regaled with food and wine and Christmas pudding, as we sat beneath the trees in the back yard. When Mary passed out gifts to the family, she had a package for me—which amazed me, since I didn't know until yesterday that I was invited. She gave me a huge map of Australia and a fine-point marking pen, so I can outline my whole trip around the continent. What a thoughtful family.

Mary's children are delightful. Peter (5-1/2) is charming, clever, good looking, and loves an audience. Karl (4) is quieter, able to entertain himself (though he loves to play with anyone who's willing), and is more serious than Peter. Johanna (2-1/2) is a cherub, and is quite smitten with Uncle Stephen. It's wonderful to see her face light up whenever he pays attention to her. She's a real flirt.

Robert, Mary's husband, was a very cordial host. He took great pleasure in keeping me supplied with macadamia nuts off their own trees. He enjoys engaging in deep, probing discussions, and the two of us had some pretty lively conversations (when I wasn't playing ball with Peter and Karl).

One of the highlights of the day for the family was a long-distance call from the wandering Damien, who is currently in Scotland. Wonderful invention, the phone.

Around 5 o'clock, we said thank you all around, then headed off to visit Bernadette's family. Bernadette's mother led us out to the back yard, where father was filling the picnic table with snacks, soft drinks, and home-brewed beer. I sipped soda pop, nibbled nuts and lollies (basically any sweets or candies—especially hard candies—are called lollies), talked, and listened to the amiable banter of two families looking forward to their children's wedding.

It was nearly 10 o'clock when we finally headed home. For the last few hours of the day we sat about chatting, making plans for the coming week. It was a very pleasant day: hot, brilliant, and friendly. I still have trouble believing that it's Christmas, but it was certainly merry and bright.

Monday, December 26
Today is Boxing Day. Celebrated the first weekday after Christmas, this holiday is shared by most countries of

the British Commonwealth. It is the day on which postmen
and employees are traditionally given their gifts.

We had a busy morning around the house, with cleaning
and laundry, but all work ceased in time to watch (on TV)
the beginning of the Sydney-to-Hobart yacht race. Sydney
Harbour was blanketed with boats of competitors, escorts,
officials, and fans. Then they were off, great spinnakers
unfurling as the graceful yachts ran before the wind. It was
a glorious sight. Now, before them lies 735 miles of open
water, across the Tasman Sea to the southern tip of
Tasmania. It is said that this is the roughest course in the
world. The yachts skimmed across the sparkling, crowded
harbor, nosing into the waves, clearing the stone-walled
entrance to Port Jackson and heading out to sea.

After lunch, Stephen, Anne and I went for a drive up the
coast. We wound our way north, along numerous lovely
beaches and through much National Park land. In some
places the trees and mountains ran right down to the
water's edge. The many bays and inlets we passed were
filled with bright sails.

We crossed Kuring-Gai Chase Park, up through the hills
and cliffs and numerous gum trees that make the place so
beautiful. We drove along Broken Bay and then out to
Palm Beach, where we stopped. Here, the road was a narrow ribbon between the beach and a high, unbroken wall
of rock. Trees and houses perched on the cliffs above us,
overlooking the sea.

Though it was warm, the day was gray and windy, so
Anne opted for returning to the car after walking down to
the water with us. Stephen and I continued up the beach
for about half an hour, wading in the waves that lapped the
shore. The sand was incredibly soft and shifted in the
wind, eddying around island-boulders at the base of the

great, craggy cliffs, which were like a second shore. We could see the breakers crashing on the rocks in the near distance, where the hills came down to the water. Despite the clouds, surfers, swimmers, and fishermen were out, enjoying the holiday.

We stopped for ice cream before starting the drive back down the coast. We stayed along the ocean for most of our return trip. Flowers and palm trees lined much of our route, and small towns gave way to beautiful, cliff-cradled beaches, most filled with surfers, swimmers, and fishermen.

During the evening, we went through many of the slides Stephen shot in the Red Centre. It was really grand seeing the places we'd been, the people we'd been with. It makes me want to go back.

Tuesday, December 27

We spent the day at home. Stephen and Thomas are trying to get the house painted during their days off, so they worked while I helped Anne inside, before settling into reading, writing, and thought. This place is a comfortable limbo, a place to suspend myself for a while, a place that is not part of my past, but is not really part of my dream, either. Little domesticities remind me of "real life," while my mind is occupied with "what next." It is a good time to rest, to step outside the torrential rush of my travels and reflect on what has happened and where I'm headed.

In the afternoon, Ed, an old friend and traveling companion of Stephen's, came by. We spent much time talking about travel, in and outside Australia. Both Ed and Stephen have been to the U.S. a couple of times, so we compared notes and exchanged anecdotes. Ed is another railroad enthusiast, and he and Stephen were delighted with the extensive rail systems and impressive train stations they'd seen in the U.S.

After dinner, Stephen showed his slides of the Flinders Ranges. Located in South Australia, the Flinders Ranges are stark and wild, with jagged granite peaks, colorful quartzite, limestone, sandstone, and shale cliffs, razorbacked ridges, broken purple foothills, and sweeping valleys. The ranges are renowned for the crimson, yellow, and purple blankets of flowers that cover the mountains in springtime. Wilpena Pound, a dramatic, enclosed valley in the heart of the ranges, looked fascinating, but it was all quite astonishingly beautiful. (Add it to the list.)

Wednesday, December 28

Today we headed south, beneath a soft, gray sky. We passed out of Sydney's suburbs and entered a world of narrow, tree-lined country roads and green, rolling hills. Around us, sheep stations, paddocks full of horses, and fields of flowers were only occasionally interrupted by tiny towns.

In one of those tiny towns, Thirlmere, we stopped to stretch our legs. I walked back along the way we'd come to get a photograph of the Commonwealth Bank of Thirlmere, a one-room hut that looks like a road-side fruit stand and opens only three days a week. Outside Thirlmere, we passed the Rail Transport Museum, a large complex of trains, tracks, and buildings, which features, among other things, the oldest locomotive (1864) still found in Australia. This is where Stephen worked most weekends in his younger days.

Then, again, the lovely N.S.W. countryside spread before us. Cows, horses, sheep, and goats grazed in the thick grass. Huge blue gums towered over us. The forest closed in on both sides, only to open up again at the next old homestead.

After Moss Vale, the road swung slightly west, leading us to the edge of Morton National Park, a 50,000-acre nature reserve renowned for its deep gorges and beautiful waterfalls. Just inside the park, we left the car and continued on foot. We walked across a tree-sheltered field, past a rustic ranger's cabin, and over a rise, to the head of a broad, ragged slash in the great plateau, a precipitous, golden-walled valley that stretched before us, disappearing into a distant blue-green haze.

As we approached the cliff edge, Fitzroy Falls came into view. The broad, white waterfall leaps over a great sandstone cliff and descends seven or eight hundred feet to a tumble of boulders, where the water foams and rushes before disappearing over another considerable drop. It ends in a stream that winds down the length of the valley but can only be detected as an occasional glimmer amidst the throng of trees.

A narrow, winding bush track led us into the dense eucalypt forest that crowns the cliffs around the tree-filled canyon. As we hiked between the gum and banksia trees, we saw fringed lilies, mountain iris, bottlebrushes, pink mountain devils, and trigger plants. Birds flitted and perched everywhere. There were rosellas, wrens, finches, silver eyes, currawongs, and more. Steep, rocky paths branched off the gentler main track, taking us down cliff faces or out onto ragged outcrops for unobstructed views of the valley and waterfall.

We wandered for hours, following the rim of the canyon

around to another waterfall—Twin Falls. We rock-hopped
across the clear, fern-bordered stream, which flows to the
rim of the canyon, where it splits and descends in two
thin, silver sprays

We eventually turned our steps back toward the head of
the valley. Passing our starting point, we continued around
to a spot above Fitzroy Falls. An almost glass-smooth river
undulated toward us, reflecting the trees that crowded its
banks. A few feet from where it disappears over the cliff,
the river is spanned by a bridge, which we crossed, stopping to admire the watercourse meandering through the
forest and, on the other side, the river's rushing leap into
space.

We finally walked back to the car and headed off again.
We climbed up through the mountains and descended into
Kangaroo Valley, an area of rich farming and grazing land.
Rolling, green, tree-fringed fields nestle among the rugged
mountains. A river runs down the center of the valley, and
across it is a strangely medieval bridge of far grander pro-
portions than one might expect in this little rural community.

As we strolled around, Anne and Stephen told me that
the valley is almost unbelievably changed from when they
last saw it, two years ago. It was in the midst of a severe
drought then, and the hills were brown and the fields
burned out. It's hard to imagine now.

From Kangaroo Valley we turned toward the coast, coming out at Nowra and following the shore northward.
Above Wollongong we stopped at a spot popular with
hang-gliding aficionados. It was too late to see any launch-
ings, but many hang-gliders were out. Because of the
amount of wind coming off the ocean, combined with the
effects of heat and the nearby mountains, pilots can keep
their gliders aloft for hours, actually climbing on the

updrafts high above their take-off point. We stood on a cliff overlooking the ocean, watching the brightly colored gliders hover and swoop and climb like giant butterflies.

The road on which we continued north curved around bays and clung to mountains that, in places, came right down to the ocean. We entered a shaded, emerald tunnel, which, Stephen informed me, is Royal National Park. This was the first national park in Australia, and only the second in the world (Yellowstone in the U.S. was the first). It was lush with ferns, flowers, trees, and meandering streams. The park's narrow, winding road climbs and falls quickly, so I don't think poor Stephen had much time to enjoy the scenery, but I loved it.

Thursday, December 29

Stephen had to go back to work this morning, and I wanted to see some of the sights that were still waiting to be seen, so the two of us caught an early train into town. Stephen got off the train at Town Hall, but I continued on to Circular Quay. When the train doors opened, my pulse quickened; directly before me were the harbor, the Bridge, and the Opera House. What a dazzling sight.

I walked around the Quay and over to the Opera House. I browsed through the displays of costumes, props, and photographs in the Exhibition Hall, then purchased a ticket for the guided tour of the rest of the building.

The inside of the Opera House is as interesting as the outside, because you can see much of the design of the internal structure of the building, the "skeletal system" of the great sails, with their graceful webs of concrete ribs radiating upward.

The tour took us through several of the Opera House's theatres (this is really a performing arts complex, not just an opera house). We saw the Drama Theatre and Opera Theatre, but the massive Concert Hall was not available for viewing today. Artwork abounds, and includes the seemingly obligatory Sidney Nolan mural. The complex also includes smaller theatres, a cinema, two restaurants, a recording hall, offices, exhibition centre, and more.

In addition to showing us through the various theatres and describing the productions and mechanics of them, our guide (an energetic, enthusiastic little blond who is an actress when she's not conducting tours) dazzled us with some of the statistics and figures that are part and parcel of the Opera House.

The cost was $102 million, the bulk of which was raised through lotteries. The roofs, which are held together by 217 miles of tensioned cable, are made from 2,194 concrete sections, and are covered with more than 1,056,000 white and cream ceramic tiles from Sweden. The tiles have a special, slightly roughened surface that resists dirt, on which nothing can grow, and which rinses clean in the rain. The roof weighs 157,800 tons and is supported by 580 concrete columns. A special glue was developed to hold the tiles in place, and it is supposed to last for 500 years. In case it doesn't, a small robot runs over the roofs every now and again and records if any tiles have loosened. So far, none have.

The specially made, topaz-tinted, double-thickness, bulletproof, French-produced windows have a total surface area of 67,000 square feet. There are, in all, about 2,000 panes in 700 sizes. The pink granite of the exterior and interior floors, walls, and stairways, as well as the white birch and brush boxwoods used in much of the decorating, all came from New South Wales. But, as interesting as they are, the statistics don't fully describe the Opera House. Perched on its point of land, between sun and water, the vaulting, white-spinnakered building that Danish architect Jørn Utzon designed is more than just the sum of its parts.

The tour concluded around noon, and I wandered once more toward The Rocks, to get a spot of tea. I stopped at Mary Reiby's Coffee House in the old Argyle Arts Centre. It's named after a girl who was, during the convict days of Sydney, transported from England at the age of 13 for riding a neighbor's horse without permission. After finishing her seven-year sentence, Mary was released. She stayed in Australia, became a successful businesswoman, married well, and finished her life a wealthy, respected mother of seven. She lived until the then ripe old age of 60 years.

Next I made my return to Marine Specimens. Exercising every possible ounce of self-control, I managed to get away with a purchase of only 15 shells. One specimen, a Miraculous Thatcher shell *(Thatcheria mirabilis),* looks like it was designed at the Bauhaus, it has such awesomely clean, precise lines. I got cone shells garnered from the Great Barrier Reef, and expanded my collection of cowries. I became enamored of a number of exquisite murexes, but curbed myself, as they exceeded the upward limit I had set to what I could spend. I was very happy when I left the shop.

I headed up George Street, window shopping and browsing my way across town, stopping for nearly every book sale I encountered. I eventually cut across to Hyde Park, then crossed over to Macquarie Street and the Mint.

The Mint, no longer used in that capacity, as coins are now minted in Canberra, has become a museum of decorative and useful arts. The building was originally a wing of the Rum Hospital, so called because it was donated to the city in the 1880s by a group of merchants in exchange for a monopoly license on rum importation. The exterior is pale peach with white trim and pillared veranda. The high-ceilinged, wood-floored rooms have been carefully restored and filled with wonderful objects that reveal much about how life was lived in the colony's earlier days.

The museum displays furniture, china, clothes, jewelry, large collections of stamps and coins, rugs, glass, curios, and many other items that graced homes and inhabitants when Sydney was younger. One thing that was interesting to note was how, as the colony grew in confidence and pride of place, strictly Australian motifs crept into decorations. Furniture retained the simple, elegant lines of English design, but marquetry inlays were now of gum leaves and gum, wattle, and waratah flowers. Kangaroos and wallabies were etched on glasses, and koalas clung to vases. The plant and flower designs were the loveliest, though, and the most widely used, on china and furniture, in embroidery and metal work.

When I finally reemerged into Macquarie Street, I headed back to the shopping streets, where I bought ingredients for making shortbread and a bottle of Bailey's Irish Cream, as a special treat for the New Year's weekend. Then, at 5:30, I met Stephen at his office, and we headed for the Town Hall train depot and the train to Sefton.

Friday, December 30

I was up early again to catch the train into town. It was a gorgeous day, bright and sunny and clear. I walked

across town, through Hyde Park, and over to College
Street, where I photographed the imposing and beautiful
St. Mary's Cathedral, a soaring, ornate, buttressed edifice
of gloriously Gothic design. I continued on, past the lawn-
bowling greens, to the Australian Museum, to find out
when it opens. Then I turned my steps toward Centre
Point, for a trip to the top of Sydney Tower.

Sydney Tower, a 1,000-foot golden needle rising up
from the city's center, offers splendid views of all of
Sydney, the harbor, and the surrounding countryside.
Between long bouts of admiring the vistas of land and sea
spread before me, I watched a short film on the building of
the tower, its figures, statistics, and safety factors. The
cable used to stabilize the tower, if placed end-to-end,
would stretch from Sydney to New Zealand (or Sydney to
Alice Springs, if you read the brochure instead of watching the film—either way, about 1,300 miles). The tower is
designed to withstand catastrophic cyclones and earth-
quakes and anything else that might happen, though these
things rarely occur in this area (according to the literature,
about once every 500 years).

Descending to the street once more, I continued exploring, finally making my way back to the Australian
Museum. I spent my afternoon there, happily studying
exhibits on the deserts and arid regions of Australia, the
oceans and marine life around the continent, and early
Aboriginal culture.

In the arid-regions section, I saw photographs of the
notorious Australian rabbits. I'd heard that serious problems had arisen due to the proliferation of rabbits introduced from Europe, but had not imagined how awful it
really was. A few rabbits released from a farm near
Geelong, Victoria, in 1859 grew into a plague of appalling

dimensions. In 1887, 27 million rabbit skins were turned in for bounty—but that hardly made a dent in the estimated billion-plus rabbits happily eating away the countryside.

The photographs were astonishing and horrifying—like something out of an Alfred Hitchcock movie—with acres literally blanketed by rabbit hordes, water holes drunk dry, farms eaten to the ground, a nightmare of huge, rapidly multiplying, voracious, wild rabbits. It was not until the late 1950s that scientists discovered a way to control the vermin plague, with a combination of virus and poison. Even now, rabbits are not popular animals here.

Saturday, December 31

I can't believe the year is at an end. It has gone by much too quickly.

We had a leisurely, sunny day, with the real fun beginning after dinner. Thomas, Bernadette, Stephen, and I piled into the car and headed downtown. We parked the car near The Rocks and spent the rest of the evening getting around on foot.

The city was radiant. The Harbour Bridge and Opera House were lighted up, and boats covered with lights cruised around the darkened harbor. The streets were filled with noise, music, and merry-makers. We wound our way through the crowds and down along the waterfront.

We bought wine at one of the old pubs at the edge of The Rocks, then stood on Dawes Point, under the bridge, admiring the view of the sparkling Opera House and harbor stretching before us. It was a glorious evening. The sky was clear, the air silken warm, with a gentle, fresh breeze blowing off the water.

After we finished our wine, we wandered through The Rocks, around Circular Quay, and out onto Bennelong Point to the Opera House. We stayed there for a while, watching the harbor ferries filled with New Year's celebrants drift past, checking out the costumes sported by some of the people on shore, enjoying the lights, the night, the frivolity and beauty of it all.

Turning our steps up Macquarie Street, we headed out beyond the Conservatory of Music, through the Domain, and down along Mrs. Macquarie's Point. In addition to being a singularly spectacular spot from which to view the harbor, Opera House, and Harbour Bridge, it was also the site of a concert, with the band on a barge anchored just off-shore.

Out on the water, a glittering armada of decorated and illuminated craft wound through the coves of Sydney Harbour. The harbor fire-fighting boat leading the procession offered one of the most resplendent displays in the parade: fire hoses lining both sides of the boat shot thousands of gallons of water skyward while an ever-changing rainbow of spotlights bathed the towering, arching walls of water in a shimmering kaleidoscope of colors.

Stephen bought us ice cream, and we sat on the sloping lawn near the water's edge, talking, watching boats and people, and listening to the music. At midnight, there was a dazzling fireworks display over the harbor. The exploding colors and showers of fire were all reflected in the water. What a glorious end/beginning to the year. I wouldn't mind welcoming in a few New Years this way.

Sunday, January 1

Happy New Year!

We had hoped to go to the mountains today, but it was raining, so we had a lazy morning and leisurely brunch. By noon, the weather was clearing a little, so Stephen, Anne, and I headed into town.

Almost the entire month of January is given over to the Festival of Sydney, and there are events of various sorts every day. Today it was bagpiping, and we stopped for a while to listen to the exciting skirl of the pipes, which delighted me, but which Stephen merely tolerated.

Anne wanted to see the new Power House Museum, so we walked up town. The Power House Museum, which is built in and around an enormous old powerhouse, is a museum of applied arts and sciences. It houses everything from costume jewelry to lunar landing modules.

The outdoor train yard, with its collection of wonderful, old engines and train cars, gladdened Stephen's heart. After a few moments of rapture, we entered the main building, where we were all dazzled by the variety and breadth of the displays. There were musical and mechanical gadgets, scientific and technological wonders, toys, weapons, clothing and costumes, cars and boats, pottery and glass, satellites and box kites, antique implements, and anything invented in Australia, from wine in boxes to the Owen sub-machine gun.

The museum's box kite is a replica of one built by its inventor, Lawrence Hargrave. Hargrave also developed a rotary engine and produced power-propelled model flying machines in the late 1800s. He was a visionary aerodynamics theorist as well. Hargrave might have anticipated the Wright brothers' successful flight by several years, but he was too isolated by Australia's distance to benefit from main currents of practical aviation development. Still, he had a positive influence on airplane design in the early 1900s.

A fragile Bleriot monoplane hangs from the ceiling. This plane carried the first official airmail between Sydney and Melbourne in 1914—a nine-hour journey that was the longest recorded flight at the time. In fact, the distance that hampered Hargrave proved to be a tremendous catalyst for the development of aviation in Australia. Records were set, and broken, regularly, and every ocean in the world was crossed first by Australian aviators, with the single exception of the North Atlantic.

The size of the museum and diversity of exhibits kept us busy until closing time. Then the three of us walked back through town, past the enormous Sydney Entertainment Center, and on to the car.

Monday, January 2

It was a rainy day, so our plans to visit the mountains were foiled again. We spent our time looking through books we've purchased during the post-holiday sales (I've picked up some terrific volumes of Australian natural history, bush ballads, and folk lore), showing souvenirs from various trips, listening to music, viewing slides, and talking. It was a nice, comfortable, homey sort of day, as gray days often are.

Tuesday, January 3

I awoke this morning with the overwhelming feeling that I must get back to the bush. Fortunately, staying with

Stephen's family has saved me enough that I can easily afford the luxury of this passion. So I pulled out my books, and made lists of what I still want to see.

My heart is torn between forest and desert, but by the time I'd narrowed my list down to a reasonable number of destinations, it appeared rather heavily weighted toward the arid end of the scale.

The guys returned to work today, so the house was quiet. I stayed in and thought and planned and read, then wrote letters to the people who haven't heard from me in a while, which is everyone.

Wednesday, January 4

I was up early to catch the train into Sydney. At the N.S.W. Tourist Bureau I made a reservation to ride with the riverboat postman tomorrow and picked up brochures on available camping trips.

I turned my steps toward The Domain and crossed the broad, shaded lawn to the Art Gallery of New South Wales. The gallery's excellent collection of works by Australian artists, as well as some fine European and American works, kept me entertained for several hours. From the original, turn-of-the-century section of the building, where older artwork is housed, I wandered into the bright, new contemporary wing, where more modern works compete for attention with views of the park and nearby harbor.

Leaving the gallery, I walked back toward the Mid-City Centre, where I ate lunch while perusing camping brochures. Australian Pacific listed a tour that takes in almost every place on my wish list—Mildura, the Murray

River, Coober Pedy, the Birdsville Track, Flinders Ranges, Broken Hill, and even a stop in the Red Centre—but it leaves in three days. I figured there was no way I could book it on such short notice, but I'd never know if I didn't try, so I headed over to ANZ Travel.

After 15 minutes of phoning and waiting for confirmation, the travel agent said that if I could pay immediately I could get on the tour. I was fairly quivering from the excitement and suddenness of it all as I signed over the appropriate number of traveler's cheques. I can't believe it. In three days I'll be heading back out to the Outback. I'll be seeing much of what I still want to see—and I'll be returning to the Centre. Oh, joy and exultation!

Thursday, January 5

English Victorian novelist Anthony Trollope, on visiting the Hawkesbury River, wrote, "To me it was more enchanting than those waters of either the Rhine or the Mississippi." Today, I was headed for the Hawkesbury, for a trip with Australia's last riverboat postman and an opportunity to assess Mr. Trollope's opinion.

From Strathfield station, it took my northbound train a little more than an hour to reach Brooklyn, the tiny port on the Hawkesbury River where the postman begins his run. The homes that receive their mail on this route are otherwise inaccessible. The postman also delivers groceries, medicine, visitors, and whatever else needs to go to the islands and isolated beaches in this area.

We pulled away from the Brooklyn wharf at precisely 9:30, under sunny skies. I leaned on the railing of the riverboat's upper deck as we wove out through the fishing vessels and small pleasure craft moored about the bay. Our skipper, the postman, introduced himself and began his running commentary on where we were going and what we were passing.

I was startled to see a large number of jellyfish in the water. This is a tidal river, saltwater much of the way inland, so there are saltwater creatures in abundance here. (It's one of the biggest oyster-farming areas in N.S.W.) But I didn't expect to see the swarms of large, reddish-brown jellyfish that slid past our hull and bobbed in our wake. It explains why so many homes have netted-off swimming areas.

Our first stop was at Dangar Island, where most of the tiny community was at the pier waiting for the mail. Each of the small, clean, lavishly gardened houses on the little island has its own dock, and these were crowded with sea gulls and young boys with fishing rods. Men in shorts and stockmen's hats helped unload the mail sacks and morning newspapers, laughing and talking with the postman, waving back at the boat's passengers.

Then we turned up river, passing Mullet Creek, a big oyster-farming area. We passed under the new highway and railway bridges and past the massive supports from the old bridge. Our skipper informed us that the old supports were so well built that an explosion big enough to destroy them would significantly weaken the supports of the new bridges, so they've left them standing—tall, lonely stone sentinels guarding the mouth of the river.

We cruised through the river's twists, turns, and inlets, among the numerous, little green islands. On both sides of the river the tall cliffs rise up, covered with gum trees, palms, and bright, red-flowered Christmas bushes (so called because they bloom around Christmas time). In places, the cliffs and walls of sandstone are dramatically exposed, bold strokes of gold amid the green, rising from the silver-blue water.

In the midst of all this grandeur, clinging to the occasional narrow strip of level ground along the water's edge, are little communities and single dwellings. We cruised through Milson's Passage, stopped at Fisherman's Paradise, dropped mail at Bar Point Estate. At Glenwood, we pulled into Davidson's Wharf. Then we headed to Milo Creek, the farthest point out on the postman's run. Beyond that, everyone can be reached by road.

Everywhere we stopped we were greeted by cheerful residents glad to see the mail and the postman, who always had a bit of a chat before continuing on. Children playing along the shore waved merrily to the passing boat.

We turned back down river, making stops now on the other side of the wide expanse of water. A few minutes later we looked upstream to see rain sweeping towards us. It was magnificently dramatic, with white mist haunting the valleys and black clouds towering overhead. We all stayed topside as long as we could, enjoying the rapidly changing scene, watching the weather prowl down the valley, roaring. The storm soon passed, and we completed our cruise under clearing skies.

At Sunny Corner, we passed one of the river's several restaurants accessible only by water. Then we continued on to Milson Island. This former prison is now being refitted as a holiday camp for children. (That sounds like a bad joke, somehow.) Across from the island we saw the wreck of the *H.M.S. Parramatta,* the last torpedo-class riverboat built during W.W.II. After the war, it was sold to a private firm that used it for hauling building materials up the river, but it broke its moorings one night, drifted, and foundered on the rocks at the base of the nearby cliffs.

We pulled back in at the Brooklyn dock a little after 1 o'clock. I climbed the stairs to the train depot and caught the train into Sydney. The ride into the city was beautiful. Gum trees, palms, red-flowered Christmas bushes, and streamers of white or deep purple clematis lined the track for most of the journey. I saw kookaburras perched in trees and on telephone poles all along the route. The sun was out by now, dazzling and bright, sparkling on the ocean and illuminating the hills.

In the city, I dashed around doing errands for Saturday's trip (get cash, buy sun visor, get sunglasses repaired—this time it'll be summer in the desert). I met Stephen in front of his office at 5:30, and we caught the train to Sefton. He'd gone to the motor club during his lunch break and gotten maps for me of all the places I'll be going, so we studied them as we rode along.

We passed another pleasant, quiet evening, with most of the discussion centering around my impending trip.

Friday, January 6

I stayed in today, to prepare for the trip—airing out my sleeping bag, doing laundry, packing, catching up on my letter writing, and generally getting ready to "go bush" again.

Tonight I'm making shortbread, so the family will have something to munch in my memory.

Tomorrow I'm off again.

The adventure continues.

WALTZING
FINAL TOUR&FLOOD

Saturday, January 7

It was a gloriously beautiful morning, the sun warm and the sky blue. Departing the Liverpool station just after 8:30, our coach headed out along the Hume Highway, climbing steadily higher as we proceeded southwest. The road ascended through hills and great stands of trees, over rivers, by gentle valleys and dramatic gorges. Then, as we neared Camden, the landscape opened up. Around us, rolling golden and green fields were dotted with huge gums and grazing cows.

At the beginning of the 19th century, sheep would have been a more common sight in this district. In 1804, with a grant of 5,000 acres of land, a few Merino sheep of his own, and a gift of nine additional Merinos from King George III, John Macarthur founded Australia's wool industry here. Camden was named for Lord Camden, Secretary of State for the Colonies, who had convinced the King to donate the sheep. Macarthur carried out important experiments in breeding the Merino sheep, and before long, Australia eclipsed Spain, once the sole producer of fine wool. Though now predominantly a dairy region, this area is still known as Macarthur Country.

Our climb took us up into the Southern Highlands, into prosperous wheat and sheep country. Yellow flowers bloomed beside the road and in the fields. We passed through historic Berrima, a village of golden sandstone buildings rising from the golden earth. This town, which has been preserved as it was in the first half of the 19th century, is where Aborigines came to trade with settlers during the early days of the colony. The solid, handsome, old buildings were built in the 1830s and 1840s. Many have now been converted into antique shops and craft galleries.

We rolled on through an alternately wild and domestic countryside. The day around us was dazzling and warm. The leaves on the trees glistened in the brilliant sunlight. The sky was deep blue and dotted with small white clouds. I saw my first "willy willy" on a dusty side road. A willy willy is a whirlwind, comparable to the dust devils of the Southwestern U.S. Normally only a few stories high, they are generated by heat.

Gazing out the window, I felt as if the open road was welcoming me back, seeping once more into my spirit, wooing me, and I rejoiced that I was, again, getting away from it all. However, I was also aware that this would be my last big adventure in Australia, so my excitement was augmented by a hungry eagerness to burn every part of what I was seeing and experiencing into my mind—or at least get it all into my notebook.

The bright yellow flowers that crowded the fields earlier gave way to blankets of purple-blossomed Paterson's Curse. Then we were surrounded by miles of golden wheat. Lining the fields were great stands of Scottish this-tle, two to three feet high, topped with masses of purple flowers.

We stopped for lunch in Yass, an important wool town that still has iron hitching posts in spots along the main street, and to stretch our legs in Cootamundra, birthplace of Donald Bradman, Australia's most famous cricket player. However, the main objective of day one is getting from point A to the farthest possible point B, so we did not tarry in either town.

As our sunny afternoon wore on, we could see, far away across the endless, open plains, an awesome storm with black clouds, heavy rain, and great ribbons of lightning brightening its dark face. It was off to our left for a long time, but we eventually turned into it, losing our lovely weather.

Around 5:30 we drove into West Wyalong, a former gold-mining town, which is our stop for the night. About half an hour later, another bus pulled in, this one bringing the rest of our tour group up from Melbourne. We are all booked at the imaginatively named Central Motel on Main Street.

This is our last night in beds for a while, but being indoors is especially appreciated because of the rain. Our room- and tentmates were assigned here, and I found myself paired with Gik (rhymes with sleek or chic, which she is) from Indonesia—a secretary in Djakarta. She's smart, pretty, and a few years younger than I am. She is rather shy and a bit overwhelmed by the exuberant Australians in the crowd. Having identified me as being safe, she stuck with me through dinner and mingling. I was quite happy to play mother hen for her first solo foray outside her native land.

Sunday, January 8

This morning, the sky looked like it might be trying to clear, but was still fairly ominous. Great, wide, arching bands of cloud stretched from horizon to horizon, like an immense, puffy, white rainbow, with light on one side and storm on the other.

We were now traveling through the Riverina district, location of the world's most productive rice paddies. The rice is irrigated by water from the Murrumbidgee River. The lush, green paddies are beautiful, and contrast sharply with the image commonly had of what farming in Australia is like.

Hundreds of galahs and cockatiels rose in huge flocks from the rich fields as we passed. We also saw large numbers of magpies, and a few parrots and emus.

Before long, the natural vegetation began to change, becoming shorter, hardier, with more "native pine" (casuarinas) and mallee. *Mallee* is an Aboriginal word meaning "many stemmed," and refers to a variety of scrubby eucalypts in this region, all of which are characterized by many slender trunks growing from a single root base.

We had morning tea in Hay, a town to which many of the old stock routes ran. The railhead was here, and from Hay, cattle could be transported to Victoria. Hay was also once an important stop on the Cobb and Co.* stagecoach route, as well as the location for one of the company's coach building shops.

Hay is surrounded by wide, nearly treeless, black soil plains. One often encounters the treacherous black soil plains in songs and stories of the droving days. They become a sea of soft, sticky mud whenever it rains, and wagons, horses, cattle would slip and sink, and become almost irretrievably bogged.

We crossed the Murrumbidgee River and continued heading west. The sky was beginning to clear as we launched into formal introductions. The group is large, so this occupied a good deal of time. Our coach captain, Carl, is an Australian for whom native land is also favorite

*See appendix

hobby. Jill, our hostess/cook, is a transplant from New Zealand. As my fellow travelers told about themselves, I jotted down names and enough information to try to keep names associated with the right people. In addition to Gik, my travel mates included:

Karen - Danish - high school teacher, in history and sports—blond and intelligent looking, with a great smile—has traveled widely

Laureen - from New Zealand—teacher—sweet, pert, and seems very sharp

Sandra - another teacher from New Zealand—slender, wistful-looking, with dark hair and dark eyes

Margaret (Marg) - from Ottawa, Canada—chemist—bright, exuberant blond

Peter W. - another Ottawan—organizes world-class yachting competitions—tall, blond, friendly—handed out Canadian Maple Leaf pins

Helen - Australian, from near Ballarat, Victoria—teacher—dark, curly hair, great smile

Peter S. - Australian, from Queensland's Goldcoast—greens keeper on a golf course at Tweed Heads—looks not unlike a surfing enthusiast

John - Aussie—Perth, W.A.—administration officer—very tall (6'3"), dark hair, dark, intense eyes

LaVonne - Canadian—from Pincher Creek, Alberta—university student—seems like a real live wire

Les - Aussie - Richmond, N.S.W.—senior technical officer in Navy—tall, among the few older group members

Pat - originally from Wales, now lives in Parramatta, N.S.W.—teacher—traveling with Les—seems very enthusiastic

Chris - Australian—Canberra—Parliamentary office

advisor—tall, classy, intelligent

Dave - Canadian—another Ottawan—hydrologist-geologist—in Australia for a year on a work-study-tourist pass—dark eyes, curly, light brown hair, very athletic build—looks more like a surfer than a scientist

Andy - Melbournian—training instructor with the social services department, and part-time professional musician—sleepy-eyed redhead

Tom - from St. Louis, Missouri—ice cream seller—young—light brown hair and a mustache

Amanda - Aussie—Queenslander—a "sister" (in Australia, as in Britain, a sister is a nurse)—blond and bubbly

Paul—French Canadian (Montreal)— flight attendant—tall and very tan

Michael—Melbournian—car salesman—funny, a real talker—tall, blond, muscular

Blue - from Caramut, which is near Warrnambool, Victoria—sheep shearer, horse breaker, and farm hand—a real slice of Australiana—red-gold hair and blue eyes—soft spoken

Jim - also from Caramut—a banker—dark hair, blue eyes, and an infectious laugh

Peter K. and Mary - Melbournians, though he's originally from Scotland—he's an electrician, she's a teacher—both are attractive and cheerful—he seems a little on the rambunctious side, but she appears to handle him deftly

Lee and Lara - Peter and Mary's daughters—Lee is 11, is cute, bouncy, and a little tomboyish—Lara, a 13-year-old, is already showing signs of becoming a real beauty—both girls are joyous creatures

Sally - from New Zealand—a clerk—a pretty, quiet girl with dark, curly hair

Mandy—from Sale, Victoria—singer and guitarist—blond, tan, slender

Maree - from Sydney—nurse and mother of five—outgoing and enthusiastic—slender, tan, and a sharp dresser

Allison - Maree's daughter—does drafting for an electronics firm—very pretty, very quiet

Naida - another Sydneysider—nurse—very quiet, but seems friendly

Simca—also from Sydney and also a nurse—pleasant and outgoing

Robyn - Melbournian—research assistant in microbial physics—dark hair, dark eyes, very athletic

Quite a crowd. In fact, I wondered to myself if it was too much of a crowd. I haven't been on any tours with this many people. Everyone seems quite nice, but will a large crowd make the splendid isolation of the Outback seem, well, a little less isolated? I'm not really worried, but I do wonder how this adventure will feel, compared to being with much smaller groups.

The weather was glorious by this time, and we continued on under a dazzling blue sky. We passed through rich, fruit-growing land. Vast vineyards spread from the road's edge toward the horizon. Trucks heaped full of oranges were coming from the citrus groves. Olive, peach, plum, and apricot trees stood in tidy rows in large, handsome orchards. Then Lake Benanee, which is fed by the Murray River, came into sight.

Just outside Gol Gol we saw the Murray River for the first time. This is one of Australia's most important and historic rivers; its role and significance make it roughly comparable to America's Mississippi River. The river, which rises in the Snowy Mountains, runs westward for

1,609 miles. It forms the border between New South Wales and Victoria, then flows into South Australia, not far from Adelaide, to the sea, at Encounter Bay.

The Murray was once a major transportation route, before it was superseded by trains. It is still vitally important, though, as it irrigates the farms and orchards lining it, and supplies fresh water to desert communities hundreds of miles away. It is a "lazy" river, with a slow, easy current.

Traveling through Buronga, we crossed the river, and the state border, into Mildura, Victoria, center of the Sunraysia district.

Mildura was once one of the most important ports on the river for paddle steamers, and the graceful, paddle-wheeled boats still ply the waters here, now filled with tourists and fun-seekers rather than the merchandise of commerce. We stopped to watch one of the handsome, white, red-trimmed paddle steamers coming through the locks.

About four miles beyond Mildura, we pulled into a campsite right on the banks of the Murray. Immense river red gums dotted the campground and outlined the river, their broad, ancient trunks hugely twisted by time and the elements.

After setting up camp among the trees, we jumped into our swimsuits and then into the river. We watched hawks soar over the water and boats glide along its surface. Gik, my tent mate, and I talked intermittently, getting to know each other better. We splashed and played and floated in the placid, silver water. It was gloriously refreshing, and we swam until dinnertime.

After dinner, a group of us decided to go for a walk. Within half an hour, most had headed back to camp, but four of us—Marg, Peter W., Karen, and I—kept on going, walking all the way back to Mildura. We walked across town, trying to locate the Working Men's Club, site of the world's longest bar (298 feet long—it's even in the *Guinness Book of World Records)*, but the place was closed when we arrived. So we decided, since it was nearly 10 o'clock, that we should turn our steps toward camp.

As we walked back along the dark, tree-lined country road, we stopped frequently to enjoy the beautiful nighttime sky. I pointed out the Southern Cross to the newcomers, and we were delighted to see a couple of shooting stars.

When we finally got back to camp, we found that most of the group was still up, singing around the campfire. But before long, we were ready to douse the fire and, in the peace and darkness that surrounded the old trees, to roll out our swags and bed down.

> *"Save for the weird rush of the stream and the kookaburras' good-night, all is still, with a mighty far-reaching stillness which can be felt."*
> - from *My Brilliant Career* by Miles Franklin

Monday, January 9

After a very sound sleep, I awoke at 5:30 to the wild and delightfully insane laughter of the kookaburras. As we didn't have to get up until 6, I just lay in the tent listening to a million birds sing, many familiar by now, a few new. At six I rolled out of my sleeping bag and got ready to face the day. We had camp broken and packed on the coach and were on the road by 8 o'clock.

First we had a tour of Mildura, a sunny town of wide avenues and green parkways, which Carl announced is

"One of my favorite towns." (Of course, every town we
see is one of Carl's favorites—but that's not too hard to
understand, as they all have a special charm, whether
antiquity or setting or something else.) We drove through
the center of town, passing the Working Men's Club, the
war memorial, and a beautiful fountain donated by the citizens of Mildura to the city.

At the edge of Mildura stands a large, elegant, old house
that has been converted into the Mildura Art Gallery. Once
known as Rio Vista, this was originally the home of the
Chaffey brothers. Canadian-born and Californian-by-adop-
tion, the Chaffeys, both irrigation specialists, were invited to
Australia in the late 1800s to try and solve the problem of
farming in this region. The problem was you couldn't—
there was no water, so there was no farming. The Chaffeys
started in South Australia, then moved to Victoria, where
they turned the desert into the rich, fruit-growing district it
is today. Across the street from the Chaffey house is a small
park decorated with large mechanical devices, including the
Chaffeys' first irrigation pump, which was in operation for
nearly 60 years, finishing its service in the 1940s.

Leaving Mildura behind we cruised through the countryside, enjoying the wonderful trees, the flocks of galahs, and
the bright sunlight on the river. We passed a dam-created
lake, where the sun-bleached branches of drowned trees
rose above the water. The trees' branches were filled with
hundreds of corellas (small, white cockatoos), with the
great, dense cloud of birds reflected in the still water around
the trees. They reminded me of magnolia trees in bloom.

When we crossed the border into South Australia we had
to set our watches back half an hour. We also had to stop
at the Agricultural Department quarantine station and dis-
pose of any uneaten fruit we were carrying, to avoid carry-

ing any blights into the next fruit-growing district we would enter.

We crossed the Murray again, as its winding course brought it across our path once more, though not for the last time. We drove through Renmark, the South Australian town where the Chaffeys had their first Australian success, and soon reached Berri, one of the centers of the Riverland fruit-growing area. Originally, Berri was just a fuel-wood stop for Murray steamers, but it has grown considerably since then.

Just beyond the town of Berri, we came to Berri Estates, Australia's largest winery. The winery offers an amusing mixture of quality wines and weird, cheap varieties (disparagingly referred to as "plonk"). But it was delightful to see how unserious they were about their lesser wines. They had one called Fruity Gordo. The Inisdorme Port was my favorite, with a label claiming that the liquid was dedicated to the memory of an inept ship's captain who almost discovered something important, but got lost and had to seek refuge where he could when the weather changed; hence, any Port Inisdorme remembers his efforts to make safe harbor. The wine costs $2, and may or may not be drinkable (I didn't find out) but would almost be worth buying for the story on the label.

Outside, Carl pointed to a large gum tree with a graceful, buff-colored trunk and slender, olive-green leaves. He told me it was a lemon-scented gum, and I headed off to investigate. I picked a leaf and broke it, and the scent of lemons assailed my nostrils. I tasted the leaf, and it tasted even more like lemon than it smelled, only delicate, without the tartness. It's easy to imagine how the custom of throwing gum leaves into billy tea might have started.

We continued on our way, through old Barmera, on the

shores of Lake Bonney, toward Waikerie. Outside
Waikerie, high, limestone cliffs rise above the Murray
River. Birds have long taken advantage of these cliffs and
the thermals coming from the sun-baked plains. The contrast between the warm land and cooler water creates shifting patterns of air, which has made this spot a favorite,
too, of gliding enthusiasts worldwide. We passed the
Waikerie Gliding Club, which was founded in 1937.
Named for the abundant birdlife, but also appropriate for
the gliding club, *Waikerie,* in the local Aboriginal tongue,
means "anything that flies."

We crossed the Murray again, this time on the Morgan
Ferry, a cable-drawn punt just big enough for our coach.
We all got out to photograph the placid, tree-lined river as
we crossed it. Just upstream, massive, old, dark wood
wharves, 36 feet high, stretched along the shore. In its
prime, Morgan was the busiest river port in Australia. We
disembarked in Morgan (one of Carl's favorite towns),
where weatherworn buildings lined the road, overlooking
the river.

We drove out of town and into the wilderness. We were
now in saltbush country—miles and miles of dry, reddish
flatlands covered with a lacy blanket of silvery-green saltbush. This useful bit of vegetation thrives in arid regions,
surviving by absorbing atmospheric moisture through its
leaves; cattle and sheep enjoy eating it because of its high
salt content. Bluebush, an equally hardy scrub with smoky
blue-gray leaves, also abounds here.

Our lunch stop was in Burra. This small, delightful town
has a fascinating distant past, but of at least equal interest
to me is its more recent past: this is where they made the
movie *Breaker Morant,* one of my all-time favorite films.

Burra, in its more distant past, was a company town for

the copper mines located there. These were among the first mines in Australia, dating back to 1845. The mines were tremendously rich in copper. Related minerals, such as azurite and malachite, were also found in abundance. Remnants of the town's heyday included an iron-lace rotunda in Market Square; sturdy, hewn-stone miners' cottages; Town Hall; and white-trimmed houses, shops, and hotels.

Around 2,000 of the many miners and laborers working the area during the town's early years lived in "houses" dug into the high banks of Burra Creek. Some of these dugouts still exist, and we went to explore them. The mud-walled dugouts were small and damp, but wonderfully cool.

Most of the early workers were bachelors or had left families behind while they sought their fortunes, so the one-roomed dugouts were sufficient in size. Unfortunately, the proximity to the creek, which not only kept things damp but also served as bath, water supply, toilet, and sewer, made it a fairly disease-ridden spot, and many of those early miners died before they could get back home.

Though mining was carried on for only 30 years, and ceased more than a hundred years ago, scars remain. During the heyday of the copper mines, the company at Burra hired German foresters to cut wood for shoring up the mines and for fueling the pumps that drained the mines. The pumps alone required 1,000 tons of wood per day. As a result, the hills around Burra are barren; a brown, treeless landscape rolls away for miles in all directions. It's sad, yet it does provide a rather dramatic backdrop for the pretty, green, little town. And, though the mining altered the landscape, the richness of the mines saved the economy of South Australia, which was in serious trouble at the time. Also, the newly created grasslands provided excellent sheep grazing, and Burra became a pastoral center after the mines closed in 1877.

Skirting the town, we saw several "chimneys," actually air vents for the mines below. There are two types of chimney: round, which are Cornish, and square, which are Welsh. On top of one of the round chimneys we saw a small, dancing figure, which Carl identified as Johnny Green, mascot of the Cornish miners.

Just outside of town we came to Redruth Gaol, which was built in 1856. Aside from being Burra's one-time local lock-up, Redruth Gaol was also used as the barracks, munitions store, and jail in *Breaker Morant*. It is a low, solid building, rugged stone walls spreading to either side of the finished, white-washed entry, with its arched windows and large, wooden, double doors.

On the road again, the Australian countryside continued to flash past our windows. We passed sheds where sheep shearing was in full swing, looking just like it does in paintings of shearing sheds of 100 years ago.

Mountains rippled the western horizon, growing larger as we drew nearer to Mt. Remarkable National Park. In a few hours we reached Melrose, the oldest town in the Flinders Ranges (and one of Carl's favorites). The location was beautiful, with Mt. Remarkable rising directly behind the tiny town, and a creek bordered by huge river red gums paralleling the only street.

We climbed into the foothills of the Flinders Ranges, through Horrocks Pass. The pass is named for John Horrocks, an early explorer, who would probably have been among the country's greatest if he hadn't had the misfortune of accidentally dying at the age of 24. Horrocks was testing the practicality of using camels in desert exploration—a mode of transportation that eventually became the standard. He was getting his muzzle-loading rifle off his camel's saddle one day, when the camel suddenly started bucking, which set off the rifle. The bullets passed through the explorer's shoulder and jaw, a wound that proved fatal. Horrocks's last words were, "Shoot the camel."

In the nearby hills a thin ribbon of smoke from a grass fire rose in the warm, clear air, drifting on the breeze. As we descended from the pass we could see Spencer Gulf and Port Augusta in the near distance. The late afternoon sunlight glinted off the glassy water. Avocets scurried along the shore and other birds wheeled slowly overhead.

We drove through Port Augusta, and rolled into camp around 6:45. It was a lovely evening; the stars were bright, and a fresh breeze blew from the sea. After dinner, some of us talked and stargazed until midnight. Then I crawled off to my tent and immediately fell asleep.

Tuesday, January 10

Today we swung north, keeping the lovely, strange, rolling, lavender-brown Flinders Ranges to our right. We were heading into the Outback now. Soon we were surrounded by myall trees (*myall* means "wild" in Aboriginal dialect), occasional casuarinas, acacias, and other scrubby vegetation, all of it a wonderful, silvery celadon color.

The landscape changed rapidly and frequently—suddenly, bare ground, then miles of saltbush, then short trees and fragrant brush. Every so often we'd come upon a salt "lake"—an area where there is water on rare occasions, but which is dry most of the time, with a thick, blindingly

white crust of salt covering the mud below. The great
sheets of salt are so reflective that they look like water in
places, picking up the blue of the sky. It is wonderful
country, strange and hauntingly beautiful.

> *Back to the road, and I crossed again*
> *Over the miles of the saltbush plain*
> *The shining plain that is said to be*
> *The dried-up bed of an inland sea.*
> *Where the air so dry and so clear and bright*
> *Refracts the sun with a wondrous light,*
> *And out in the dim horizon makes*
> *The deep blue gleam of the phantom lakes.*
>
> *At dawn of day we could feel the breeze*
> *That stirred the boughs of the sleeping trees,*
> *And brought a breath of the fragrance rare*
> *That comes and goes in that scented air;*
> *For the trees and grass and the shrubs contain*
> *A dry sweet scent on the saltbush plain.*
> *For those that love it and understand*
> *The saltbush plain is a wonderland.*

- from "In The Droving Days" by A.B. "Banjo" Paterson*

Off in the distance we could see the table-topped Oakton
Hills. A large, red kangaroo started out of the brush and
tried to outrun us, turning suddenly in front of the coach
and crossing to the other side of the road before disappearing in a cloud of dust.

The new Ghan—the Adelaide to Alice Springs train—
was coming as we approached the only railroad crossing
on this road, and we had to wait for it to pass. It runs

*See appendix

infrequently enough to make the crossing of our paths in the middle of nowhere seem noteworthy.

Woomera was our first stop of the day. This town grew out of the Woomera rocket testing range and satellite-tracking station. Testing is no longer being done, so the town is depopulating. However, it's no ghost town, since its space-tracking facilities are still needed. In the center of town there is a large outdoor display of rockets and missiles that were tested here. Les, our Naval technical officer, who at one point worked in the defense field, explained the use of many of the rockets, from defense to upper atmosphere research.

As we strolled around town, the thing that most held my attention was the sky. It was beautiful and remarkable. The blue seemed far more intense than usual, and the clouds were wispy and elongated, like the strokes of a nearly dry brush, curving, and crossing at right angles.

From Woomera, we headed back out into the desert. Our next stop, miles later, was for morning tea at Spuds Roadhouse in Pimba, a "town" with a population of three. A camel and donkey were grazing nearby, and I wondered if they were among the three.

The camel was waiting for us when we stepped back outside. I've read that camels are both cheeky and playful, and the nibbling and nuzzling and chasing that ensued seemed to bear this out. The degree of amusement with this varied among individuals, though the camel was obviously enjoying it more than anyone else. We managed to get back on the coach without mishap, and without the camel, who was left standing forlornly, watching the back of the receding bus as we continued on our way.

Down the track a bit, we stopped at Island Lagoon. The shining salt of the deceptive lake stretched brilliantly beneath the blue sky. Farther along, after crossing Eucolo Creek, we came to shimmering Lake Hart.

Surrounded by heat and light, we stood at the edge of the blinding, white lake and looked out over the great, rolling wilderness. I shivered with joy, and wished the others were a thousand miles away. I took a few slow, almost involuntary steps toward the emptiness.

"Be careful," Carl said quietly. Perhaps because he, too, is drawn to this land he recognized the symptoms in me. "Head out there without water and you'd be dead in eight hours. Few years ago, a family wandered off the track. They didn't take water, and they all died. It's beautiful, but it's not real forgiving."

Lunch time found us in Glendambo. This small town was founded around 1980 by people from nearby Kingoonya. It is not a metropolis, but it is bigger than Pimba. There's an impressive motel/restaurant/pub building, a general store, fuel pumps, and a few houses. The locale is flat, red, and dotted with mulga trees, hardy, slow-growing members of the acacia family.

I loved the look of the place, the red desert around it. I sat on the porch of the motel, watching the desert, which begins directly across the road from the small cluster of buildings. The startling sky I had noticed first at Woomera seemed even stranger and more beautiful here, over the red earth and pale-green, spreading mulgas. The wispy tails of clouds no longer crossed each other, but all seemed drawn to a single spot on the distant horizon.

After Glendambo we hit the dirt—the dirt road, that is. No more comfortable cruising on asphalt pavement. Now it was time to brace ourselves for a rough ride. It will be a little disappointing when they get it all paved. The roughness suits the place, adds to the feeling of remoteness. Ah well, so runs the course of progress.

As we drove through the seemingly endless miles of wilderness, the scenery was interrupted only occasionally by sightings of the dog fence. The dog fence is the longest fence in the world. It stretches for more than 6,000 miles, surrounding the Centre of Australia, separating the deserts and their attendant dingoes from sheep country.

Around 4 p.m., we rolled into a weird, undulating land of golden-beige earth flecked with the white of exposed rock: Coober Pedy. In this bizarre town, nearly 80 percent of the floating, multi-national population lives underground. Water tanks and chimneys sprout from hillsides and open cut or deep shaft mines fill backyards. Huge mounds of rock and pieces of strange equipment stand everywhere.

People live underground to escape the heat. In dugouts— "houses" carved into the sandstone, gypsum, and white clay stone of the district—the temperature is fairly constant and quite cool, which is a real advantage in a town where summer temperatures average around 120 degrees.

Besides the heat, Coober Pedy's biggest problem is that there's no fresh water. Wells have been sunk several hundred feet deep, but only salt water has been struck, so all water must be treated. The treatment, desalinization by osmosis, is not cheap, so water is conserved rigorously. The district only gets about four inches of rain per year, so there is no real help there.

Why do people stay? Opals. Residents readily admit that the dream of wealth acquired from mining the precious stone is the reason they're in Coober Pedy. Approximately 80 percent of the world's opal comes from this town. Independence is another big draw. Local law bars large-scale mining operations, leaving the opal fields to the rugged individuals who want to try their luck and have a go at treasure hunting.

Coober Pedy was named by the Aborigines. *Kupa* means uninitiated person: a young boy or, as in this case, a white man. *Piti* is a hole in the ground, generally a waterhole or burrow. Coober Pedy, then, is "white man's hole in the ground," referring to the dugout homes and mines.

One resident was expecting us. We entered his dugout home through an ordinary front door bolted to a golden hillside. The pleasantly cool house was surprisingly spacious, with kitchen, dining room, bedrooms, living room, and recreation room with an indoor, saltwater swimming pool. The only reminders that we were underground were the airshafts in the corners. The walls of the house were the unadorned, pale beige of the stone from which the dwelling was carved, still showing chisel marks in places.

Next we visited one of Coober Pedy's underground churches, a long, low, narrow cavern carved from the same stone as the dugout home. The alter was modest, the walls, rough and simply adorned. However, the decorations, though few and handmade by local miners, were largely crafted from opal.

Carl ran us up to the Opal Cave, a dugout store. The owner, a simply dressed, dark-haired woman in her late 40s, leaned amiably across the glass counter as she recounted, in the unhurried speech of the Outback, the "secrets" of mining in Coober Pedy. On locating a claim, she said, "Stand where you like, face any direction you choose, toss your hat over your shoulder, and dig where it lands." Dig long enough and you may strike opal: "It sounds like china breaking when you hit a vein." Of course, she did not fail to mention that buying opals would save you all the trouble, and added that, "All that stuff you've heard about opals being bad luck was made up by the people who sell diamonds." I didn't buy anything, but I enjoyed perusing the displays of opals, other local minerals, and fossils.

Tonight we're camping in a dugout, which pleases me immensely. Our dugouts are not of a luxurious nature—just large, bare rooms carved straight into a hill. We rolled our swags out on the smooth, stone floor. All of us have been fitted into two, long rooms, so it's much like a giant slumber party. However, since men and women are not separated, we learned how to get dressed without leaving our sleeping bags.

Shower and toilet facilities are in a separate building (they are for most dugouts). Showers cost 60 cents for three minutes, but seemed a bargain, since we were pretty hot and dusty. Since the water in the hand basins is salt, we had to brush our teeth in the shower, too.

It's not hard for me to appreciate the peculiar, rugged appeal of Coober Pedy. Here, just getting by is an adventure.

Wednesday, January 11

It was cloudy when we arose this morning, and there was a light drizzle. It was evident that it had been raining for a while. But, undaunted, we packed the coach after breakfast and headed back out onto the dirt road.

We continued to drive through spinifex and mulga wilderness. Carl said some of the slow-growing mulgas are in excess of 400 years old.

We spotted a family of Aborigines walking by the road, which prompted Carl to relate to us the many uses the Aborigines have found for the local plants. They make their spears from straightened branches of mulga trees, and fasten the barbs on with spinifex wax. Carl told us that an Aboriginal stockman he knows once repaired the pierced tank of a motorcycle with a plug of mulga sealed with spinifex wax, which kept the thing running till he got to a repair station. Also, the mulga tree's seeds can be soaked and used for food, except for certain times of year, when they become poisonous.

Occasionally we came upon great bursts of greenery and tall gum trees, which strung out along the desert, marking the courses of creeks, usually dried up. We continued to enjoy the company of great flocks of galahs and budgerigars.

The rain began to pick up its pace. Carl plowed through the puddles that now filled the rutted road, sending up sprays higher than the coach's roof, which was greeted by loud yahooing from nearly all on board. (The entire under-carriage of the coach is water- and airtight, so there are no worries of damaging anything. In fact, these safari coaches are so designed that the water can come up to the wind-shield and they can still keep on going—provided they don't get bogged.)

In the ever-increasing downpour, the red desert was tak-ing on a green tinge right before our eyes. Pools and streams became larger and more frequent. The coach rocked from the onslaught of the rising wind, and the rain became torrential. The desert was beginning to look like a lake.

Carl played a Slim Dusty tape for us as we drove on. (Slim Dusty is The Father of Australian Country/Western music. He is an institution here. Though he packs the big stadiums, he still drives around the country, stopping to play at Aboriginal reserves, Outback rodeos, and small towns. His songs celebrate Australia, Australians, and life on the road. His music is terrific—and I'm not a big C&W

fan.) Carl selected the song "Send 'Er Down, Hughie!"—
the tale of a truck driver stranded on a muddy road during
an Outback downpour—the appropriateness of which
elicited a burst of appreciative laughter.

After a few more Slim Dusty numbers, Carl slipped on
the song "Oh Lord, it's Hard to be Humble," which we all
sang along with enthusiastically. Pat took this as a signal
for a great time for a sing-along, which she proceeded to
lead. After a rousing chorus of "Row, row, row your boat"
the entire effort sort of deteriorated, and the guys at the
back of the bus managed to end every song with "Merrily,
merrily, merrily, merrily, life is but a dream." These were
the last sounds we heard before pulling in, for lunch and
information, at Marla Bore.

By now, the rain was coming down with awesome feroc-
ity, so Carl went off to see if the track ahead was negotiable. A little exploring and a few phone calls later the
word finally came through—no way out. Greg, the owner
of the Marla Hotel Motel (which, with its staff and their
homes, is pretty much the whole town of Marla) offered us
special arrangements for the night—six or seven of us in
each room, we use our sleeping bags and towels, not their
linen, and we pay only $1.50 each. The alternative is
camping out. Needless to say, we all opted for rooms. We
unloaded our baggage in fire brigade fashion, passing it
from the bus to the roadhouse's sheltered patio, then we
made a dash for our rooms. I'm in with Gik, Helen,
Simca, Maree, and Naida. It's a large room, and even with
our swags rolled out we can move about easily.

The kitchen trailer was backed into the spacious
garage/machine shed behind the roadhouse and pub section of the motel complex, and it was to this cavernous,
gasoline-scented shelter that we repaired for our evening

meal. In an effort to compensate the group for the inconvenience of being trapped here, Jill made dinner a bit more lavish than usual. Everyone set up camp stools around the inside of the shed, amidst the oil cans, tools, and engine parts, and we toasted each other and the weather with wine-filled tin cups, and heaped metal camp plates with lamb chops and veggies in cheese sauce. It was beautifully weird. Everyone enjoyed the meal, and the camaraderie was noticeably increased by the shared difficulty.

After dinner was done and the dishes were all cleaned up, we slogged to the pub to while away the balance of the evening. We are not alone here, and it was interesting to look around the room and see who our fellow strandees are: the 24 passengers from a Greyhound Express bus bound for Alice Springs; a gathering of locals who can't get home; a few families traveling by road; a truck driver, two police, and the hotel staff. The trucker sits in the corner reading an Alistair Maclean novel; a number of people are looking at magazines, writing letters, or playing cards; Tom is sewing travel patches on his camera case; I'm writing; children are playing the video games; most of our guys and many of the locals are engaged in consuming beer and playing pool; a few individuals are busy with the jukebox near the bar; and someone is always at the window, checking on the status of the storm, staring in mute astonishment at its escalating fury. The front drive is littered with cars, utes, 4WD vehicles, a truck, and the two buses. Beyond the drive, all that is visible is water.

Eventually, we all wandered off to our rooms and bedded down for the night. The weather, however, is not particularly conducive to sleeping. The torrential rain and fierce wind lash the single-story buildings of the motel with vehemence and great noise. The walls shudder at the onslaught. But at least we have walls, and a roof, and we're safe and dry. It's not a bad place to be stranded.

Thursday, January 12

I rose early for kitchen duties this morning (we all take turns helping Jill with meals). I grabbed my duffel bag, which had been leaning against the wall, and found that it and the clothes in it were soaking wet. Actually, one thing was still dry—my swimsuit. Having been built for a desert climate and not for a sub-aquatic existence, the motel walls had allowed some of the rain to slip through. But I had the advantage of pre-wet clothes—everyone else had to wait till they went outside.

Breakfast was set for the optimistic hour of 8 o'clock, so Jill, Marg, and I had to be in the "kitchen" by 7. Even as I crossed the nearly submerged courtyard through the still unabated torrents I suspected we wouldn't be going anywhere.

Despite the dreary outlook, the whole group was up for breakfast (much to our surprise) and on time. Hope springs eternal. Many of us even rolled our swags up in anticipation of imminent departure. Carl promised nothing, but continued to check all possibilities for getting us out.

Everything that is not under water is wonderfully green. Watching the downpour, if not encouraging, is at least fascinating. The desert frogs, which survive the climate by burying themselves, staying underground for as long as seven years waiting for rain, are out in great numbers and having a grand time—as are the children trying to catch them.

The morning disappeared in chatting and napping, wandering in the rain and surveying the damage, or playing frisbee in the by now completely submerged courtyard. At lunch we were told that we will be here for another night, which we'd kind of guessed, since the rain was descending with new force. We've already had more than the area's total annual rainfall within 1-1/2 days, and no let-up is predicted.

Jill announced that we would have a cabaret this evening, and everyone would be expected to do something, no matter how simple or strange. I spent the afternoon writing a poem to present at the cabaret: "Sturt's Revenge or The Return of the Great Inland Sea." (Charles Sturt was an early and important Australian explorer who was so convinced that there must be an inland sea that he carried a small boat on his first expedition into the interior. Actually, at one time there was an inland sea, but Sturt was a few million years too late to see it.)

Several more members of our group braved the rain in order to view the devastation. The water on the highway is five feet deep and rising fast. The new Ghan "all-weather" railroad is destroyed—the earth has been washed out beneath it and the rails have collapsed. It is broken in four places. We were among the last to see the train running when it crossed our path Tuesday.

At dinnertime a list was passed around for everyone to sign, along with the name of their "act." By 8:30, we were assembled in the main lounge of the roadhouse. All the other inhabitants of our newly formed island were on hand as well, which, though it appeared daunting at first, contributed tremendously to the success of the evening.

Andy brought the house down with the opener, "I'd like to thank you all for being here tonight." He and Mandy got the show off to a good start, singing songs about rain. There were renderings of various folk songs, and Les read

"Ode to the Dunny" (a dunny is an outhouse), which is printed on one of his T-shirts. Margaret and Peter W. presented a clever quiz on Canadianisms vs. Australianisms, pitting the men against the women in an effort to see which group is most nearly bilingual.

Chris and Sandra did a charming and humorous skit titled "Beauty and the Beast," in which a charwoman attempts, with her cleaning utensils, to imitate the primping of a fastidious socialite. A group of the guys sang (what else) "Row, row, row your boat." There were games that got people from outside our group involved, from an obstacle course walked blindfolded, with volunteers guided by comments from the audience, to a hilarious competition where people had to guess the meaning of vague instructions and do what they thought was wanted. I read my poem, which was very well received, with many requests for copies and even autographs!

The cabaret ended with a sing-along, then we broke into smaller groups to chat until well after midnight. It was a delightful evening, and broke down any barriers that existed between the various groups stranded here.

Sturt's Revenge or The Return of the Great Inland Sea
The rain came down and tried to drown
The great, red, sunburnt land.
We swam ashore at Marla Bore,
Though it's not what we'd planned.
We thought that we would see Ayers Rock,
But now we are stuck here.
It's rather sad, but not so bad—
At least the pub's got beer.
The sky is gray, it rains all day,

The wind howls through the night.
The coach won't float, we have no boat,
And no relief's in sight.
There's water, water everywhere,
But we'll need stronger drink
To see us through till skies are blue
And vehicles don't sink
Beneath the waves and sticky mud.
It's sad to say, but true,
We're stuck encore at Marla Bore,
No hope of getting through.
The Red Sea parted at a word
From Moses. Why can't we
Find someone who could pray and then
Part the Red Centre's sea?
We'll eat and drink, and sleep and drink,
And then we'll drink some more.
We're high and dry—well, at least high,
And stuck at Marla Bore.

(Note: The end of the second quatrain is an allusion to a very famous, humorously mournful, Australian song, "The Pub With No Beer," which states that "There's nothing so lonesome, morbid or drear/ as to stand at the bar of a pub with no beer.")

Friday, January 13
   After coming down all night long, the rain continued with unrelenting force this morning. Breakfast was set back to 9 o'clock, so we got to sleep in a little before stumbling off through the mud and water to our waiting

coffee and toast.

At breakfast, Carl asked for volunteers to help him plot a possible escape. His plan was that he and a small band of adventurous souls would head down the track, wading through the water on the road to see how deep it is and how far it goes. Then, if it seemed even remotely passable, the rest of us would form a human chain along the side of the road to show Carl, driving the coach, where the edges are. The coach can handle about five feet of water, but the big danger is leaving the road—the coach would sink in the mud and it would be days, possibly weeks, before we'd get it out. John, Michael, Paul, Peter S. and LaVonne set out with Carl within the hour.

It was hours before the "search party" returned, and the news was not good. Even John, our tallest guy at 6'3", couldn't touch bottom a hundred yards from where the road disappears into the water. After swimming for more than a mile they found it got no shallower, and they could see no end to it. So they swam back, returning to us wet, cold, and tired, with the disappointing news.

In the meantime, there had been a little action in camp for our nurses. A two-year-old girl had fallen and hurt her arm, possibly cracking a bone. Simca, Naida and Maree scurried about, gathering magazines and tape for an improvised splint, borrowing a sling from the coach's first-aid kit, checking into getting the flying doctor out here, and reassuring the mother and child.

During the day our numbers continued to increase. Many of the houses on the surrounding stations are flooded by now. Marla is one of the highest points in the area, so it is one of the few spots still above water.

At lunch, Jill announced that, because we weren't getting out, we'd have a fancy dress dance this evening. This was greeted at first with mixed enthusiasm—great idea, but: 1) who wants to dress up in lousy weather, then slog through the mud and rain to the pub; or 2) it's a camping trip; I didn't bring any fancy clothes. But as the afternoon progressed, everyone began to view the idea of a dance with increasing pleasure.

In the late afternoon, the sky began to lighten, and, though the wind was still wild, the rain began to ease up a little, stopping for a few minutes before starting again. The cloud cover began to break up, and we could see our first tatters of blue sky in three days. There were still bursts of torrential rain, but there were also moments of relief. Spirits began to rise.

A huge crane had been brought out previously for surveying the devastation and sighting people lost in the floods. (Due to Marla's proximity to the tracks, Australian National Railways has a lot of heavy equipment here, so the presence of such machinery is not unusual.) Now, as the weather was improving slightly, and the crane crew was stranded and bored, too, they began giving rides to the top in the iron bucket. The wind made the trip up a bit dicey, but the view was amazing. We could really get an idea of how extensive the flooding is. All roads lead to lakes. Signposts stand like lonely reeds in the seemingly endless sea. The tops of fences trace geometric patterns along the surface, or act as breakwaters, accentuating the swiftness of the current in places where the water is flowing. But the trees and bushes that stand above the waves are tremendously green, as are the fingers of land that stretch out into the water.

When we got back down from our crane ride, Helen and I walked to the "lake," where the road and railway tracks disappear into the water. Walking along the sleepers (railroad ties), we followed the rail down to where the earth has been washed away and the track has collapsed—the end of the line. The great, twisted rails plunged into the murky torrent, and the swift current foamed as it rushed past the sunken tracks. The wind was raising white caps on the surrounding water.

The swirling water was gunmetal gray. The trees that rose above the flood were silhouetted darkly against the billowing white and black clouds that still filled the sky. The distant mountains were an undulating, deep purple specter rising from the silver plains at the horizon's edge. It was hard to believe we were standing in the middle of the great Australian desert.

We finally returned to our room to prepare for dinner. As several of the rooms have lost electricity and/or hot water, we see a lot of the members of our group this time each evening, as they appear one by one at our door to request time in the bathroom. Soon, it was dinnertime, and we all braved the mud, wind, and (thankfully) diminishing rain as we headed back to the machine shed.

The dance was set for 8:30. A portable stereo was set up in the main room of the roadhouse, and tables and chairs were pushed back to make room for a "dance floor." It took a few minutes to get things going, but soon almost everyone was on their feet, with members of the hotel staff and work crew joining in. We laughed and danced and talked until 3 a.m.

Saturday, January 14

The combination of last night's fun followed by a sound sleep had my spirits soaring. The sky was clearing and the temperature was rising—it looked like it would be a glorious day.

The big excitement this morning was the evacuation of the little girl with the injured arm. There was nowhere for the flying doctor to land his plane, so an emergency helicopter that had been making food drops at isolated stations was routed this way. The little girl and her mother are the first to escape our island home.

We found out today that one of the couples from the Greyhound group is missing their daughter's wedding. They were headed for Alice Springs, where the wedding was scheduled for today, when they got trapped here. We haven't heard, yet, whether the event has been postponed, but we all hope so.

After lunch, Peter K. organized a cricket game on the small bit of relatively dry road out front. We had a cricket bat, a tennis ball, and wastebaskets for wickets. All the little kids joined our group, as the Aussies (some of them really good cricketers) taught us foreigners how to play. Normally, a batter is up till they're out, but we set a limit of six runs, so everyone would have a chance to bat. We also all tried to bowl (pitch) and field. Fielding was wild, as we slid through the mud and water all around us, trying harder to stay on our feet than to catch the ball. It was terrific fun, and a great opportunity to learn about cricket—at last I understand.

Several of us changed into swimsuits and headed down the track for a once-in-a-lifetime chance to swim the Stuart Highway. The water has stopped rising, now that the rain has stopped falling, but it does not appear to have receded at all. I walked out till I was chest deep, then began to swim. We swam carefully, ever watchful for floating fauna—scorpions, desert centipedes and the like.

The water was refreshing, and it was a long time before we headed back to our room to shower and change for dinner.

This evening we had something of a "sport night," with virtually everyone here joining in the crazy events. There was a race with children on grown-ups' shoulders, a really wild game called "pass the body" (which produced our only injury of the evening), and a thong-kicking contest. An auction for "racing frogs" (race to follow) was held by our two policemen. Eighty percent of the proceeds from the auction would be divided among the top three placers, with the final twenty percent being donated to the Royal Flying Doctor Service. It was a great success. Most of us formed "syndicates" for bidding on the frogs, so the going prices for these "thoroughbreds" shot up to nearly $10 each as we pooled our resources. The race wasn't as much fun as the auction.

During the evening, another truck was added to the collection of vehicles on the drive. The two hapless drivers got stuck on the road when the floods hit, and have spent the last three days bogging and digging out their rig, over and over again. They didn't have anything to eat for those three days, either. Needless to say, they were happy to get to Marla Bore.

People drifted off as the night progressed. I stayed up talking with Blue. He told me tales of horse breaking, its joys and dangers. The excitement is exhilarating, but he now has a permanent limp from the time a horse slammed him against a tree, crushing his knee. He spoke of shearing season, when he takes leave from his regular chores and travels from shed to shed in about a 150-mile radius, working wherever another shearer is needed for a few weeks. He described rural pleasures, from fishing to country dances, and he told me about his family—Scottish in origin, but Australian for many generations.

At around 3 a.m., we were joined by the hotel kitchen staff. We chatted until 4 o'clock, at which time the cook said that, if I'd stay until they opened the kitchen in two more hours, he'd fix anything I wanted for breakfast. However, when I started suggesting ideas for a good "brekkie," I heard the woeful tale of how thoroughly depleted the supplies really are. It was just as well, though, as I really felt more like sleeping than eating breakfast. So I dragged off to my waiting sleeping bag and was soon blissfully unconscious.

Sunday, January 15

A pleasant but uneventful afternoon was spent playing cards. Almost more amusing (to me) than playing the games was watching John play. He sat for a long time, with his feet up, his hat down so we couldn't see his eyes, looking for all the world like Clint Eastwood in one of those spaghetti Westerns. He was silent, unmoving, and seemed uninterested. But when he finally did play, he knew every trick everyone had, every twitch that might give them away. Obviously, the man is an artist.

After dinner, the troops gathered once more in the lounge for an evening of good company. A few people are feeling the strain of being stranded, and there are some sad faces around the room. I admit I'm disappointed to miss the sights I've come so far to see, but my spirits are still pretty high. Besides, how many people can say they've swum the Stuart Highway.

I played cards with Gik, Paul, and Michael for a while, and played video games with Dave. Eventually, everyone wandered outside, where we sat, talking and enjoying the cool evening breeze, which was refreshing after a day of blazing sunshine.

Scorpions and desert centipedes are a bit of a nuisance, now, having been driven to higher ground by the water. Australian scorpions are not very large—maybe 3-4 inches long—and are not lethal. They are nocturnal, eat primarily insects, and would rather retreat than sting. They are actually less repulsive than the large (4 or more inches long), venomous centipedes.

I did enjoy seeing some of the other, non-venomous insects driven toward us for refuge: stick insects, praying mantises, several flashy-looking beetles, and some gorgeous, huge moths.

Miscellany

The history of Marla Bore stretches back considerably further than the town and hotel of Marla. The original bore (artesian well) at Marla was used in the cattle-droving days as a watering point for livestock moving from the northwest of South Australia and the Northern Territory to southern markets.

Monday, January 16

This morning, about 20 of us went for a long walk, to see how far our island extends, now that the water is retreating. We headed down the road till we came to water, then we cut cross-country, following the shore. The sky was blue, the ground, dark red, and there was green everywhere. The mulga is in bloom, with its delicate yellow flowers, as is the pink grevillea and the purple-flowered wild tomato.

We played kick-the-can whenever we came across a washed up tinny, and we talked, and Peter K. kicked over anthills (which, should you ever be in this part of the world, you ought to know cannot be done unless the anthills have been submerged for some time). We were gone for 2-1/2 hours, and returned warm but exhilarated.

Railroad and Department of Highways workers began to appear today. A few of the supervisors told us that this is only the second time in more than 100 years that this much flooding has occurred in this area. That's why the new railroad succumbed to the ravages of the weather—it was built to withstand more common catastrophes. I'm impressed. I mean, if you have to be stuck in a flood, it might as well be one that makes the record books.

At lunchtime we found that the coach had been moved out of the machine shed and onto the rapidly drying drive. The kitchen was set up alfresco, and we enjoyed our first meal outdoors since the rain began.

Following lunch, we all congregated in the pub for announcements. Our police officers first told the gathering that interest-free loans were available to anyone running out of money. This applied mainly to the Greyhound people and other travelers, as our group came equipped with sleeping bags, clothes, and a mobile kitchen full of food, so we're in pretty good shape. Then they went on to explain that, though most of us will be here for a while longer, there will be an evacuation of people with sufficiently good reasons for leaving.

A work train caught on this section of track will be brought from Kulgera, the next big break in the line, to the far side of our break. Those who must leave will be taken out on the work train. At Kulgera, a Greyhound bus will meet the train and take the "refugees" to Alice Springs. Every one of the stranded Greyhound passengers opted for this out. In our group, only Peter J. and Marg had to leave. They have an international flight to catch by the end of the week, and no one knows when we'll be getting out of here.

Almost everyone waded out to see the evacuees off. The train arrived at 5 p.m., and departed moments later with a capacity load. After wading back through the mud and waist-deep water, we cleaned up, changed our clothes, and got back into enjoying our enforced stopover.

After dinner, a number of women gathered in our room, to borrow our shower and electrical outlets, or just to chat. Maree produced a bottle of wine, and we had an impromptu party. When the bottle was empty, I soaked off its labels. The back label bears the statement: "This premium wine was specially selected to commemorate the joint opening of the town of Marla and the Marla Hotel Motel on November 20th 1982 by the Premier of South Australia." How could I resist a souvenir like that?

Leaving the room, I wandered over toward the pub lounge. Most of the group was sitting out on the patio. Andy was playing the guitar, and he and Mandy were singing. Helen joined us, and she and I talked, listened to the music and the desert breeze, and enjoyed the pleasant coolness of the evening.

Tuesday, January 17

We rose early today and moved out of our rooms. Our tents were pitched on the now dry front lawn, which only four days ago was under nearly a foot of water. The great heat (it has been over 100 degrees every day since the rain stopped) and continuing winds are helping to dry up the shallower pools, although the "lakes" seem unaffected. It seems strange to be in tents and still be here, but the general consensus is that this feels like a step in the right direction.

We were sitting on the lawn, enjoying the sunshine and talking, when word came that Carl, ever seeking a way out, was bogged somewhere up the track. Volunteers were solicited, and four of our guys slogged up the road, shovels in hand, to dig out our fearless leader.

The roads are deceptive (those that are above water), as the surfaces have dried quickly in the extreme heat, but there are still several feet of mud beneath the thin crusts. Carl's is not the first vehicle to get bogged.

After lunch, a number of men assisted the Australian National Railway crews in filling holes and clearing an emergency road for getting repair equipment out to the railroad and a food shipment from the rail to Marla. The rest of the group spent the afternoon soaking up the brilliant sunshine or retreating to the coolness of the pub's cards, pool table, or video games.

My time was spent swimming and sunning. At Marla, a water tank has been converted into a swimming pool of unusual dimensions—a circle about 10 feet across and 8 feet deep. In fact, we didn't realize at first that it was supposed to be a pool, as it still looks a lot like a storage tank. Anyway, I swam and "sunbaked" (as the Aussies say) until 4:30, by which time I was well and truly cooked, but feeling wonderful.

An evening that would otherwise have been identical to other evenings was highlighted by a brief, boisterous celebration of John's 21st birthday. We gave him a Marla Bore

T-shirt and a cardboard "key to the city" that we'd all
signed, and Jill brought out two decorated cakes. Then we
settled once more into amiable conversation and enjoyment of the evening breeze.

Wednesday, January 18

I joined our morning marching group for our semi-
daily stroll down the track, but our walk was interrupted
before it really began. A TV7 news crew from Adelaide
and reporters from a number of newspapers arrived by helicopter, here to get the story of how we're getting on.
While they were setting up, the news came in that we
might be getting out today. We began to get ready for the
eventuality that we might be leaving when word came that
we would definitely be on our way before day's end.

With the cameramen and reporters still running around,
now documenting the imminent escape, we redoubled the
speed of our preparations. The excitement ran through
camp like an electric current. The only people saddened by
the news were the inhabitants of Marla, the staff and management of the hotel-motel complex, who said that the
place won't be the same without us. That I can believe.

We had a leisurely, joyful lunch, not yet knowing when
we'd be leaving, but ready and raring to go. We all wandered off after eating, believing our departure was hours
off. Only moments later the cry went up: "It's time—we're
going—everybody on the track."

The timing had remained uncertain till the last minute
due to the nature of the escape. Carrying all our hand luggage, we had to hike out, using the railroad's emergency
access road, then follow the tracks, skirting the "lakes"

and mud holes, then walk five miles to the first spot that could be reached by four-wheel-drive vehicles, and we had to time it so the 4WDs arrived when we did.

It was brutally hot, with not a cloud in the sky to diminish the effects of the blazing sun. The air shimmered, and burning mirage melted into standing water. We walked past the bleaching bones of animals that had died in drier years. The scorpions we spotted were dead, too—drowned—but we still avoided them.

Pools and puddles left by the flood stood everywhere, but around them, dust already drifted in the hot wind. As we trudged along, occasionally, the thin dry crust of the road would break through, and someone (myself included) would have a sandal sucked off by the thick mud below. We'd retrieve our footgear, rinse it in a nearby pool, and walk on.

When we reached the Australian Pacific 4WD desert cruiser, we were overjoyed to find a case of canned soft drinks waiting for us—sitting in the sun, and almost at the boiling point, but wet, and consumed with great relish. Then we piled into the cruiser or onto the utes that came along with our luggage and food supplies, and we were off.

The ride was rough but interesting. We saw where trucks and road graders had been severely bogged, and where normally dry creeks had cut across the road, taking the road with them. Two glorious wedge-tailed eagles watched our progress from a nearby tree before lifting gracefully into the air and gliding away. The Musgrave Ranges rose up off to our left, dark and purple against the red desert.

Near Chandler, a stream had carved a little too deeply to permit our passage, so we had to stop. We climbed out of our vehicles and wandered off to amuse ourselves until a backhoe could be brought in to break down the banks that had formed on either side of the temporary watercourse.

It was a wonderful spot, bordered by river red gums, with enough clear, cool water left in pools along the streambed to be really pleasant. It was obvious that the water had come through here with some force. Bushes and shrubs that had been in its path were completely flattened. The now exposed mud showed current patterns, like the floor of the ocean.

Many of the pools were full of tadpoles which, if they can attain full size before the water disappears, will absorb water through their skins until they're tightly bloated, then bury themselves deep in the ground, where they will survive until the next big rainfall. LaVonne spent a great deal of time rescuing tadpoles from nearly dry puddles, catching them and carrying them to deeper pools.

Most of us waded in the largest ponds, cooling off and rinsing away the dust we'd accumulated during our long walk. Dave climbed a big gum tree, and sat up there surveying the situation. After a bit of splashing, I wandered off to explore and take photographs.

Within an hour, Greg, from Marla Bore, arrived with the earth-moving equipment. He got a fair amount accomplished before he, too, became bogged. One of the ute drivers hopped into the cab to help Greg and, using the machine's front and back power shovels, they pushed and lifted the vehicle out of the deep mud. With the wheels almost completely buried and the two mechanical claws flailing and thrashing about, it looked for all the world like some metallic crab-creature from a Japanese horror flick.

When the backhoe was again free, and the crossing was sufficiently level, the 4WD vehicles forded the stream. We waded along behind them.

After another half hour of driving, we arrived at the spot

where our new coach awaited us. Someone had thought-fully filled the water drum on the back of the coach. We stopped to drink as much water as possible and filled our canteens. Then we rapidly transferred the contents of the 4WDs into the coach and climbed on board. The doors closed, Carl started the engine, and all the guys at the back of the coach burst joyously into the refrain, "Merrily, mer-rily, merrily, merrily, life is but a dream." And we were off, heading north once more. Before long we were back on the Stuart Highway.

The roads were barely passable, a morass of mud and water-filled gullies—but we were moving. Carl stopped at the state border, so we could photograph the "Northern Territory—Outback Australia" sign welcoming us into the territory. Across the border, the landscape began to change almost immediately. There were great tumbles of boulders and outcrops of red rock, and scattered corkbark trees and desert oaks. It was beautiful. The Ayers Range rose before us as we approached Kulgera. It was a spectacularly clear, fresh night, filled with bright stars.

At Kulgera, a trailer awaited us, with tents and cooking gear to replace what we'd left behind. It was nearly 9 o'clock when we arrived, so we all pitched in to unload gear, haul water, put up tables, and move kitchen supplies so Jill could get to work on dinner. Then we put up our tents.

There is no hot water in the ladies' half of the ablution block, so we took turns showering in the gents' half. This was not much of a problem, since our group is the only one here, and we all know each other pretty well by now.

Most of us headed over to the pub for some refresh-ments before dinner. Last week there was two feet of water running through this place, and it still looks pretty hard hit. But nobody seemed to notice the hole in the wall, the loose boards, the paneling peeling away from the walls, or the high-water mark on the bar, and a good time was had by all. We're here and settled in, and it's not Marla Bore, so we're happy.

Thursday, January 19

When we rose this morning, the nearly full moon had not yet set. The sky was bathed in pinks, lavenders, and golds, and the distant hills and a lone windmill were silhouetted against the light. I moved through the cool, pre-dawn silence, slowed only by my need to watch the desert's day begin.

By 6:30, breakfast was finished, the coach was packed, and we were on the road. It was a gloriously sunny day, and our drive north, then west, was filled with beauty. We saw a profusion of birds; Nankeen kestrels, green and black Port Lincoln parrots, butcher birds, galahs, Major Mitchell cockatoos, budgerigars, and a wedge-tailed eagle. Everything is very green, and there is still a lot of standing water. Purple-blossomed wild tomatoes line the roads and the acacias are in bloom. The green of new growth and blue of the pools of still-standing water soften the area's vibrant red, enhancing its beauty.

We turned down the Lasseter Highway toward Ayers Rock. At one point, Carl stopped the coach, leapt out, and returned with a thorny devil, a ferocious looking but harmless lizard that I saw on my previous trip to the Centre. Carl passed it around, and I was surprised to find that the thorns covering the animal's body are as hard and sharp as they look. The creature behaved itself admirably, and was soon placed back in the dust by the road, where it strolled off as slowly and calmly as if this happened everyday.

In the distance, to our left, Mount Conner slowly rose into view. When we were parallel to the massive, flat-topped mount, we all climbed out for a photograph and a clamber up the sand dunes across the road to see the salt lake. What a change. The great, shining, white expanse of salt I saw on my previous visit was now a real lake, with miles of water.

Back on the coach, we continued our journey toward Ayers Rock. The desert oaks became more frequent. It's good to see them again. Carl pointed out the desert poplars to us, explaining that these trees normally grow for about seven years, and then slowly fall over.

I gazed intently into the rolling, red, green-veiled distance. My heart beat faster as the curving hump of Ayers Rock edged above the horizon, like a dim, stone sunrise, then grew greater as we drew closer. Even the second time the Rock is awesomely impressive. As William Christie Gosse (the explorer who, in 1873, named the monolith Ayers Rock) exclaimed on his second trip to this site, "This rock appears more wonderful every time I look at it, and I might say it is a sight worth riding over eighty-four miles of spinifex and sandhills to see."

Uluru, sacred giant, desert "island," is said to have dropped from the sky in Dreamtime. Every mark, bump, cave, indentation, or old tree is significant, the reminder of a battle, a spell, a ceremony, an event from that mythic time when the line between humans and other desert creatures was blurred, or nonexistent. The trails of the Kunia (carpet snake people) and Liru (poisonous snake people) formed gutters along the Rock's sides. Caves and rocks mark where the Linga (sand lizard people) and Mala (hare wallaby people) slept, and boulders around Uluru's base are the women and children from the Kunia camps. Mulga trees were once the spears of the Mala men. The lichens on the towering walls are the smoke from the burning camp of the sleepy-lizard (Metalungana) people, and the blood of fallen warriors forms dark streaks along the rocks.

The tremendous winds that swirl around the Rock, even when the desert is still, are the monolith's own creation. The stone absorbs enormous amounts of heat during the day, and cools rapidly at night, with the temperature fluctuating as much as 75 degrees. These dramatic temperature changes cause the roaring winds that rush up the steep stone walls as Uluru heats up and down as it cools off.

We circled the Rock, stopping at spots already familiar to me. But I loved seeing them again, and photographed everything as if I'd never been here before. Of course, it has been changed by the rain. The waterfall at Maggie Springs was flowing this time, and the pool beneath it extended far beyond its previous boundaries. The water stretched out long, silvery fingers that curved around the base of the Rock, and the well-worn stone arched up and over the clear, still, impromptu streams. Reeds and flowers grew thickly along the shores of the enlarged water hole. We visited the nearby caves, then continued on around the Rock to the Kangaroo Tail and the Brain.

We drove next to the Ininti store, where I picked up an "I climbed Ayers Rock" T-shirt, not having purchased one after my first climb. Then we turned our wheels toward the Olgas.

Because I'd already made the hike into Olga Gorge, I decided to head in the opposite direction. I cut across country, walking through the strange, beautiful scrub. It was so devoid of human noise, it was as if I were the only person in the whole desert. It was glorious. Even a hover-ing wasp, back-lighted by the late afternoon sun, seemed amazingly beautiful to me.

I wish I could capture the sound of the wind as it blows across the desert, around the trees and through the Valley of the Winds, and the songs of the birds that sing when the wind dies down and you stand still and silent and they've forgotten that you're there. I was completely alone. There was nothing but the sound of the birds, wind, and humming insects; the red desert; the towering rocks of the Olgas; the mulga, desert oaks, and other fragrant brush; and the heat. I wandered slowly around the sage-colored bushes and rippling red earth, listening, breathing, enjoying, trying to absorb it all so I could take at least some of it home with me.

Two hours disappeared into the timelessness of the desert, and I had to rejoin the group. Back on the coach, we returned down the rugged, stony track toward "Sunset Strip." We startled a dingo from the scrub, and watched it run along side us before it vanished again into the brush.

The Strip, the popular spot where camera bugs gather to record the Ayers Rock sunset, was almost deserted. But, unaware of the diminished audience, nature put on a spectacular show, drawing the shimmering, red Rock, the clouds, the trees, the entire desert into the play of light, color, and shadow. We stayed until the sun disappeared behind the rolling dunes and the distant domes of the Olgas. Then we headed for camp.

At dinner, we celebrated Sally's 19th birthday. Then most of the group boarded the coach for a visit to the chalet, to see the slides of the many moods of Uluru. I opted out, having seen the presentation during my last jaunt out here, and enjoyed instead some quiet stargazing and a second cup of tea, followed by a long shower.

Standing alone in the shower, I had the slightly eerie sensation that no time had passed since I was last at Yulara, using these same showers. Four months dissolved, disappeared, and I almost felt as if I should be able to step out of the shower and be back in September. But someone called my name, shattering the reverie, and it was January again.

Friday, January 20

Some people only do this once in a lifetime!
I had forgotten how tough the first ascent at Ayers Rock was, although negotiating the ridges and rocky meanders of the top seemed easier than I remembered. A fear of heights conquered more prospective climbers than the actual difficulty of the climb, however. One is so exposed on that great, unrelieved monolith. A nervous climber can find nowhere to hide, nowhere to escape the view of endless space and precipitous stone walls.

Of all those who didn't achieve the summit, the one for whom I felt sorriest was Maree. She said that she had wanted so terribly to succeed, that climbing Ayers Rock was a life-long ambition. She had hoped that her determination and desire would overcome her fear. She made it up the first ascent, then could go no farther. She just sat down and cried out of frustration and disappointment. She had to wait until Allison was on her way back down, then followed her during the descent, focusing all attention on her daughter rather than on the climb.

A wedge-tailed eagle soared past as I reached the top of the first ascent, and I turned to share his view. The transformed desert spread below me, a haze of green blanketing the red dunes, and pools everywhere, blazing in the sun, like a thousand silver mirrors.

I was delighted to see pools on the Rock's upper reaches filled with shield shrimp, survivors from the time of Australia's great, prehistoric, inland sea. These creatures, which look like miniature horseshoe crabs, live their lives in the duration of these pools, hatching, maturing, mating, and laying eggs before the water disappears. The eggs can lie dormant for years, hatching only when there's enough rain to fill the odd, circular "holes" in the Rock's back.

When we reached the summit, we found that the book had been removed from the cairn because of all the wet weather. However, someone from another tour who had been up before us had left a scrap of paper with the note, "Even though the book's not here, I want to leave some record that I made it to the top."

Our group gathered near the cairn, with the sprinters waiting for the stragglers. The aid of another climber, someone not in our group, was solicited, and the poor man was soon surrounded with cameras, the owners of which all wanted photographs of our intrepid band.

We rested near the cairn, enjoying the oranges we'd brought with us, the limitless view of the desert, the sunshine. Then it was time to scramble again across the hugely rumpled back of the beast, and negotiate The Climb in reverse.

When everyone was down at last, we reboarded the coach, then swung around to Maggie Springs, to pick up the non-climbers. As we headed away from Uluru, we passed a deserted Aborigine camp. Carl explained that a member of the tribe had died recently, and Aborigines desert a camp when someone dies there, to avoid having to deal with restless or vengeful spirits.

Then we were on the main road again—destination: Alice Springs. At Erldunda, Carl stopped to call and check road conditions before turning north on the Stuart Highway.

We crossed the Palmer River, which was already dry on the surface but still showed signs of the recent flood. The Finke River still had water in it, but we forded it easily. This river is said to be the oldest river in the world. The watercourses are beautiful, with their rocks and pools and ranks of huge river red gums, snaking across the wonderful red-gold land.

Soon after crossing the James Ranges we stopped at a camel farm, where we met the fascinating owner, Noel Fullarton. Actor (whenever a camel driver is needed in a movie), philosopher, and political activist (best known for riding his camels through Canberra), Fullarton was, according to some sources, the first person to undertake the grueling task of capturing and breaking in wild camels, both for domestic use and export.

A full, gray beard with a generous, curling mustache, and long, braided hair framed a tanned, animated face. Fullarton talked, with much encouragement from us, about the history of camels in Australia, how he would solve a number of the country's current political and labor-related problems, the traditions of local Aboriginal tribes, and his approval of the work of Yirara College (one of two free colleges for Aborigines in the Northern Territory).

"All my grandchildren have Aboriginal blood," Fullarton said in explanation of his interest in the Aborigines. He expressed concern over the continuing inequality of women among more traditional groups and the increase in drinking, as alcohol tolerance becomes (at least among those in Alice Springs) the new standard by which a warrior's greatness is assessed. Fullarton worries not only about the injury to individuals, but also about the impact these things will have on the survival, and acceptance, of Aborigines on the whole.

Fullarton's discussion of the history of Aussie camels began with the introduction of the beasts into the country by John Horrocks, the unfortunate young explorer who died before he could see how suited camels were to the deserts here. He described early exploration, and told about the huge loads camels were often employed to carry—even pianos. Fullarton explained that the trading route that was opened up was dubbed the Ghan, short for Afghan, which all camel drivers, whether Afghan or not, were called in the old days. Because it followed the old camel route, the Port Augusta to Alice Springs railroad was named the Ghan.

We examined Fullarton's collection of antique camel saddles, then followed our host to the corrals where the camels were penned. I watched the camels being saddled, but while others in our group tried their luck at camel riding, I wandered off to enjoy a grove of huge desert oaks nearby. A cloud of pink and gray galahs rose into the air as I approached.

Then it was on to Alice Springs (really one of Carl's favorite towns). We are camping this time at Heavitree Gap, the natural gap in the MacDonnell Ranges where I first viewed the dramatic, skyward thrust of the range's immense, stone layers. I read once that the Aborigines, who call it Pitchi Ritchi—break in the range—say that if you pass through this gap, you will never leave the Centre. I almost believe it. I stood once more at the base of the bare, striated, red walls, loving the sight of them. It was good to see the ghost gums again, too.

The big news in town is us. Our escape from Marla Bore is on the front page of the *Centralian Advocate*. We all raced to buy copies and cleaned out the local newsagent. Page two details the ordeal of the truck drivers who joined us Saturday night after three days without food. Page three shows a photo of the flooded Stuart Highway and has interviews with several members of our group. Page four has a cartoon of the ruined railroad, and page five has shots of our camp and stories about the frog races, the cabaret, cricket games, and other diversions with which we passed our days. Great fun.

We set up camp at the foot of the red cliffs, near the banks of the Todd River (which actually has water in it this time), among the ghost gums and river red gums. Then Carl took us for a quick spin through Alice—a trip down memory lane for me and an orientation tour for the rest.

After dinner, we learned from Carl that an Aussie country/western singer named Jimmy Howard was on hand, if we'd like a bit of entertainment. This brought home to me once more what a "small town" Australia is. I heard Jimmy sing nearly four months ago on his last night, and my first, in Broome, W.A. We gathered around Jimmy and enjoyed a couple of hours of fun music, joining in whenever the songs were familiar.

After Jimmy finished, Mandy was cajoled into doing "Clancy of the Overflow," a song, based on a Banjo Paterson* poem, that we've requested often of her in the last two weeks. We sang and talked, until there was no reason left to stay up, then we headed for our tents.

*See appendix

Saturday, January 21

This morning, we had several hours free to wander around town and spend money, which I did fairly prodigiously. At the Centre for Aboriginal Artists and Craftsmen, after perusing the large collection of traditional Aboriginal items—spears, woomeras, coolamons, bark paintings, etc.—as well as nontraditional pieces designed or decorated by Aboriginal artists, I bought a necklace made of desert seeds, a tea towel hand-printed with an ancient kangaroo motif, a coolamon, and booklets on Aboriginal painting, sculpture, dance, and weapons. I worked my way up Todd Street, stopping in souvenir shops and Aboriginal art stores. I bought a bullroarer, a didgeridoo, an Alice Springs/Northern Territory T-shirt, and four records: three of Slim Dusty's and one of traditional Australian songs.

Finally, at 12:30, we returned to camp. At lunch, we made presentations to Carl and Jill of the gifts and cards we'd gotten for them. This was Jill's first time on the tour, so we had a T-shirt made commemorating "Australian Pacific—AP16—Maiden Voyage." Carl also received a T-shirt, this one with a map of Australia and the legend "My Favorite Place."

Then it was back on the coach, for a run up to Anzac Hill for the view of Alice Springs. Again, I was delighted by the sight of the tidy, wilderness-wrapped town with the jagged, dancing, red wall of the MacDonnells rising along its far side. All is, of course, far greener than on my previous visit, so the town stands out more against its surroundings, like a ragged patch sewn into the billowing, red fabric of Australia's heart.

We headed next for the Telegraph Station and the spring named Alice. The water hole was broader, the growth around it was more luxuriant, and more happy children were there, splashing and wading. I strolled around the grounds, among the wonderful, old buildings, studying things I had not had time to examine closely before.

At the Telegraph Station there is a fenced yard that is home to several emus, which prompted Carl to relate to us the reason the emu and kangaroo appear on Australia's coat of arms. The country's motto is "Advance Australia," and both the emu and the 'roo can only advance—neither animal can go backwards,

Crossing back through town, we came to a small, dusty, nearly shadeless cemetery, where we visited the graves of Albert Namatjira, the famous Aboriginal painter, and Lewis Lasseter (later known as Harold), the ill-fated fortune seeker.

In 1908, Lasseter was found wandering near the edge of the Gibson Desert, horseless, delirious, clutching a bag of gold ore. While looking for rubies in the MacDonnell Ranges he'd become lost. Stumbling about the countryside, he'd chanced upon a great reef of gold. He returned once with a surveyor and (he claimed) relocated the reef, but their bearings got scrambled, and its location was not correctly recorded. Others tried to find the gold, but ran into trouble with thirst and Aborigines. Finally, in 1930, Lasseter returned to the Centre and, with two camels, set out alone to find the reef once more. Fragments of Lasseter's diary and letters to his wife found later relate that he located the reef, which he described and said he'd photographed. However, during his return, his camels bolted, carrying off his water and supplies. His death—attributed by Aborigines to a curse placed on him for crossing a sacred site—was not long in coming. To this day, Lasseter's reef, if it exists, has never been rediscovered.

As we walked between the two noteworthy memorials, my attention was caught by a little, ragged red stone set over an untended grave. Nailed to the front of the small, broken rock slab was a piece of metal with the following epitaph scratched on it:

In Memory of
W.O. (Bud) Bailes
from
His old bush MATES
Of BY-GONE DAYS
Died - 12/10/1965
-- AGED 73 YEARS --

This small testimony of friendship delighted me. It seemed almost to be an object out of legend, this modest, bushman's grave.

The sunset this evening was spectacular. The sky seemed to be set aflame by the lowering sun. The clouds blazed yellow and orange, fading outward to deep purple. Then they turned bright pink, gold and lavender, all reflected in the water still standing in the Todd River. I climbed the hill behind our tents and just sat on a rock and watched the brilliant, changing colors.

After dinner, it was time to dress up for a night out at the Casino. It was amazing to see smartly dressed, freshly scrubbed, powdered and perfumed individuals emerging from the dusty tents. Moments later, we walked into the Alice Springs Federal Hotel Casino.

Some of our group members played, some won, some lost. Paul didn't find out until it was too late that, when you rack up credits on the poker machines, you have to push a button to receive your winnings. He walked away in disgust because he never got any money, only credits.

Most of us simply watched, waiting for 9:30 and the opening of the disco.

Tipped off, probably by Carl, the disco's DJ extended a warm welcome to the Marla Bore refugees (we cheered) and dedicated a song to us: a number that, with its lament, "It's been raining for so long," was certainly apropos to our former situation. We tripped the light fantastic until closing time at 3 a.m., then taxis were summoned to haul us home to our waiting tents.

Sunday, January 22

We were up for breakfast at 7:30 (yawn). It was a splendid, bright, and extremely hot day, with just touches of white cloud in the shimmering blue sky. On the coach once more, we headed west, along the MacDonnell Ranges. The red hills and rolling desert were even more beautiful than I had remembered. The deep, forest green of newly sprouted spinifex and the celadons and olives of myriad shrubs accentuated the beauty of the red land. The white trunks of the ghost gums seemed even lovelier and more graceful surrounded by the burst of luxuriant new growth. The dark, rich green of the corkbark trees glistened in the brilliant sunshine. Wildflowers dotted the fresh grass blanketing the red earth.

We stopped first at the grave of John Flynn, then headed on to Simpson's Gap, to enjoy the beauty of its broad pool and dramatic rock formations. As we waded through the pale sand of the sometime river, the great, red and beige stone walls closed in, towering above us. The ancient quartzite that makes up the walls of the gap has been weathered and shattered into jagged-edged, smooth-sided, many-layered shapes that overhang the water hole, jut out of the sand, and reach skyward in ragged spires. We spent an hour there, soaking up the beauty, and watching the rock wallabies hop through the tangle of boulders lining the gap.

We visited Namatjira's twin ghost gums, then continued on down the track. It was not long before we reached Standley Chasm. Here we had two hours to wander as we willed.

The gorge that leads to the chasm was greener, with fresh pillows of spinifex clinging to the sloping walls of the valley. Jay Creek gurgled and splashed vigorously among the trees and moss-covered rocks. Beside the path, four slender ghost gums sprang from one burnt, ruined, massive, old trunk. The hardiness and resilience of these trees never cease to amaze me.

The marvelously shattered rocks lining the gorge looked as if they were carefully cut into layers, some appeared almost sculpted. I saw one stone that looked like the horse's head from the Elgin Marbles. The stone walls got higher, steeper. The path took a sharp, right turn, and led into the deep, narrow, sheer-sided fracture that is Standley Chasm.

Dragonflies danced in the hot sunlight at the center of the otherwise shady path between the perpendicular orange walls. The pools left by the heavy rains were cool and clear, and several people waded through them to climb the steep tumble of boulders at the far end of the chasm. Blue sky and wisps of white cloud were only a bright strip far overhead.

I looked at everything, intently, intensely, lingering over every unusual rock, every clump of spinifex. I was the last member of our group to leave the chasm, and I wandered slowly back through the wonderful gorge. I am beginning to feel the pain of knowing how soon I must leave all this behind. I have come to love this strangely beautiful and exciting land even more than I had dreamed, back when the dream began. Saying good-bye will not be easy.

During the drive back to Alice Springs, Carl stopped several times to let us photograph the magnificent, oddly compelling landscape. We climbed a hill in the midst of a broad, rolling plain, and saw the ranges stretch to the horizons, gently bounding the otherwise limitless sweep of land around us. The ancient mountains stood worn and red against the blue sky, with the sea of newly sprung greenery lapping at their feet.

Even the hill on which we stood was fascinating, with its jagged rocks and wild diversity of plants. There were bright yellow blossoms growing close to the ground, with pale green leaves shaped like holly; vivid pink flowers with tiny, gray-green leaves; intensely orange blooms on a short shrub with bright, shiny foliage; fuzzy, purple and silver mulla mulla; and red, trumpet-like flowers of the needle-leafed emu bush.

I wondered again, as I have wondered before, why this place moves me so. I am drawn to the remoteness, to the vigor, the fierceness, and the unfettered innocence of this land, and its spirit whispers to my spirit, and its song sings in my veins. I don't know if this is cause or effect, but I do not need to know. I simply surrender myself to the pleasure of feeling it one more time.

This evening, word came that we will be leaving in the morning. The roads are still in bad shape, but more rain is on the way, so it's now or never. The news was greeted with mixtures of disbelief, sorrow, joy—we're getting out, but no one wants the party to end.

Since this is our last real night together, no one wanted

to go to bed, so we sat around by lamplight, chatting. Someone finally asked what many had wondered—how did the handsome, soft-spoken Carl come by his large collection of tattoos? He explained that when he was 15 he was pretending to be 18, and he thought they made him look older. He enjoyed them for about one year, then regretted them ever since. He showed us scars from when he tried to have a tattoo removed by laser, and detailed the grisly and painful process. It's sad that at so early an age we can make decisions of such longstanding consequence.

Everyone was punchy from lack of sleep, and a bit silly from the euphoria of the trip and desire that it should not end, so the evening disintegrated into a chaos of tent collapsing and shaving cream and water fights. The majority of us were soon dripping wet, which was delightful as, even though it was nearly midnight, it was still awfully hot.

Carl approached our merry band with what appeared to be a small bird cupped in his hands. It turned out to be the most enormous moth I've ever seen—about four inches long, with a wing span of seven or eight inches.

Thanks (?) to the rain, there has been an astonishing proliferation of insects: moths, beautiful or huge, leaf insects, jewel-like beetles, some insects the likes of which I've never seen before, and, of course, mosquitoes.

At around 1 a.m., I finally climbed into my tent. Though it was hot, we closed the tent flaps, to keep out the insects, and just slept on top of our sleeping bags. It was going to be a short night anyway.

Monday, January 23

We were awakened at 5 a.m. and, in an amazing burst of speed and efficiency, had the camp down, the coach packed, breakfast finished, and ourselves in our seats by 6:30. It was a beautiful morning, the sun finally getting up about 45 minutes after we did. The gentle colors of the breaking day bathed the red cliffs, ghost gums, and water in the river in an almost surreal light. Eagles circled above the desert nearby. The air was a gentle cool/warm that slid over the skin like silk. The fresh, early hues flickered across the cloud-dappled sky. It could have made a stone weep to see such a dawn. The noise in camp was subdued, hushed by the morning's serenity, but also filled with the mixed emotions of knowing we were leaving.

There were a lot of people trying to get out of Alice Springs. The roads were still in pretty bad shape, so coaches traveled in pairs on the worst stretches, to avoid getting stuck without assistance. We departed under a sky that was rapidly filling with clouds. We would be driving straight through, basically non-stop except for meals.

We drove south on the Stuart Highway, crossing again the gloriously strange, rugged, red land. Soon the skies began to clear, though some frail wisps of white still trailed across the blazing blue. The lovely, tree-lined Finke River was still full when we forded it, and most of the creeks we passed had some water in them. We all enjoyed seeing what the rain had wrought in this normally dry area. It would hardly be recognized by anyone familiar with the Red Centre—green everywhere, with the red only peeking out along the road, in riverbeds, and between the plants on the rolling sand dunes. We passed numerous desert oaks, which are always beautiful, but which were fuller, greener and even lovelier now. The splendid landscape flashed past us, always changing, always wonderful, as we rolled along.

Carl stopped momentarily in Kulgera to make a phone call and ascertain whether we really could get through, then we continued on. Soon we left the sealed road behind, and once more hit the dirt. We traveled now in the company of an Ansett bus. Ahead of us the Stuart Highway was still out of commission, so we retraced our steps down the track we'd used for our escape, though that was not in great condition, either.

Before long we reached an impressive expanse of water and mud. The Ansett bus headed across, and about half way through became bogged, listing so badly to starboard that we thought she'd go over. All the strapping young men from our group waded into the murky pond to join the effort to push the bus to safety, but to no avail. Everyone was cleared away from the site and, with a bit of a running start, Carl powered our coach through, going around the bogged bus, sending huge sprays of muddy red water high into the air. When he reached the other "shore," Carl produced a towing cable, which was strung between the two vehicles. There was a lot of rocking and straining, and we still weren't sure the bus wouldn't capsize, but slowly, ponderously, the Ansett bus emerged from the mud, to a chorus of wild cheering.

Since it was only a standard express bus, rather than a safari coach like our vehicle, the luggage bins were not watertight. We looked on in amazement, the others in horror, as the water poured out of the compartments. It looked like a surfacing submarine blowing its tanks. We felt sorry for those unfortunate passengers, as we watched them drain the water from their sodden luggage.

Our valiant boys rallied again, rushing to the aid of the

occupants of a rapidly sinking ute. This vehicle, too, was rescued from the red swamp, after which the soaking wet, mud-stained heroes returned to our coach.

Under way once more, with Carl still negotiating a less than ideal road, it was a couple of hours till the next crisis, so we all settled into the jarring routine of careening down the shattered roadway, enjoying what little amusements we could devise.

Things began to get a bit rougher when we reached the part of the track where we'd been ferried by the 4WDs a few days earlier. The coach danced through the bull dust that had collected on the rutted road as the water dried. We were glad to see that the creek crossing that the backhoe had worked on for us had been considerably improved, and we crossed it with little difficulty.

A bit farther on we weren't so lucky. We came to a spot that was totally impassable. All of us got off the coach, both to lighten the load and so Carl had nothing to worry about except driving. Then Carl turned off the road and set off around the perimeter of the massive quagmire. Soon the coach was down to its axles and still sinking in the thick mud. Michael was the first to have his shirt off and a shovel in his hands, with as many others as were needed following suit. There were only two shovels, so digging was done in turns. It was almost an hour before we could see the rear tires again.

It was about 2 o'clock when we got bogged, and the blazing sun was at its hottest (over 100 degrees in the shade, and almost no shade). Those of us who were unnecessary for excavating tried to hide from the relentless sun under what sparse cover we could find at the bases of some of the larger bushes.

There was a road grader working nearby, manned by our

friends from Marla Bore, and it was brought to our rescue. The tow cable was run from it to the coach. The trailer had to be disconnected, as there was no way it could all be extricated at once. Even with the diminished load, and with as much mud dug away from the tires as could be reached, the strain of pulling the coach back onto dry land bent the thick tow cable connection pin, and it was difficult to release the cable once the coach was safe.

We walked the long way around to where the coach waited for us. We skirted the water, then climbed up to the train tracks, walking along the sleepers and crossing a large culvert. Below us, we could see multitudes of scorpions that had been washed up by the flood, now frying (as we were) in the intense heat.

The road grader crew went back and rescued the trailer. They were going to haul the trailer the rest of the way to Marla for us, but the grader blew one of its immense tires and had to limp back on its own. So we reconnected the trailer and drove, without further mishap, down the five-mile track we'd walked during our "escape" just five days earlier. Then it was up and over the railway tracks and down to Marla Bore. Near the seemingly undiminished Stuart Highway lake, lawn chairs and an umbrella-top table had been set out and a sign erected welcoming visitors to Marla Beach!

It was 3:20 when we pulled into our former home— nearly eight hours since leaving Alice Springs. We had an hour for lunch, so we ordered our food, then most of us grabbed our towels and rushed off for a quick, cool shower, so we wouldn't feel quite so sticky when we got back on the coach. Also, none of us knew when we'd get another chance to indulge in such a luxury.

Water from my still wet hair dripping down my back

made the sun seem more amiable, as I headed back to the coach for the next leg of the journey. While at Marla, we acquired a second driver. By trading off, Carl and the new driver could keep us going straight through the night.

The land around us flattened out, though the constantly changing vegetation continued to be fascinating. Driving was a lot like bronco busting. In places, the torrential, rain-swollen streams had turned the road into a miniature Grand Canyon, and often there was little room between our tires and the edges of these ragged, soft-sided erosion channels.

The desert continued to awe us with its newly verdant beauty. Wedge-tailed eagles wheeled in the sky above us, and a surprisingly large number of horses were out enjoying the lush grass that had so recently appeared.

We thought we were trapped when we reached one "lake" that extended as far as the eye could see. Carl had the back-up driver wade out to check the depth, and it didn't look good. When Carl began to back the coach up, we thought he was going to take a running start and attempt to forge through the water (we'd already made it through several smaller ponds). We were half relieved and half disappointed to find out he was just going back to a set of very faint tire tracks that indicated a safe way around the water.

Gik and I talked, as we have talked for the last two weeks, about everything. People will say things she doesn't understand, or some of the guys, knowing how sheltered she is in Indonesian society, will tease her, or make provocative comments, and she comes to me to find out what things mean. I have enjoyed the lively intelligence with which she has absorbed everything, her frequent dissolving into giggles with hands over her mouth, and her wide-eyed, "Do you truly have such things here?" She has told me a lot about Djakarta and has invited me to visit.

Now, as we sped homeward, she gave me an Indonesian coin to remember her by.

The sunset was splendid, as it tends to be in the desert. The clear, pale, silver sky shimmered above the endless, uninterrupted horizon, which blazed with the oranges and golds of the disappearing sun. Opposite this flaming sky-line, the stars were already appearing in the darkening sky.

Not long after sundown we traded the rolling desert for the lunar landscape that surrounds Coober Pedy. At 9:15 we rolled into Coober Pedy for dinner. It was not easy finding a place to dine at that hour, as most of the few shops were already closed. We did locate one take-away place that would serve us, then we headed out into the dusty, barren streets with their innumerable Christmas beetles, stray dogs, and wandering Aborigines.

One thing that was still open was the town's pub, and it didn't take our group long to find it. After standing in the dark, quiet street while eating dinner, it was pleasant to relax in the bright, laughter-filled pub, enjoying cold cider, soft drinks, or beer before heading off into the night once more.

At 10:15 we reboarded our coach for the continuation of the run for home. Star gazing, talking when we were awake, and intermittent attempts at sleeping filled the hours. The nighttime sky was fabulous, utterly clear and, as we were so far from civilization, awesomely dark. As a result, the stars were almost overwhelming. The Southern Cross rose in the south before us, the Milky Way washed across the center of the sky in a dazzling concentration of stars.

I could identify Orion, the Magellanic Clouds, and a couple of planets, but mostly I just enjoyed the general intoxication of the sparkling universe spread above and around us, uninterrupted, from horizon to horizon, by buildings, trees, or anything else.

It was a spectacular night,
which eventually turned into. . .

Tuesday, January 24

Moonrise was around 2 a.m. The moon was just past full. It sat on the horizon, reddish-gold and enormous, then slowly began its heavenward climb.

We pulled into Port Augusta at 4:45 a.m. Here we were met by a second coach and another pair of drivers. All Sydney-bound passengers had to switch to the new coach, which we did in a somewhat dazed manner, before stumbling off to breakfast. Fortunately, the two buses would be traveling together until Mildura, so we didn't have to try to wake up enough to bid a final farewell to the Melbourne-bound group.

At 5:45 we were on the road again. The sunrise was magnificent. The water of Spencer Gulf was like glass. Mist drifted around the foothills of the Flinders Ranges. The mountains, the mist and the pale, pastel-tinted sky were all reflected in the mirror-like water. Sailboats rode silently at their moorings, unmoving, duplicated by their reflections.

After the lift we got from the exquisite dawn, the dozen of us who were Sydney bound began to feel fairly acutely the letdown of having the party really over. We spread out all over the nearly empty coach and pretty much flaked out after a night with little or no sleep.

Morning break was in Burra, where we wandered like zombies for the allotted half hour, doing little else but use the public restrooms and buy Cokes in the only shop in town open at 8:30. Then we were on the road again, "dead bodies" once more littering the seats of the coach as our many days of non-stop activity finally caught up with us. We continued to retrace, in reverse, the first part of our trip, passing through Berri and Renmark on the way to Mildura.

Carl, driving the Melbourne-bound coach, opted once more for the ferry crossing at Morgan. We went cross-country and arrived in Mildura about 20 minutes ahead of the other coach. Our driver told us we had one hour for lunch, but Chris, Sandra and I decided we just wouldn't make it on time, as it would mean leaving without saying good-bye to everyone on the other coach.

The three of us bought sandwiches at a nearby take-away shop, then ate in the park, enjoying the warm sun and fresh air after being cooped up for so many hours. Before long, we saw people from the other coach wandering around town. Peter K., John, Blue, and Jim beckoned to us to join them. We crowded around a tiny table in a small café and talked, but were a bit more subdued than on previous occasions. As the guys finished their lunches, they asked when we were due back, and we responded, "Ten minutes ago."

We walked slowly back to where the coaches were parked. Apparently, the rest of the Sydney crowd had gotten the same idea we had, and started drifting back, late, in the company of Melbourne-bound group members. We lined the windows on one side of the coach, waving to our friends clustered by the curb, waiting till they were out of sight before settling down in our seats again.

It was easier to say good-bye earlier in my travels, because there was every likelihood that I'd run into some of the people later in my journey. Now, I feel as though, instead of saying farewell to people, I'm saying farewell to Australia. I wish I could start all over again—go home for a month or two, see family and friends, look at my slides, edit my journal, then come back and begin the entire six months over, returning to the places I love, seeing the friends I've made, visiting all the places on my long and still-growing "next time" list.

The road we were now on was good—we had been driving on sealed roads since sometime in the middle of the night. Fatigue made us grateful for the smoother ride. Still, I'll be sorry when everything is paved here. When the roads are all sealed, so much of the excitement of crossing these remote regions will be lost. However, I guess for the people who live along these roads, who drive them regularly, it isn't exciting, just rough, frustrating, and tiresome.

We traveled on through the wonderful, changing landscape. Everything here has its own special beauty—desert, scrub, mountain, plain, all is affecting, with a delicate, seductive magic that winds around your heart and gets into your blood. There is, as D.H. Lawrence observed, a "strange, as it were, *invisible* beauty...a sense of subtle, remote, *formless* beauty more poignant than anything ever experienced before." Even the difficulties are somehow part of the spell this land casts over you.

We passed through miles of silvery, green scrub, by creeks lined with coolibah trees, before emerging onto the Hay plains. At 5:45 we rolled into the town of Hay. We only had 20 minutes, but we were a fair way off from our dinner stop, so we dashed down the wide, veranda-lined street, to get soft drinks and snacks to tide us over. Then it was back on the road again.

Mile after green mile of sheep-raising country flashed past our windows. Again we saw the mallee and native pine, again the gum-bordered paddocks. We passed the rice paddies of the Riverina, the wildflowers along the roads, the meandering streams. We saw numerous emus, cockatoos, and other birds as we crossed the open plains. It was a splendid day, and the scenery, though tamer, was still a pleasure to see, even if the circumstances in which it was being viewed were less than ideal.

At 9 p.m. we pulled into West Wyalong, driving past the Central Motel, where we'd first gathered more than two weeks earlier, and stopping at a roadhouse on the edge of town for dinner. We bought chicken and chips and sat on the driveway to eat, as there were no seats or park benches around. But somehow, sitting on the pavement in the middle of the night at a roadhouse in West Wyalong seemed sort of in keeping with the general tenor of things so far. We ate, chatted, and fed our leftovers to the sad, scruffy-looking dogs that appeared soon after we sat down. Then at 10 o'clock we were back on the coach. The second driver took over for this last leg of the trip. And we rolled on into the dark quiet of the Australian night.

Wednesday, January 25

As Tuesday night faded into Wednesday morning, I enjoyed watching the Australian nighttime sky—possibly for the last time, at least under the ideal conditions afforded by our being so far removed from the lights of civilization. It comforted me to lie back in my seat and watch the Southern Cross as it ascended the sky. It rode high above the horizon, and was more brilliant than I can ever remember seeing it before.

I was not sleepy, having been lulled into that state of too tired to move but not tired enough to sleep that comes of hours of inactivity. But the sky was worth staying awake for. The Milky Way was dazzling, sweeping across the heavens like a jeweled shawl against the black velvet of night. But my gaze was always drawn back to the Southern Cross. The words of Stephen Stills's song "Southern Cross" kept rolling through my mind. "When you see the Southern Cross for the first time, you understand now why you came this way." The first time, yes, and now the last time, even more so.

The darkness closed in more completely, as we climbed, then descended through the forest-clad Blue Mountains. Finally, at a little after 4:45 a.m., we arrived at the Central Railway Station in Sydney, almost 46 hours and 2,000 miles after leaving Alice Springs. There were groggy farewells as we parted company with most of what remained of our intrepid band. Only Chris, Sandra, and I remained in the nearly deserted station, talking about the trip and the people we'd spent it with, as we waited for the rest of the world to awaken.

A little after 7 o'clock I rang Stephen's house, to make certain someone would be home when I arrived. I bid a fond and rather sad farewell to Chris and Sandra. Then, gathering up my duffel bag, camera equipment, sleeping bag, and large collection of souvenirs from this trip, I headed for the ticket office and the train platforms.

I caught the 7:47 train to Sefton. When I arrived, I was pleasantly surprised to find Anne waiting for me. I had planned to walk, but, after what was by now 49 hours of traveling, I was thankful for the ride. Anne made me a cup of coffee when we got home, and I recounted to her some of my adventures. Then I had a very welcome shower, followed by an even more welcome nap.

The balance of the day was spent in writing, chatting, and recounting tales to Thomas and Stephen when they came home. I calculated that the more than 4,000-mile round trip on this last tour shot my journey total to well over 18,000 miles traveled inside Australia. Actually, it's probably closer to 20,000, if you throw in the little side trips, day tours, and runs into the mountains from Sydney. Hard to believe I could cover so much ground and still have so much more I want to see!

WALTZING
LAST DAYS

Thursday, January 26

Today was pretty unexciting—thank goodness. I spent a few hours going through piles of *Sydney Morning Heralds* that Stephen had saved for me, clipping out articles on the floods. I got caught up on my writing, which had gone pretty much by the boards during the 2-1/2 days of our return. I also listened to the Slim Dusty albums I purchased in Alice Springs, delighted that I had purchased them. So passed the afternoon.

Evening brought the return of the menfolk, and amiable conversation filled the balance of the day's hours.

Friday, January 27

This morning, Anne and I caught the train to Circular Quay. As the train doors opened, my pulse again quickened at the sight of the Opera House, Harbour Bridge, and Sydney Harbour directly before me. It is not a view of which one tires readily.

The two of us descended to the wharf, where we boarded the ferry for Taronga Park Zoo. The weather was dazzling, and the harbor glittered joyously around us.

Taronga Park Zoo occupies an exceptionally gorgeous piece of real estate. This locale was once (in the 1890s) a favorite haunt of Australian painters Tom Roberts and Arthur Streeton. It's easy to see why. The verdant hills rise directly out of the water, and from almost every vantage point there are glorious, panoramic views of the harbor (*Taronga* is Aborigine for "water view").

The grounds of the zoo were green and shady, with palm and fig trees, cascades of bougainvillea, clusters of white ginger, bushes of brilliant pink grevillea, and vines covered with deep purple clematis. Waterfalls sparkled, and pools reflected the abundant foliage. The animal enclosures, all densely planted as well, were nestled in the midst of this exotic verdure.

We visited some of the non-Australian animals, but spent most of our time viewing the Aussie fauna—wombats, dingoes, echidnas, platypuses, sea lions, and kangaroos. The aquarium was a delight, as were the native birds: parrots, cockatoos, lyrebirds, wrens, finches, and many others.

A large number of wild, non-captive birds are attracted by the presence of the birds in the aviaries, plus the abundant food and water. Innumerable ibises make their homes in the park's trees, and compete with myna birds, sea gulls, and pigeons for leftovers and handouts in the picnic areas.

After many delightful hours amidst the flora and fauna, we caught the ferry back to Circular Quay. We browsed for a while through wonderful shops at The Rocks, particularly enjoying a bookstore specializing in Australian history, then caught the train back to Sefton.

Saturday, January 28

The big excitement of the day was buying a handful of Queensland boulder opal chips from a friend of Anne's. The friend and her husband go fossicking each year along the Queensland/New South Wales/Northern Territory borders, and they usually bring back an interesting assortment of boulder opals. They have some real beauties, too.

It's fascinating to see how ribbons and trickles of bright opal run through the dark rock, every crack and crevice of the boulder filled by the pale, once-liquid mineral. Sometimes a vein of opal is so narrow you don't even notice it until the light hits it and it shoots out a flame of color.

Someday, I shall have to try my hand at fossicking. It would have to be a real kick to go out rummaging around a bunch of old rocks and come up with a handful of opals. But for now, I am pleased just to have a few small, colorful fragments of Australia to take home with me.

Otherwise, the day was passed quietly, thoughtfully, in pursuit of such activities as reading and writing, organizing, keeping Anne company, and locating a box in which to ship things home—all liberally interspersed with increasingly frequent bouts of staring out the window, thinking, dreaming.

The closer I get to the end of my trip, the less I want to think about the future, and the more I must. But mostly my mind is set on "replay," and all the beauty and freedom of the places I have known rise before my eyes and fill my head and heart with a happy, poignant ache. This has been the best six months of my life. When I go, I shall leave part of myself behind, yet I am more complete than when I came.

Sunday, January 29

Despite the appearance of a number of ominous-looking clouds, we set off optimistically, as well as relatively early, for a day in the Blue Mountains. Bernadette and Thomas do a considerable amount of bushwalking in the mountains and were planning on taking Anne, Stephen, and me to some of the choicest spots.

We wound through Sydney's suburbs, out through Richmond and onto Bell's Line of Road. The road wound up and into the mountains. Around us was that wonderful, rugged, gum tree-clad scenery that I have so frequently described, and I was no less pleased by it on this occasion than on previous visits. As we ascended Bellbird Hill, we heard first one bellbird, then increasing numbers, until the air rang with the crystalline tones of their remarkable, bell-like song.

Unfortunately, as we got higher, the clouds began to settle on the mountain's shoulders, and our surroundings were enveloped in a gentle fog—not dense enough to impede our progress, but sufficiently thick to remove "the view." Still we forged on.

We came to the lookout for Govett's Leap, a dramatic, 1,000-foot waterfall that I'd only seen in pictures—which, in fact, I have still only seen in pictures, since the fog wrapped snugly around the lookout completely obliterated the scene.

We parked the car and walked out to the lookout. Beside the path, strung between trees and bushes, large spider webs covered with droplets of water looked like spun crystal or diamond necklaces suspended on air. There were delightful flowers on all hands: pink mountain devils, fringed lilies, buttercups, banksia, and many with which I was not familiar. New growth showed everywhere, as the plants and trees responded joyously to the recent rains. We stood for a while at the lookout, peering into the cottony, white blindness for a glimpse of the falls that we could only hear. Then we strolled back through the damp, fragrant forest.

Since the decreasing visibility made hiking along the mountain paths seem a less than ideal option, we headed instead for Mt. Victoria, a charming little town of antique shops and book stores. We stopped at the town's edge and slowly browsed our way up the short, main street.

In a second-hand-book shop I found a book I wanted to buy. I couldn't locate a sales clerk anywhere, but finally came across a note pinned to a shelf near the front door: "If shop is unattended, please pay at the antique store up the street." Ah, the joys of small town life.

Because a light rain had begun to fall, we had our picnic lunch in the car. Then we were off again, rolling through the gloriously green though only vaguely visible mountains. From the snatches I could see it was possible to guess at the magnificence of the views on clearer days, especially along the appropriately named Cliff Drive. I must return.

Around teatime we arrived in Leura, which is not far from Katoomba. We had tea in one of the charming little coffee shops on Leura's main street, then wandered through several of the town's arts and crafts galleries and antique stores.

Back on the road again, we began our descent. The fog was slowly lifting, so our view began to improve. We stopped at a bridge built in 1825, one of the older constructions still standing. The sturdy, golden sandstone bridge was quite handsome, which surprised me only because it is in the middle of nowhere, over a small stream and narrow gorge between two hills, surrounded by dense forest.

We parked the car and spent a little time exploring. We climbed down the hill and walked along the ledge under the bridge. Greenery crowded in on both sides of the stream, closing over it entirely a few yards either side of the stone arch. There were innumerable flowers, including Christmas bushes and flowering gums. I could have stayed for hours, listening to the merry chortling of the water, basking in the beauty of the forest.

Finally, I had to peel myself away and climb back to the car. We continued down through the mountains, then out onto the plains and, at long last, back to the city. My own gentle fog settled in. I felt a little disappointed; I missed the mountains today, and who knows when, or even if, I shall ever see them again. I really wanted this one last hike in the bush. I guess I've just gotten a little greedy for beauty and peace. And Australia. What will happen to me, and to my dream, when I leave?

Monday, January 30

Today was a public holiday—one of those arrangements where you work the actual day then get the following Monday off so you have a three-day weekend. The holiday is Australia Day, and the actual date is January 26. This day commemorates the arrival in Australia of Captain Arthur Phillip and the First Fleet* in 1788, and the unfurling of the Union Jack on January 26 by Captain Phillip at Sydney Cove, which he had just given that name the previous day, in honor of Lord Sydney, Secretary of Colonial Affairs. No one had to work, so we piled "the gang" into the Toyota and rolled out into the dazzling sunshine of a

*See appendix

beautiful Australian summer day.

We drove through the southern suburbs, rising and falling with the hills, catching frequent glimpses of the water. When we reached the elegant suburb of Vaucluse, every turn offered spectacular views of the harbor, which was, today, filled with light and sails. We drove along The Gap, seeing the lovely Greenway lighthouse and the steep cliffs that drop to the sea at that spot. We finally pulled in at Watson's Bay, parking the car and continuing on foot, along winding roads and down to the shore. Right at the water's edge is Doyles On The Beach, a well-known, well-loved, century-old seafood restaurant and our destination.

We got a table by the wide picture windows on the second floor, where we had an incredible view of Sydney's magnificent waterway, with the Opera House and Harbour Bridge in the distance. The sky was a bright and changing fantasy of blue and white, and the silvery sunlight fell upon the hills and danced across the water. White sails floated between heaven and the diamond sea, and the moving clouds dappled coves, cliffs, forests, and roofs. It is hard to believe such views exist except in dreams.

This was sort of my farewell party, and certainly my last chance to indulge in local delicacies, so we ordered with abandon. Soon our table was buried under an avalanche of fabulous Sydney seafood. Sharing appetizers and main courses "family style," we feasted well beyond the point of satiety. We'd brought an excellent Hunter Valley white wine with us (this is a BYO restaurant), so everything was perfect.

It was nearly 3 o'clock when we finally left Doyles. As we were a little less than comfortable, we appreciated having a fair distance to walk to the car. We strolled through the nearby beachside park, among the enormous and complexly rooted fig trees, and up the hillside streets, which

lead between white-walled, red tile-roofed houses. It's
hard to imagine anything more intoxicating than waking
up to the view these houses have.

The air was heavy with the scent of frangipani and hon-
eysuckle, which bloomed everywhere, in company with
masses of bougainvillea, hibiscus, and uncounted thousands of other bright blossoms. The sun poured down on
us, the water, the flowers, the hills—everything was brilliant and beautiful, and my spirits soared.

Glorious place.

Glorious day.

Tuesday, January 31

I can't believe January is almost gone. How can days
that are so full move so quickly?

Today was reserved for a final trip into Sydney. For my
farewell visit the weather outdid itself—dazzlingly sunny,
hot, sparkling. I wandered from one end of the city to the
other, from Central Station to Circular Quay and The
Rocks. I had a lot to do, but I still managed to spend a
good deal of time just looking at everything, enjoying the
beauty of the day, the city, the harbor.

Down by the Quay, on the lawn near The Rocks, there
was an old, gray-haired Aborigine demonstrating and selling boomerangs. He was attired in stockman's dress and
was solemn and silent as he stood, skillfully throwing and
catching the boomerangs. I watched him for a while and
was sorry that I'd already bought my boomerang.

I spent much of the day shopping. After filling the
empty places on my gift list, I turned to my own desires. I
picked up one more Slim Dusty record and tried, unsuc-

cessfully, to find a recording of the version of "Clancy of the Overflow" that Mandy so often sang during the evenings at Marla Bore. Other than that, my purchases were almost entirely of books—history, poetry, geography, folk tales, and songs. There's so much to know and so much to remember. I want to take it all with me, and though I realize I can't, I do at least seem to be trying.

By the time all my buying and farewelling to Sydney were accomplished it was time to turn my steps up town. It was a half hour walk to the Java Restaurant, where I was meeting Anne, Stephen, Thomas, and Bernadette for one last Indonesian meal. Then, as the others were off to the theatre for the evening, I walked alone to Central Station and headed back to Sefton.

I spent most of the evening packing books (14 of the 16 I've purchased here) and unneeded clothing (sandals, cottons—it's winter back home) into a shipping box. I managed to fit enough stuff in the box that I should now have room in my big suitcase for my sleeping bag. But I'll deal with that tomorrow.

Leaving is difficult enough emotionally—it shouldn't be this hard physically.

Wednesday, Feb. 1

Today was spent packing, writing, sunbathing (glorious, hot day) and generally preparing to leave. "To leave"—how harsh and impossible a concept that now seems; "to travel onward"—I like that better. This is not the end of the dream, just part of the beginning.

Anne prepared a lovely last dinner of Australian favorites—lamb and Pavlova (an indigenous confection of

meringue, cream, and passion fruit). Aside from enjoying
the meal, I was also, again, amazed and delighted with
Anne's thoughtfulness and kindness.

Thursday, Feb. 2

It was a very busy day, which helped. In the morning,
I boxed up all my books, then dashed into Sefton to mail
them home. Back at the house, I washed my hair, then
dried it outside in the brilliant summer sun. I can't believe
I'm going back to winter. Finally, I finished packing.

Figuring out how to juggle my carry-on luggage was a
trick. I had my canvas flight bag, my camera case, didgeridoo (which is about 3-1/2 feet long and weighs a few
pounds), records, shell collection, gifts, stockman's hat,
and oilskins. I tied much of it together, stuffed some of it
inside other things, and wore some of it. Though it was
ungainly, I got it all out to the car, along with my suitcase
and duffel bag, and we were off.

Anne drove me to the airport, and Stephen met us there,
coming straight from work. I checked my bags and got my
seat assignment. I then headed down to the currency
exchange to trade in the balance of my colorful Australian
notes for that funny-looking green currency they use in the
United States. Anne, Stephen, and I talked until it was
time to go, then said fond farewells, and I headed out
through immigration and security.

On the jet, I sat by the window and gazed intently out at
the skyline. Before me, Sydney shimmered gold in the late
afternoon sun. As we taxied down the runway and took
off, I was clicking away with my camera, taking last shots
of the harbor, city, and coastline, none of which will prob-

ably turn out, as the sun was in the wrong place, but it made me feel better. It was getting late, and the light was failing fast. And so, with the setting of the sun, my lovely and dearly loved Australia disappeared from my sight.

Sadness overtook me like a great wave, washed over me, pulled me down. Scenes from the past six months flashed past my inward eye. I ached, but did not cry. I leaned against the window and stared into the night, hugging my oilskins, breathing their residual fragrance of wood smoke, gum leaves, and leather. Already I miss everything.

I shall, of course, be glad to see my family again, to share with them all the things that can't be shared in letters and on post cards. I shall be glad to see my friends. But right now, sorrow prevails. Australia is behind me.

I thought of the words of T.E. Lawrence, another dreamer, who loved another dry country: "All men dream: but not equally. Those who dream by night in the dusty recesses of their minds wake in the day to find that it was vanity: but the dreamers of the day are dangerous men, for they may act their dream with open eyes, to make it possible. This I did."

So, too, did I. But "did" is not enough; I want to continue to do, to dream and make it come true.

So now the fight begins, the fight to keep the dream alive. Australia is mine and will always be part of me, now. But there are other aspects of the dream that must be explored, must be refined. It would be so easy to go back to what I was—easy, comfortable, safe, and wrong. I have come too far.

The adventure must continue.

The dream must go on.

EPILOGUE

WALTZING THE NEXT STEP

I never went back, never returned to what I was before. That's not to say I didn't glance over my shoulder occasionally, at first. But I've never again let expectations and security eclipse the dream.

The second step was not as dramatic as the first, but it took more time. I gave up a lot to follow my dream, and I had a lot of rebuilding to do. But I never stopped believing it was worth it. Even when I was eating potatoes for every meal and driving a car that only cost $800. Even when I was working evenings and weekends in retail, to pay the bills, and writing 10 hours a day. It was always worth it—though I can say that with greater conviction now that this hard and wearying step is behind me.

Slowly, the dream gained strength. I sold a magazine article and bought an answering machine. I wrote a computer course and could afford film again. An educational publisher asked me to write the "Australia" section of a high school geography book. Editing and production work followed. I sold some photographs. More writing assignments came in. I quit retail. I was going to make it.

The dream has grown and changed as it has gained strength, and so have I. My world is wider, and I am, I think, a little wiser. No life is perfect or free from pain, but I have found much contentment in having searched for what I really wanted and in having paid the price to gain it.

Australia is still part of the dream. Of course, I have the photos, the journal, the memories. The shoulder I injured while riding in the High Country still aches—the rotator cuff is permanently damaged. The oilskins, Snowy River hat, didgeridoo, and Slim Dusty albums are much-loved souvenirs. But Australia gave me more than these.

Friends I made on that first trip are still part of my life. Jo and I have traveled together since our adventures in Western Australia. She has visited me in Chicago, and I have visited her several times in England. Nikki went on one last outback tour after we parted company in Perth, fell in love with her bush guide, married him, and stayed in Australia. She and Richard also have visited me in Chicago, and I have enjoyed their hospitality in their charming home in South Australia. I still correspond with Judy "of the white crash helmet," from the horse riding trip, and have visited her and her husband, Geoff, at their beautiful little ranch in the mountains outside Melbourne.

Yes, I have returned to Australia. Though the world holds many delights for me, and I have truly loved other countries I've visited, there is something about Australia that keeps drawing me back. No other place feels so right to me. For my return trips, I have only managed four weeks each time—the six-month journey will likely be irreproducible, but perhaps that is best.

On my second trip, I rented a car for a couple of weeks (driving on the left was, in and of itself, an adventure), so I could see exactly what I wanted. I returned to some places I loved—Queensland's rainforest, the Red Centre—and I saw some things I'd promised myself for "next time." I spent only three days in cities, and the rest of the time I was out bush, hopping from National Park to State Forest to Nature Reserve, from mountain to desert to craggy, wind-swept coastline. I visited friends, and spent a lot of time alone, just looking at things.

For my third trip, I again visited friends, but spent most of my time on a camping trip in an area so remote (the Kimberley Ranges in northwest W.A.) that it is believed that nothing has become extinct since Western civilization reached the continent. They haven't even named all the plants. I drank again from waterfalls, slept beneath the Southern Cross, and hiked through a wilderness of astonishing strangeness and beauty.

Trip number four found Nikki, Richard, and me camping in the magnificently rugged Corner Country (so rugged, in fact, that in two weeks their 4WD had four flat tires and a broken rear windshield—and I've been told that's on the light side of average). We traveled along rough tracks. Around us stretched miles of beauty and emptiness, rocks and dry rivers, and more kangaroos and emus than I'd seen on any previous trip. I finally got to travel down the Birdsville Track, and it was far more wonderful seeing it with two friends than it would have been on any tour.

When Nikki and Richard had to return to work, I continued on to see Judy and Geoff again. The cool, green mountains where they live contrasted sharply with the arid, red land I'd left behind, but were loved, though differently, as much. And Judy and Geoff, like Nikki and Richard, are warm and generous friends who more than share my enthusiasm for Australia.

Australia's cities are bigger now. Even some small towns have grown or changed (Alice Springs has a large, downtown shopping mall, and Broome has become so upscale I almost couldn't recognize it). More roads are sealed, and there are hotels in places I bush-camped previously. But the cities are beautiful, and progress has not reached everything. The land has not changed. It is still ancient and haunting, filled with rocks and gum trees and parrots.

Leaving is never easy, but each trip is reassuring— Australia is still there, and I can go back. Each time, I've left with a different sadness, but the same refrain: "Next time, next time."

My career, my life is not always what I expected, but it is always rich. Not every day is filled with beauty, but I know now to seek it when I hear its call. The love of adventure that I discovered on that first trip has stayed with me, and has carried me far and wide, from the bazaars of Istanbul to Mongolian nomad gers in the Gobi Desert, from a dugout canoe in the Ecuadorian rainforest to the temples of Tibet and Cambodia, from Iceland's chill to India's heat. Beauty, wonder, and things that are just a little bit difficult have maintained their hold on me. Happily, I have also reconciled the two halves of the "split personality" that once concerned me, discovering that sleeping bags and billy tea do not preclude theater tickets and French food.

I write, I take pictures, and these things are sustaining me, though I always hope to move in new directions. I'm not at the end of my journey, but the journey itself has become part of the reward.

The dream is still alive.

The adventure continues.

WALTZING
GLOSSARY

The Australian language is very similar to American. There are, however, differences. British expressions not heard in the U.S. are commonly used in Australia. A large number of Aboriginal terms have been adopted. And even a few familiar-sounding words have slightly altered meanings. This is by no means a complete list of Aussie words and phrases, but simply a compilation of terms employed in the book, as well as some objects, animals, and abbreviations with which American readers might not be familiar.

A.C.T. – Australian Capital Territory
Anzac – Australia New Zealand Army Corps

barramundi – also called giant perch, a delightfully tasty fish, found from Queensland to the Kimberleys—grows to about 100 lbs. (its name means "big fish")
billabong – cut off bend of a river; a water hole created when a river changes course, leaving a pond "stranded"; or a backwater or water hole in an otherwise dry riverbed—from Aboriginal *billa* = creek, river or water, and *bong* = dead.
billy – black metal bucket used for boiling water, usually over a campfire—origins uncertain, but possibly derived from Aboriginal *billa,* for water.

billy tea – tea made in a billy—a handful of tea is put in a billy full of boiling water and, traditionally, a few gum leaves are tossed in, then the can is swung by its handle to force the tea leaves to the bottom before serving.

biscuits – (or bickies, for short) – cookies or crackers

boab – Australian relative of the African baobab—a strange tree with a bulging, barrel-like trunk that can reach a diameter of 30 feet—sometimes erroneously called a bottle tree—the bottle tree, another Australian native, is a member of the cacao family, and is unrelated.

bogged – stuck, immobilized, usually in mud, sand, or soft dirt

boomerang – throwing stick—returning boomerangs belong to the tribes of the east and west—they are generally playthings, and are only used in hunting to flush wildfowl, not to kill or wound—hunting boomerangs do not return—central desert aborigines make only hunting/killing boomerangs; Arnhem Land aborigines don't make boomerangs at all, as they would be useless in the thick bush—originally, every tribe had a different name for their throwing sticks, but boomerang has now become pretty universal.

bore – a well sunk in the Artesian Basin to supply water to stations and towns in the more arid regions—of such importance that they usually appear on maps—for example, Marla Bore.

brolga – Australian crane

brumby – wild horse

budgerigars – (budgies, for short)—members of the parakeet family—usually green or blue in the wild.

bull dust – soft, dry silt or dust that drifts over Outback roads, obliterating them, or fills in holes and ruts, disguising them—its consistency is so fine that it has the sticky quality of talc. Bull dust is so odd that scientists have awarded it a special geological identity.

bullroarer – Aboriginal artifact—a flat, oblong piece of wood which, when whirled about at the end of a string, gives forth a deep, continuous "roar"—used to gather tribe or call up spirits.

bush – wilderness, wild wooded and sparsely populated area—derived from the Dutch *bosch,* meaning forest— imported from South Africa before 1820.

bushed – lost

bushranger – originally escaped convicts who lived as robbers in the wilds to avoid recapture—later became term for any wide-ranging outlaw, such as the famous Ned Kelly* or Ben Hall.

casuarina – family of graceful, narrow-leafed trees (leaves look almost like pine needles, but are more round-ed and softer), which includes swamp oaks, desert oaks and sheoaks—also sometimes called Australian pines.

chemist – pharmacist

chemist shop – drug store, pharmacy

chips – French fries

chock-a-block – packed to capacity, full, crowded

churinga – sacred Aboriginal stone, believed to embody spirits of mythical times—also occasionally spelled tjeringa.

coach – a bus that has been modified for touring or long-distance travel—usually includes special features not found on ordinary buses.

coolamon – long, curved, wooden bowl—used by Aborigines, depending on its size, for everything from gathering food to carrying infants.

*See appendix

cordial – a normally fruit-flavored, uncarbonated soft drink, usually made from a syrup.

corroboree – gathering of Aborigines for song and dance, either ceremonial or social.

crayfish – rock lobster (the small, freshwater crustaceans we call crawfish are called yabbies in Australia)

damper – traditional bush fare, this is a very basic bread made of flour, water and baking powder, usually cooked in an iron camp oven buried beneath the coals of a camp fire.

dead horse – Cockney rhyming slang for tomato sauce (catsup)—this expression, along with other rhyming slang phrases, is more likely to be heard in the Outback (though use is declining) rather than in the big cities.

didgeridoo – an Aboriginal musical instrument consisting of a hollow piece of wood four or five feet in length—it is a drone "trumpet" which produces an undulating tone.

digger – originally a miner, later an Australian soldier

dingo – Australian wild dog—also known as a warrigal—similar to the American coyote in size and habits.

dinkum – genuine, sincere, honest—frequently used in the exclamation "fair dinkum," i.e., the absolute truth—also in the expression "dinkum Aussie," a true, home-grown Australian.

Dreaming – Aboriginal totemic traditions, spiritual life—each person has his or her own Dreaming, the rituals, places and stories for which he or she is responsible in order to sustain the continuity of past with present, to maintain the power of the spirits of the land and of Dreamtime.

Dreamtime – the time of Aboriginal myths and legends, of the creation of the world and the beginning of traditions—

the time of spirits and giants, of ancestors that were both man and animal—a time outside of time, from which all magic and power emanate.

echidna – also called a spiny anteater—looks like a large, flattened hedgehog with a tube-like snout and spines on its back embedded in a coat of bristly, brown hair—eats ants and termites—it is a monotreme, a primitive, egg-laying mammal.

emu – large Australian bird similar to an ostrich—stands more than five feet tall, and may weigh more than 100 pounds—flightless, but can run 30 miles per hour.

eucalypt—eucalyptus (either form is acceptable and correct, but it's usually "eucalypt" in Australia—or else they just call it a gum tree)—any of a genus of mostly Australian evergreen trees or shrubs (in fact, of roughly 650-700 different species of eucalypt, only seven occur naturally outside Australia)—about 75 percent of the trees in Australia are eucalypts (including the jarrah, giant karri, ironbark, bloodwood, mallee, and many others that do not have the tell-tale "gum" appended to their names).

fair dinkum – see "dinkum"
flat – apartment
fossicking – gem hunting
4WD – four-wheel-drive vehicle
freshie – freshwater, or Johnston, crocodile

galah – (accent on the second syllable) a pink and gray parrot related to the cockatoo.

gaol – jail (pronounced the same as "jail," too—this is

the standard British spelling)

goanna – Australian monitor lizard, of which there are about 19 species in a wide range of sizes—the largest is the giant perentie, which can grow to more than eight feet in length

gum (or gum tree) – eucalypt

jabiru – Australian stork, also sometimes called a policeman bird, because of its black and white coloration.

Joe Blake – Cockney rhyming slang for snake

joey – baby kangaroo or wallaby

kite – bird of prey in the hawk family

Kiwi – New Zealander

koala – also called koala bear or native bear, it is not a bear at all, but a marsupial—it is probably most familiar to Americans in its role as representative for Qantas Airlines.

lilo – (pronounced lie-low) an air mattress

loo – restroom, toilet—except when it's a bush loo, then there's just bush, no loo

lugger – small fishing or pearl-diving boat that carries one or more lugsails.

mallee – *mallee* is Aboriginal for "many stemmed," and refers to a variety of short, scrubby, many-stemmed euca-lypts which grow in southern, semi-arid regions.

marsupial – mammal that carries its young in a pouch (the *marsupium*—Latin for pouch or purse) on the abdomen while they develop, such as the kangaroo, wombat, koala, possum, Tasmanian devil, bandicoot, wallaby—the majority of native Australian mammals are marsupials (more than 170 species, most of which occur nowhere except Australia).

monotreme – primitive mammals, of which only two species exist, the echidna and platypus, both indigenous to Australia—they are warm-blooded, yet lay eggs—they feed their young milk, though they have no teats; milk simply exudes from the skin on the mother's belly and is sucked off the tufts of fur.

mozzie (also, mossie) – mosquito

mulga – a yellow-flowered tree of the acacia family which grows primarily in arid regions.

myall tree – another of the numerous acacia trees that dot the Outback—*myall* is Aborigine for "wild."

Never-Never – the Aboriginal term for the Outback, the land of no time, and of endless time, the land of Dreaming, of always and never. The term is actually a lose translation of the Aboriginal *Nulla-Nulla*

note – paper currency, what we call a bill

N. S.W. – New South Wales

N.T. – Northern Territory

pademelon – a very small wallaby which favors thicket and undergrowth.

platypus – small, rabbit-sized monotreme (primitive, egg-laying mammal), with thick, fine fur like an otter's, webbed and clawed feet, and a leathery duck bill.

plonk – cheap wine

pokies – poker machines, slot machines

prawns – shrimp

pub – public house—usually includes a bar, lounge, and lunch counter or other dining area—generally a great place to get a good, inexpensive lunch—more of a community center than simply a drinking hall (especially in smaller towns).

road grader – a large vehicle/machine used for leveling dirt roads.

roadhouse – depending on its remoteness, anything from a gas station with a take-away counter, to complexes that offer showers, rooms, necessity shop, and restaurant, in addition to gas and auto repairs.

roo – kangaroo

S.A. – South Australia

saltie – saltwater, or estuarine, crocodile

sauce – tomato sauce, i.e., catsup

sealed – paved, as in sealed roads

shout – buy, treat—if you shout a round of drinks, you're picking up the tab.

sleepers – railroad ties

squash – beverage, usually citrus, made from "squashed" fruit—lemon squash is basically lemonade.

station – a large, pastoral property and its homestead—a ranch.

stockman – cowboy—also known as a ringer, because he rings the mob (rounds up the herd).

stubbies – bottles of beer

swag – bed roll, sleeping bag—usually includes any

clothes or personal effects rolled up in it—also called
Matilda.

take-away – carry-out
Tassie – Tasmania
tinny – beer can
torch – flashlight
tram – streetcar
tucker – food

Uluru – Aboriginal name for Ayers Rock
unsealed – unpaved
ute – short for utility – a type of pickup truck

Vegemite – a concentrated yeast extract, and an
Australian staple—it can be used to flavor soups, stews,
etc., or spread (in small amounts) on bread with butter—it
is very savory and tastes a bit like beef bouillon.

W.A. – Western Australia
walkabout – Aboriginal term for traveling around on
foot or a holiday in the bush.
wallaby – a small member of the kangaroo family
wattle – acacia – Australian settlers built wattle-and-
daub huts after the English manner, using twigs of the
abundant acacia trees, which hence became known as wattles—the beautiful, sweet-smelling golden wattle is the
national flower of Australia.
the Wet – the monsoon season, the summer rainy season

(northern Australia, only)

white ants – termites

wombat – a short, stocky, powerfully built marsupial—a chubby virtually tailless, tunnel-building ball of dark fur.

woomera – spear thrower—also, Woomera – a missile testing range and satellite tracking station in South Australia, and the town nearby.

WALTZING
APPENDIX:
WRITERS, EXPLORERS, OUTLAWS,
AND OTHER KEY ELEMENTS OF
AUSTRALIAN HISTORY

Burke and Wills

Robert O'Hara Burke and William John Wills led a famous and ill-fated expedition, crossing Australia from south to north. Burke was a fiery romantic with little practical knowledge of the bush, a well-educated Sergeant of Police who had served in the Austrian cavalry and the Irish constabulary before coming to Australia. Wills was an astronomer-surveyor whose precise maps and notes recorded the progress of the expedition. He was younger (26, to Burke's 39) and was second in command. Wills was more familiar with the bush, but he was no explorer.

On August 20, 1860, Burke, Wills, an Irish soldier named John King, and fifteen others set out from Melbourne. The government of Victoria wanted to flaunt its new-found, gold-rush wealth, so the group was insanely over-equipped, with horses, camels, wagons, and tons of equipment—so much equipment that three wagons had broken down before they even got out of Melbourne.

By September 6, after crossing a hundred miles of plains to Swan Hill, Burke had decided to lighten the load, auctioning the extra equipment and supplies to the locals. While there, Burke hired a former sailor named Charles Gray. Five days later, the party continued north.

The rough travel began to take its toll, and by the time the group reached Balranald, nerves were fraying, members were bickering, and the first discontented traveler left. Burke dumped more gear and then continued on.

It was 160 difficult miles from Balranald to Menindee. The horses and camels struggled alternately through thick mud and blowing sand drifts. The weather turned malevolent, with thunderstorms and frost. Only now were they nearing the true frontier. Beyond Menindee lay unsettled country, wild tribes, and the great, fierce deserts. More people turned back.

The supply wagons had fallen behind the main group, but Burke and Wills pushed on. They left six men at Menindee to wait for the wagons to catch up. They were to follow along as quickly as possible.

Slowly working their way north, the party reached a branch of Cooper Creek by November 11. They were nearly half way across the continent. Burke decided to split the group again, leaving four men as a "rear guard," to set up a depot and wait for the supply wagons and the rest of the party. Burke, Wills, King, and Gray would attempt to dash across half the continent and return to this depot before their supplies ran out.

The "dash" north turned into a torturous grind. "I am satisfied that the frame of man never was more severely taxed," Burke wrote. It was another two months before they reached the Gulf of Carpentaria. Still, though they had succeeded in reaching the gulf, the saltwater swamps and mangrove forest that border the water along that coast denied them sight of the sea.

With only four weeks' rations left, they began the long journey back to the depot at Cooper Creek. One by one they killed and ate all but two of the camels. The weeks turned into months as they staggered south.

On April 17, 1861, only 70 miles from the Cooper

depot, Gray died, and Burke, Wills, and King slowly dug his grave. So exhausted were the three men that this took nearly the whole day.

Meanwhile, the men back at the Cooper depot were running out of supplies. They had already waited a month longer than Burke had instructed, each day searching the horizon for some sign of the explorers. The supply wagons had never arrived (they were pinned down by sickness and hostile Aborigines just 110 miles south), and one of the men was dying of scurvy. They finally gave up hope, and decided to return south.

As impossible as it now seemed that Burke, Wills, Gray, or King would ever return, one of the men at the depot, William Brahe, buried a cache of dried meat, flour, sugar, oatmeal, and rice, along with a note in a bottle. He marked the place by carving on a coolibah tree the notation:

DIG
3FT
NW

He and his compatriots then left camp, traveling slowly because of the sick and dying. They covered only 14 miles before camping for the night.

Only 14 miles and 9-1/2 hours away from the Cooper depot they camped in the bright moonlight. Beneath that same moon, Burke, Wills, and King finally staggered into the depot, only to find it deserted. After eight months of traveling, they missed their back-up by 9-1/2 hours.

Burke, Wills, and King found the food that Brahe had left, and this sustained them a bit longer. Believing they could never catch up with Brahe, they decided to strike off to the southwest. For a month they tried to find a way to cross the desert. One camel became trapped in mud and had to be shot, the other simply gave out. Packing supplies on their backs, they tried a forced march, but after 45 miles gave up and retreated back to Cooper Creek.

In the meantime, Brahe and his group had found the embattled relief party, led by William Wright, who had just fought off an attack by hostile natives. While the others rested, Brahe and Wright rode back to Cooper Creek to see if Burke had arrived. The explorers were nowhere to be seen, so the weary riders left. The survivors of the two rear camps withdrew toward Menindee, leaving behind the graves of the less fortunate (during the siege, three members of Wright's group had died, and before long, Brahe's sick companion died as well).

Back near the Cooper, the three explorers continued to search for a way out. They were on the point of starvation. On June 29, realizing that he could not go on, the dying Wills asked Burke and King to continue without him. Two days later, Burke collapsed. King found a tribe of Aborigines who befriended him, and he lived, though he was terribly wasted by the hardships he had endured.

On September 15, the pitiful, emaciated King was at last found by a rescue party. The remains of Burke and Wills were located and taken to Melbourne, where they rest beneath a granite monument. Wills's detailed maps and notebooks and Burke's last scrawled notes are now in the State Library of Victoria in Melbourne.

Just 9-1/2 hours and 14 miles had separated them from safety and triumph. However, triumph could hardly have made Burke and Wills any more famous than tragedy did.

Cobb and Co.

Cobb and Co. was a mail and passenger coach company whose fame became legendary in Australia. When Freeman Cobb arrived in Victoria, during the early days of the gold rush, the only reliable transport to the gold fields were bullock-drays. Cobb was familiar with the U.S. coaching firm of Wells Fargo, and recognized the need for a similar service in Australia. In 1854 he formed a partnership with Americans John Peck and James Swanton, and imported American coaches, first-class horses, and experienced Wells Fargo drivers. The company had an immediate success, and regular services were started from Melbourne to Bendigo, Ballarat, and Castlemaine.

After Cobb had made his fortune, he sold the company to another American, James Rutherford. The company extended its services, established local coach-building works, obtained a mail subsidy, and replaced the American drivers with Australians.

When the railways eventually drove these horse-drawn vehicles from the busiest routes, Cobb and Co. moved to the back country of eastern Australia. By 1870, they were harnessing 6,000 horses a day, and their coaches were traveling 28,000 miles per week. Not until 1934 did the company go out of business, usurped in the end by buses and other motor transport.

The success of the company lay partly in the quality and comfort of the coaches, but its real fame derived from the reliability and resourcefulness of its men. Some of the drivers were real heroes, and their feats and characters were well known by all in their day. Tales of the exploits of Cobb and Co.'s crack drivers are as exciting as any told of Wells Fargo, and are an established part of the lore and legend of Australia's frontier days.

Behind six foaming horses, and lit by flashing lamps,
Old Cobb and Co., in royal state, went dashing past the
    camps.

-from "The Roaring Days" by Henry Lawson

The First Fleet

Since the recently independent United States was no longer available as a dumping ground for criminals, political malcontents, paupers, and other undesirables, too-crowded England needed somewhere new to settle her "colonists." Also, having lost the U.S., England needed a new source of raw materials—especially flax and timber—and there were reports of superior quality flax and tall, straight pines covering Norfolk Island, north of Sydney and just off Australia's east coast.

James Matra, an American loyalist who had sailed with Cook on the Endeavour, described this new land in glowing terms to Lord Sydney, Secretary of Colonial Affairs, and pleaded that a settlement be established for loyalists who had been dispossessed of their goods and property after the American Revolution. So there were numerous reasons for seriously considering fresh colonization—though the greatest factor was still the need to empty the jails and hulks. (The hulks were demasted ships, lining the river in London, that served as overflow prisons.)

Captain Arthur Phillip, a man with a fine naval record, was appointed to lead the First Fleet, which would convey the first convicts from London to Botany Bay. The Fleet consisted of six transports, three storeships and two ships of war carrying a total of 1,138 people, of whom 821 were convicts, male and female. To police the expedition, Phillip had been allotted four companies of marines, over 200 men, some of them with their wives and children.

On May 7, 1787, Phillip boarded *HMS Sirius,* flagship of the First Fleet. Traveling with him were Captain John Hunter, second in command, and Philip Gidley King, Second Lieutenant, both close friends of Arthur Phillip, and both destined to succeed him as Governors of the new colony.

Phillip was an intelligent man, kind but firm enough to make his authority respected. Above all, he was intensely humane. The crossing in those days, which took nearly eight months, was grueling for everyone involved, convict or free, but Phillip made every effort to make the trip safe, healthy, and relatively comfortable. He argued with the authorities, bargaining for more supplies for the voyage and greater provision for establishing the colony on the other side of the world.

Even with a humane Commander and sympathetic doctors, the trip was a torturous one for the convicts tethered between decks on the over-crowded transports. Still, the convicts received better treatment from Phillip than was meted out by some prison officials back in England or by Commanders on later Fleets. On the whole, prisoners' health actually improved during the voyage.

After a stop at Cape Town in South Africa, Captain Phillip, taking the three fastest ships in the Fleet, went ahead to make preparations for the landing, leaving Hunter in charge of the other ships. On January 7, 1788, this advance guard sighted the South Cape of Tasmania. On the 18th they anchored at Botany Bay, where, two days later, they were joined by Hunter and the remaining vessels.

It was found that the anchorage at Botany Bay was dangerously exposed to the prevailing southeast winds and was too shallow to provide protection. In addition, the surrounding country was marshy and low-lying, with an inadequate water supply. So two days after his arrival, Captain Phillip set out, with a party of marines in a rigged longboat to explore Port Jackson, a few miles to the north. The Port, which had been named but not investigated by Captain Cook, proved to be an excellent, well-protected harbor, with lovely bays, golden beaches and a thickly wooded shoreline. Phillip picked a small cove that offered good anchorage and a freshwater stream, and named it after Lord Sydney. He then hurried back to his Fleet.

En route to Botany Bay, Phillip sighted two ships flying French colors making way toward the Bay. As soon as he got back to the Fleet he boarded his ship and sailed for Port Jackson, with Captain Hunter instructed to follow him with the rest of the ships as soon as the wind and weather would permit.

On the following day, January 26, Captain Phillip landed at Sydney Cove and unfurled the Union Jack, claiming New South Wales for England. Volleys were fired and toasts were drunk. The new colony had begun. The French, when they arrived, were welcomed as guests of the British government—they were too late to claim the new territory as their own.

January 26 is now celebrated as Australia Day.

Adam Lindsay Gordon

Dashing, educated, adventurous, melancholy, English-born Adam Lindsay Gordon was the first poet to celebrate and capture Australia in verse—and he is the only

Australian poet with a bust in Westminster Abbey's Poet's Corner.

Though he was an exceptionally fine writer, during his lifetime, his reputation rested mostly on his ability as a horseman—which was fine with Gordon. He had an iron nerve and a seemingly magic influence over horses, and his exploits on horseback were famous. Probably the most renowned of his feats is known as Gordon's Leap, a jump that was reckoned to be impossible.

His favorite sport was to lead a field at follow-the-leader and leave everyone behind. One day his riding companions had managed to keep up with him all day, and they were vociferous with their own praise, ribbing Gordon for being unable to loose them. "Well, damn well follow me now," Gordon retorted, and put his horse at a high guard fence.

Beyond the fence, as they well knew, was a narrow ledge at the top of a 400-foot drop to the jagged rocks bordering Mt. Gambier's Blue Lake. Gordon's horse took the fence, turned in mid-air, and landed steady on its feet parallel to the fence. If Gordon had made the slightest slip, both he and his horse would have fallen to their deaths. His companions had to dismantle a section of the fence to let Gordon back through. (The ledge was so narrow, he couldn't safely dismount.) Today, an obelisk marks the site of Gordon's Leap.

Gordon—a lonely, moody, introspective man—arrived in Australia in 1853, when he was 20 years old. He enlisted in the South Australian Mounted Police as a trooper. The freedom, excitement and, above all, the provision of a good horse made the occupation irresistible to the young Gordon.

He eventually left the police force and traveled back and

forth between South Australia and Victoria breaking and racing horses. In 1862 he married Maggie Parks, a woman who took little notice of his poetry but admired greatly his abilities as a horseman. They were happy together, and Maggie's cheerfulness soothed his dark and brooding nature for a while. Yet his ingrained melancholy still colored his outlook on life and often was reflected in his verse.

In 1864, Gordon inherited some money from his mother, which enabled him to dedicate more time to study and writing. He would often compose his verses while riding, stopping occasionally to scribble poems down on odd pieces of paper. The rhythm of hoof-beats seems indeed to have established the meter of his rhyme, especially when riding was the theme.

And faster and faster across the wide heath
  We rode till we raced. Then I gave her her head,
And she—stretching out with the bit in her teeth --
  She caught him, outpaced him, and passed him, and led.
                    - from "From the Wreck"

In 1865, Gordon was elected to the South Australian House of Assembly as Member for the District of Victoria. However, he had no gift for public speaking, so he took his inheritance money and opened a livery stable at Ballarat. While at Ballarat, he won his first great race, the Melbourne Hunt Cup. He won three steeplechase races at Flemington in one afternoon, two of them on his own horse. It was a record that put him at the top of the list as chief amateur steeplechase-rider in Australia.

Though he was a skillful and brave rider, Gordon was very nearsighted—hardly able to see beyond his horse's ears, he said. This resulted in frequent, serious accidents. More than once he fractured his skull, and in 1870 he had a particularly bad fall from which he never fully recovered. Pain, insomnia and depression plagued him. "Since that heavy fall of mine, I have taken to drink," he wrote. "I don't get drunk, but I drink a good deal more than I ought to for I have a constant pain in my head."

Despite growing recognition for his poetry, Gordon's despondency deepened. He believed himself friendless and unlucky. His ill-health and money worries exaggerated his habitual state of melancholy, and on June 24, 1870, the 37-year-old Gordon rose at dawn, walked off into the scrub and, propping his rifle in a fork of a ti-tree, shot himself.

Ned Kelly and the Bushrangers

"Game? Why, he's as game as Ned Kelly."

-old Australian saying

In the earliest days of Australian settlement, bushrangers were convicts who escaped into the wild and sustained themselves by robbery, while trying to avoid recapture. However, the mid-1800s saw the emergence of a whole new type of bushranger, the Australian-born "wild colonial boys."

This new generation of young bushrangers was generally made up of selectors (small-scale, often poor farmers) and selectors' sons. Some were spurred on by wrongs suffered at the hands of wealthy squatters (pastoralists) or local police, many went along in sympathy for friends, and a few joined in for the adventure.

For a while, bushrangers multiplied at a frightening rate. There were bushrangers of every nationality and color:

European, Aboriginal, and Asian. Some were maniacs, lunatics, or terrorists, but these are not the ones who became legendary.

Men like Ben Hall, Frank Gardiner, Johnny Gilbert, John Dunn, Jack Doolan, and, later, Ned Kelly and his gang became popular folk heroes, symbols of the fight against injustice and the oppressive practices of the squatters. Few of these bushrangers committed brutal or cold-blooded crimes, and usually took pains to avoid unnecessary violence. Some were admired as much for their dashing appearance and charm as for their courage and exploits. It was claimed for them that they never robbed the needy, that they were the enemies of the greedy pastoralists, that they treated women and children with gallantry, that they fought fairly, and that they "died game." In fact, the young law-breakers took some pride in their reputations and were generally careful to behave accordingly.

However, bravery, charm, and even widespread support did not save the bushrangers from retribution. They died game, but they still died.

The last and most famous of the bushrangers was Ned Kelly. The Kelly gang, which included Ned, his brother Dan, and two friends, Joe Byrne and Steve Hart, ranged throughout northeast Victoria for three years, ending their adventures, and their lives, in 1880.

Ned, who was born in June 1855, bore a deep-seated resentment toward the authorities, at least some of it justified. The local Superintendent of Police considered the family—Ned's mother, a widow, and the eight Kelly children—to be troublemakers, and he harassed them in the hopes of driving them out of the territory. Ned's brother, Jim, was arrested and sentenced to five years in jail for horse stealing. Dan, only 16-years-old in 1877, was arrested on trumped up charges, but was released. Sister Kate was allegedly assaulted by a trooper, who was pistol-whipped by an outraged Ned. Finally, Mrs. Kelly was arrested as an "accessory" and sentenced to three years in prison.

It was this final incident that precipitated the formation of the Kelly gang. The boys immediately offered to surrender in return for Mrs. Kelly's release, but the proposal was ignored, and a manhunt that would last three years was begun by the police.

Ned Kelly possessed charm, a sense of chivalry, and a wonderful flair for dramatics. He saw himself as a latter-day Robin Hood (though, in robbing banks, he stole from both rich and poor) and a defender of the free against the oppression of the English overlords. When the gang graduated from horse stealing to the holding up of entire country towns, Ned would make speeches full of Irish patriotism, Australian republicanism, and sentimental pathos to his literally captive audiences.

While the working classes generally saw him as a hero, the upper and middle classes viewed Ned Kelly (who was not above killing police or informants, and shot one officer in front of the man's pregnant wife) as a bloodthirsty ruffian. As his popularity increased in one quarter, concern grew in the other. Eventually, Aboriginal trackers were brought down from Queensland, and the authorities began to close in on the gang.

Finally, in June 1880, the police hot on their heals, the gang descended on the town of Glenrowan. It is likely that they could have gotten away, but, as Ned later explained, "A man gets tired of being hunted like a dog in his native land. I wanted to see it end." So, attired in armor fashioned from iron moldboards, they made their last stand at the Glenrowan Hotel.

Donning the heavy (90 pounds) armor, the men lumbered out of the hotel and into the moonlight to face the 50 police and trackers gathered against them. The armor so impeded the men's movements that they were forced to retreat back into the hotel. Ned, the only one with a helmet, worked his way around back and, as dawn was breaking, his huge figure, the armor covered with a long gray coat, advanced on the astonished police through the timber and swirling ground mist. Bullets bounced off the ponderous apparition, and the police were momentarily confounded. But soon the weakness was discovered, and a dozen double-barrel shotguns were aimed at Ned's exposed arms and legs, and the outlaw sank to the ground.

The gun battle lasted ten hours. By the end, Ned, seriously wounded, was captured, and the other members of the gang were dead.

Ned faced jail and court with calm dignity and self-control, commenting during his trial only that "the public. . . should remember that the darkest life may have a light side, and after the worst has been said against a man, he may, if he is heard, tell a story in his own rough way, that will lead them to soften the harshness of their thoughts against him."

Ned's last visitor was his mother, herself still an inmate of the Melbourne prison, whose last words to her son were, "Mind you die like a Kelly, Ned."

"I fear [dying] as little as to drink a cup of tea," Ned told his keepers. He passed his remaining days cheerfully, singing bush ballads in his cell. Then, on November 11, 1880, Ned Kelly was led to the gallows. Still calm, he simply said, "Such is life," and was hanged.

Lachlan Macquarie

Fifth Governor of New South Wales, replacing William Bligh, Lachlan Macquarie was to become "The Father of Australia."

Macquarie's accomplishments during his twelve years of office were astonishing. He put up 265 buildings, ranging in scale from cottages to guard-barracks large enough to accommodate 800 men. He built a hospital, founded churches, inaugurated townships, and laid down hundreds of miles of turnpikes and carriage roads. No Governor in any colony of similar size and remoteness has ever come close to his achievements as a constructor. By the time Macquarie left, he had completely rebuilt Sydney's main public edifices, all upon a scale he felt more appropriate for what he saw as Australia's glorious destiny. He had done the same at Parramatta and Windsor, and had literally created some dozen other townships, carving them out of the wilderness. In Tasmania, he replanned Hobart and Launceston, which were to become the island's major cities. In addition, he introduced the colony's own currency in 1813, replacing the informal rum trade, and in 1817 he helped establish the colony's first bank—the Bank of New South Wales.

When Macquarie arrived at Sydney Cove on New Year's Day, 1810, with his regiment of Highlanders and his bride, Elizabeth, the colony had been settled for 22 years. Yet the entire population—by this time nearly 6,000—clung to the coast, living in Sydney and a few small settlements. The formidable Blue Mountains had never been crossed and barred settlement of the rest of the continent.

Of the conditions that prevailed upon his arrival Macquarie wrote, "I found the colony barely emerging from an infantile imbecility and suffering from various privations and disabilities, the country impenetrable, agriculture in a languishing state; commerce in its early dawn; public building in a state of dilapidation and mouldering to decay; the few roads and bridges formerly constructed almost impassable; the population in general depressed by poverty, no public credit, no private confidence; the morals of most in the lowest state and religious worship almost totally neglected."

In Sydney itself, the careful, orderly plans of Arthur Phillip had been encroached on. During Johnston's period of control (Johnston was the Major who arrested Governor William Bligh at the outbreak of the Rum Rebellion), officers of the New South Wales Corps had been allowed to pick the most desirable sites, regardless of the fact that the properties they had chosen might interrupt the sweep of an intended avenue. As a result, streets needed straightening, and trespassers had to be evicted. A law was passed to keep people from allowing their livestock to roam freely in the city—pigs or goats found encumbering the city proper would be seized and sold at auction, with the proceeds going to charity.

Knowing that Macquarie would deal with a difficult situation, the Colonial Office in London had given him considerable authority to handle the government, and he used his authority deftly and extensively. His policy towards Aborigines was the most liberal since Arthur Phillip had been Governor. His attitude towards convicts—that their former state should not be remembered or held against them, and that they should be allowed to work on an equal basis with other colonists—was enlightened. He overcame the boundaries that hedged in the area; by 1813 there was a road over the Blue Mountains, opening up the interior of the continent. Sydney began to take on a new look as Macquarie's edicts on law and order, town planning, and

building took effect. Macquarie now decided that a change
of name was in order: the Colony of New South Wales
officially became Australia.

Macquarie's farsighted approach to his considerable
challenge brought vociferous complaints from the
entrenched and generally corrupt Exclusives—free men
who owned great farms and depended on convict labor to
run them. Fortunately for the new colony, it took eight
months for the accusations and vilifications to reach
London, and more time than that for the Colonial Office to
act in delivering decisions back to Australia. The Governor
ignored the threats of the Exclusives, and continued to
build the nation he envisioned. He laid out towns where
ex-convicts could live. He personally pushed back the
wilderness, spending long hours in the saddle, overseeing,
exploring, working.

Macquarie hired a convict, Francis Greenway, a talented
architect who had been found guilty of forging a contract,
to help him build the lighthouses, churches, public buildings, and other edifices that were to grace the growing
towns. This policy of adorning a convict settlement was
quite beyond the comprehension of the government officials in London, and they were astonished when
Macquarie appointed Greenway, to whom he had granted a
pardon, Civil Architect.

The Exclusives were outraged when Macquarie, despite
all their protests, continued to place the most outstanding
of the freed convicts into positions of responsibility. They
blamed him for all the ills of the world, and, as time progressed, their half-truths, misstatements and lies began to
be believed by the home office. Governor Macquarie treated such calumnies with contempt. But now time and distance were against him. By the time he heard the sub-

stance of the accusations and had responded to them, 16 months had passed, and the charges were being accepted as facts in London. Besides, the British Treasury had its eye on the money Macquarie had been raising for improvements in the colony.

In 1817 Macquarie was severely censured by the Colonial Secretary. The Exclusives had won. Macquarie had been judged on the basis of their testimony. But he was not allowed the dignity of resignation. He was required to stay in the colony for another four years, while a commission investigated his administration based on the distorted and unfavorable reports of his enemies.

Before he left New South Wales, Macquarie took one last tour of the land he had grown to love. What he saw reassured him that the 12 years he had spent there had not been in vain. In addition, he could be consoled by the fact that the House of Commons decided to restore to the ex-convicts and their Emancipist supporters all the rights which the Exclusives had tried to deny them.

Macquarie returned to England in 1822. The last two years of his life in London and Scotland were clouded by his efforts to clear his name. The unfortunate findings of the investigation were known and believed by everyone. His strong defense of his work in Australia succeeded in making the Colonial Office realize that Great Britain now possessed a new land of vast size and potential, but it did not improve Macquarie's status. He was granted a pension, but approval and recognition were denied him.

Disconsolate, Lachlan Macquarie, in life never accorded the praise he deserved, died on July 1, 1824. He is buried at Gruline on the Isle of Mull, off the west coast of Scotland. His weathered gravestone is engraved, "The Father of Australia."

Australia itself is his real monument. Macquarie's name can be seen everywhere in Australia today. His work, his planning are still very much in evidence. The Georgian-influenced architecture of Francis Greenway, now known as Macquarie style, still graces Sydney, Parramatta, and Windsor. Macquarie's colony has spread across the continent. His vision of Australia as a great country has been realized.

New South Wales Corps

The New South Wales Corps was a British military unit formed in 1789 for service in the convict colony of New South Wales. They were an often-excellent group of soldier-settlers who figured prominently in early Australian history.

With the arrival of the corps in 1791, the colony gained a new dynamic force. Many officers became involved in business ventures, most notably the rum trade. The ranks of the corps provided the colony with explorers, surveyors, and scholars.

The corps, under the command of Francis Grose, administered the new settlement during the interim between Governor Arthur Phillip, who departed in December 1792, and Governor John Hunter, who arrived in September 1795. During this period the corps succeeded in extending the border of the colony to the Hawkesbury River. The corps distinguished itself by quelling the 1804 Castle Hill Rising, a rebellion of Irish convicts. The officer in charge of this operation, Major George Johnston, was later one of the leaders of the Rum Rebellion.

An insufficiency of coinage in the colony lead to an

extensive barter system, with rum the primary medium of exchange. Rather than trying to curb this practice, many of the corps officers became foremost among the monopolists in the rum trade. In 1805, William Bligh was installed as the fourth Governor, and he set about trying to alter this state of affairs.

Relations between Bligh and the N.S.W. Corps were strained. Bligh accused the corps of ineptitude and corruption. But it was not just the officers who were implicated in the rum trade, but all the free settlers, and they resented Bligh's strict interference. A petition was signed by the citizenry, asking Major Johnston to depose Bligh and take charge of the colony himself. In January 1808, the New South Wales Corps took over the government of New South Wales, and Bligh was placed under arrest.

The corps controlled the colony until the arrival of Governor Lachlan Macquarie. The preceding year, the name of the corps had been changed to the 102nd Regiment of the Line as a preliminary to its recall to England. In May 1810, half of the regiment accepted reassignment, but the rest chose to remain in Australia.

A.B. "Banjo" Paterson

A. (Andrew) B. (Barton) Paterson was an Australian lawyer, poet, and journalist who published his verses under the pen name "The Banjo" (after a racehorse of that name). Paterson achieved great success in 1902 with his book *The Man from Snowy River and Other Verses*. In 1917, the now famous "Waltzing Matilda" appeared in another collection of his poems. Almost all Paterson's poems celebrate the Outback: the people, places, and events of rural and frontier life. "Waltzing Matilda" has become the unofficial anthem of Australia, and "The Man from Snowy River," a well-loved Australian classic, was made into a wonderful movie that, in Australia, made more money than Star Wars.

CPSIA information can be obtained at www.ICGtesting.com
Printed in the USA
LVOW12s1347210714

395315LV00001B/79/P